D1500140

W.B.
YEATS
and his contemporaries

By the same author

Monographs on *Walter Pater*, *Beaumont and Fletcher*, *Swinburne* (Longmans and Scribbners) *Beardsley* (Twayne)

Edited: *Romantic Mythologies*, *Meredith Now* (Routledge & Kegan Paul); *Decadence and the 1890s* (Arnold), *British Prose and Verse 1870–1905* (Oxford)

Poetry and Translations: *Orisons*, *The Lover's Martyrdom*, *Motets*, *A Restoration Comedy Version of Iliad XIV*, *Lauds*

With John Stokes: '*Wilde*: An Annotated Bibliography' in *Anglo-Irish Literature: A Review of Research* (1976 and 1982)

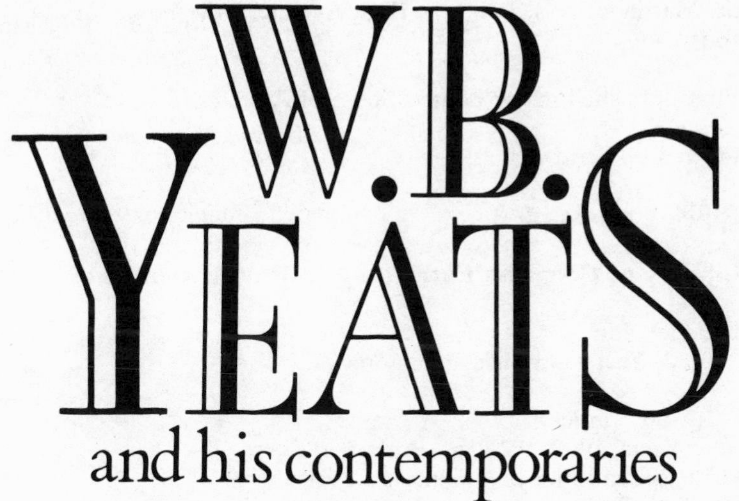

W.B. YEATS

and his contemporaries

Ian Fletcher

Professor of English
Arizona State University

St. Martin's Press
New York

 For information, write:
Scholarly & Reference Division,
St. Martin's Press, Inc., 175 Fifth Avenue, New York, NY 10010

First published in the United States of America in 1987

Printed in Great Britain

ISBN 0-312-85306-8

Library of Congress Cataloging-in-Publication Data

Fletcher, Ian.
W.B. Yeats and his contemporaries.

Includes index.
1. Yeats, W.B. (William Butler), 1865-1939—Criticism and interpretation. 2. Yeats, W.B. (William Butler), 1865-1939—Contemporaries.
3. English poetry—19th century—History and criticism.
I. Title.
PR5907.F58 1987 821'.8 84-40573
ISBN 0-312-85306-8

for

John Lucas, David Howard and Carl Pidgeon:
survivors of the Reading of the 1950s and 1960s &
veterans of 'The Flat'.

Contents

Acknowledgements

Grateful acknowledgement is due to Messrs A.P. Watt, acting on behalf of Michael Yeats and Macmillan, London, for permission to quote from the poetry and prose of W.B. Yeats.

I should like also to thank the Prior Provincial of the Dominican Order and to Fr. Allan White, O.P., for allowing me to use extracts from the writings of John Gray; and to Professor Denis Donoghue for the quotation from his introduction to the *Memoirs* of W.B. Yeats.

I.F.

Note: A number of the pieces reprinted below have appeared before; all have been revised, and several expanded.

Preface

These essays veering over three decades, amount to a suite of pieces on end-of-century topics and writers. Most involve W.B. Yeats, discussed at several phases of his career. The notion that Yeats is not three or more but one poet is now more or less acceptable. In re-reading him I conclude that after the leap in the poet's art around the year 1908, there is a high proportion of thin and even failed poems in the ensuing three books, though there are sharp successes also, signs of the healthy range of his dissatisfactions. As to revision, which is commonly assumed to liberate an energy in early poems buried under the drapes of the early style, it cannot be denied that in, let us say, 'The Lament of the Old Pensioner' the early version is merely a fretful old man's 'whingeing' while in the second version, written at the height of the poet's power in 1925, the old man spits into the face of time, and that spit is now organically connected with the life-giving rain of the first stanza. But the revision, with its extra middle stanza, becomes a new poem, not the liberation of a poem too oppressed by the furnishings of the earlier text.

The centre of the book is Yeats and particularly the Yeats of Autobiographies, of persons and places, of a theatre where myth and anecdote collide; I do not find the notion of the book as a text for explication in terms of the 'system' like, say 'The Phases of the Moon' particularly rewarding. Quite exemplary is the episode of Verlaine's burial in 1896.

The episode of Verlaine's funeral is turned into typical truth. Verlaine becomes Yeats's own defence against the objective phase. Louis XI Bibi-la-Purèe, Verlaine's pimp, hanger-on and straight man, acts a supporting part in this *commedia dell'arte* production, still playing on his opera hat, that badge of festivity and respectability, acquiring still more respectability and absurdity by the precision of *fourteen* umbrellas (see p. 161). How in God's name could he have carried them all off? Clearly they belonged to Verlaine's fellow poets, busily eulogizing and the deed is Louis XI's comment on the aftermath of Verlaine's passion. Louis XI parodies Verlaine and so somehow preserves the dead master from entire deflation. In the revision we have not less but more accident, an accretion of wit and humour that solicits the reader but not in the direction of the 'system'. The typicality is that of the visual image, though Yeats was more moved by the human image than the painter's, even if not unmoved by that. Physical truth, though, reflects the truth of the soul in a manner decidedly Platonic: form doth the body make or, as Yeats puts it in his 1893 commentary on Blake, essence requires body for its full presence.

It remains only to recall the name of two colleagues at the University of Reading who in very different ways loved W. B. Yeats for himself alone—D. J. Gordon and Douglas Brown—and to record my gratitude to the Warburg Institute for their habitual generosity to all pilgrims and strangers. I should also like to thank Jonathan C. Tutor for a sight of his excellent and as yet unpublished essay on John Gray.

I. F.
December 1985

PART I

AMBIANCE

I

Some Aspects of Aestheticism

The Aesthetic Movement is still somewhat misted despite much acute and arduous research.[1] Words such as 'aesthete', 'aestheticism', 'soul', 'art for art's sake', 'intense', and so forth, seem to derive from no centre, touching groups or circles as briefly as Walter Pater's 'forces' in the Conclusion to *The Renaissance* as they pass on their way to the beyond. It is not easy, moreover, within the limits of Aestheticism to isolate literary texts that are purely 'aesthetic'; that are indeed all 'soul' and with no more of gross meaning than the accidental play of light on some Eastern carpet. With art, or with the abstract gestures of decoration, the evidence is less tenuous: Albert Moore, for example; could those frailly robed, langorously posed girls of his ever mean anything? Are they—are not we too—pleased simply by their weightlessly being? Even the most fragile offerings of the Rondeliers, though, a rondeau of Dobson, a kyrielle of Lang, can never quite formalize themselves out of meaning. And is there not a little too much of the 'aesthetic teacher' about Walter Pater: what is Walter, we might say, but George Eliot in petticoats? And Swinburne seems too bent on teaching too, teaching us to be more naughty, caught in the puritan–antinomian dialectic. As for Oscar, well, he presents so many masks and does the fat boy in so many voices that it is not altogether safe to say anything about him at all. And in any case, Oscar and Algy may be safely gathered under the orchidaceous shade of Decadence.

Considerations such as these doubtless led Ruth A. Temple in 'Truth in Labelling'[2] to suggest that 'aestheticism' as a term applied to literature might disappear from our discourse. There was no movement: there was only an inventive spasm of the higher and the lower journalism. Artists of the 1880s and the 1890s care for Beauty no more and no less than other artists; nor should 'aestheticism' be confused with 'art for art's sake'; aesthetes were not all decadents; the one genus did not mechanically mutate into the other. Altogether the term was the outcome of much confusion, chauvinism and moralism: it was not British; it was effeminate, it was … damme, Sir, it was French—'poisonous honey'.

Elizabeth Aslin in her magistral *The Aesthetic Movement: Prelude to Art Nouveau*[3] managed to evade imaginative literature altogether; she makes one incidental reference to Pater as the inspirer of Wilde, who is accorded some space as the publicist of the movement. Attempts have been made to locate the absent centre: Robin Spencer rather implausibly canvassed for Whistler; others, more plausibly, promoted E.W. Godwin; Albert Moore (who wrote poetry) may yet have his turn.[4] Wilde as sedulous ape and impresario condemns himself to the margins. And if the flavour of, say, 'art for art's sake' is mid, even later nineteenth century, there may be grounds for starting elsewhere than in France and much farther back (or out of time altogether). But the line of development, if well enough known in Germany and in France, is somewhat veiled in Britain. A.G. Lehmann isolates two instants in time that really matter.[5]

French Aetiologies

The first instance is when the slightly rickety syncretisms of the Romantic group in France go out of date and fall to pieces: the 'good and the true and the beautiful' come to power in 1830 for an eighteen-year reign. Art for art's sake, which is the thread to follow, meant nothing in the *cénacle* of Victor Hugo, Alfred de Vigny, Sainte Beuve, and so on, but for them 'art' is a portmanteau word covering not the plastic arts but rather implying cultivation of moral sentiments (with which we may compare Wordsworth's stricter discipline). The Good and the Truthful are accented distinctly more than the Beautiful. The *cénacle* in 1828 was still very much of a minority, but hoped in the person of Victor Hugo to break down resistance to its messages: his voice and his claque will tumble Jericho. But for personal and other reasons, the army disintegrates after the fall of Jericho in 1830, and art for art's sake appears as a form of *non-possumus* from Théophile Gautier above all, who in a new climate of ideas will have nothing to do with civilizing the people of Jericho. Now art becomes at once a *monumentum aere perennius* and a refuge, Pater's cloister of calm; at once a world of consoling hopes and dreams *and* a rehearsal for future humanity.

The first document of importance is, of course, Gautier's introduction to *Madamoiselle de Maupin* (1835), a short but emphatic affair that speaks for a generation; that is still current for Wilde. The tone is off-handedly polemical, intended to frighten the bourgeoisie and spit at both respectability and revolt. If the bourgeois moralizer wants literature to improve the reader, then what happens to dramatic art if one takes 'thou shalt not kill' seriously?[6] Gautier's notions about obscenity in literature prefigure the campaign for dealing with all aspects of life, culminating in *Ulysses*, when man can be altogether described, masturbation, farts and all.

As for the so-called *Utilitarian* critics of Gautier's friends' books: socialists, Saint Simonians—great acrobatics about the word 'utility'—of what use are music and painting; what good Utilitarian would be mad enough to prefer Michelangelo to the man who invented white mustard? 'Nothing is truly beautiful, but what is useless; everything useful is ugly.'[7] Utilitarianism, in Gautier's use of the term, implies progress; but progress is a mirage; no one nowadays can eat as much as Milo of Croton who ate an ox, and there are no more deadly sins now than the seven there have always been.[8] Progress and utility and politics are inelegant as well as inoperative. The most becoming occupation for a civilized man is to do nothing or else smoke his pipe or cigar analytically.[9] Gautier has a high regard too for billiard players and also for good verse writers. Various forms of art are a game and a luxury, and the equivalent of this in narrative literature is disengagement.

And Baudelaire and Flaubert continue the polemic against progress ('a doctrine of Belgians': Baudelaire) and Utilitarianism ('a California of lunacy': Flaubert.) Among the French, 'art for art's sake' remains an aesthetic of exclusion. Symbolism will change all that, while in England, Ritualism, the Kyrle Society and other movements attempt some modest inclusiveness.

Some English Sources

And as for England, Max Beerbohm's clever–silly dating of the Aesthetic Movement won't do: 'Beauty existed long before 1880. It was Mr Oscar Wilde who managed her debut. To study the period is to admit that to him was due no small part of the social vogue that beauty began to enjoy.'[10] Beauty had been taken up by smart society before 1880. Max's essay appeared in 1894 when the Aesthetic Movement was dead, though all the aesthetes were not, and he was thinking of the birth of the 'Souls' and of the mellifluous Lady Elcho and of Lady Archibald Campbell, Whistler and Godwin's patroness; but Aestheticism spread to the suburbs and the Aesthetic aristocrats took up bicycling. But of course Aestheticism and the Aesthetic type had existed long before 1880, and Beauty had made something of a debut long before that, though not perhaps altogether in the best circles. Graham Robertson made the disconcerting suggestion that the origins lie in the 'passionate Brompton' of the 1860s with old ladies stitching those lumpy shepherds, milkmaids and stylized flowers, that reconditely anticipate Kate Greenaway and the children's books of a mature Aestheticism.[11]

As for the connections between the Queen Anne period and Aestheticism, in 1860–61 the novelist William Makepeace Thackeray, who had a cult of that period, built himself a house in Palace Gate that could be fairly described as being in a vaguely early-eighteenth-century Victorian style. But Queen Anne in purer form existed well before Thackeray's house: John Shaw's Wellington School dates back as far as 1852. But Shaw was as unversed in publicity as the dear old Ladies of Brompton. Moreover, it was in the 1860s that the manuals on the House Beautiful, furniture, dress and the Book Beautiful begin to appear. Those constitute one of the main literary manifestations of the movement and will be looked at later.

But to return to the art-for-art's-sake thread within the Aesthetic Movement, we might begin with Richard Payne Knight (1750–1824), dilettante, landowner, gardener, aesthetician, poet and most other things, who might have understudied for Mr Rose of the *New Republic* with his enthusiasm for that naughty book *Les Cultes secrets des dames romains*, since those mysteries we may presume were not to be celebrated without some aid from Monsieur Dildo. Knight's offering was concerned more with nature than with art: *A Discourse on the Worship of Priapus* ... (1786). Its author, so the rumour runs, alarmed by the distress of the Philistine, tried to buy up all copies he could find. It is, however, his views on the 'picturesque' that involve him in the art-for-art's-sake story, though the phrase was far from having become formulaic at that time in England or France. Painting, Knight asserts, does not portray objects comprehensively; it isolates their visual qualities: painting is a language, existing for its own sake. And great painting by no means necessarily depends on noble subject. The great painter can dignify any object: flabby women (Rubens) or a flayed ox (Rembrandt) where the reality might merely disgust.[12] Indeed, the corollary might seem to be the *jolie laide* of decadent theorists: the novel beauty of ugliness.

Two other significant figures in the development of visual beauty for its own sake are Sir Charles and Lady Eastlake. In the latter's famous review of Ruskin's *Modern Painters* in the *Quarterly Review* of 1856, she argues that 'thought' and 'ideas' are separable from, and not superior to, the language of painting itself. We seem to be listening to a Baudelaire or a Whistler when she declares, 'art was *not* given to man either to teach him religion or morality.... Art [is] not a direct moral agent to all.'[13]

Janice Nadelhaft in a recent article[14] has furnished evidence that *Punch*'s polemics about those who advocated the autonomy of art touched only one of the aspects of Aestheticism of which that periodical disapproved, and that its attacks on Aestheticism had begun as early as 1841. The target was a group of dramatists, influenced by German Idealist philosophers (Kant and Schiller), who called themselves the Syncretic Society, an offshoot of the London Aesthetic Institution. The Syncretics' views were anti-rational, and *Punch*'s attacks may be seen in the context of the mid-Victorian reaction against Romanticism. Westland Marston, John Abraham Heraud, and their colleagues attributed a high role to the poet. Like Gautier, the Syncretics were anti-Utilitarian; they remained, though, naively devoid of Gautier's scepticism about the vulnerability of Jericho. For the Syncretics, the poet mediated between the spiritual world and *lumpen* humanity; the poet was not necessarily alienated from the public, and by definition poetry should be devoted to the exploration and expression of the poet's inner life. Poetry should also expand the areas of experience commonly treated in literature. Its concern is with the cultivated individual rather than in any immediate sense with society. Marston, Heraud and their associates admired Shelley, Keats, Blake and Browning—advanced taste in the 1840s. In spite of their élitism, the Syncretics' ambition was to conquer the stage, but their programme failed at its onset. In the 1840s also, R.H. Horne in his

'Essay on Tragic Influence' anticipated Pater in stressing relativism and art for art.[15] Throughout the decade, *Punch* ridiculed the Syncretics, whose self-image was Prometheus (rather than the Narcissus of the later Aesthetes).

In 1850 the Roman Catholic Church re-established its hierarchy in England, and *Punch*, like your average Protestant, interpreted this action as 'Papal aggression'. Celibate priesthood and floridly Italianate ritual were an affront to the English, who liked their sexes to be well differentiated. The tepidly subversive role of the Syncretics was continued by a group of young poets nicknamed the 'Spasmodics', puffed by a Scots critic George Gilfillan. Their plays were intended only for the study, allowing still more indiscipline, though 'Spasmodic' heroes were culled from the same moody stock as the Syncretics. Their brief fame, as everyone knows, was brilliantly extinguished by W.E. Aytoun's *Firmilian* (1854), presented to the world under the pseudonym of T. Percy Jones, the humdrum name contrasting sharply with the language, incidents and ambition of the offering. Goethe and Byron furnish models for the hero, though, as Aytoun consolingly insists in his mock review of *Firmilian*, T. Percy Jones does not carry his imitative admiration of *Faust* to the extent of personally evoking Lucifer, Mephistopheles and Co. The review lists the principal beliefs of the Spasmodics; that is, poetry is a sacred calling and anything that limits the poet's development must be disregarded or even destroyed. The group rarely, if ever, attempt anything as obvious as a plot, and they tend to the prurient. *Firmilian*, though, Aytoun gravely tells us, is a favourable specimen of its kind since, if not exactly burdened with a plot, it at least has 'some kind of comprehensible action'.[16] To accomplish his drama on the topic of *Cain*, the hero concludes that he must himself commit murder in order to feel the exquisite pangs of remorse; but after disposing of a benefactor and a number of friends, and even blowing up a cathedral crowded for a service, the hero remains unable to feel anything of the sort, and his integrity forces him to abandon *Cain* altogether. The parody still reads amusingly. The hero braces himself to 'Be great in guilt!' but falls into bathos when addressing his blackamoor lady (he intends a *menage à quatre*): 'the fiery song/Which that young poet framed, before he dared/Invade the vastness of his lady's lips,'[17] lines which could hardly be published in these more liberal and sensitive days. Firmilian assures us that he plans to push his best friend off a tower: 'think not he dies a vulgar death/The poetry demands the sacrifice.'[18] The unfortunate victim squashes in his fall. Apollodorus, alias Gilfillan, on the hunt for yet another obscure proletarian genius, and announcing the fact vaporously: 'I've dashed into the seas of metaphor/With as strong paddles as the sturdiest ship/That churns Medusae into liquid light.'[19]

The Un-Aesthetic Novel

Aytoun satirized proto-Aestheticism more tellingly than the random cartoons of *Punch*, and in 1857 Charles Kingsley published a novel, *Two Years Ago* (the title looks back to the close of the Crimean War), that is the first of a series with 'spasmodic' or 'aesthetic' anti-heroes. John Briggs, a sensitive, Shelleyan youth, small of stature and feminine by nature, is brought up with, and bullied by, one of Kingsley's thuggish heroes, Tom Thurnall. Tom advises Briggs, self-styled 'priest of the beautiful' to change his name if he wishes to succeed: there can be no Briggs by the Helicon. When the two next encounter one another, the poet has taken the sneering advice and renamed himself 'Elsley Vavasour'. Elsley's uniform is described by another muscular, not too Christian lout as 'nasty, effeminate, un-English foppery'.[20] Poor Elsley is tall on *weltschmertz* and severely devoid of humour. Averse to action, he fails to help out in the village when cholera strikes.

Kingsley admits that Elsley has genius and that his earlier poems move the audience to a love of moral and spiritual beauty, but (unforgivable in a poet) he allows his imagination 'to run riot' in Chapter 24, and his poetry becomes progressively less concerned with the state of England, with 'needlewomen and ragged schools'. Instead he devotes himself to the political subjection of distant Italy (Kingsley may well have had in mind Sydney Dobell's pseudonym Sydney Yendys, Dobell's closest drama *The Roman* and his Crimean War poetry; he had met Dobell a year or two earlier). As Elsley grows older, more moody and self-absorbed, his poems lose all pretence of subject; they become mere 'word-painting'. The work of art's subject is—itself. Far from dissipating his melancholy by cold baths and jogging, Elsley takes to opium: a logical end for one who believes that he is sent into the world to see and not to act.

Behind such a notion of self-culture lies the philosophy of Goethe, a culture-hero for the mid-Victorians, and the great

German is duly savaged: 'Self-education, and the patronage of art and the theatre—for merely aesthetic purposes.... [He] thinks himself an archangel, because he goes on to satisfy the lust of the eyes and the pride of life. Christ was of old the model, and Sir Galahad was the hero. Now the one is exchanged for Goethe, and the other for Wilhelm Meister' (p. 128). And one of Kingsley's several fierce women—fit mates for the straightforward Anglo-Saxon christianized male—tells off an American aesthete: 'You, the critic ... the highly organized do-nothing—teaching others how to do nothing most gracefully; the would be Goethe, who must, for the sake of his own self-development, experiment on every weak woman whom he met' (p. 130). And the poor transatlantic aesthete is shamed into thanking the fierce one for rousing him from that 'conceited dream of self-culture ... into the hope of becoming useful, beneficent'. Stangrave, the New Englander, overfastidiously shrinks from action and indulges in frivolities:

> Poetry and music, pictures and statues, amusement and travel, became his idols, and cultivation his substitute for the plain duty of patriotism; and wandering luxuriously over the world, he learned to sentimentalise over cathedrals and monasteries, pictures and statues, saints and kaisers, with a lazy regret that such saints 'forms of beauty and loveliness' were no longer possible in a world of scrip and railroads; but without any notion that it was his duty to reproduce in his own life, or that of his own country, as much as he could of the said beauty and nobleness (pp. 132–4).

'A mediaevalising impressionist', Stangrave, and it is barely surprising that the same page leads to an attack on Pre-Raphaelitism, praised for its local honesty but condemned for its unnatural ugliness (Millais is presumably the object). Why 'copying nature', wrinkles and all, is to be eschewed is because 'the double vision of our two eyes gives a softness, and indistinctness, and roundness, to every outline' (p. 135). Stangrave is, of course, converted to action. 'Life', he tells us, 'is meant for work and not for ease; to do a little good ere the night comes ... instead of trying to realise for oneself a Paradise; not even Bunyan's shepherd-paradise, much less Fourier's casino-paradise; and perhaps least of all ... my own heat-paradise—the apotheosis of loafing ... Ah! Tennyson's Palace of Art is a true word—too true, too true!' (p. 381). Another penitent character observes

> that his Goethe fever is long-past.... Easy enough it seems for a man to educate himself without God, as long as he lies comfortably on a sofa, with a cup of coffee and a review; but what if that 'daemonic element of the universe', which Goethe confessed, and yet in his luxuriousness tried to ignore, because he could not explain, what if that broke forth over the graceful and prosperous student, as it may any moment (pp.432–3).

It certainly breaks forth over poor Elsley, who is in a worse case as he creates rather than merely contemplates the beautiful.

Anti-intellectualism is not the only object of polemic in *Two Years Ago*. As we might expect from the sour allusions to cathedrals and monasteries, revived medievalism (even Patristic enthusiasm) in any form is suspect. Puseyites are mocked at more genially than Mr Punch, though the implication is the same: they are wolves in sheep's clothing—addicted to 'bowings', 'crossings', and 'chanting' at St Nepomonic's; 'brotherhoods', 'sisterhoods', and 'all ... gorgeous and highly organized appliances for enabling five-thousand rich to take tolerable care of five hundred poor'. The decade was one when several Anglican brotherhoods and sisterhoods were established.[21] The hysteria stems not only from patriotic and Protestant affront, but from Kingsley's own psychology. He distrusted celibacy as a Manichean invention, encouraging effeminacy in men. His own view of marriage is to be gathered from those amazing drawings in which himself and his wife, nude, are presented making love, corded to a cross that floats on tumid waters, though this image fades beside one where Kingsley and his wife, at the general resurrection, wing nudely upwards in actual coition.[22] Bondage was one of Kingsley's major stimulants; one of his longer poems is on the subject of Andromeda, and in the closet-play *The Saint's Tragedy* we encounter lines that might have been written by the earlier Swinburne, though it is Kingsley's men who tend to lash the women:

> Those cushioned shoulders' ice,
> And thin soft flanks with purple lashes all,
> And weeping furrows traced.[23]

Kingsley's novel, then, presents the type of the effeminate aesthete, whether artist or critic, associated with High Churchness or an aestheticized Catholicism. Such polemical presentation becomes the model for such later novels as Mrs Margaret Hunt's

Thorneycroft's Model (1874), Vernon Lee's *Miss Brown* (1881) and Robert Buchanan's *The Martyrdom of Madeline* (1882), to mention only a few. The figure of Lewis Seymour, painter and lounge lizard, in George Moore's *A Modern Lover* (1883), has all the characteristics of the type, but rich women and a latent philistinism, becoming a Royal Academician rather than an aesthete (self-culture and morbid inaction), are now the polemical substance.

Kingsley's Elsley had been a composite, but it was not long before a model from life was typed as 'Aesthete' through an existing polemical vocabulary. In the *Saturday Review* of 10 October 1863, an Oxford contemporary wrote a hostile obituary essay on the Latin Catholic convert. Oratorian, and poet, Frederick William Faber, reacting ostensibly against the 'gaudy' *éloge* of the Catholic newspaper *The Tablet:* 'To its author, the life of ... Frederick William Faber seems something like a superhuman marvel. To us it seems as natural and explicable as if the owner of it had been plain William Smith'[24] Or for that matter, John Briggs. Faber was flashy, not solid. As one of his fellow-converts is reported to have regretfully murmured, 'no bottom, no bottom'. His handsomeness, we learn, was of 'a feminine sort'; his manner affected, and he had initially offended his Oxford contemporaries by transforming his 'scout's hole' into an oratory. Already Faber was refinedly self-indulgent (Mr Rose of *The New Republic* was to have two main topics: self-indulgence and art), preached 'lady-like sermons' and turned his gardens into 'an aesthetic promenade' (whatever dubious activity that harmless phrase may mask). When converted, 'he carried with him a dozen or so of his parishioners, including certain choir-boys whose parents made some unpleasant references to the fifth commandment.... In all the non-masculine virtues he was admirably suited to shine, he was popular' with 'a small and rather spoony set'.[25] 'Spoony', a synonym for sentimental devotion, though generally applied to schoolgirl 'crushes', was applied increasingly to Uranian lovers. In the 1870s Oxford aficionados of adolescent boys were described as 'spooning'. The anonymous *Saturday* author's piece is unified by harping on effeminacy and Uranianism: 'Even his weakness for attracting (some people called it kidnapping) schoolboys was turned to its use, as a recent and unpleasant instance has shown the unadmiring world'.[26] Like Gautier's tone, Faber's freedom of speech 'people in general were inclined to characterise as flippancy'. The conclusion is that Faber was if little else 'decidedly ornamental'.

Eight months earlier, the *Saturday* had been at it in a piece entitled 'Aesthetical Delusions', protesting against the word 'artist' indiscriminately applied to any fine art, whether the art of acrobat or rope dancer or any other romantic person who is doomed to 'live his poem' instead of 'writing it'. Those with 'aesthetical sensibilities' or 'artistic temperament', we are told, manifest a discontent with common life, and the author finds precedents in Lydia Languish, Maria Edgeworth's tale of the 'unknown Friend', Byronism and Wertherism, though young men in England generally evade suicide and do not become bandits. But these young men *do* believe that the artist is a 'law unto himself', born to follow his own impulses; if he does not harmonize with society, then so much the worse for society. Sensibility consequently substitutes for morality: the subjectively good and beautiful become the end of life.[27]

From its neutral origins in the eighteenth century and its prestige among Idealist philosophers, the word 'aesthetic' is by the late 1860s rapidly becoming a pejorative term. We are told that a great scholar is able to observe of a young man that though he is 'remarkable for his aesthetical tastes', he 'yet evinced considerable ability'. And the aesthetic young man no longer asks if this or that is right or wrong, but 'how will it look if worked up into a poem and what new subtlety in human nature can I discover?' Nor does 'poisonous honey stol'n from France' revolt him: no sentiment is too painful for his scrutiny. Self-analysis becomes a new and satisfying employment and, like Firmilian, the ever so aesthetic young man performs strange acts purely from *frisson*; loses all 'elementary rectitude of response' and soon 'yearns morbidly for pain'. Swinburne, of course, has happened since the *éloge* for Faber; 'art for art's sake' has been asserted in the recently published William Blake essay; Prometheus has ceded to Narcissus and the course of Aestheticism melting into Decadence has been predicted.

Visual Satire

Visual satire connects Pre-Raphaelitism and Aestheticism. The 'china craze' originated with Rossetti and Whistler early in the 1860s, and by the close of that decade the demand for blue Nanking was high. It was not, however, until December 1874 that *Punch* and Du Maurier first mentioned 'chinamania'. A little girl blubbers to her mama: 'O! O! N-N-Nurse has given me my c-c-cod liver oil out of a p-*plain white mug*.'[28] In the following year chinamania has become acute when a small child fails to console her mother for the loss of a favourite pot: 'You child! You're not unique!! There are six of you—a complete set.'[29] Aestheticism can distort normal family affections, and the types of the aesthete are already embodied in *Punch* for 2 May 1874:[30] the haggard eye, drooping mouth, and long jaw of the wife; the husband, proleptically drooping-shouldered and ineffectual. The mother mourning over her broken pot has a flowing dress and loosened hair that suits both with grief and 'aesthetic' tendencies in the context of a tastefully simple room with bare polished floor-boards and high wainscot.

Charles Lock Eastlake, nephew of Sir Charles, in the first of the manuals devoted to the 'House Beautiful', *Hints on Household Taste in Furniture, Upholstery and other Details* (1868), observed that the collecting vogue of the 1860s was not confined to china, but that the smallest example of rare old porcelain, metals, venetian glass, enamels, and so on, 'which illustrate good design and skilful workmanship, should be acquired whenever possible and treasured with the greatest care ... a little museum may thus be formed'.[31] As far back as 1860, *Punch* had a young man offer a perplexed uncle a decanter of fantastic design, and in 1873, a girl presents her cousin with a 'bit of Japanese enamel'[32] which he desecrates by dropping ash into it.

The taste for *japonaiserie* was also associated with the aesthete, particularly with E.W. Godwin and Whistler. Japanese fans as wall-decoration are present in 1872, and the appearance of Oriental motifs—blossoms, cranes and tall female figures on firescreens and room dividers—rapidly follow. In February 1876 in 'Intellectual Epicures'[33] surrounded by artistic wallpapers, blue china, Japanese fans, medieval snuff boxes and his favourite periodicals of the eighteenth century, the dilettante De Tomkyns complacently boasts that he never reads a newspaper and that the events of the outer world possess no interest for him whatever.[34] De Tomkyns's pose is spineless enough, though he has not yet developed the fully attenuated aesthetic physique. His absorption in 'culture' has led him into total withdrawal from everyday life, and the eighteenth-century enthusiasm is notable.

Mr Rose of the *New Republic* and Walter Hamlin in Vernon Lee's 'aesthetic' novel *Miss Brown* similarly approve of withdrawal from the ugliness of the present. De Tomkyns is juxtaposed with an old charwoman in the right panel of the drawing, who expresses similar failure of interest in wars and 'sea-sarpints'.[35] And as Elizabeth James points out, *Punch*'s inhumanitarian style makes the charwoman as laughable as De Tomkyns so that the moral comment tends to evaporate. A similar ambiguousness—Du Maurier after all shared aesthetic tastes with his victims—can be detected in later *Punch* cartoons. What is interesting in the 1878 narrative and illustration 'The Rise and Fall of the Jack Spratts',[36] an indigent painter and his 'girl-wife' with Pre-Raphaelite tastes, is that Aestheticism has spread to shabby Bohemia: the Spratts live in a rundown red-brick house, built at the time of Queen Anne; it is only the dust on their muddle of objects that harmonizes them.

Correspondences between the arts is a familiar symptom of the Aesthetic Movement. *Punch*'s 'Jack Easel' had commented as early as 1860 on Whistler's first work exhibited in England at the Royal Academy 'At the Piano': 'The tone which he has produced from his piano is admirable, and he has stuck on it a chord of colour which I hope will find an echo in his future works'.[37] It was three years before the painter's first 'Symphony in White' was painted. Satire of such features was not limited to the cartoon or the novel. *The Grasshopper* which ran at the Gaiety Theatre in 1877 has a character, Pygmalion Flippit, featured as a 'Harmonist in colours.... Like my great master Turner, I see things in a peculiar way, and I paint them as I see them.'[38] The audience was invited to behold 'a dual harmony in Red and Blue. You observe before you ... the boundless ocean lighted up by one of those Gorgeous Sunsets.... Reverse the harmony thus, and you have the equally boundless Desert ... slumbering peacefully beneath an Azure sky.'[39] In *Fun*, an even brasher organ than *Punch*, the confidence-trick element in Aestheticism (with corroboration from the Whistler–Ruskin trial) seems to confuse the production of Nocturnes with Tachism. The medium is 'a pair of shoe brushes on my feet, and a bucket of any colour'.[40]

Where the earlier Aesthetes appear as harmless, effeminate, dangerous mainly to themselves, by the end of the 1870s, both in drama and novel, they tend to be portrayed as more self-conscious and sinister. Lambert Stryke, in the editor of *Punch* F. C. Burnand's *The Colonel* (1881),[41] is a confidence trickster pure and simple with his flotation of the Aesthetic High Art Company Limited that aims to cultivate 'the Ideal as the consummate embodiment of the Real and to proclaim aloud to a dull material world the worship of the

Lily and the Peacock Feather.'[42] Stryke's enjoyment of good food has to be concealed to maintain the pretence that he feeds on beauty alone. Most of Stryke's disciples are aristocratic devotees.

The Aesthetic Manuals

Punch's Mr Fernando F. Eminate in 1877, if epicene, is nimbly topical in recommending for drawing-room decoration 'lattice windows glazed with opaque glass', 'sage-green or dull yellow for walls, and black furniture; not carpets' but 'straw matting' on the floor and dado.[43] Pictures, of course, by 'E.B. Jones and Whistler' and 'delf and blue china'. In one of the 'Aesthetic' novels, Walter Besant's and James Rice's *The Monks of Thelema* of the same year,[44] the plan for a cottage might have been designed by Fernando or appropriated by him:

> The windows were to have diamond panes, *en grisaille*, to open on hinges: the rooms, each with a dado, were to be prepared and painted in grey and green: Dutch tiles were to adorn the stoves and the fenders were of brass: no carpets, of course, but matting in wonderful designs: cabinets for the inexpensive blue and white china: chairs in black wood and rush, with tables to correspond.[45]

Eastlake's *Hints on Household Taste* (1868) had no successor—apart from its later reprintings and revisions. In 1875, though, *Punch* ran a series, 'The House and the Home' by Leonardo della Robbia de Tudor Westpond Tomkyns ... Hon. Member of the Dulidillitanty Society, of the 'low-toned papers' and tiled dado—the first dado in *Punch*,[46] it seems, for the dado was in *Punch*'s view both ridiculous and indispensable to the aesthetic 'House Beautiful'; perhaps the noise of the word itself was pruny and prismy enough to encourage giggles.

'Soft indescribably' colours were promoted in reaction to the harsher primaries of the earlier nineteenth century. The Misses Garrett in *Suggestions for House Decoration* (1877) urge the suitability for the bedroom of 'shades of soft olive and sage green' not only are they 'particularly pleasant and restful to the eye but altogether safe because freer from the arsenic used in the brighter greens'.[47] Eastlake had advised a 'delicate green or a warm grey tint' and 'silver grey' as suitable backgrounds for pictures in living rooms, embossed white or cream colours for walls where watercolours were hung.[48] However, all the manuals associated with the movement did not agree: W. J. Loftie, for example, in *A Plea for Art at Home*, orthodoxly plumps for a dark-red ground as best for oils,[49] while Jakob von Falke sounds a note of caution in his rigorously and Teutonically detailed *Art in the House* (1879). The wall, he tells us, should be 'absolutely quiet in tone'; it must 'harmonize in colour with all, or with as many of the pictures as possible, it should be of a neutral tint....'[50] Red, that is to say, 'a dark broken red, neither too fiery nor too rusty ... of a flat tint' should be used with a border, flat in tint, or with a simple conventional hue of the same group. Alternatively, Falke would allow 'a decidedly broken and subdued green, something like the colour of green tea, or a dull drab'. No trace of Whistlerian or Godwinian chaste light colour here, though any mention of straw matting will suggest those sources. The engravings of the Garretts' book are specially tasteful: Godwinian coffee-tables, Morris wallpapers and so on.

All this indicates the distance we have travelled from Eastlake's *Hints on Household Taste*. As Aslin has remarked, the illustrations there (although Eastlake replaced some of those in the first edition) have a mid-Victorian look that does not altogether reflect the book's modern elements. Eastlake's accenting of industrial art looks back to Sir Henry Cole's preoccupations and the establishment of the Schools of Design; but also accents his sober and pragmatic tone. Unlike the authors of later manuals, he is aware that establishing what is bad and what should not be done is easier than to 'indicate the road to excellence'. His prejudices are strong. He prefers the English and the Gothic: French taste, so vulnerable to the rococo—'curves with everything'—and the curvilinear in furniture, rarely functional, he considers vicious. What is 'modern' is Eastlake's approval of 'fidelity to material': function must not be hidden; substance conditions form; ornament depends on the nature of the material: and art is degenerate when it directly imitates natural form, though nature remains a norm. Students should study natural form, and colours should, as in nature, be 'graduated'. Drawing room chairs may be light, though not rickety. The dado (presumably toned distinctively) is required to prevent monotony in the expanses of wall, floor and ceiling. And confirming his nearness to Morris and Art and Craft, Eastlake is insistent on the superiority of wrought to cast iron, of handcraft to manufacture; he deplores stucco. His own sympathies are clearly with the Gothic, but he recognizes that it is a condition of civilization that taste should move in cycles, and he himself seems to have moved in later editions to a guarded approval of the Queen Anne style for domestic uses, though he remains uneasy over nineteenth-century eclecticism. On the other hand, total art is condemned and, unlike Morris, he does not approve of the four poster. Most of his rhetoric involves 'we', as appeal to consensus, now that he detects continuous improvement in public taste. Occasionally, he uses the first person and the lively contemptuous note that is frequent in the later manuals: English carpet design, with its naturalistic flora, is only fit to cover the floor of the Chamber of Horrors at Madame Tussaud's; as for Irish porcelain, it 'glistens like wet barley sugar'.[51] A circular rosette is an obviously appropriate feature for the joint where the rods intersect in an iron bedstead instead of the small boss generally introduced. The designer 'insists on inventing a lumpy bit of ornament, which, possibly intended to represent a cluster of leaves, more closely resembles a friendly group of garden slugs, and this excrescence is repeated not only a dozen times in one bedstead, but in some thousands of the same pattern.'[52]

Eastlake shows a concern with manufacturing industry that is not always typical of the more florid and devoted manuals of the high Aesthetic period. Many such works were written by women, Eastlake appears to be writing more for men than women. He has, for example, more to say on the topic of men's than women's clothing, but apart from deploring male dress and observing that the old hoop is better than its modern version, he is not at all prescriptive.[53] Falke, on the other hand, devotes a chapter to 'Woman's Aesthetic Mission'. It is man who is responsible for all beautiful works of art: female artists are few and minor and succeed best in the minuter arts. Woman's domain is the home where she can create the 'House Beautiful' for her menfolk, who are too busy with business to visit museums. 'Shall the gates of the kingdom of beauty be therefore closed', he asks, 'to the countless myriads of men who cannot visit museums and collections, and to whom all possibility of coming under the influence of art is denied?'[54] No, for the Useful and the Beautiful shall lie down together in the House of Art, a temple whose artificer and priestess is the wife. 'Her husband's occupations necessitate his absence and call him far away from it. During the day his mind is occupied in many good and useful ways, in making and acquiring money ... and even after the hours of business have passed, they occupy his thoughts. When he returns home tired with work he takes pleasure in the home which his wife has made comfortable ... and has beautified with works of art.'[55] The home should be a temple for the tired businessman, where he can brood more agreeably on the goodness and usefulness of acquiring money, and a means also of keeping lonely wives out of mischief. Falke accents the influence of beautiful objects on children, and in England, certainly, children's clothes and books became expressions of the Aesthetic Movement.[56] Books, for example, were visually agreeable, entertaining and did not peddle morals. Finally, Falke insists that the woman of the house should dress up to her 'artistic surroundings', should herself be 'the noblest ornament in the ornamented dwelling'.[57]

Neither of the two manuals already glanced at can be termed imaginative literature; but Mrs M.E. Haweis's *Beautiful Houses*, a set of articles contributed to *The Queen* in 1880–81 and in the latter year published in book form, is firmly within the Aesthetic Movement and amounts arguably to a set of prose poems about the interiors of houses belonging to and largely designed by artists such as Lord Leighton and architects such as William Burges and the Queen Anne style architect J.J. Stevenson. She looks also at several wealthy virtuosi and the interior of the British Embassy at Rome. The volume is itself a total work of art, designed for 'time-travelling' through museums not altogether imaginary, 'a modern vision of the past' and it involves the 'beauty of inclusion', a controlled eclecticism that can contain wide margins, catchwords, the long 's', side notes (anterior to Whistler's *Gentle Art*) and the occasional black-letter words looking back to the sixteenth century, wood-cut initials and running heads that rather remarkably extend beyond the sidenotes, so unifying the page, and with rich italicizing of the text.

> In Lord Leighton's house the main feature is the gradual progress and ascent to the studio, and the arrangement of the ground floor, where hall opens out of hall, reviving now antique, now mediaeval, now *Renascence Italy*, from *Florence* to *Rome*, down through regal *Naples*, on to *Cairo* itself; and yet it is not *Rome*, nor *Sicily*, nor *Egypt*, but a memory, a vision seen through modern eyes.
>
> Turning aside from the foot of the stairs, we pass through peacock-greeny arches, with deep gold incisions, into the third Hall, called of *Narcissus*, which strikes a full deep chord of colour, and deepens the impression of antique magnificence. A bronze statuette of the fair son of *Cephisus*, from that in the Naples Museum, stands in the midst of it. Here the walls are deepest sea-blue tiles, that shades made dark; the floor is pallid (the well-known mosaic of the *Caesars'* palaces), and casts up

> shimmering reflected lights upon the greeny-silver ceiling, like water itself. There is something poetic and original in thus echoing here and there the points in the story of *Narcissus*—not repeating point-blank the hackneyed tale, or showing the fair boy adoring his mirror'd self in the 'lily-paven lake', but just recalling it piecemeal—the lilies in the pavement, the shining lake above, and all the joy and sorrow, the luxury and pain of his loneliness and aberration, told by the colours, the purple and the gloom, and by the boy's own attitude.
>
> There is undoubtedly here an imperial stateliness and strength of flavour; and the silence is like a throne. The deep shades of the corners are filled with tarsia work and porcelain; but, as in a well-coloured picture, these are absolutely subservient; and the impression given is purple; like a Greek midnight, circling round a point of softest green (the bronze boy), and falling into a warm grey on the floor.
>
> But further on—beyond this vestibule—dwells the sun! and here springs up the lovely dome as of the *Alhambra*, made of the dust of the earth, but quickened by the rainbow, even as man's body sprang from dust and received a soul. People who have not a real sense of colour cannot understand the joy in it of those who have. Fine colour comes like food, like joyful news, like fresh air to fainting lungs.[58]

Disclaiming any intention of dissecting the Moorish Court, Mrs Haweis still lingers intensely on disparate detail and evanescence of colour:

> The delicate tracery of the lattices brought bodily from the *East*, and which rise to right and left, having the complexity and colour of the skeleton of a leaf, and guarded by glass outside; the fine *alhacen* of carved wood which lines the central alcove facing us, with its four rare *Persian* enamels of women's figures, and its shelves of Persian plates; the brilliant little windows that break the sunshine into scarlet and gold and azure flame; the snow-white columns of marble that stand against red at every angle; the fountain that patters and sings in its pool of chrysolite water—most perfect *colophon* to all the colours and the outer heat. Again and again we wander round and enjoy the toss of its one white jet from a bed of water wherein descending ridges step-wise have the semblance of the emerald facets of a great green stone.[59]

In describing J.J. Stevenson's house, designed like Leighton's and Burges's by the owner, Mrs Haweis is severe on Bedford Park: 'Its handsome russet *façade* and niche holding a *Nankeen* vase, has been continually parodied by cheap builders possessed by the idea that red brick, a blue pot, and a fat sunflower in the window are all that is necessary to be fashionably aesthetic and *Queen Anne*'.[60] And on a sour, concluding note: 'To explain the apparent confusion of terms, I may remind readers how I have elsewhere shown that the slang term "*Queen Anne*" means almost anything just now, but it is oftenest applied to the psuedo-classic fashions of the *First Empire.*'[61] Mrs Haweis's book on aesthetic topics appeared during the year that the Movement began to decline.

Four years later, the patron and disciple of E. W. Godwin, who produced his open-air pastoral plays with their costumes delicately toned to the woodland ambiance in the grounds of her house at Coombe Warren in Surrey, Lady Archibald Campbell, published a strange slim essay *Rainbow: Music or the Philosophy of Harmony in Colour Grouping*, a faithful reflection according to her lights of the doctrines of Godwin, Whistler and, more remotely, Wagner. Her notion that certain laws, 'as true, though not as self-evident, as those of mathematics', operate in any work of art, was illustrated by what she predictably considered to be successful applications: the colour schemes of Godwin's pastoral performances and Whistler's 'Peacock Room', which achieved harmony through counterpoint of blue on gold, gold on blue. And the essay concludes with a lecture on the chromatics, 'by which the seven primary colours are said to harmonize with the seven gaps in the octave'.

Lady Archibald, though accurately described as the 'Queen Bee' of the Aesthetes, is sharply opposed to the 'House Beautiful' manuals. As for the art-works described by Mrs Haweis, Burges's *salle de reception* in the Castle of Pierrepont is 'like sitting in a Kaleidoscope'. Without theme, room-decoration is approached through inductive reasoning and didactic method, hardly impairing the flight of imagination. Decorative unity 'is alone worthy to be designated the Grand Style'. So the Imaginary Museum and the 'beauty of inclusiveness' approach is rejected. Lady Archibald gives us a close analysis of the Peacock Room, which concludes: 'In the mustering and opposing of these birds in feathered strife, in counterchange of golden plumes on field of azure plumes on field of gold—from the glancing movement of multitudinous eyes and erected feathers and interchange of fiery tone is evolved Peace—Unity—as of ONE Plume.'[62]

Lady Archibald's prose can be as lush as that of Mrs Haweis. 'The Iris Parlour' presumably refers to a real room (though this is not certain) at Inverary Castle, or her own house in Argyll, Ard Cheannglas, or even perhaps her other house at Coombe. The room is not the result of handcraft but of light and natural objects:

> Far from the sea, yet so much of the sea that within its glimmering walls the in-dweller may almost feel its air, listen for the lapping of a languid

tide, and dream that from jewelled sands have been gathered all the wealth of strange conceits which bedeck the room.

It is so far true, in that nothing but sea-wonders here find a place. Shells, large and small, shimmering with iridescent light, Venus's ears, the horned murex, rose-lipped conches, tender-coloured pectens, Triton's horns in amber and white, the graceful nautilus, the spikey spondelli, the pearl house of the sea-snail, the oyster, and the mussel—all are here. Corals peep pendant from nook and corner. A giant craw-fish from the Malay Straits combines in the tracery of its strange characteristics all the dominant hues of the room. These dominant hues are golden pink (or aurora), amethyst fading to pearl-grey, sea-green (aqua-marine), all melting in tone like the blushing dawn reflected in a calm sea. There are three lattice-windows of quaint but simple construction, all slightly differing; but as it is now evening, we see them closely curtained with aurora-colour satin of the same tint as that on the walls. On these walls are painted and on these curtains are embroidered many an Iris in delicate tint and fantastic form. Their fluttering heads and waving reeds bend hither, as if swayed by contending breezes; while others lie stricken to the ground, as if by a passing storm; their flowers vary in every tint of amethyst, pearl-grey, blue, pink, and white, and the reeds in aqua-marine and every tint of sea-green. Of nervy and resolute outline, it is the Iris of pure convention in form and treatment; for, painted in flat colour with little shading, it suggests the spirit rather than the substance. Here and there a crystal dew-drop glistens on a petal; here and there one stands out in bold relief, shining in *Iris* tints and bathed in light; and again the water-splashes from which they rise glance with the hues of a fading rainbow; the faint water-bow itself shimmers on the wall, through which flags and flowers are seen tipped with changeful colour; gold and silver mists hover among the reeds and add their witchery to the whole arrangement. The eye travelling the rainbow-path, or following the caprice of these wayward flowers and flags, is carried up first to a row of lustrous shells which, fixed rectangularly and about two feet apart on a pearl-grey velvet belt, support a slight shelf of gilded oak. The gilding is very pale and seems to repeat the self-same lustre as that of the shells. This shelf divides the aurora wall from an aqua-marine frieze above, and higher still, as the eye wanders upwards, the aurora appears again on cornice and ceiling cut into by an aqua-marine oval, thus leaving the surrounding corners of aurora free, whereon ghost-like Irises have room to wave their pennons, and beck and nod their shadowy heads; a golden fishing-net at a certain angle is looped across the ceiling, and within its folds glisten the changeful light of many shells. On the pearly-grey velvet curtain, drooped low across the wide bay-window we see embroidered a tangle of ocean plants in all the colours of the room. On the door are emblazoned Landor's famous lines on the sea-shell.[63]

A description follows of M. Chevreuil's colour-organ, of 1851, though later she alludes to that of the eighteenth-century Abbé

Castel. One is led to wonder if Lady Archibald had been reading *A Rebours*. That her 'Iris Parlour' is decadent and *symboliste*, we may gather from her rationale of the decoration.

> I have been asked why I selected the Iris to accompany the sea-shell as a joint element in this decoration. On the surface of things there is, indeed, a wide divergence between the pearly tombs of the deep and the sedgy margin of some shallow pool. Yet their point of concord and bond of union is a close one. By inter-marriage of Shell and Iris is simplicity, a certain singleness of purpose accentuated—pattern given through contrast of form and line, unity throughout the colour-scheme: the Shell contributing the ever-changing curvature of the volute, the spikey reed and flower-barbed shaft of the water-plant the required opposition in design. This sinuous Shell and Iris are, indeed, not only depositories of, but the symbols of, one and the same treasure—the message of peace. The Shell recording in its hollows the gift of Iris; the flower, true to its name, keeping the sign of its baptism when, long ago, the goddess stepped from her rainbow-path on the white lily, which men henceforth were to call *Iris*.[64]

The Aesthetic manuals belong to the high years of the Movement, 1878 to 1882, though the articles on which Mrs Haweis's *The Art of Beauty* was based had appeared several years earlier in *St Paul's*. There is then a hiatus, the years of the Guilds—Century and Art-Workers, among others—until *The Art of the House* (1897) by the poet Rosamund Marriott-Watson, who protests against the latest fashions:

> Unhappily the same movement that dethroned the bloated common places of the day before yesterday has given birth to ... monstrosities, human and inanimate. The decadent, the art 'square', the symbolist, the hand-painted looking glass, bedizened to distorted simulacra of Iris and Mary-lily; the 'art' wall-paper with its misbegotten sunflowers and poppies, its inane mediaeval dicky-birds intermixed with geometrical patternings, its living complexion, now sour, now sallow, but ever revolting.[65]

She consoles herself, however, that the monstrosities 'have mainly ebbed on to the suburbs'. Her book presumably appeared because of an ambitious art library scheme promulgated by the publishers, George Bell.

The Aesthetic Novel

That *Two Years Ago* furnished the model for the aesthete anti-hero is evident enough. We are told by *Fun* on 23 February 1881 that like Du Maurier's Pilcox, Basil Georgione was a chemist before he took to art; and John Briggs himself had run away from a chemist shop to be a poet. Briggs anticipates Henry James's *Roderick Hudson* of 1875, a morally weak artist and the type continues with the Hamlin of *Miss Brown* and Moore's Lewis Seymour.

Elsley Vavasour had a principled dislike of the horrible. *Punch* on 24 February 1877 devotes some attention to a nasty criminal case: a couple had brutally mistreated a servant they had been sent from an orphanage. As soon as the girl arrived, the mistress of the house had complained about her servant's appearance. She was too plain and 'she wished her child from the first to look only on what was beautiful'.[66] Mrs Perry applies the same criterion in *Miss Brown* and *Punch*, solemn for once, drew a moral about 'the absolute independence of Ethics and Aesthetics and the entire absence of correlation between Art and Morals'.[67]

The cold aesthete is memorably imaged in the Osmond of *Portrait of a Lady* (1881). James's Gabriel Nash, who 'announces' Nick Dormer's talent as a painter in *The Tragic Muse*, is an aesthete of another type; but Nash too objects to ugly words that denote an ugly world: 'Mr Pinks, the member for Harsh? What names to be sure.'[68] And Mr Rose in the *New Republic*, when he enters ugly houses, often takes 'a scrap of some artistic cretonne with me in my pocket as a kind of aesthetic smelling salts'.[69]

In *The Monks of Thelema* (1877) those who confront and those who evade the ugliness of common life are sharply contrasted. Alan Dunlop, a solemn young aristocrat, is under Ruskin's influence and has done his bit for the road-building project, unlike his friend Paul Rondelet, Fellow of 'Lothian College' (his name may owe something to the French and English Parnassian poets—or to the Rondoliers, who in their rondeaux, rondels, kyrielles and other old French forms, pursued the ideal of formal purity). While Dunlop applies himself to improving his estate, Rondolet lurks effetely, like the type about to appear in *Punch* with his 'long white fingers, which played plaintively about his face.... He spoke in a low voice as if exhausted by the effort of living among humans, and he spoke with melancholy, as if his superiority were a burden to him; he affected omniscience.'

Besant and Rice offer an aetiology of Aestheticism as a 'school of prigs ... some of them are still at Oxford; but some may now be found in London. They lounge about sales of china ... and they worship at the Grosvenor Gallery. Rondolet called himself, sadly, an agnostic, but he was in reality, a New Pagan.'[70] Whether this anticipates Wilde's New Hedonism is not clear. Rondolet is indifferent to the Ritualism of the Aesthetes, refuses to take orders, affects to be unable to pronounce his r's, and his poem 'Aspasia's Apology' is a companion piece to Rossetti's 'Jenny', only 'even more realistic'. 'Above all', Rondolet tells us, 'the man of Higher Culture is a critic', anticipating Pater and Gabriel Nash once more: 'Literature, you see, is for the convenience of others. It requires the most abject concessions. It plays such mischief with one's style that really I have to give it up.' Rondolet is an élitist, who finds it 'useless and even mischievous to promote culture. Especially when such efforts lead to personally interesting oneself with the lower classes.'[71] This attitude is the 'Paterian' as opposed to the 'missionary' attitude towards culture.

Thelema itself is a genteel, hardly Rabelaisian commune devoted to aesthetic dilettantism, with lectures and a gazette promulgating the Higher Culture. The agreeable life of the inhabitants of the Abbey (actually Alan's country house) is presented idyllically rather than ironically, though the tone drifts sometimes into irony. At Thelema, 'dining was no longer the satisfaction of an appetite; it became the practice of one of the fine Arts'.[72] The canon's daughter 'was aesthetic, dressed in neutral tints, parted her hair on the side, and corrected her neighbours in a low voice when they committed barbarities in art. She was not pretty, but she was full of soul, and she longed to be invited to join the order.' But invited, she is not. Her 'soul' is not smart enough. Alan, the landowner, has a total lack of success with aestheticizing the local proletariat. Briefly he finances Rondolet's magazine, more *raffiné* than any other review. It fails, and Rondolet resorts to the lower journalism, not 'writing for the common herd', but now 'swaying the masses'.[73]

Robert Buchanan in the Preface to his *Martyrdom of Madeline* (1882) hedges his bets by attempting to distinguish between 'Aestheticism proper'—he is still trying to exculpate himself from the Fleshly School Controversy of 1872—and 'the cant of Aestheticism'. Vernon Lee's Hamlin in *Miss Brown* of 1884 is both poet and painter and is certainly based on Rossetti, the main target of Buchanan's polemic, though he comes from the landed class. His refusal to ameliorate the condition of the villagers on his estate is compounded by incorporating their incestuous vice into his own poem. The analogue with Elsley Vavasour's impassive surveillance of a shipwreck as raw material for a poem is plain enough. The Pre-Raphaelite set in this novel is a simplified, coarsened version of William Michael Rossetti's circle at Fitzroy Square in the 1870s and 1880s.[74] In Buchanan's novel, Gavrolles represents the 'new Aesthetic set', influenced for the worst by 'poisonous honey' not exactly 'stolen from France' since Gavrolles is himself a Frenchman. This set supersedes the old Bohemia, though Gavrolles seems to add a missionary keenness to his 'art-for-art's sake' heresy. He is described as 'having Communist views'.[75] Buchanan's views of communist views probably owed more to contemporary reporting of the Commune than to Marx. Hamlin's exotic cousin Sacha is another evil graft on the native Bohemia. Elitism in Aesthetic circles is confirmed by the species of mutual admiration Buchanan disliked in Pre-Raphaelitism. He saw it as inevitably connected with the practice of several arts and the close connections between the arts. The poet writes a sonnet on the painter's 'poetic' image, while the painter illustrates the painterly qualities of the poet by illustrating his work, and both are praised by the 'aesthetic' critic. And Buchanan and 'Vernon Lee' share an attitude of pained sensitivity to the 'aesthetic' mode's accommodation to the erotic, though this becomes involved with Buchanan's genuine sympathy for the wrongs of women under the Victorian double standard. Even so, Buchanan still exalts woman for her traditional virtues of self-sacrifice, suffering and patience. He does not recognize any virtue in the Pre-Raphaelite and Aesthetic Movement's concern with women of the lower classes and with the 'unchaste' woman. What he observes is the reduction of woman to the role of sex-goddess: the Lucrezia Borgia of Swinburne's verse or her worship by Vernon Lee's Cosmo Clough (a version of Arthur O'Shaugnessy); the physical distortion of Rossetti's later mannerism, the convulsed necks in the *Astarte Syriaca* corresponding to the painter's psychic distortion of woman and that Zolaesque lingering over the degradation of women in the person of the prostitute. The stately Lecky, speaking for enlightened Victorian males, eloquently salutes the fallen woman as antinomy incarnate:

> herself the supreme type of vice [she] is ultimately the most efficient

> guardian of virtue. But for her, the unchallenged purity of countless happy homes would be polluted, and not a few who in the pride of their untempted chastity, think of her with an indignant shudder, would have known the agony of remorse and despair. On that one degraded and ignoble form are concentrated the passions that might have filled the world with shame. She remains, while creeds and civilisations fall, the eternal priestess of humanity, blasted for the sins of the people.[76]

To descend from that paean—we need only chaperone, not lock up our daughters—let us glance at the heroine of Mrs John Lillie's novella *Prudence*, who in Chapter 1 appears at an 'aesthetic gathering' in 'passionate Brompton' alarmingly without a chaperone. A male friend has brought her to the door and will call for her at one o'clock in the morning. *Prudence* was to be published in Britain, but appeared first in *Harper's New Monthly Magazine* between December 1881 and May 1882, altogether appropriately, for the action conforms to the now familiar contrast between Europe (ruined paradise) and America (wilderness becoming Eden), a *topos* doubtless deeply reassuring to its transatlantic audience. Aestheticism is part of that ruined paradise, but is mildly treated. The principal characters, with the exception of an absurd and absurdly named English aristocrat, Barley Simmonson (desperate evasion of libel?), are all transatlantic. Aestheticism has been taken up by Society and has claimed two charming cultivated sisters. The younger, Helena, is unmarried and is a sympathetic critic of the Movement. Prudence, a simple sweet thing from Ponkamak, precipitates the action when the Aesthetes take her up as an animated Boticelli or, as one genial hostess observes: 'The child is like the Pompeian Psyche'. In fact, she is like her pretty silly self, but plays her role capitally by acting as passive vehicle for specially designed Aesthetic dresses; like the girls of Albert Moore (whose work is alluded to when the Bromptonians visit the Grosvenor Gallery), Prudence *means* nothing at all. Her hopeful suitor, an American clergyman, discovers this. Helena falls in love with this young Hickory figure, who seems to her a forcible emblem not of London, Washington or Boston, but 'the fervider, more intrinsically American life which has for its background, as it were, the cañons of Colorado, the ranches of California' (p.455), very much 'as it were'. Helena nobly precipitates the two towards one another's arms, but Prudence is already absorbed in being the idol of the Aesthetes and the watercolouring, arpeggio doodling Barley

Simmonson is on the verge of proposing. Fortunately, another wealthier, moderately Hickory young American turns up and marries Prudence instead. Barley rapidly transposes his loss into sentiment and the reader is left wondering idly if Helena will ever again see her 'fervider intrinsically' Yankee preacher. But even the fervider one sees some good in Aestheticism, and Helena gravely observes that 'the false ground of aestheticism is only in the establishing a standard of feeling'. This rather baffling remark is given point by Barley, who clearly is quite unable to establish any standard of feeling. It hardly requires the narrator to mock Aestheticism when he is on stage. Even a peerage it seems can be aestheticized: 'Then we may wear laurel in Westminster; then we may assemble as one palpitating, perfect soul.'

The preoccupations of the novels of Kingsley, Mrs Hunt, Vernon Lee, Mrs Lillie and others, are more magisterially addressed by Henry James through *The Tragic Muse* of 1889, and in Gabriel Nash we at last encounter a sufficiently subtle species of 'aesthete', though one with a decadent fear of his own image: he seems to lose identity as Nick Dormer's portrait of him advances, and finally, like the Cheshire Cat, even his epigrams disappear.

The Kyrle Society

'Missionary' Aestheticism is best exemplified by the history of the Kyrle Society. It would require a far abler and more sociological pen than mine to write that history; all I can do is to mention and let fall salient moments. The Kyrle's origins have been traced to the appearance of a brief pamphlet in December 1875, 'A Suggestion to Those Who Love Beautiful Things' by Miranda, sister of the famous housing reformer Octavia Hill. Miranda suggested that a 'Society for the Diffusion of Beauty' along the lines of the 'Society for the Diffusion of Christian Knowledge' might be formed for 'helping the great work of making beautiful places for the poor … our towns are growing so enormously … there is less and less possibility of beautiful country objects being within the reach of the poor in their daily lives' for they were beyond walking distance.[77]

A small committee had actually begun work in October 1875, and its first, paradigmatic efforts included the planting of flowers on barren land, the draping of ugly buildings with creepers, the provision of window boxes and flowers, the painting of walls in St

Jude's church among the slums of Whitechapel with panels of wild flowers, and those of an institute building with sketches of the countryside, along with the carving of brackets. Miranda wrote plays for slum children and organized drama for the adults; oratorios were sung at churches in poor areas of London before working-class audiences and in public gardens on evenings of summer. More than a tinge of Ruskinism seems to colour such activities. The Kyrle Society published its first annual report in December 1876, and became a national organization in June 1877, when it acquired Prince Leopold and Princess Louise as, respectively, president and vice-president. The real work, though, was done by devoted bands of middle-class persons up and down the country. Often the same family would provide officers for the various activities through several generations. The national committee members included William Morris, G.F. Watts, Mrs Alfred Hunt, whom we have encountered already as author of *Thorneycroft's Model*, and the faintly incongruous figure of G.A. Sala, journalist and very *bon viveur*.

The society's name derived from the philanthropist John Kyrle of Ross in Herefordshire, celebrated in lines 249 to 280 of Pope's *Epistle to Bathurst* as one who on distinctly limited means provided considerable service to the local poor. The Kyrle was never to control much money, and appeals in the newspapers for funds and volunteers were not infrequent. Octavia,[78] the more forcible of the Hill sisters, was active in the more public activities of the Society, the Open Spaces Committee, which began by transforming old churchyards of the inner city into gardens, preserving open spaces in the suburbs, so becoming the ancestor of the present National Trust. *Punch*, which seems not to have become aware of the Kyrle Society until 1881, directed its satire mainly against the notion of offering beauty to the poor in place of bread, and feared the unsettling of those whose labour sustained the social order. A few verses from 'A Kyrley Tale' to the tune of 'A Norrible Tale' will make the point:

Oh a curious tale I am going to tell
Of the singular fortunes that befel
A family which late resided
In a slum by High Art much derided.

They never dreamed of the Weird Intense,
Though a family of undoubted sense,

Till a Kyrle Man came with his lyre and lily,
And drove that unfortunate household silly.

He came, soft carolling, 'Lo! I Come!
My mission's the bringing of Beauty home!'
And he opened the door, and he led her in,
A weariful damsel pale and thin.

With eyes as dusk as the veil of Isis,
Like an incarnation, she seemed, of Phthisis.
When in he ushered this spectral Psyche,
The family's comment all round was 'crikey!'

But the spell was on them, they stood and gazed
Till their souls grew dim and their sight grew dazed;
From the youngest child to the father burly
Their views of life straight before, grew Kyrly.

The father—he was a hearthstone vendor—
Strove to make his street-cry as subtly tender
As Chopin Nocturne, and pined to a shade.
And ruined his voice, and lost his trade.

The mother—she used to go out to 'char'—
Fell madly in love with a Japanese jar,
The pot, with cold scraps, in her basket left,
And was quodded for taste, which the law called theft.

The eldest son—and he carried a hod—
Yearned his ladder to mount with the grace of a god
In Attic story, but failed and fell
From the Attic story, and ne'er got well.

The eldest daughter—a work-girl plain—
Would touzle her hair and wear gauze in the rain;
Caught cold, sought cure in a peacock's feather,
And died of High Art and the state of the weather.
...

Clearly the satirist was ignorant of the Society and its aims.[79] But not all those involved shared the same aims. For William Morris, speaking as a convinced socialist to the Society on 27 January 1881, asserted that the group's purpose was to fight 'Carelessness, Ugliness and Squalor', and in another address at Nottingham on 16 March of that same year he used the occasion to attack *laissez-faire* capitalism and dilettantism: if those who work with their hands will not have art, then 'we the cultivated and rich people cannot have it; if they cannot have it, if our social system forbids it to them, be sure that the day is not far distant when the cultivated part of our society will refuse art also, will have grown utterly blind to it'.[80] The aim of the Kyrle Society must be to 'resist such a return to barbarism, nay to a state of degradation far worse than barbarism, for that was hopeful'. The Society has begun at the right end, with art. Any discussion about art as its own end, rather than for a purpose, is fruitless: a 'real artist does his work because he likes it ... when done 'tis a blessing to his fellows'.[81] And Morris anticipates the natural rage of the deprived against art: the slashing of pictures, vandalism, graffiti. The Kyrle's work is not mere palliation of a steady social state. A note of warning is added: any decoration for the poor should be up to the standard of marketable work.

Octavia Hill in an article of 1884, 'Colour, Space and Music for the People' adapted from a paper given to the Society at Grosvenor House on 24 March 1884, stresses that the Kyrle Society, in bringing joy to the poor, does not claim to bring them 'the principal sources of joy'. These are religious: music, colour, art, space and quiet are 'secondary gifts', but distributed with a sad inequality. For Miss Hill, the stencils on the walls of parish halls and the coloured prints in squalid houses amount to a species of *biblia pauperum*; they speak of 'higher things' to those who are too weary or uneducated to read. Miss Hill emphasizes the importance of helping the deserving poor, and she attacks those who have 'a depraved hunger for rags, sharp need, and slums.... "I should like to go where there is condensed misery", a lady said lately in the cheeriest tone ... there is a certain excited temper abroad which almost amounts to a longing to see extreme want.'[82]—rather in the spirit of those who earlier in the century had enjoyed public executions. Unlike Morris, Miss Hill does not take large philosophical views of society: there is work to be done, economically, and in a devotional spirit.

By 1884 associations had been founded at Liverpool (1877), Birmingham (1880), Glasgow (1882), Leicester, Bristol and Nottingham. The Birmingham Society is particularly well documented, and its activities included plays and concerts. What this illustrates is that the Kyrle was responsive to movements of taste in the arts. Its history of *Work Done and Proposals for New Developments* has a rousing cover design by Walter Crane, an angel festooned by a streamer with the bracing device 'Art for All: The

New Social Order Work for All', and this is reinforced by the familiar 'All for One and One for All': socialism, art and craft, and trade unionism. The programme illustrating Pinero's 'The Schoolmistress' given at Edgbaston on 13 and 14 December has *art nouveau* poppies (recalling MacKnurdo's famous design for *Wren's City Churches*). Pinero, indeed, was the favoured Kyrle dramatist, but the dramatic entertainments were probably directed to the volunteers rather than to the poor. The songs, however, given at musical evenings were popular, sentimental and insipid, and well illustrate Morris's warning about aesthetic condescension to the working class. Morris's influence can be detected in the record of the Society's aims in 1894 as being 'to revive the handicrafts amongst men to whom work has become drudgery rather than delight'.[83] The most ambitious activity of these years was the new building designed by W.H. Bidlake in 1892 for the Kyrle Hall Workshops. This embraced the activities of the Society and the Birmingham Guild of Handicraft, founded in 1890, seven years after the Century Guild. 'Bookbinding, woodcarving and doorplates' were among its activities. The 'simple type' of Flemish building, 'quaint and unobtrusive', contained a hall, a stage, a boy's club, men's workshops and a library.

In 1896 a May Festival was given. The programme printed by the Guild of Handicraft has a Celtic-type initial letter with an elaborate tail, showing that the Kyrle was once more at the frontier of fashion. MacFarren's cantata, 'May Day' was given by the Kyrle choir, and we are reminded of the May entertainments at girls' schools under the auspices of Ruskin. The programme included also a song by the notorious Lord Henry Somerset, in exile for his unorthodox sexual tastes, 'Come to Me in the Silence of the Night'. This, along with sentimental, morally wholesome *lieder*, set the tone.

Annual reports of the Birmingham Society continue until 1908, but the Kyrle society survived till much later: *The Kyrle Hall Flash* (incorporating *The Wag and Perch*), magazine of the boys' and girls' union, respectively, was still being published between 1942 and 1953, though by that time its original connection with the Society may well have faded. The Liverpool Society 'quietly ceased to exist' in 1919. Its activities had been increasingly taken over by the Corporation, and more intense local government spending on tree planting, seats, music for the ratepayers, and so on, rendered its programme nugatory.[84]

One of the more ambitious enterprises undertaken by the Society was the production and publication of the Kyrle Pamphlets. The second of those was *The Guide to the Italian Pictures at Hampton Court* by Mary Logan, Bernard Berenson's disciple, mistress and, finally, wife. Mary's description of the pictures combines historical survey, brief appreciation and a species of re-attribution associated with the connoisseurship of Morelli, Frizzoni, Richter and Berenson himself. The arguments in favour of such re-attributions are not given, we are blandly assured, in order 'to bring the work within the limits of similar publications of the Kyrle Society'.[85] Still, there can be no doubt that these pages are for the educated, not the poor. The disciple of Pater stands revealed in Mary's description of Giorgione's temperament as Greek, though with a subtlety, a refinement and feel for landscape in, for example, the Dresden Venus that goes beyond the reach of Greek art. We then pass to the 'blonde manner' of Palma, and the story of the Venetian school ends with Tintoretto and Bassano's 'jewel-like colouring and mysterious effects of twilight and night'—hardly unorthodox descriptions. Mary will have no truck with mannerism or the rococo: we are hastily shuffled on to the *ottocento*, and the piece concludes with a long examination of the Mantegna *Triumph of Caesar*.

Like Octavia Hill's housing schemes, the Kyrle was a symptom of the old paternalism; it was to be succeeded not only by the National Trust but by a new impersonal paternalism of state benefits that has now, it seems, run its course. The need for a revival of the best type of private effort as represented by the Kyrle is pointed.

The Dress Reform Movement

A further activist area was dress reform, a movement that began somewhat late and cohered only sporadically. It was to reach its consummation in the United States rather than in Britain with the apotheosis of the Bloomer. The Dress Movement's comparative failure on this cisatlantic shore stems from its proponents being highly various: men, women, aristocrats, the middle classes, with often divergent aims. Though it involved Art-and-Craft figures no less than Aesthetes, and coincided with the moment when the Aesthetic Movement was already faltering, the Dress Movement (which could sometimes be construed as an 'undress' movement) was certainly patient of a 'decadent' accent, particularly in its more Hellenic form.

The first generation of Pre-Raphaelites had reacted against Victorian constrictions. Rossetti, as Leonee Ormond has pointed out,[86] disliked the 'unnatural' taste of modern costume, and since reformed dress existed in painting from the 1850s it is the more remarkable that systematic reform should have taken so long to come about. But for the exalted, the beautiful and/or eccentric, all of whom might ignore fashion, dress was essentially a matter of individual style. Some generalizations emerge. That the Aesthetic ladies of the late 1870s and the earlier 1880s did affect shapeless garments that ignored the waist and failed to accent the *derrière* was not evaded by *Punch* and other unkind observers. And documentation of a distinguished minority's wear can be found in Frith's well-known picture of the *Private View of the Academy*. There, highly fashionable dresses suavely brush the more fluent spaces of the female Aesthetes. Disciples of Art and Craft tended to stress the healthy and the useful, though the Aesthetic element saw the end as beauty of form and colour: nature demanded the use of natural colours rather than synthetic (the aniline dye had been recently perfected). The artist Henry Holiday, prominent in dress-reform circles, suggested indeed that Beauty should rank higher than either Health or Utility. In nearly every publication of the Movement, the three values were interrelated with free motion. This interrelationship involved an attack on the tyrranous supremacy of the corset, stiffly whaleboned to create the waist. As early as 1860, Wilkie Collins in *The Woman in White* had praised the natural form of the female waist, 'occupying its natural circle ... visibly and delightfully undeformed by stays'.[87]

The earlier reformers, we are told, damaged the cause by insufficiently accenting beauty and instead stressing the fact that nineteenth-century woman's costume rendered her unfit even for light home duties, frequently indeed causing those faints, so much an index of the sensibility of the heroine in contemporary novels. These arguments were barely germane to, say, Lady Elcho, who had evolved her own style of loose dress and whose home duties were seldom more arduous than entertaining Arthur Balfour in the East Room at Stanway, their 'right paradise', occasionally proffering a little light flagellation. Holiday, in the first issue of the dress-reform periodical *Aglaia*, suggested a modified form of rational dress for working, whether about the house or in the fields (another instance of the Aesthetic mission to all classes), a loose over-dress which could be looped into sashes for walking and practical work or let down to ankle-length for a house-dress, modelled on European peasant costumes and the costumes of classical Greece, with cross-sash fastenings. Dress played a large role in dividing the sexes, and at a period when 'liberation' was beginning, women became aware that dress was actually constraining their physical potential, muting health and general activity.

The Pre-Raphaelite taste was for the vaguely medieval; the taste for the Greek style was furthered by the elaborate machine paintings of Leighton and Alma Tadema and the glowing, timeless idylls of Albert Moore. E.W. Godwin, another hierarch of the Movement, wrote extensively on dress reform, advocating 'freedom of the body' and designing Greek costumes for his meticulously archaeological reconstruction of a Greek theatre at Hengler's Circus. Regent Street, where John Todhunter's play, some way after Euripides, *Helena in Troas* (1886), was performed, with Mrs Oscar Wilde swirling whitely among the chorus. However, the taste for Greek costumes dates as far back as the neo-Grec movement of the early nineteenth century, to Lord Guilford's vision of the boys of the Ionian Academy at Corfu at work and at play in the chlamys. Whatever the nature of Lord Guilford's antiquarianism, boys in chiton and chlamys became part of the vision and vocabulary of the 'New Hellenism' of Wilde and others, and the photographs of Sicilian youth so prized by homoerotic collectors show them, when not nude, in Greek apparel, appropriate to that island's antique past. The late-nineteenth-century versions of Greek dress are hardly precise archaeologically, since the loose long robes were fastened with stylish unconcern at the shoulders so that they could take the wind and be curved into fetching arabesques. Oscar Wilde, it need hardly be said, approved, suggesting that such designs would form the costume of the future. Such recourse to Greek practice, so April Dunnett points out, lent authority and respectability to dress reform. This was indeed part of the time-travelling inherent in the Aesthetic Movement (compare the costume conversazione popular at Bedford Park round about 1880). Leonee Ormond reminds us of how the Aesthetic ladies had loose, long, flowing, waistless dresses with 'leg of mutton sleeves and no bustles—a mixture of motifs, from any period that was sufficiently distant and romantic. They favoured large floral patterns and restrained colour schemes'.[88] The dresses were worn without petticoats and they produced that drooping effect familiar from *Punch* cartoons.

In the late 1880s, a few issues of a gazette had been published by the Rational Dress Society, but the full spectrum of the Movement is better gathered from the periodical *Aglaia*, which ran to three numbers between July 1893 and October 1894. *Aglaia* was the official organ of the Healthy and Athletic Dress Union, which included men and women of several social classes. The general principles involved no corsets; free play for the limbs and low heels for shoes; lightweight clothes for work and recreation; economy in general through simple dress, free of changes in fashion.

Throughout the English Movement towards dress reform, beauty may have nominally been the highest factor, but Health seems to predominate—certainly as a means to Beauty. *Aglaia* alludes to one of the Graces, Adornment. Her sisters, Thalia and Euphrosyne, who share the cover design, represent pastoral health and joy, along with the practice of homely skills such as weaving (we are reminded of Morris at the loom). Only under Aglaia's aegis may Health and Utility flourish. As April Dunnett remarks: 'the stated principles of the Union fail to mention Beauty or artistic taste at all; only health and economy'.[89] But both are probably taken as read. *Aglaia*'s tone is persuasive; even the corset is mildly censured. The dresses illustrated combine classicism with the folk and the medieval, signs of Art and Craft once more, merging with older Aesthetic influences. Several years later such dresses were advertised in Liberty catalogues, but by the end of the century—rational, utilitarian, brashly medical (think of Jaeger suiting!)—the English movement faded.

Yet Aestheticism survived the century and precisely in those artistocratic circles where it first became prominent. In Oxford, as in London, 1895 and all that had finally blanched the Movement of its frivolity, its elegance and its public. But in their country houses the 'Souls'—their nickname which, like the Decadents they sometimes shruggingly accepted—continued to be hospitable to literature and art and in turn inspired the authors of *Dodo* and *The New Machiavelli* and the somewhat more tepid fictions of the Honourable Maurice Baring.

'Soul' and 'The Souls'

A lustre of ladies, like elusively tinted moths fluttering round the thin flame of Arthur James Balfour, statesman and philosopher (of whom it has recently been remarked that though the flesh was willing, the spirit was bleak), were themselves not only inspirers of literature and art, their images descending to us from the hands of Poynter, Watts, Burne-Jones and J. S. Sargent, but talented artists also: Violet, Duchess of Rutland was painter; Nina Cust (never quite accepted into the group, the too grave wife of one of the more dashing members), sculptress; while Lady Elcho created her own luminous ambiance, tasteful yet inexpensive. Poynter's watercolour illustrates her, aesthetically habited, among the vases accented with flowers, Oriental screens and flame-coloured fishes mildly drifting through their vast bowls in that paradisal, if piercingly cold 'East Room' behind Stanway's warmly golden stonework (light flagellation of Balfour by Lady Elcho) may well have been a physical as much as a psychological solatium). Her exquisite and ingeniously designed playing cards are as evocative in their manner as Conder's fans. Lady Desborough, an alarming beauty, was captured by Sargent as Selene in black chalk, the upcurved moon tangling faintly in her hair. The Duchess of Rutland, it was said, found Morris's colours too vulgarly bright and would put out his curtains and rugs on the lawns to fade them in the sun, Morris reportedly acquiescing. In their intellectual gaiety, their intense interrelationships, their treatment of politics as game and the drawing-room games of their own devising with a high seriousness, they carried life as art far beyond the interiority of Pater and the iridescent talk of Wilde.

As Mark Girouard has splendidly shown, the 'Souls' inherited, consummated rather, the chivalric ideals of the century: the women of the circle tended to be the more formidable and claimed the right to pursue a cult of passion between the sexes: 'Unlimited licence in love, save for the one connubial act', and some (Lady Desborough certainly) exceeded that limit when it so pleased them, though her finer pleasures seem to have consisted in the subjugation of numbers: 'the chase was more important than the kill'. In conflating siren with *grande dame*, the women of the sect practised a species of *amour courtois*, and indeed not merely their decor but their friendships and ideals also were more than tinged by the revived medieval and the Pre-Raphaelite: the *Morte D'Arthur* furnished *exempla*, all banners and adultery. And as Mark Girouard points out, they were wealthy enough to build or better refurbish actual castles. Those ladies needed richly suggestive backgrounds, though Stanway, most beautiful of backgrounds, was modest enough. Pre-

Raphaelitism, Aestheticism, they inherited many of the cultural ideals of the nineteenth century and their enthusiasms extended to Wagner, Rodin and bicycling, while Balfour, in moments not given to Lady Elcho and the House of Commons, threw off his sombre theorems as to Philosophic Doubt. The painters they admired were admitted to the circle, and even to its rites, as the tensely passionate friendship between Burne-Jones and Lady Windsor witnesses.

The 'Souls' had inherited their attitudes from an older generation of hostesses, the 'Aunts' as they called them, but their children were not to inherit. For twenty years the women moved, of society, yet superior to it; the men were continuously and conspicuously in government, but their male children in particular were shadowed by their splendid mothers. The world shifted in 1914 and the trenches claimed, almost without exception, those sons, some gifted but all restless. Still, Barrie, George Moore, and others were to be found at Stanway in the early 1930s. 'Anima dilectissima', Lady Elcho died in 1937. Perhaps the 'Souls' were not as elect, not so clever as they themselves thought, but not since the Heian world of Japan in the tenth century, and not for a long time to come, is such a circle likely once more to cohere.[90]

But where does all this leave us? The Aesthetic Movement, we may conclude, is only marginally connected with literature. It subsisted in satire, in parody and in the furtive cadences of Pater; and it subsisted in art, the remote glow of Albert Moore's flower maidens lost in timeless reverie, their world, in Ruskin's phrase, 'without facts', as though they only lived as part of the design of an Oriental carpet. Essentially centrifugal then, Aestheticism, before it finally dissolved, became fully embodied in a total art of love and friendship, vivacity and style, more passionate than Brompton could ever have kindled.

Notes

1. See, for example:
   Elsie B. Adams, *Bernard Shaw and the Aesthetes* (Columbus, 1971).
   Amy Cruse, *The Victorians and Their Reading* (Boston, 1962).
   Marotino D'Amico, 'Oscar Wilde between "Socialism" and "Aestheticism"', *English Miscellany* 18 (1967), 111–39.
   Lorentz J.H. Eckhoff, *The Aesthetic Movement in English Literature* (Oslo, 1959).

Hoxie N. Fairchild, *Gods of a Changing Poetry*, Vol.V of *Religious Trends in English Poetry* (New York, 1962).
Albert J. Farmer, *Le Movement esthetique et décadent en Angleterre (1873–1900)* (Paris, 1931).
William Gaunt, *The Aesthetic Adventure*, rev. edn (London, 1975).
Albert Guerard, *Art for Art's Sake* (Boston, 1936).
R.V. Johnson, *Aestheticism* (London, 1969).
R.V. Johnson, 'Pater and the Victorian Anti-Romantics', *Essays in Criticism* 4 (1954), 42–57.
Morse Peckham, 'Aestheticism to Modernism: Fulfilment or Revolution', *Mundus Artium* 1 (1967), 36–55.
Louise Rosenblatt, *L'Idée de l'art pour l'art dans la littérature anglaise pendant la période victorienne* (Paris, 1931).
Irving Singer, 'The Aesthetics of "Art for Art's Sake",' *Journal of Aesthetics and Art Criticism* 12 (March, 1954), 343–359.
John Wilcox, 'The beginnings of l'art pour l'art', *Journal of Aesthetics and Art Criticism* 11 (June 1953), 360–77.
Wilkie Collins's Frederick Fairlie (*The Woman in White*) is a brief and unsympathetic study in languid dilletanteism; Miserrimus Dexter (*The Law and The Lady*) is a legless aesthete with whom Collins (always partial to deformity) has an ambivalent relation. An inscription illustrating his own paintings reads 'Persons who look for mere Nature in works of Art ... are persons to whom Mr Dexter does not address himself with the brush. He relies entirely on his imagination. Nature puts him out.' (*The Law and the Lady*, New York, n.d. p.307).

2. 'Truth in Labelling: Pre-Raphaelitism, Aestheticism, Decadence, Fin-de-Siècle', *English Literature in Transition* 17 (1974), 201–22.
3. (London: Elek, 1969).
4. *The Aesthetic Movement: Theory and Practice* (London, 1972).
5. A staff seminar paper given at the University of Reading in May 1956.
6. Lehmann, p.6.
7. *Ibid.*, p.7.
8. *Ibid.*
9. *Ibid.*
10. *The Works of Max Beerbohm*, 5th edn (London, 1923), p.46.
11. *Time Was* (London, 1931), p.36.
12. *The Dictionary of National Biography*, peddles the story about Knight censoring himself, but the latest scholarship is dubious. For Knight's views, see *An Analytical Enquiry into the Principles of Taste* (London, 1805), pp.70–2, 181, and especially 102 and 151. For recent views about the suppression of *An Account*, see *The Arrogant Connoisseur: Richard Payne Knight 1751–1824*, ed. Michael Clarke and Nicholas Penny (Manchester, 1982).
13. *Quarterly Review* 98 (1856), p.433 and *passim.*
14. '*Punch* and the Syncretics: An Early Victorian Prelude to the Aesthetic Movement', *Studies in English Literature* 15 (1975), 627–40.
15. Horne's essay appeared as a preliminary to his tragedy, *Gregory VII* (1840).
16. *Poems of William Edmonstoune Aytoun* (London, 1921), p.499.

17. *Ibid.*, p.311.
18. *Ibid.*, p.330.
19. *Ibid.*, p.333.
20. *Two Years Ago* (London, 1881), I, 57.
21. A useful book which summarizes the history of guilds and sisterhoods in the Anglican Church is Arthur W. Crickmay, *A Layman's Thoughts on Some Questions of the Day* (London, 1896).
22. See Susan Chitty, *The Beast and the Monk* (London, 1974).
23. *The Poems of Charles Kingsley*, with an introduction by Ernest Rhys (London, 1927), p.32.
24. *The Saturday Review*, 10 October 1863, p.488.
25. *Ibid.*, p.489.
26. *Ibid.*
27. *The Saturday Review*, 31 January 1863, p.138.
28. *Punch*, 26 December 1874, p.270.
29. *Punch's Almanac for 1875*, 17 December 1874, unpaginated.
30. *Punch*, 2 May 1874, p.189.
31. Charles L. Eastlake, *Hints on Household Taste in Furniture, Upholstery and Other Details*, 4th edn (London, 1878). Eastlake along with Edis is particularly considered in Sir N. Pevsner's *Victorian and After* (Princeton, NJ: Princeton University Press, 1968). See 'Art Furniture of the 1870s', a piece first published in *The Architectural Review*, XI, 1952.
32. *Punch*, 17 March 1860, p.107.
33. *Punch*, 5 February 1876, p.33.
34. *Ibid.*
35. *Ibid.*
36. *Punch*, 7 September 1878, pp.98–100; 14 September 1878, pp.110–12; 21 September 1878, pp.122–4; 28 September 1878, pp.134–5; 5 October 1878, pp.144–5; 12 October 1878, pp.159–60; 19 October 1878, pp.178–9; 26 October 1878, pp.183–9.
37. *Punch*, 17 July 1860, p.9.
38. 'The Grasshopper', Lord Chamberlain's Papers, British Library Add. MSS. 52722, pp.78–9.
39. 'The Grasshopper', p.117.
40. *Fun*, 11 December 1878, p.235.
41. 'The Colonel', Lord Chamberlain's Papers, British Library Add. MSS. 52722.
42. 'The Colonel', p.78.
43. *Punch*, 12 May 1877, p.216.
44. Reprinted from *The World*.
45. *The Monks of Thelema*, Library Edition (London, 1887), pp.313–14.
46. *Punch*, 31 July 1875, p.24; 25 September 1875, p.124.
47. Rhoda and Agnes Garrett, *Suggestions for House Decorations* (1877; reprinted New York, 1978), p.69.
48. *Ibid.*, p.119.
49. W.J. Loftie, *A Plea for Art in the House with Special Reference to the Economy of Collecting Works of Art* (London, 1876), p.68.
50. *Art in the House* (Boston, 1879), pp.216–17.

51. Eastlake, p.226.
52. *Ibid.*, p.207.
53. *Ibid.*, p.259.
54. Falke, p.314.
55. *Ibid.*, p.315.
56. See, for example, Aslin, pp.106 ff.
57. Falke, p.319.
58. Mary Eliza Haweis, *Beautiful Houses*, 2nd edn (London, 1882), pp.3–5.
59. *Ibid.*, p.6.
60. *Ibid.*, p.91.
61. *Ibid.*, p.106.
62. Lady Archibald Campbell, *Rainbow-Music or the Philosophy of Colour Grouping* (London, 1886), pp.6, 14. See also, John Stokes, *Resistible Theatres* (London, 1972), pp.58–60.
63. Campbell, pp.16–18.
64. *Ibid.*, p.29.
65. *The Art of the House* (London, 1897), p.9.
66. *Punch*, 24 February 1877, p.84. For the reference to *Fun*, see v.33, p.74.
67. *Punch*, 24 February 1877, p.84.
68. *The Tragic Muse* (London, 1891), p.31.
69. W.H. Mallock, *The New Republic*, a new edition (London, 1879), p.262.
70. W. Besant and J. Rice, *The Monks of Thelema*, pp.36, 37, 286.
71. *Ibid.*, pp.288–9.
72. *Ibid.*, p.126.
73. *Ibid.*, p.22.
74. *The Diary of W.M. Rossetti 1870–1873*, ed. Odette Bornand (Oxford, 1977), furnishes a useful context.
75. Robert Buchanan, *The Martyrdom of Madeline* (London n.d.), p.171.
76. W.H. Lecky, *History of European Morals from Augustus to Charlemagne* (London, 1911), II, p.283.
77. See Alice Corkran, 'The Kyrle Society', *Merrie England*, July 1884, p.154. 'The Kyrle Society', *Oxford and Cambridge Undergraduates Journal*, 3 February 1881, pp.182–3, praises the Society and calls for volunteers. Other literature on the Society includes *Extracts from Octavia Hill's 'Letters to Fellow Workers' 1864–1911*, confided by her niece, Elinor Southwood Ovry (London, 1933). J. Rutter, *The Nineteenth Century: A Poem in Twenty-Nine Cantos* (London, 1900), pp.53–6, outlines the Society's aims in amiable doggerel. The Mitchell Library, Glasgow, has the annual reports of the Glasgow branch for 1886 and 1887; the Bristol Central Library of the Bristol branch from 1908 to 1913. I have not found any manuscript materials from the papers of Octavia or Miranda Hill relating directly to the Society's foundation.
78. For Octavia Hill, see Charles E. Maurice, *The Life of Octavia Hill as Told in Her Letters* (London, 1913).
79. *Punch*, 19 February 1881, p.84.

80. May Morris, *William Morris: Artist, Writer, Socialist* (1936; reprinted New York, 1966), I, p. 199.
81. *Ibid.*, p. 200.
82. 'Colour, Space and Music for the People', *Nineteenth Century*, 15 (May 1884), 745. Another article by Octavia Hill, 'Open Spaces of the Future' also mentions the work of the Society.
83. The annual reports of the Birmingham Society extend from 1882 to 1912. *The Birmingham Kyrle Society and the Birmingham Guild of Handicraft* report for 1890 reprints a speech by Montague Fordham, which actually quotes approvingly 'the socialist poet, Morris', p. 7.
84. Letter from Mark P. Rathbone in *Liverpool Daily Post*, 21 December 1921. The Rathbones were a family of Liverpool merchant princes. See also issues for 30 and 31 December 1927. Brief references to the Liverpool Society appear also in Ivy A. Ireland, *Margaret Beavan of Liverpool* (Liverpool, 1938) and Margaret B. Simey, *Charitable Effort in Liverpool in the Nineteenth Century* (Liverpool, 1951). The earliest reference to the Liverpool Society appears in a letter from Mr (late Sir) Lewis Beard, the Honorary Secretary to the Liverpool Corporation in October 1883. Articles on the Liverpool branch can also be found in *The Liverpool Review*, 4 December 1886, p. 1006; 19 November 1887, p. 110; 15 December 1894, p. 3.
85. Mary (Smith) Berenson [Mary Logan], *Guide to the Italian Pictures at Hampton Court, with Short Studies of the Artists, The Kyrle Pamphlets, No. II* (London, 1894), p. [v].
86. L. Ormond, *Costume* II (1968), p. 33; and Aslin, pp. 145–59 and *passim*. See also, *Costume* VIII (1974), p. 26, for Rossetti's views. The standard work is S.M. Newton, *Health, Art and Reason: Dress Reformers of the 19th Century* (London, 1974).
87. *The Woman in White* (London, 1875), p. 21.
88. A. Dunnett, 'Breeching the Atlantic', Reading University MA Thesis, 1977, p. 29.
89. *Ibid.*, p. 29.
90. There is no general study of the 'Souls' as such. They appear in numerous autobiographies, biographies and memoirs, and in novels such as H.G. Wells, *The New Machiavelli* (1911) and E.F. Benson, *Dodo* (1893). An account of their origins may be found in A.G.C. Liddell, *Notes from the Life of an Ordinary Mortal* (1911) pp. 212–13; this suggests gatherings at Wrest, Bedfordshire, the seat of Lord Cowper in the earlier 1880s. *The Souls: An Exhibition*, compiled and catalogued by Jane Abdy and Charlotte Gere, March 1982, at the Bury Street Gallery, Cork Street, London, may be said to begin a study of their aesthetic milieu. See also Jane Abdy and Charlotte Gere, *The Souls: An Elite in English Society* (London, 1984). Mark Girouard relates them to nineteenth-century notions of chivalry and gentility in *The Return of Camelot* (New Haven and London, 1981), pp. 208–13 and 225. For the hints about Balfour's 'spankings', see *Balfour: A Life of Arthur James Balfour* by Max Egremont (London, 1980), p. 63. Lady Elcho's 'home duties' included, of course, presiding over many house-party guests.

2

Bedford Park: Aesthete's Elysium?

In the early 1880s, the London suburb of Bedford Park became associated rather vaguely with that vague movement Aestheticism. An image of it as a paradise of aesthetes has survived in memoirs, some, such as those of W.B. Yeats and G.K. Chesterton, distinguished. A second, perhaps more secure image of Bedford Park presents the first recognizable English garden-suburb. The suburb preserves also a modest place in the history of domestic architecture, for it contains buildings by Norman Shaw, E.W. Godwin and one striking house by C.A. Voysey.[1] Yet because of difficulties in the attribution of buildings, and because an account of Bedford Park involves architectural history, literary history, and even some mild sociology, little has been recorded of its early years. My concern is to recount its origins; to give some details about those who lived there: what they did, what they thought of themselves as a community.

G.K. Chesterton opens his novel *The Man Who Was Thursday* with this paragraph:

> The suburb of Saffron Park lay on the sunset side of London, as red and ragged as a cloud of sunset. It was built of a bright red brick throughout; its skyline was fantastic, and even its ground plan was wild. It had been the outburst of a speculative builder, faintly tinged with art, who called its architecture sometimes Elizabethan and sometimes Queen Anne, apparently under the impression that the two sovereigns were identical. It was described with some justice as an artistic colony, though it never in any definable way produced any art. But although its pretensions to be an intellectual centre were a little vague, its pretensions to be a pleasant place were quite indisputable.[2]

Saffron Park is Bedford Park. Chesterton knew it well: he courted Frances Bloggs, his future wife, there in the 1890s. The image he elaborates in his novel and later in his *Autobiography*[3] is somewhat fantastic, somewhat inaccurate. The inaccuracy stems from Chesterton's constant quest for birds of paradox and his habit of dramatizing people in terms of their beliefs. But the point is that Bedford Park provoked images: Chesterton's was merely one of a series. It was seen as Arcadian, Aesthetic, Bohemian; as an unconscious example of a romantic socialist co-operative. Its physical presence alone was striking, different, isolated. In the late nineteenth century it was peopled by a close community of artists, poets, academics, journalists, actors and cultivated members of the professional classes; self-conscious and articulate persons, very much aware of themselves as a community.

A little west and a little north of Hammersmith the grey chaos of building is clarified. Emblematically almost, the entrance to Bedford Park is marked by a level crossing over a disused railway. The noble anarchist, Sergius Stepniak, one of the few inhabitants of Bedford Park, who might himself have stepped straight out of one of Chesterton's fantasies, seemed also to have been under the impression that the line was disused. It was Stepniak's custom to walk along a small length of this railway, perhaps for the same reason as Descartes is said to have joined the Dutch Army—as a place where one could be sure of a little peace and quiet. While reading the agenda for one of his meetings of exiles, a train came down the line and Stepniak was killed. This rather brutal anecdote is told merely to show that fact in Bedford Park seems easily to touch fiction.[4]

On the farther side of the railway, one finds oneself among winding roads richly loaded with trees and houses that have been inaccurately termed 'early Oscar Wilde' in allusion to the 'aesthetic' past. In one road, Priory Gardens, we have a vista of houses with East Anglian-type gables and eighteenth-century shell-hood doorways. But the main east–west artery is the Bath Road with flowing gables and ornamental brickwork from plans prepared by Norman Shaw and E. J. May. The houses stand in ground that still faintly preserves the appearance of orchard land. And at the west end of the Bath Road we come to what was clearly intended to be the centre of a complex: a church; what was once a co-operative stores, and an inn. Bedford Park was planned as a self-contained village unit, and to enter it, as the painter Edward Abbey observed, was like 'walking into a watercolour'.

It was in 1875 that Jonathan T. Carr (1845–1915), brother of J.

Comyns Carr, an art critic closely associated with the 'greenery-gallery' Grosvenor Gallery, where the painters popular in Aesthetic circles exhibited, initiated the project.[5] By the 1890s Jonathan Carr had come to be regarded, according to Chesterton, not merely as

> the patriarch or the oldest inhabitant but in some sense as the founder and father of the republic. He was not really so very old; but then the republic was very new: much newer than the new republic of Mr Mallock, though filled with philosophic gossip of much the same sort, over which the patriarch benevolently beamed and brooded. At least to quote a literary phrase then much quoted, he was older than the rocks which he sat among, or the roof he sat under; and we might well have murmured another contemporary tag; a little vaguely, perhaps, from memory:
>
> Match me this marvel save where aesthetes are,
> A rose-red suburb half as old as Carr.[6]

Carr began by acquiring 24 acres of land adjoining Bedford House, the midmost of three eighteenth-century buildings at the entrance of the estate.[7] This property took its name from the brothers Bedford, who had owned the land up to the earlier nineteenth century, when it passed to John Lindley, Professor of Botany and Fellow of the Royal Society, who planted many trees in the area. When Bedford Park was detached from the vestry of Old Brentford to Chiswick in 1878, it consisted of 29 acres 18 poles.

The first half-dozen houses were built in the Avenue to the designs of Coe and Robinson, and six at least by Ernest William Godwin (1833–86), father by Ellen Terry of Gordon Craig, friend of Wilde and Whistler and, like his son, a daring theatrical designer. Godwin's corner houses are simpler than the later designs for Bedford Park: English vernacular, without Renaissance detail. Godwin had been asked to provide economical designs, after Carr had seen a vicarage designed by him, near Northampton. The early Avenue houses were ready for occupation in the autumn of 1876 and were illustrated in *The Building News* for 22 December of that year. Later, Godwin complained that his designs had been altered and it is doubtful if they can be considered among his better work.[8]

Building was carried on during 1877 to the designs of Coe and Robinson and to that year belong the semi-detached villas in the Bath Road, which strongly suggest Norman Shaw in style. Shaw designed nine types of house altogether. The Bath Road houses have large, studio-type windows, though these face south. Later designs were by Wilson, E. J. May, Shaw's assistant, and Maurice B. Adams, editor of *Building News*, who was responsible for the rather nasty eclecticism of the parish hall and for a number of Passmore Edwards libraries.[9] Both May and Adams became residents. We have an account of the early building from H. Fox-Bourne, editor of *The Bedford Park Gazette*:

> Continuing the old roadway known as The Terrace, leading from Turnham Green towards East Acton, the earliest road opened up was The Avenue, from which the Woodstock Road and the Bath Road branched out on the right-hand side ... while this initial scheme was in process, moreover, it was being expanded by the construction of the Blenheim Road, the Bedford Road, and Queen Anne's Gardens, quickly followed by Queen Anne's Grove, Newton Grove, Marlborough Crescent, The Orchard, and the other roads and their houses now grouped in artistic variation, but in harmonious agreement with the original conception of the architect and projector.[10]

As Moncure Conway, another resident, observed in 1883, 'the pattern of streets and gardens was largely decided by Dr Lindley's trees'. Carr and a surveyor whose name is not known had laid out the roads themselves. For the *Daily News* of May 1880, the effect was rather that of a *camera obscura*. The roads are described as being designed

> with cunning carelessness to curve in such wise as never to leave the eye to stare at nothing. But one straight thoroughfare runs through the estate, and even this is bounded by the wooded hill of Acton. All the others appear closed at the end by trees and houses, and form a succession of views as if the architect had taken a hint from Nature, who, when in pleasant, lazy mood, will dispose such mighty rivers as the Rhine and Hudson to form a series of lake views.[11]

What was admired about Bedford Park was primarily the country quality rather than the complex of buildings; not so much its sense of community expressed in its co-operative stores and clubhouse, as its insinuation into the landscape. Stories about nightingales singing in the Bedford Park gardens were current in the 1880s and 1890s. Bedford Park was *rus in urbe*. The stress falls on the natural, the homely and, of course, on Craft and Art. *The Sporting and Dramatic News* for 27 September 1879, stresses the homely and functional aspects of the architecture, presumably, like the *Daily News*, echoing the views of Carr and Shaw:

We have here no unchangeable cast-iron work, but hand-wrought balustrades and palings; no great sheets of plate glass, but small panes set in frames of wood which look strong and solid, although, the windows, being large, they supply ample illumination for the spacious rooms within. There is no attempt to conceal with false fronts, or stucco ornament or unmeaning balustrades, that which is full of comfortable suggestiveness in a climate like our own—the house roof; everything is simple, honest, unpretending. Within, no clumsy imitations of one wood to conceal another, but a preserving surface of beautifully slatted paint, made handsome by judicious arrangement of colour. Mere brick is openly brick, and paint openly paint. Nothing ... pretends to be that which it is not. Varnish is unknown. There is an old-world air about the place despite its newness, a strong touch of Dutch homeliness, with an air of English comfort and luxuriousness, but not a bit of the showy, artificial French stuffs which prevailed in our homes when Queen Anne was on the throne, when we imported our furniture from France and believed in nothing which was not French.[12]

By January 1880, 100 acres had been laid out in some 220 houses. By 1883, the number of occupied houses was 333 and later in the 1880s had risen to more than 400. The first public building, the club-house, was begun in 1878 and opened on 2 May 1879. The original design looks like the work of E. J. May, and the enlargement a few years later was certainly under May's direction.[13]

The architectural press, no less than the popular press, maintained a vivid interest in Bedford Park. *The Building News* for 30 January 1880, describes exterior and interior of the club-house:

The exterior is that of a plain red brick and tiled building, roofed in two divisions and decorated with a deep cove in plaster on the principal fronts. A porch with heavy wooden head, opens through a hall into an assembly room, 36 × 24 feet; on the right of the entrance in a small card room; on the left are a reading room, and a billiard room, each 25 × 20 feet. The walls are hung with Japanese paper of dark tone, and with choice specimens of old tapestry; some genuine old furniture, including an arm-chair carved in oak and dated 1636, is interspersed with chairs by Godwin, Morris and Jackson, and here and there a piece of old china, sets of a cabinet or whatnot. In the assembly room there is a mantelpiece exhibited by (Aldam) Heaton in the last Paris Exhibition, the work is painted with clear green colours and relieved by gesso-work in transparent colours and large gilded human figures, the general effect being rich and handsome, though it fits badly with the cornice and frieze of the room. At the rear of the room, a stage is being fitted up, and will be thrown into it when complete, and a ladies' billiard room is nearly finished. The oak dado and pedimented doorway to this room are from the late Church of St Dionis Backchurch ... the light is from three small windows on the east, and from glass prisms, in the ceiling, and a series of

> half a dozen Suggs gas burners, furnished with hoods and placed at equal distances over the table. The fireplaces have open grates set with tile-borders, by De Morgan.[14]

In his *Travels in South Kensington*, Moncure Conway gives us a further glimpse of the interior. In the assembly or ball-room, were 'panels, with classical subjects wrought in gold on ebony which fill the wall space above the mantelpiece. There is a stage with a drop-scene, representing one of our streets.'[15] According to a pamphlet on the Clubhouse, dating from some time between the two world wars, the green and gold over-mantel of the assembly or ball-room was part of an old organ case, presumably also from Wren's St Dionis Backchurch.[16] The gilded human figures, according to W.B. Yeats, were, in fact, Cupids.[17] *The Bedford Park Gazette* describes the bay windows as lined with broad oaken seats, with coffers under them, modelled on the antique. Flowers and ornamental shrubs, book-shelves, settees and pieces of furniture of the dark perforated pattern made in India completed the *ensemble*. The stage itself was built with a convex inner wall. Carr was devoted to trees and this rather awkward design was to ensure that a large tree in his own garden which backed on to the clubhouse should be saved from the axe. Consequently, it was impossible to proceed from one side of the stage to the other without being seen by the audience, though this state of affairs was later remedied.

By the close of 1879, club membership had risen above 150 and increased steadily over the next four years. The entrance fee was three guineas and the annual subscription two. The assembly rooms could be hired for balls, concerts and dramatic performances for five guineas. No betting was permitted and light 'general daily and weekly papers were taken and the chief monthly magazines'. A library was formed in 1883 and a constant flow of new books supplied by the Grosvenor Gallery library. Each member had the right to put forward the name of two ladies (members of his own family) who might use the club facilities at a cost of ten shillings and sixpence a year.

Tower House, the largest residence on the estate, was the seat of Jonathan Carr himself. Designed by Shaw, it was completed in 1879 and unfortunately demolished towards 1932. It boasted a cupola and balustrade and resembled a country house of the Inigo Jones school. Its chimney stacks were taller than usual. The back elevation had two large projecting bays with Georgian panes which were fully glazed on the ground floor and joined by another continuous strip of glazing marked as a conservatory on the plan.

Here once again were the choice hangings; what is described as 'Early English', that is Jacobean-type furniture, dado and fireplace, this time carved out of the organ loft of St Dionis Backchurch, along with papers by Morris and Jeffrey and Co.[18] Japanese paintings hung on the walls and the hall windows had tinted glazing. We know that Carr wished everywhere to use wood rather than stone or brick inside. Cheapness as much as aesthetic theory was the probable motive. Even so the building and decorations cost £4,000. Here Carr dispensed, as the squire of the village, liberal and continuous hospitality. A fête was held every year in the garden, generally in July, to which Ellen Terry and other notabilities often came.

In 1880 Norman Shaw's church of St Michael and All Angels was consecrated. The exterior presents a *mélange* of Perpendicular, domestic Renaissance and cottage vernacular features: a cupola, cornices, balustrade with coved gables over dormer-windows. Shaw's aim was not to overpower but to harmonize with the surrounding buildings. The interior has a Jacobean-type screen and much woodwork. Shaw was probably influenced by the mass of dark Carolean woodwork of the Laudian church of St John, Leeds, which he had restored.

Early in January 1880, a group of members of the Architectural Association visited Turnham Green and in *The Builder* for 31 January 1880, after an account of Shaw's church, there are some comments on the new buildings opposite:

> the buildings will comprise a row or terrace of seven gables, like the old row in Holborn, and will include, beside the stores, a private house for the manager, an old-fashioned inn[19]

The reference here is probably to Staple Inn, then unrestored. But here, as in Swan House, Shaw seems to have had in mind for his heavily projecting bays, Sparrowe's House at Ipswich (1670).[20] This again asserts the English vernacular theme. The old-fashioned inn was given the name of the Tabard, recalling Chaucer's pilgrims, with a sign showing a trumpeter, painted by T.M. Rooke (who had begun as a Pre-Raphaelite and later did much topographical drawing from Ruskin). Rooke was a resident in Bedford Park.[21]

The Tabard owed its origin to the need for a licensed house 'within easy access of numerous workmen employed in the estate' and, as the editor of *The Bedford Park Gazette* rather darkly continued, 'to obviate the danger and annoyance of the otherwise inevitable sale of alcoholic liquors to those workmen through other channels'.[22]

The role of the stores was 'to meet the demand [for] larger and more various household necessaries than was within reach of the inhabitants and to relieve them of the necessity of frequently sending to London to make purchases.' By 1883 it had ten separate establishments, and one could obtain from it groceries, provisions, meat, poultry, greengroceries, furnishing, fancy goods, coal, wines and spirits, china and glass, stationery, drugs, turnery, ironmongery, house decorations and so on.[23]

The impression gathered from the architectural papers and from the *Gazette* is of a ye-olde-England, Ruskin and Morris medievalism. But although the exteriors of the Bedford Park houses do indeed form an architectural unity within diversity and pleasingly react against contemporary taste for stucco and Italianate Villas, the general effect remains, particularly if we take the interiors into account, of an imaginary museum, eclecticism. Both externally and internally, Bedford Park houses leave an impression of time-travelling in taste, and this is typical of Aestheticism; the sense in Pater's words that 'all periods, types, schools of taste are in themselves equal,'[24] a remark reflecting acute historical self-consciousness.

The impression of the artist T. Raffles Davidson, who visited Bedford Park in the later part of the year 1880, was not, however, one of eclecticism. In a description published in the *British Architect* of 3 December 1880, Davidson stressed the suburb's picturesqueness, its spontaneity and asymmetricality, but, oddly enough, also found its general effect monotonous, mainly owing to the materials used. Instead of brown and purple tiles, green and yellow, purple and red bricks, there was, he remarked, a generally dull use of one thin red colour for bricks and tiles. He also mentions that many of the furnishings had been placed in the houses by order of the architects. Morris would certainly not have approved Davidson's prescriptions, and we may be grateful to Godwin, Shaw and May for avoiding the shrill polychromatic brickwork of a Butterfield. The vocabulary that Davidson and others apply to Bedford Park is the 'quarter', the 'village', the 'colony'. Emphatically, it was not a suburb.[25] This social distinction was to be sharply drawn by the inhabitants themselves.

According to Moncure Conway, purchasers or leasers of houses could choose their own wallpapers and colours for woodwork. The occupants were allotted a fixed amount for decorations, and for the most part they chose Morris papers. Conway opined that the firm of Morris & Co. would shortly have to open a branch in Bedford Park.

The prices of houses to be leased ranged from £35 to £120. *The Builder* for 24 April 1880 reports that a Bijou Villa in the Queen Anne style was sold at an auction for buying freeholds for £610 and was bringing in £50 a year with a ground rent of £91.[26] The early houses, however, were reported to have inadequate drainage and this may account for the stress laid on the topic in the early advertisements, along with the marriage of utility and beauty: few houses had basements or cellars, according to the recommendations of Dr Richardson, *The Bedford Park Gazette* informs us:

> Hitherto it has been generally supposed that perfect sanitary arrangements and substantial construction are inseparable from ugliness. But it is especially claimed for Bedford Park that it is the most conspicuous effort yet made to break the dull dreariness of the ordinary suburban villa ... an effort has been made to secure, by artistic treatment of plain bricks and tiles rather than by meretricious ornament, an effect hitherto never attempted. By placing houses varying in size and design side by side the dull monotony so often seen is avoided.[27]

But Jonathan Carr had over-reached himself. The account of his financial fall, told to Chesterton by Lucien Oldenshaw, a resident, is probably too picturesque:

> The 'patriarch' who 'benevolently beamed and brooded' over his suburb had gone bankrupt in the making of it. He lived for the rest of his life with the bailiff as his butler. He and his equally impoverished brother would spend long hours playing cards together and getting highly excited when three shillings changed hands.[28]

Fox-Bourne, the editor of the *Gazette*, is naturally more tactful:

> In order that assistance might be given to Mr Carr in further developing a project which had already assumed far larger proportions than he had contemplated, the Bedford Park Co. Ltd was established in the Autumn of 1881. The portion of the estate then transferred to the company was valued at £265,850.[29]

Carr seems to have continued speculating. In 1884 we hear of him in connection with new buildings in Northumberland Avenue.

But Bedford Park was more than a speculation. It was as consciously artistic as it was conscious of any shortcomings in sanitation. The main purpose was 'to set up' a London suburb that should possess 'artistic and sanitary advantages superior to those to be found in any other suburb of London.'[30] In some ways, Bedford Park certainly anticipated Port Sunlight, Welwyn Garden City and Hampstead Garden Suburb. Indeed, Port Sunlight is, in part, an anthology of features derived from Shaw's Bedford Park houses. But Bedford Park was related by at least one of its inhabitants, as we shall see, to the romantic socialism of the earlier nineteenth century. John Silk Buckingham's Victoria pre-dates the Public Health Act of 1848, which stimulated a succession of model towns, projected by philanthropists and enlightened employers of labour. In *Tait's Edinburgh Magazine* for December 1848,[31] a project which would have made Ilford in Essex the first garden village was suggested. The numbers involved were to have been of the order of 5,000 to 6,000. Like the advertisements for Bedford Park, the scheme stressed air and space, wood and water, schools and churches, shrubbery and gardens, around pretty self-contained cottages, in a group not too large to deprive it of a country character, nor too small to diminish the probabilities of social intercourse. The Ilford scheme was, however, commercial and based on class selection. Like Bedford Park, it was to be a paradise for the professional class. Bromborough on the Mersey had had its paternalistic co-operative store, free school, library and sports grounds. But the nearest analogue to Bedford Park belongs also to the year 1876, when Alexander Stewart's Long Island model estate began. Like Bedford Park, it was for the middle-class and had no industry attached. In 1879 the first houses were built at Bourneville, rather gaunt and grim architecturally, but of reasonable density. Bedford Park, then, certainly has its place in the development of the garden-suburb. It was not Utopian like Buckingham's Victoria nor, like Saltaire or Bourneville, was it the product of enlightened paternalism. At the same time it cannot be related too rigidly to the Long Island estate. For Moncure Conway, pastor of the Ethical Church and a Bedford Park resident from 1879 to 1885, Bedford Park fulfilled in its modest, undoctrinaire way an ideal of co-operation; in his book it is related both to the medieval village and to Aestheticism:

> There is not a member of the new suburb who would not be startled, if not scandalized at any suggestion that he or she belonged to a

> community largely socialistic. They would allege, with perfect truth, that they were not even acquainted with the majority of their neighbours, have their own circle of friends, and go on with their business as men and women of the world. Nevertheless, it is certainly true that a degree in social evolution is represented by Bedford Park and that it is in the direction of that co-operative life that animated the dreams of Père Enfantin and Saint Simon. All society indeed must steadily and normally advance in that direction.[32]

The equation is startling. One justification for Conway's claim was the presence of 'new women' in Bedford Park, but his argument is actually based on the low price range of Bedford Park houses and on the fact that owing to the large number of families who had agreed to buy or rent houses, Carr had been enabled to buy materials and labour in bulk. As a result the chief advantage of co-operation was assured. Conway cites the stores, the club with its newspapers and current literature in common, its tennis lawns, billiard rooms, conveniences and entertainments. The success of Bedford Park as a community, Conway considered, lay precisely in its empiricism. Earlier nineteenth-century ideal communities had failed because they had started with theory and made practice conform to that. No blueprint for development had been laid down in Bedford Park, but each of the many institutions had appeared in response to a felt want. Conway is not alone in stressing the Bohemian quality of the village. 'The entire freedom of the village and of its inhabitants is unqualified by anything whatever, whether social, political or economic.' This is all too rosy to be true, but there does seem to have been some interest in co-operatives: in February 1884, a lecture was given in the clubhouse on Leclerc's co-operative workshops.[33]

Bedford Park, then, provided several images. To Conway it appeared as an example of unconscious co-operation, with a respectable Bohemianism which cut across a good deal of class structure; to others, it appeared as a commuter's pastoral,[34] and to the architectural press it was a comfortable innovation. By the popular press, it tended to be seen as a Mecca of Aestheticism.

The beginnings of Bedford Park coincide in date with the rise of the Aesthetic Movement and journalists failed to distinguish between a liking for Morris papers and a philosophy of conduct. This is not the place to discuss the origins of the word 'aesthetic' or the narrower uses to which the word was put in the course of the nineteenth century. George Brimley, for example, in his essay on

Tennyson in *Cambridge Essays* (1855) describes the *Lotus Eaters* as 'carrying Tennyson's tendencies to pure aestheticism to an extreme point'.[35] Brimley is polemically distinguishing a poetry that is 'picture and music, and nothing more'; a poetry which luxuriates in its evasion of moral strenuousness. A.H. Hallam had made a comparable distinction in his famous review of Tennyson's *Poems* (1830).[36] Here Hallam defines a type of romantic poetry which is all imagery and confined to presenting dark subjective states.

As a self-conscious movement, Aestheticism gathers force in the early 1870s, is vulgarized in the 1880s and disappears by the end of that decade. It represents something of a shift from literature to the applied arts. Graham Robertson, indeed, rather naughtily suggests that the real origins of the movement are to be found in industrious old ladies in the 1850s and 1860s happily sewing away at their crooked milkmaids and lumpy flowers in the back parlours of Bayswater and Brompton.[37] The actual doctrine appears first in Swinburne's review of Baudelaire's *Fleurs du Mal* in *The Spectator* for 6 September 1862 (reprinted in Swinburne's *Works*, Vol. XIII, p. 419) and in Pater's essay on Winckelmann, which was published in the *Westminster Gazette* in 1867. Swinburne's *William Blake* (1868) gave prominence to the phrase 'art for art's sake', and five years later the phrase was embodied in the provocatively enigmatic conclusion to Pater's *Renaissance*. Through Pater and J.A. Symonds, the Movement acquired also an eclectic neo-Grec quality of which Godwin's Greek-type dresses which *express* rather than constrict the body; Godwin's antiquarian Greek stage sets; the paintings of Alma-Tadema, Leighton and Poynter; Grant Allen's *Physiological Aesthetics* of 1877 and the cult of pederasty, are all symptomatic. One of the constant elements in Aestheticism was a revulsion from the ugliness and materialism of the contemporary scene and the tendency to look back to 'imaginary' 'spots of time' when the sense of beauty was normative. Historical self-awareness led to a sense of freedom in time: time-travelling might be defined as central to Aestheticism, and this sharply distinguishes it from the cult of the moment, of the 'modern', which is characteristic of 'Decadence'. The Aesthetes looked back to the eighteenth century, the Jacobean period or the Middle Ages, periods represented in Bedford Park. The Movement even captured the Church through the Ritualist Movement of the 1860s,[38] and the Kyrle Society gave it social emphasis, sending well-bred young women into dim homes to spread the new gospel and to suggest that the poor might forget their lot more readily by taking to watercolour painting, buying reproductions of great paintings and visiting the South Kensington Museum somewhat more often.[39] The Movement coincided and became entangled with the enthusiasm for all things Japanese that became a mania in the 1880s. There was much *japonaiserie* in the Bedford Park houses. Japan had been opened after centuries of seclusion by the Americans in 1859, and there, frozen, perfect, was a medieval feudal society.[40]

That the vulgarizing of Aestheticism had been disastrous to a genuine art-movement was widely recognized, we may gather from Graham Robertson. Indeed, he calls its beginnings, those of the only genuine art-movement that England had ever known.[41] The patriarch of Bedford Park, Jonathan Carr himself, gave a lecture at the Clubhouse on 27 January 1883, with the title: 'The Harm Aestheticism Has Done to the Spread of Art'.[42]

Aestheticism was all too easy to ridicule. Indeed, by providing an easy role for poseurs of all types, it parodied itself. The early years of Bedford Park witnessed both alarmed and amused philistine satire of the Movement. From 1880 on, George du Maurier elaborated his gallery of Aesthetes in *Punch*: Basil Giorgione (a symbiosis, it seems, of Pater and Wilde, whose role as half-caricaturing, half proselytizing entrepreneur of Aestheticism in the earlier 1880s brought much discredit on the Movement); Leonora della Robbia de Tudor, one of those young women, amateurs of the Beautiful, who pursue art—without ever quite catching it; Westpond Tumpkyns, shining light of the Dullialilytanty Society, Cimabue Brown, Prigsby, the critic, Maudle, the painter and Jellaby Posthelthwaite, the Aesthetic poet. Literary satire kept pace with du Maurier. Pater had been satirized as Mr Rose in Mallock's *New Republic* of 1877, with its atmosphere of leisured Socratic conversation in a country-house setting. Besant and Rice's *Monks of Thelema* of 1878 also has a country-house setting, satirizes Pater and contains an aesthetic young woman who is dressed in 'neutral tints', parts her hair on the side and corrects her neighbours in a low voice when they commit barbarities on art: 'she was not pretty, but she was full of soul'. And the most famous of such satires, still within these early days of Bedford Park, was Gilbert's *Patience* of 1881.[43]

That there were several Aestheticisms in a social no less than a doctrinal sense, was recognized by Henry James in his *Tragic Muse*, which first appeared in serial form in 1889, with its rather awkwardly half-satirical, half-sympathetic portrait of Gabriel Nash, whose doctrine is Paterian but whose defensive paradoxes are Wilde's. James distinguished the 'worldly semi-smart' Aesthetes, associated perhaps with Lady Archibald Campbell and such fashionable painters as Mrs Jopling Rowe, from the 'frumpy, sickly lot who wore dirty drapery' in 'some dusky dimly-imagined suburb of culture, peopled by phrasemongers ... who had no human use but to be held up in the comic press, which was probably restrained by decorum from touching upon the worst of their aberrations.'

It was in 1882 that the new suburb was decisively linked with Wilde and the Aesthetes by Walter Hamilton in his *Aesthetic Movement in England*, where a culminating chapter of twelve pages is devoted to Bedford Park. Here, the Aesthete's programme—of applying the spirit of art to every detail of modern life—has transcended the single object of furniture, the perfectly designed book, the perfect exterior and interior design of a single house; the single artistic personality and its expression through dress and manner—for Dandyism, turning oneself into the impassibility of a statue, where the suffering that constitutes the condition of art is charmed away—was naturally part of the programme. Even the artistic group has been transcended. All is united in an ideal community: the most elaborate synthesis of the arts possible, where art has triumphed over ugliness and modernity in every detail.

Hamilton writes as an apologist, and lyrically insists on the English rather than the Japanese element in Bedford Park:

> The sunlight wavers and flickers on the red brick fronts of the houses; many of the doors are open, and the neat halls are visible with clean cool Indian matting, square old-fashioned brass lamps; comfort and cleanliness everywhere, lightness and grace abound. Even the names on the doorposts have a touch of poetry and quaintness about them. Pleasaunce, Elm Dene, Kirk Lees, Ye Denne.[44]

Hamilton notes the reaction against High Victorian (and perhaps Regency) metalwork: 'Nearly every house has a balcony, not the ordinary kind of iron abomination jutting like a huge wart on the face of the house.'[45] These wooden balconies *Punch* used for a drawing reproduced in the issue of 25 August 1883:

> Scene: Aesthetic Neighbourhood. (The background represents a gabled Bedford Park-type house.) Two figures are walking thoughtfully away. Converted Betting Man (Plays Concertina in Salvation Army): 'Pooty

'ouses they builds in these subu'bs, Mr Swagget.' Mr S. (Reformed Burglar and Banner-Bearer in the same): 'Ah! and how 'andy them little bal-co-nies would a' been in former …' A warning flourish on the concertina and Mr S. drops the subject.[46]

Three birds at a swim: Aestheticism, Philanthropy and the Working Class. The joke refers to Canon J. W. Horsley, a resident, who devoted himself to the reclamation of criminals and used to ask them to stay with him at his Bedford Park house.

But how Aesthetic was Bedford Park? Shaw somewhat incongruously decorated four of his early houses in the Avenue with sunflowers, and the sunflower like the lily and the poppy was much prized by the Aesthetes as an emblem.[47] Hamilton found Aestheticism on a visit to the School of Art.

> One young Lady was just putting the finishing touches to a very life-size representation of that aesthetic favourite, that bright emblem of constancy, the brilliant sunflower. I noticed, too, that in many instances the young ladies were decidedly of the aesthetic type, both as to the mode of dress, and to the fashion of arranging the hair.[48]

The Chiswick School of Art had been built in 1880–81 to the design of Maurice B. Adams.[49] There were two directors, E. S. Burchett, from the South Kensington Department of Science and Art, and F. Hamilton Jackson, from the Slade School, who was also a resident. The committee included Adams, Jonathan Carr and several artists, who, like Jackson, were resident on the estate. In spite of the inclusion of severer studies such as anatomy, drawing from life and the antique, the emphasis in the teaching fell very much on the decorative arts that were so prominent in Aestheticism.[50]

Moncure Conway's description of Bedford Park, like Hamilton's, comes at the climax of a volume devoted to arts and crafts. Though he described it as Thelema, an ideal village, a Utopia in brick and paint, Conway was aware that it was in danger of becoming too self-consciously isolated a community. 'Now and then the fair riders of Hyde Park extend afternoon exercise to enjoy a look at the new suburb.'[51] John Bright and Renan visited and admired. Conway's chapter on Bedford Park appeared in *Harper's Magazine* and transmitted its image to an American audience.[52]

Satire, good-humoured and less good-humoured, of Bedford Park was frequent, particularly in the early 1880s. Hamilton quotes two ballads *Ye Haunted House* and the more amusing *Ballad of Bedford Park*, which had appeared in the *St James's Gazette* of 17 December 1881. Some of the verses bear quotation:

In London town there lived a man
  a gentleman was he
Whose name was Jonathan T. Carr
  (as has been told to me).

'This London is a foggy town'
  (thus to himself said he),
'Where bricks are black, and trees are brown
  and faces are dirtee.'

'I will seek out a brighter spot,'
  continued Mr Carr.
'Not too near London, and yet not
  what might be called too far.

''Tis there a village I'll erect
  with Norman Shaw's assistance
Where men may lead a chaste correct
  aesthetical existence.'

With that a passing 'bus he hailed
  (so gallant to be seen)
Upon whose knife-board he did ride
  as far as Turnham Green ...

''Tis here my Norman tried and true
  our houses we'll erect;
I'll be the landlord bold and you
  shall be the architect.

'Here trees are green and bricks are red
  and clean the face of man;
We'll build our houses here,' he said,
  'in style of good Queen Anne.'

And Norman Shaw looked up and saw,
  smiled a cheerful smile.
'This thing I'll do,' said he, 'while you
  the denizens beguile.'

To work then went these worthy men,
  so philanthropic both;
And none who sees the bricks and trees
  to sign the lease is loth.

Bedford Park: Aesthete's Elysium

'Let's have a stores,' said Jonathan;
said Norman, 'So we will,
For nought can soothe the soul of man
Like a reasonable bill.'

'A Church likewise,' J.T. replies—
Says Shaw, 'I'll build a Church,
Yet sore, I fear, the aesthetes here
will leave it in the lurch.'

'Religion,' pious Carr rejoined,
'in Moncure Conway's view,
Is not devoid of interest
although it be not true.

'Then let us make a house for her,
wherein she may abide,
And those who choose may visit her,
the rest may stay outside;

'But lest the latter should repine
a tennis ground we'll make
Where they on Sunday afternoons
may recreation take.'

Then each at t'other winked his eye
and next they did prepare
A noble Clubhouse to supply
with decorations fair.

With red and blue and sagest green
were walls and dados dyed,
Friezes of Morris there were seen
and oaken wainscote wide.

Thus was a village builded
for all who are aesthete
Whose precious souls it fill did
with utter joy complete.

For floors were stained and polished
and every hearth was tiled
And Philistines abolished
by Culture's gracious child.

And Jonathan and Norman
found so much work to do.
They sold out to a company
to put the business through.

Now he who loves aesthetic cheer
and does not mind the damp
May come and read Rossetti here
by a Japanesy lamp.

While 'Arry' shouts to 'Hemmua':
'say, 'ere's a bloomin' lark,
Them's the biled Lobster 'ouses
as folks call "Bedford Park."'[53]

That sounds like a malicious insider: dubious drains, Aestheticism, agnosticism, speculative building, are all present. The ballad seems to have been, perhaps for its medieval associations, the chosen vehicle for verse-satire on Bedford Park. In the Supplement to the Special Number of the *Lady's Pictorial* for 24 June 1882, Horace Lennard tells how a young couple were able to marry by discovering Bedford Park. The young lady was an Aesthete and

Said she, I have for Art a zeal,
Most high and grand is my ideal,
And a very little way, now-a-day, you know,
Five hundred pounds will go, go, go.

No modern house for me will do,
All sham and plaster, damp and new;
I won't have stucco and varnished paint,
But something old and quaint, quaint, quaint.

A journey by District Railway leads them to Turnham Green:

They left the station and turned to the right,
When a picture strange arose in sight:
'O look!' cried the youth to the maiden 'Quick!
Houses of red brick, brick, brick, brick!'

A pretty porch soon came in view,
The house looked old, although 'twas new,
A lady artist there did dwell,
So the youth gave a ring at the bell, bell, bell.

And in reply to his remark
They said this place is Bedford Park,
And all these houses erected are
By Mr Jonathan Carr, Carr, Carr....'

The Tabard, the stores and the church are all featured:

A tavern o'er the way they spied,
Where marvels more they met inside,
For nut-brown ale and sack within
Were sold at the Tabard Inn, Inn, Inn.

And just next door there stood a store,
Which an Early English aspect bore,
Where each artistic serving-man
Wore a costume of Japan-pan-pan.

The Bedford Parkites are so good
They have propped up with post of wood
Their red-brick Church, because you see,
It must supported be, be, be.

In *Youth* for 6 April 1883, a certain pseudonymous 'Madge' records that:

> We ... met some people who live at Bedford Park ... I have never seen the place except from the vantage point of the window of a railway carriage, whence it appears rather a glare of red brick, which makes the eye long for trees, many and large. We were, therefore, much surprised to hear these ladies talk of the place in a curiously exalted strain. I really thought for a few moments they were conversing about Paradise, and wondered at the exactness of detail that seemed to characterize their information. Flowers always blooming, and skies always bright, sun always shining, existence idyllic, etc., etc.; these were a few of the phrases. Consequently it was quite a shock when the elder lady, including me in the conversation, remarked, 'And then our drainage is so perfect!' I was really disconcerted for a moment. She added 'and our club is so charming!' ... I then ... enquired 'Where is this delightful place?' Maud and I were regarded as outer barbarians because we not only had never been to Bedford Park, but actually knew no one who lived there. It appeared incredible to our new acquaintances: and when the elder lady said 'And have you not seen our newspaper?' and I replied, humbly, 'No, I didn't know you had one,' she seemed quite compassionate over so much ignorance. From her air of incredulous surprise one would have thought I had said I had never heard of *The Times*.... I had heard of this aesthetic colony, of course, and found that I had been by no means wrong in imagining that Tennyson must have had them prophetically in his mind's eye when he wrote the line:
>
> They think the cackle of their burg the
> murmur of the world.[54]

The identification of Bedford Park with Aestheticism is also stressed in an article contributed to *The Whitehall Review*, based, according to Fox-Bourne on material distorted from *The Bedford*

Park Gazette, which had devoted part of its first issue to an account of the origins of the suburb, along with some contemporary comment.[55]

The Bedford Park Gazette[56] first appeared in July 1883, and the editor's image of the Bedford Park community stressed Bohemianism and respectability: 'In no other suburb of London is so much individuality combined with so much hearty co-operation for the benefit of all.' He pointed out that the residents included:

> busy merchants ... a far larger proportion of officers retired from military service than are to be found in any other district of so limited a space, here meet on common ground with artists, authors, men of science, and members of professions, whether the profession be that of the Bar, or that of the Stage. And in spite of these differences and divergences—or is it not rather in consequence of them?—it happens that during these few years of our lifetime as a 'village or community' we have established so many local institutions that we now find it necessary to have a Gazette of our own in which to chronicle their doings.[57]

The status of the actor, we may note, though not yet secure, has certainly risen, perhaps owing to the prestige of the Bancrofts and Irving. In rebutting the image of Bedford Park as an Aesthetic colony, is Fox-Bourne accurate?

Out of about 500 persons listed in the *Gazette* as resident in the month of August 1885, it is possible to identify three generals, four colonels, two majors, one commander, R.N., and six captains, whether military or naval is not stated. These were probably attracted to Bedford Park after the *démarche* of 1881 and by cheap prices rather than wallpapers, or the chance of a game of billiards with a poet. None of the service persons (with the exception of the actor, Captain Percival Keene, who was manager of the club from 1879 to 1881) took any part in the social and intellectual activities of the suburb. Of declared artists, only twenty are to be found in the *Gazette* or in the *Year's Work in Art* for the year 1884, which I take to be Bedford Park's apogee. There were in addition at least six architects, one sculptor, and fifteen authors and journalists.

Among such a close group tensions were certain. A contributor to the *Gazette*, admitting some Aestheticism in the early years of Bedford Park, found that by 1883 it had become a place fit for major-generals. But, adopting a tone of friendly criticism, he observed:

> On rare occasions I have noticed costumes, male and female, which would be more noticeable in some other suburbs of London than they are in Bedford Park, where everybody seems to be tolerably free to wear and do and be what he or she likes best....[58]
>
> Your Club is, I suppose, a fair index of your whole colony. Doesn't a zealous and devout clergyman of the Established Church often play billiards there, with a short pipe in his mouth? and doesn't the wife of another zealous and devout clergyman act gracefully in farces and comedies at the amateur theatricals ... there performed?[59]
>
> Your Bedford Park Committee appears to exist for the sole purpose of starting new institutions. Out of your population of 2,000 or 3,000, only a few take an active part in the society mania. The same names occur again and again in this committee, and on that; and I fancy your 'leading spirits' must always be in a fever of excitement between amateur theatricals and amateur concerts, lawn tennis matches and playing at firemen's duties. Can they stand the excitement for long?[60]

The answer was they couldn't. A crisis rose among the governing body of the Art School. Maurice B. Adams was criticized by implication in the *Gazette* and retorted angrily and elaborately in *The Richmond and Twickenham Times*, and the next issue of the *Gazette* was the last. It had survived for a year only. A breach in the community had been made.

The number of painters or of literary persons living in Bedford Park in the first six or seven years of its existence may not have been large. The names, however, add another perspective: A.W. Pinero; John Butler Yeats and his two sons, W.B. and Jack Yeats; John Todhunter, poet and dramatist; Mark Perugini, historian of the theatre and the ballet; George Manville Fenn, prolific novelist; James Sime; Richard Bowdler Sharp, ornithologist; Frederick York Powell, Icelandic scholar and poet; Sergius Stepniak, 'Man of the Steppes', author of *Underground Russia*; Julian Hawthorne, son of the great American novelist, Moncure Conway; and H.R. Fox-Bourne, editor of the *Gazette*, who is remembered for his two-volume history of English newspapers. In later years Bedford Park was to attract Professor Oliver Elton; Sydney Cockerell; St John Hankin, the dramatist; the publisher Elkin Mathews; the novelist Edgar Jepson and others. The stage was represented by William Terriss, Harry Nichols, Dora Burton and in later years C.B. Cochran. Painters included H.M. Paget, Birket Forster, Starr Wood, Charles Pears, W.B. Wollen and T.M. Rooke.[61]

Bohemianism in Bedford Park most readily proclaimed itself in dress. Terriss and York Powell seem to have left most impression,

York Powell, in particular, booming round corners with his menacing and misleading eyebrows, immense beard and yachting-cap. But not only dress was Bohemian; Bedford Park not merely contained eccentrics who might have figured in some Chestertonian extravaganza, but the whole village itself partook of an 'attractive unreality':

> More especially … about nightfall, when the extravagant roofs were dark against the afterglow and the whole insane village seemed as separate as a drifting cloud. This again was more strongly true of the many nights of local festivity, when the little gardens were often illuminated, and the big Chinese lanterns glowed in the dwarfish trees like some fierce and monstrous fruit.[62]

So Chesterton, and not unhistorically. Such festivities were indeed frequent in Bedford Park: costume conversazione or *tableaux vivants* or fancy dress balls, they seem to have spent half their time dressing-up, like some of the early inhabitants of Welwyn Garden City. Of these tableaux, a contemporary poet, George Barlow, gives us a hostile glimpse:

> 'twas at that
> Delightful Fancy Fair at Bedford Park,
> When, you remember (did I tell you, dear?
> Oh this is my first letter: so it is)
> That Mr Barnes, the great tall clumsy man,
> Dressed as a bearded woman: it wasn't nice.'[63]

Moncure Conway is naturally more enthusiastic:

> There is … a rumour in the adjacent town of London that the people of Bedford Park move about in fancy dress every day. And so far as the ladies are concerned it is true that many of their costumes, open-air as well as other, might some years ago have been regarded as fancy dress, and would still cause a sensation in some Philistine quarters. At our last fancy dress ball, some young men, having danced until five o'clock, when it was bright daylight, concluded not to go to bed at all, but went out to take a game of tennis. At eight they were still playing, but though they were in fancy costumes they did not attract much attention. The tradesmen and others moving about at that hour no doubt supposed it was only some new Bedford Park fashion. There seems to be a superstition on the Continent that fancy-dress balls must only take place in the winter … it does not prevail here. It was on one of the softest nights in June that we had our last ball of that character. The grounds

> [i.e. of Tower House] … were overhung with Chinese lanterns, and the sward and bushes were lit up, as it were, with many-tinted giant glow-worms. The fête-champêtre and the mirth of the ballroom went on side by side, with only a balcony and its luxurious cushions between them. Comparatively few of the ladies sought to represent any particular 'character'; there were about two hundred present, and fancy costumes for both sexes were *de rigueur*, yet among all these there were few conventionally historical or allegorical characters … The ladies had indulged their own tastes in design and colour, largely assisted, no doubt, by the many artists which Bedford Park can boast.… There is hardly an evening of the spring and summer when Bedford Park does not show unpurposed *tableaux*.[64]

Though the *Gazette* hardly underwrites Conway's hectic account, there can be no doubt that costume soirées were frequent and popular. *The Richmond and Twickenham Times* carries a report of a ball given at the School of Art on the 3 June 1884.[65] Dancing lasted until four in the morning. The lights were subdued by rose and amber tinted paper, and F. Hamilton Jackson, one of Bedford Park's artists, provided 'sumptuous special decorations, and three choice tapestry hangings.' Costume, on this occasion, was partly historical: the painter, Hargitt, was robed as William Shakespeare; Dr Gordon Hogg, the Bedford Park Medical Officer of Health, appeared as Claudian; his wife as Edith Plantagenet; Moncure Conway, as a friar. Mrs Edward Wyman, wife of the President of the Sette of Odde Volumes, appeared as 'Night' in a dress of 'cut steel crescent moon, with stars to match, long black tulle veil with spangles, dress black lace and satin; trimmed with stars and spangles and silver lace, black spangled shoes, black gloves.' Miss Violet Wyman, as 'Mistress Mary', sported a primrose muslin kerchief 'festooned with crossed silver rake and hoe, pale blue floral polonaize over delicate primrose quilted satin petticoat, trimmed with diagonal wreaths of silver bells, cockle shells, chatelaine of silver garden tools, white gloves.' George Haité, another Bedford Park painter, appeared in the court costume of George IV, wearing the orders of St Estable and the Sette of Odde Volumes, with hair dressed and powdered in the fashion of the period. Miss Dawson was dressed in 'flowering robes and veil of Esther, jewelled crown and cincture'. Three of the costumes were Japanese and there were several examples of costume explicitly following contemporary paintings: Mrs T. Field Fisher's 'Roman Princess', we are told, faithfully copied the draperies in Alma Tadema's 'Colisseum', while Mrs Moncure Conway appeared as 'a lady after Rossetti'.

Barlow in his poem had related the 'fancy-fair' at Bedford Park with costume-drama at the Lyceum. Particularly with non-historical costume, however, this passion for dressing-up was not so much antiquarian as self-expressive. These Bedford Park revellers were time-travellers, escaping from the present, breaking down the limits between art and life.

Treating life in the spirit of art extended to other activities. In the 1890s, the bicycle fever shook Bedford Park, and Cecil Aldin in his autobiography describes how

> this little oasis was crowded with fat and thin, short and long, men and women, boys and girls learning, or becoming expert at the art of taking exercise on the new low bicycles. Nightly the talk in the houses and the club was about the latest gears or ball-bearings, the newest type of handle-bars, lamps or pneumatic seats. The bicycle cult became a mania. Everyone caught it, from children just able to walk, to grandmothers.

In the evening there were torch-light rides round the 'confines of our little colony'. These parades were organized at the club, a notice being put up stating the time and day. Large and small Chinese lanterns were fixed at every available spot on the bicycles, some attaching long bamboo poles to the handle-bars and hanging the lanterns from these. The first 'meet' was a fiasco. The lanterns were lit; the bicyclists began their ballet on wheels in formation of three; the night was fractured by crashes and only ten out of fifty or sixty starters managed to ride out the *mêlée*.[66]

Of the many Bedford Park societies, the Musical Society, the Conversazione Club founded in 1883, and the Bedford Park Reunion dating from 1882, and others, the most interesting and historically significant was the Amateur Dramatic Club.[67]

This began with informal entertainments in 1879, but was formally inaugurated in 1881. Subscription was half a guinea a year, with half a guinea entrance fee. On 15 July 1880, George Macdonald, poet, novelist and mystic, along with his family, gave a dramatized version of *Pilgrim's Progress*. For about eight or nine years, the Society offered on the average either three or four plays a year, mostly farces and melodramas, with *tableaux vivants*, readings, pantomimes. In 1884 a local resident, Alexander Hatchard, wrote a one-act play which was acted at the clubhouse. *The Bedford Park Gazette* found its dialogue 'witty and refined', and one or two of the London papers were favourable. There are two other instances at least of Bedford Park residents writing plays for the suburb's dramatic company: Oliphant Downs, author of a one-act play 'The Maker of Dreams', who was killed in the First World War, and John Todhunter.[68]

Todhunter's *A Sicilian Idyll* was produced over four days in the week of 5 May 1890. All the Bedford Park productions had the advantage of Bedford Park artists to design scenery and costumes. With the *Sicilian Idyll* we have the spectacle of a Bedford Park dramatist, supported by Bedford Park artists, with a cast that included a majority of residents, playing before an audience that brought in artists, men of letters and the aristocracy from the metropolis.[69]

Among the audience was the young William Butler Yeats, who had persuaded Todhunter to write the *Idyll* in the first place. In Yeats's mind was the notion that Todhunter's play should inaugurate a yearly festival, a kind of Dionysia at Bedford Park. The subject of the play, a pastoral based on Theocritus, was peculiarly appropriate to Bedford Park itself. The *Idyll* was a poetic play, depending more on words than on naturalistic scenery. Yeats saw it as the beginning of an attempt to bring back poetry to a theatre now dominated by naturalism for a small, defined 'aristocratic' audience. It was the first step in freeing the theatre from commercialism.

Yeats had been excited by the Macdonald family's presentation of *Pilgrim's Progress*, which has been played 'before hangings of rough calico embroidered in crewel work, [I] thought that some like method might keep the scenery from realism'.[70] An unpublished letter of John Butler Yeats written in April 1885 records his son's admiration for Todhunter as poetic dramatist:

> Willie ... watches with an almost breathless interest your career as dramatic poet—and has been doing so for a long time—he has read everything you have written most carefully.
> —he finished when at Howth your Rienzi at a single sitting—'the' sitting ending at 2 o'clock in the morning.[71]

Todhunter's *Helena in Troas* was given the following year at Hengler's Circus, Great Pulteney Street (chosen for its suitability for Greek settings). Every detail, whether of acting or setting, was controlled by E.W. Godwin who, in this play, as in his production of W.G. Wills's *Claudian* of 1883, carried archaeological realism to its extreme. The distance between the patient detail of Godwin's production and the non-naturalistic décor of Yeats's ideal was not as remote as might appear. Godwin, before Oscar Wilde, was concerned to use costume dramatically: the 'truth of masks', dandyism applied in the theatre (and indeed Wilde's article of that name is little more than a tesselation of Godwin's ideas: its documentation is most uncharacteristic of Wilde). The terms in which Godwin's productions were discussed show how it was possible for Godwin's scholarly recreations to be modulated into quasi-symbolist theatre. Speaking of *Claudian*, for example, Wilde refers to Godwin as exhibiting the life of Byzantium 'not by a dreary lecture and a set of grimy casts, not by a novel which requires a glossary to explain it, but by the visible presentation before us of all the glory of that great town.'[72] Costumes were 'subordinate' to the unity of artistic effect ... the artist has converted an antiquarian motive to a theme for melodies of time.'[73] Godwin himself had written: 'As speaking involves poetry and music, as architecture involves painting and sculpture, so dressing involves in principle all these.'[74] And Lady Archibald Campbell (for whose Coombe Players, Godwin had provided open-air productions of Shakespeare's and John Fletcher's pastoral plays), with special attention to blending costumes with natural scenery, found that in *Helena in Troas*, 'line and colour [took] the place of language, the play ultimately reverted to that plastic ideal which lies at the basis of all *Greek art*'.[75] Yeats did not see Godwin's production, but at the time when the *Sicilian Idyll* was being mounted he wrote of its 'solemn staging, its rhythmical chorus and its ascending incense [which moved] the audience powerfully.... Many people have said to me that the surroundings of *Helena* made them feel religious. Once get your audience in that mood, and you can do anything with it.'[76] And *Helena in Troas*, Yeats recognized, had drawn not merely the cultivated public who cared for verse-drama, but filled the theatre with ordinary run of theatre-goers. Here we have all the prescriptions for the Abbey Theatre and Yeats's Noh Drama: 'the seeming natural expression of the image', the drama communicating, in a way that is strictly analogous to Mallarmé's ideal theatre, to the laity no less than the clerisy;[77] the use of myth and of stylized painted back-drops.

But Todhunter and Bedford Park were to prove a disappointment. After the limited success of the *Sicilian Idyll* (it was played at other small theatres over the following years), Todhunter attempted to conquer the London commercial stage on its own terms, not with poetry but with Ibsenite, or more accurately, Pinero-like 'problem' plays. He failed. And the Bedford Park Amateur Dramatic Company lapsed into comedy and melodrama once again.

The principal part in the *Sicilian Idyll* was taken by Florence Farr. Miss Farr, or Mrs Emery (she was separated from her husband) lived at Brook Green, but was often at her brother-in-law's at Bedford Park. She had studied embroidery with May Morris and in that resembled a number of the Bedford Park ladies. She was also not dissimilar to the Bedford Park 'new women', though she pushed her feminism far beyond theirs.[78] It was said that she was prepared to commit adultery on principle, as a protest against the double standard of morality. A photograph of her, taken at the time the *Idyll* was mounted, shows her lolling somewhat voluptuously in a hammock. She sent the photograph to the highly respectable Todhunter (Bernard Shaw describes him as bearded like a picture of God in an illustrated family bible). On the back of the photograph Miss Farr mischievously wrote: 'Do I inspire thee?' History does not record whether this was a suggestion that she was to act as Todhunter's muse, or one of another kind.

Miss Farr's part in the *Idyll* was much praised, and Yeats remembered the beauty of her verse-speaking for the rest of his life. It had the self-forgetting passion that he demanded.[79] Miss Farr was to have some success on the London stage, but, according to Shaw, her early life had been too easy; she was always too much the dilettante. In the early years of the present century she collaborated with Yeats in reading poetry to the zither, 'cantillation', dabbled in occultism, and in journalism for *The New Age*, retaining charm and courage to the end of her life. A young man, who met her when she was just short of fifty, described her as: 'a wonderful Egyptian-looking person, habited in purples and ambers and scarlets and great hats and veils ... glamorous and vivid.'[80]

That the 'Queen Anne' style was in the middle 1880s still *di moda* and sympathetic to the publicist of a new aesthetic millenium, we may gather from a lecture given at the Bijou Theatre, St Leonards, by Oscar Wilde, on 'The House Beautiful' and reported in *The Artist and Journal of Home Culture* (5, 22–3 of 1884). 'Queen Anne suggested ... possibilities for the introduction of a balcony here, or a gabled window there, which the strictness of the pure classical school rendered impossible; and it is evident that the lecturer's sympathies are more with Fitz-Johns Avenue and Bedford Park than the Quadrant.' Genial satire persists in, for example, H. Francis Lester's *Under Two Fig Trees* of 1886, where there are all allusions to Queen Anne houses, damp, the cultivation of sunflowers and the clubhouse.

Yet in 1888, in Wilde's *Woman's World*, a Miss M. Nicolle, discussing Japanese art-ware, was to write:

> when five or six years ago, Bedford Park was supposed to be the Mecca of Aestheticism, a Philistine poet addressed a sarcastic invitation to the faithful to
>
> 'come and read Rossetti there by a Japanese lamp.'
>
> Much has happened since then. Bedford Park is no longer aesthetic (if indeed it ever was so) and the appreciation of Japanese art-wares has long ceased to be confined within its narrow bounds.[81]

By 1888, indeed, Bedford Park was distinctly old hat. The late 1880s saw some rather mean terrace-housing in Blandford Road, and one or two monotonous new roads were added to the estate on the south side of Bath Road. But its hour was not over. In the 1890s the Calumet Talking Club named after the North American Indian ceremony of the peace pipe and designed to encourage improvization and style in that art, could still bring together J.B. Yeats, York Powell, James Sime and Stepniak.[82] And in 1893 the Irish Literary Society—parent of the Irish Literary Theatre and the Abbey Theatre—was founded from the Yeats house at 3 Blenheim Road.[83]Camille Pisarro visited his son Lucien, a resident from 1897 to 1901. Lucien had been led there by Charles Ricketts, who described Bedford Park as the home 'of the elect of the art world'.[84] Bedford Park appears five times in Camille's *œuvre*. And in 1891 the most remarkable of Bedford Park's houses was built, to the design of C.A. Voysey: 14, South Parade. It is white, deliberately contrasting with the surrounding red brick, with a green roof, whose horizontality is remarkable in a period which generally shows as much roof as possible. The fenestration of the front is delightfully piquant, and is only matched in the side elevation of some houses by Shaw, May and Adams.[85]

The Amateur Dramatic Club continued with its three plays a year, children's ballet and pantomine, in which young and old would take part. And in May 1914 the last production before the First World War, Ronald Coleman, who was living near by at Ealing, took part in a production of *Hindle Wakes*. But at some time round the turn of the century, the overall subscription to the club was discontinued, and it split into separate institutions. This, more than any other factor, broke the sense of community. Some of the original residents, such as H.M. Paget, Rooke and Adams, lived on into the 1920s and 1930s, but after about 1905 Bedford Park ceased to attract artists and men of letters. The Fancy Dress Balls were dropped after the First World War, and the Amateur Dramatic Society was discontinued just before the Second. The club and its contents were sold to C.A.V. Engineering Works and is still being used for its original social purpose.

For the period around the turn of the century, Chesterton is the liveliest authority. To Chesterton, Bedford Park was a microcosm of heresy: imperialist, because it was agnostic, and man must have faith; mildly aesthetic, sometimes occultist, and because of its heresies, pessimistic. Like Yeats, in his autobiographical fantasias, Chesterton tended to see personality as an epiphany; something issuing dramatically as gesture, or stylized into pose. For him the typical Bedford Park resident of the turn of the century was St John Hankin, the dramatist. Hankin was something more atheistic than an atheist; 'a fundamental sceptic, that is a man without fundamentals ... he despised democracy even more than devotion'. Hankin, who wrote for *Punch*, was, indeed, deeply melancholy like many comic writers, and committed suicide. He wore formal dress, unlike 'the artistic garments affected by Bedford Park as a whole' and, in Chesterton's view, was typical of the era; not eccentric, but centric. 'He had a low opinion of the world, but he was a man of the world.'[86] That is one version of the decline of Bedford Park. Chesterton gives another in a ballad:

Dear Olga, it was Long Ago,
If life may be accounted long,
When by the windows (often bow)
Or on the stairways (seldom strong)
Summoned (perhaps) by copper gong
Fixed up by Craftsmen pure and stark,
We met in that amazing throng
People we met in Bedford Park.

There was a velvet long-haired beau
I could have murdered (which is wrong),
There was a lady trailing slow
Enormous draperies along.
And there was Yeats; not here belong
Sneers at the stir that made us mark

That heathen but heroic song
People we met in Bedford Park....

Princess, we both have come to know
What might have been a happier Ark
For Hankin and for Yeats and Co.
People we knew in Bedford Park.[87]

Roman Catholicism may have been a happier ark than occultism or agnosticism or aestheticism, but no one suggested it was prevalent in Bedford Park.

If Bedford Park had any common ethos, that ethos was genteelly Bohemian. Bedford Park was not co-operative; it was only self-supporting in the arts. Otherwise it depended on the District Railway that took its time-travellers back to the highly time-conscious City of London. Yet it will always provoke an image of Elysian Aestheticism. And if, as Graham Robertson suggested, Aestheticism came with dear old ladies in Brompton, Mr John Betjeman has also suggested that it went with dear old ladies in Bedford Park:

> Here until just before the Second World War gentle craftsfolk survived making celtic jewelry in their studios or weaving on handlooms among the faded sunflowers of a now forgotten cult.[88]

Notes

1. W.B. Yeats describes his reaction to Bedford Park in *Autobiographies* (1926), pp. 52–6, pp. 139–41 and *passim*. The Yeats family were resident between 1876 and 1880 and again from 1888 until J.B. Yeats left for Dublin in 1901. G.K. Chesterton has a chapter on Bedford Park in his *Autobiography* (London, 1937), 'The Fantastic Suburb', pp. 133–53. Miss Phyllis Austin records memories of the 1880s and 1900s as revised in 'The Enchanted Circle', *Architectural Review*, 133 (1963), pp. 205–7. For the architecture of Bedford Park, see H. Mathesius, *Das Englische Haus* (Berlin, 1904), *passim*; R. Blomfield, *Norman Shaw* (London, 1940), pp. 35–8. Walter Creese, *The Search for the Environment* (London, 1966), pp. 87–107. T. Affleck Greeves, *Bedford Park: The First Garden Surburb* (London, N.d., [1975]) sorts out the attributions; Andrew Saint, *Richard Norman Shaw* (New Haven and London, 1977) gives the Bedford Park Club to Shaw rather than E.J. May; it was at least published as Shaw's, p. 206. Saint also suggests 'artisan's–mannerist' buildings of the 1630s as the true

ancestors of 'Queene Anne'. Margaret Jones Bosterlie *The Early Bedford Park Community* (London and Henley, 1977) analyses the suburb in terms of 'corporate happiness' and has some information of the period after 1900; see also, Mark Glazebrook, *Artists and Architecture of Bedford Park* (London 1967) and Mark Girouard, *Sweetness and Light: The Queen Anne Manner 1860–1900* (London, 1978).

2. *The Man Who Was Thursday*, 5th edn (London, 1944), p.5.
3. For Chesterton, Bedford Park was an enclave of imperialism (materialism), agnosticism, pessimism and occultism.
4. The inquest proceedings, however, tell a somewhat different story.
5. For Carr, see the obituary in *Chiswick Times* XX, 1032, 5 February 1915, p.6, c.2. He was educated at Bruce Castle School, Tottenham, and King's College, London. William Terriss, the actor, a fellow-resident at Bedford Park, and F.C. Selous, the explorer, were among his contemporaries at school. Carr married Agnes Fulton, daughter of a civil engineer, who lived at Bedford House, one of three eighteenth-century houses on the site of Bedford Park. An enthusiastic Radical, he acted as political secretary to John Stuart Mill when Mill stood for Westminster in 1865, though this reads somewhat oddly as Mill is reported neither to have canvassed for himself nor to have allowed anyone to canvass for him. Carr had a wide variety of interests, many friends, a tenacious memory. By trade, he was a cloth-merchant; by temperament he was genial and optimistic, which probably accounts for his continuous and, in general, unsuccessful speculations in property. See *Bedford Gazette* 2 May 1884, p.140, c.2. and *Pall Mall Gazette* 11 March 1884. There is a brief description of him in an undated pamphlet *The Bedford Park Club*, p.2: 'hurrying along intent on business, top hat rather at the back of the head, low-cut, turn-down collar below the short beard, and almost always a cheerful red tie'.
6. *Autobiography* (London, 1937), p.140. The two lines quoted parody the famous couplet in J.W. Burgon's prize-poem *Petra* (1845), p.14.

   Match me such marvel, save in Eastern clime—
   A rose-red city—half as old as Time!
7. The three houses were Bedford House, Melbourne House and Sidney House. Sidney House was demolished in the 1890s to make way for a block of flats between the Avenue and Woodstock Road. See 'Changing Chiswick and Its Neighbourhood', MS. MP 3303, Chiswick Public Library, for Bedford Park before 1876. See also W.H. Draper, *Chiswick*, London, 1923, *passim*.
8. For Godwin and Bedford Park, see D. Harbron, *The Conscious Stone* (London, 1949), pp.113, 151 and 157. This, the only book on Godwin, is not altogether satisfactory as an account of the total artist. See *The Building News* 33, 9 November 1877, pp.451–2, for description of the early houses. This mentions that the plots for the Avenue were 75 feet in depth by 50 feet of frontage. Buildings were set back by 15 or 20 feet from the pavements. Godwin's houses provoked much criticism, particularly of the interiors. Rents were £95 per annum. Coe and

Robinson's houses were illustrated in *The Building News* 32, p.192. The rental of these houses was £55 per annum. Shaw's houses were illustrated in *The Buildings News* 33, p.614.

9. Blomfield, pp.133–8, states that Shaw was helped in designing Bedford Park by Adams, 'a well-known draughtsman, though not a very good one'. This is corroborated by the account in *The Building News*, 30 January 1880. Maurice Bingham Adams published *Artistic Conservatories* (London, 1880); *Everyday Life and Domestic Art* (London, 1882); *Artists' Houses* (London, 1883); *Examples of Old English Houses* (London, 1888); and *Modern Cottage Architecture* 2nd edn, revised and enlarged (London, 1912); *Cottage Housing* (London, 1914). His buildings include New Rectory House, Merton; Belle Vue, Dublin Bay; J.C. Dollman's houses at 12 and 14 Newton Grove, Bedford Park, an inventive work with attractively irregular fenestration on the side elevations; Queen's Mead Cottage, Windsor, and a house and studio on the Queen's Mead estate. See also RIBA, 72,036, pam.150, for sketches for cottages by Shaw and Adams.
10. *Bedford Park Gazette* 1 July 1883, p.2., c.1.
11. As quoted in *Bedford Park Gazette* 1 July 1883, p.2., c.1. The frequent extracts from newspaper accounts of Bedford Park in the *Gazette* is remarkable. The present account mentions that in 1880 houses were being built at the rate of five a week and stressed that they were neither mansions nor mews. It refers also to 'lofty poplars, adding infinitely to the poetry of the landscape' against which is marked the 'quaint outline of the many-gabled houses'. Poplars are prominent in a set of watercolours of the suburb by Bedford Park artists, which was reproduced in chromo-lithography and was popular in the early 1880s. Miss Phyllis Austin speaks of 'None of your London sooty planes here. Lilacs, laburnum, may (pink, red and white), mountain ash, copper beech, limes and acacias lined every pavement. To walk in the roads on a spring evening was an Arcadian adventure' (*Architectural Review*, 133, p.205). *The Building News* 33, p.451, c.1. mentions that the avenue was planted with limes.
12. *Bedford Park Gazette*, 3 March 1883.
13. *Bedford Park Gazette*, 1 July 1883, p.1., c.1. unequivocally ascribes the clubhouse to Shaw; similarly, the editor attributes the whole of Bedford Park to Shaw alone, but there was a feud between Adams and the editor, H. Fox-Bourne.
14. *The Building News* 38, p.124, c.3, and p.125, c.1. (30 January 1880).
15. *Travels in South Kensington* (London, 1882), p.228.
16. *The Bedford Park Club*, n.d. (4).
17. *Letters to the New Island*, by W.B. Yeats, ed. H. Reynolds (Cambridge, 1934), p.114. The interior was altered first in the Edwardian period and later in 1964.
18. Wallpaper was also supplied by W. Woollams & Co.; see letter to *The Builder* XXXVIII, 1931 (7 February 1880), p.169. These were of 'Queen Anne' patterns, though in many cases worked in colours specially suggested by Aldam Heaton for the estate.

19. *The Builder* XXXVIII, 1930, p.140 (31 January 1880), p.139, c.3.
20. See N. Pevsner, 'Norman Shaw', in *Victorian Architecture*, ed. P. Ferriday (London, 1963), pp.240–41.
21. For the 'Tabard', William de Morgan had provided tiles in the hall, which was panelled with cedar from St Dionis Backchurch. Insistence on the medieval robust Englishness was rather curiously diffused in the 1880s. Even the apparently French-influenced Rhymers Club in the early 1890s used Dr Johnson's 'Cheshire Cheese' for its meetings, drank beer from tankards and smoked church-warden pipes. Their programme included a reaction against so-called English Parnassianism, with its cult of old French forms. See W.B. Yeats, *Letters to the New Island, Cambridge*, pp.142f. for the Rhymers' programme and James K. Robinson, 'A Neglected Phase of the Aesthetic Movement, English Parnassianism', *Publications of the Modern Language Association* 68, II, 1953, pp.733–54. For T.M. Rooke, see 'Extracts from T.M. Rooke's letters to Sir Sydney Cockerell', *The Old Water-Colour Society's Club, Twenty-first Annual Volume*, ed. R. Davies (London, 1943), pp.16–25; and *Burne-Jones Talking: His Conversations 1895–1898 Preserved by his Studio Assistant, T.M. Rooke*, ed. Mary Lago (London, 1981), pp.4–9. Plans of the Tabard, St Michael, the stores and Tower House, are in the Victorian and Albert Museum, 1705–25, Press Mark DD II.
22. *Bedford Park Gazette* 1 July 1883, p.1, c.3.
23. A leaflet dated 1886 is among the Bedford Park archives in the Acton Central Library (Acc. No. ME 5195). The heading is 'The most Liberal Stores in the World'. Items not listed above as sold include artist's colours (Winsor & Newton's), Patent Medicines, Perfumery, Wines, Cigars, Cigarettes and Tobaccos. 'Livery. Every description of work, at the lowest prices. Carriages well turned out, with experienced coachmen.'
24. *The Renaissance: Studies in Art and Poetry*, 2nd rev. edn (London, 1877), p.x.
25. 'A Visit to Turnham Green', *British Architect* XIV, p.240, c.2. Moncure Conway and the popular journalists tend to use the word 'suburb' more freely.
26. *The Builder* XXXVIII, 1942, p.520.
27. *Bedford Park Gazette* 1 July 1883, p.15, cc.1–2.
28. M. Ward, *Return to Chesterton* (London, 1952), p.25.
29. *Bedford Park Gazette* 1 July 1883, p.3, c.1.
30. From the *Daily News* of May 1880, as quoted in *Bedford Park Gazette* 1 July 1883, p.2, c.3.
31. 'London Lanes and the Village Association' in *Tait's Edinburgh Magazine* XV, 845–52. The scheme stressed sanitation, and an ideal plan of the village shows steeply gabled houses in gardens. The density was low and there were small public open spaces. For another early ideal city, see James Silk Buckingham, *National Evils and Practical Remedies, with the Plan of a Model Town* (London, 1849).
32. *Tait's Edinburgh Magazine*, XV, p.232.
33. *Bedford Park Gazette*, 10 April 1884, p.116, c.4.

34. A poem called 'The New Arcadia' was published in the *Bedford Park Gazette*, 5 November 1883, p.54, c.1. The tone is whimsical. The poem features an Aesthetic shepherdess sketching in her garden.
35. *Essays*, 3rd edn (London, 1868), p.24. G.M. Young suggests that definitions of Aestheticism owe much to the lectures of James Garbett (1802–79), Professor of Poetry at Oxford from 1842 to 1852. Its manifestations are various and include word-painting and sonnets for works of art, in literature; formalism and 'The Truth of Masks', poetic archaeology, in the theatre.
36. This essay was in part republished in the *Remains in Verse and Prose* (London, 1862), pp.294–305. For the full text see *The Poems of A.H. Hallam, Together with His Essay on Alfred Tennyson*, ed. R. Le Gallienne (London, 1893), pp.87–139. It had a strong influence on the early W.B. Yeats and the Rhymers' Club in general.
37. *Time Was* (London, 1931), p.36.
38. A good source for the Ritualist connection with the Guild Movement and its capture by Christian Socialism in A.W. Crickmay's *A Layman's Thoughts on Some Questions of the Day* (1896).
39. The Kyrle Society was founded in 1876 by Octavia Hill and Miranda Hill, for the purpose of 'Diffusion of Beauty'. Its activities included collecting flowers for decorating the houses of the poor, planting small gardens in crowded urban areas, providing entertainments and oratories for poor parishes and providing a choir for singing in such parishes. Its members painted panels; they illuminated texts and carved brackets and decorated blank walls in clubhouses and parish halls. The Society was deeply involved also in the provision of open spaces, and this branch of their work was taken over by the National Trust. Octavia Hill was a close friend of Charles Loch, secretary of the Charity Organization, poet and a resident of Bedford Park. Miss Hill built and managed cottages. Her attitude, like Loch's, was strictly practical and paternalistic. The Kyrle Society's published pamphlets include some on the appreciation of paintings. The Society was continuously satirized in *Punch*.
40. For the reception of Japanese art in the 1850s and after, see particularly, J.A. Michener, *The Floating World* (London, 1955); Hugh Honour, *Chinoiserie: The Vision of Cathay* (London, 1959); and Elizabeth Aslin, 'E.W. Godwin and the Japanese Taste', in *Apollo*, 1962, pp.779–84. Oriental art seems to have been known to some Parisian artists in the middle 1850s. The periodical *Once a Week* started to publish an account of Japan in July 1860, and this article was illustrated by prints, while Sherard Osborn's *Japanese Fragments* (London, 1861), also continued reproductions of prints. In 1854 an exhibition of Japanese applied art had been held in London in the gallery of the Old English Water Colour Society in Pall Mall, though the impact of the applied arts was, in England, to be felt somewhat later than that of the prints. Japanese lacquer, bronze and porcelain were shown in London at the 1862 Exhibition. In the earlier 1860s, Whistler and Rossetti were enthusiasts in the collection of Oriental China. When the Victoria and Albert Museum of Practical Art at South

Kensington was founded in 1882, two-thirds of the exhibits were Japanese though these were not of high quality. W. Burges in an article on the International Exhibition (*Gentleman's Magazine* CCXIII, 10 July 1862) had associated Japanese art with Gothic. Burges stressed the asymmetricality of Japanese art and Godwin's designs for wallpapers are noticeably asymmetrical, e.g. as Miss Aslin has pointed out, the sparrow and the bamboo design of 1872. We may relate, perhaps not too fancifully, the asymmetricality of the Bedford Park Houses with the Bohemianism of its inhabitants. Porcelains, screens and prints had been available from the 1860s at Farmer and Rogers' Oriental Warehouses in Regent's Street; Liberty's was founded in 1875 at the height of the Japanese mania.

41. Graham Robertson, *Time Was*, 3rd impression (London, 1931), p.36.
42. *Bedford Park Gazette* 1 July 1883, p.9. c.1. Other relevant topics of club lectures include: 'Dress Reform' and 'The Responsibility of Women to the State'. John Todhunter, another prominent Bedford Park resident, had satirized Aestheticism somewhat affectionately in a sonnet 'An Utter Person Uttered Utterly', in *Kottabos*, 1882, and reprinted in Hamilton, p.31.
43. See also F.C. Burnand's 'The Colonel', which was produced in February 1881 at the Prince of Wales Theatre. Here Lambert Streyke, the principal Aesthete, is distantly modelled on Wilde, though as Dudley Harbron observed, he more nearly resembles Charles Augustus Howell. The play is amusingly described in *Punch* LXXXIX, 'The Colonel in a Nut Shell', pp.81–2, and in F.C. Burnand's *Records and Reminiscences*, 4th revised ed (London, 1905), pp.358–69. Godwin enjoyed the play, but found the 'Aesthetic Room' rather inadequate and suggested how it should have been decorated, see D. Harbron, p.153. N.H. Kennard's *There's Rue for You*, 2 vols., (London, 1880), has an Aesthetic villain-hero and some evocative descriptions.
44. *The Aesthetic Movement in England* (London, 1882), p.117. Hamilton tells us that his attention was directed to Bedford Park by a friend 'whose interest in the Aesthetic Movement was intense'.
45. *Ibid.*, pp.117–18.
46. *Punch* LXXXIV, p.87. See also R. Blomfield, pp.37–8.
47. Sunflowers were certainly much cultivated in Bedford Park. 'Do you remember how they used to mock at me because years ago, when we were here before, I said I would have a forest of sunflowers and an underwood of love-lies-bleeding and there were only three sunflowers after all? Well, I am having my revenge. I planted the forest and am trying to get out the love-lies-bleeding....' *The Letters of W.B. Yeats*, ed. A. Wade (London, 1954), pp.68–9. *The Bedford Park Gazette* refers to the local painter G. Haité's 'excessive reverence for the sunflower', but Haité assured the editor that he 'deprecates the false worship of the flower by the aesthetes.' Aston Webb declared: 'We have now certain well-known aesthetic villages not far from town, where people live in "cots" and fill their gardens with sunflowers,

where ladies dress to suit the houses,' in obvious reference to Bedford Park.

48. Hamilton, pp. 121–2.
49. This was one of Adams' better buildings and, as the coloured pen-sketch at the Chiswick Public Library shows, its flowing roof-line modulates in a very attractively with the gabled houses on either side. However, a letter from Shaw to Lethaby now at the RIBA makes it clear that Lethaby worked with Shaw's sketch (also in the RIBA library V. II/123 for the front). Shaw inserted the large central dormer. The building was bombed during the Second World War and has been rebuilt.
50. *Bedford Park Gazette* 1 July 1883, p. 14, cc. 1–2.
51. M. Conway, *Travels in South Kensington* (London, 1882) p. 232.
52. *Harper's Magazine* LCII, CCCLXX, March 1881, pp. 481–90. There is a brief, anonymous description of Bedford Park in *Chambers's Journal*, Fourth Series, 31 December 1881, pp. 839–40. This stresses asymmetricality in the housing, the variety of size, from family mansion to 'cosy little dwelling which brings the idea of "love in a cottage" from the realms of fancy'.
53. *Bedford Park Gazette* 1 July 1883, pp. 12–13, cc. 2 and 1 quotes twelve verses and R. Blomfield, pp. 34–6.
54. Indignantly quoted in *Bedford Park Gazette* 10 April 1884, p. 125, c. 2 and p. 126, c. 1.
55. Quoted in *Bedford Park Gazette* 5 November 1883, p. 52, c. 1.
56. The unique file of the *Gazette* is held in the Chiswick Public Library. It appeared first at twopence and the price was increased to threepence in January 1884.
57. *Bedford Park Gazette* 1 July 1883, p. 3, c. 2.
58. *Ibid.*, 3 September 1883, p. 30, c. 1.
59. *Ibid.*, 5 November 1883, p. 51, c. 1.
60. *Ibid.*, 3 September 1883, p. 30, c. 1. The article estimates that there are 400 houses in Bedford Park with a total population of between 2,000 and 3,000.
61. In 1882 Bedford Park artists not mentioned in my text included T. G. du Val; Dover Wilson; F. Hamilton Jackson (1848–1923), illustrator of many travel books and the author of *True Stories of the Condottieri* (London, 1904) and *Intarsia and Marquetry* (London, 1903); E. Blair Leighton (1853–1922), a costume and anecdotal artist who was particularly attracted to illustrating Tennyson. For Blair Leighton, see A. Yocking in *The Art Journal* (1913); Mrs Turner, figure painter and draughtsman; Charles Pears, illustrator; Edward Hargitt, painter in watercolour; Sutton Palmer; Joseph Nash; W. B. Wollen (1857–1936), who later became a war artist in the South African War; J. G. J. Penderel-Brodhurst (1859–1944); L. A. Calvert; Miss M. Barry; Miss A. S. Fenn, daughter of Manville Fenn; C. G. Hindley; A. W. Strutt; H. M. Paget and his brother, Walter; J. C. Dollman (1851–1939), chiefly known as an illustrator. The work of five or six of these artists appeared regularly in Grosvenor Gallery exhibitions.
62. *The Man Who Was Thursday*, 5th edn (London, 1944), p. 6.

63. *An Actor's Reminiscences and Other Poems* (London, 1883), pp.67–8. This extract along with a few more lines was reprinted in *The Bedford Park Gazette*. The poem itself is dated June 1882. Robert Owen's model co-operative colonies were to have included fancy-dress balls, with the ladies attending in bloomers. The 1880s witnessed the sudden appearance of a number of books on Balls. A. Holt's *Fancy Dress* in its second edition, London, 1881, keeps topical with an Aesthetic Pierrot modelled on Gilbert's Bunthorne.
64. Conway, pp.228–9.
65. 7 June 1884, p.3, c.6.
66. *Time I Was Dead* (London, 1934), pp.69–71.
67. The Reunion met on the last Saturday of the month.
68. For Todhunter's verse, see the article contributed by W.B. Yeats to *The Magazine of Art* (Buffalo) in 1889 and reprinted in W.B. Yeats's *Letters to Katharine Tynan*, ed. R. McHugh (Dublin and London, 1953), pp.152–4, and *Letters to the New Island* (Cambridge, Mass, pp.174–92), for Yeats's review of *The Banshee and Other Poems* (London, 1888). In the early 1900s, Todhunter was to write on the non-naturalistic drama in 'Blank-Verse on the Stage', *Fortnightly Review* LXXI, n.s. (1902), pp.346–60.
69. Yeats mentions, as present on the third night, theatre personages such as Alma Murray, Winifred Emery, Cyril Maude and William Terriss; Lady Archibald Campbell; Mrs Jopling Rowe, the painter; the poet, Mathilde Blind, Theodore Watts-Dunton and May Morris. The *Sicilian Idyll* was reviewed favourably in *The Theatre* 15 June 1890, p.330. Costumes were designed by A. Baldry, a pupil of Albert Moore's.
70. *Letters to the New Island*. This may refer to a later visit by the Macdonald family, since Yeats places the event a few months prior to the production of the *Idyll*.
71. Unpublished letter in the library of the University of Reading.
72. *Intentions* (London, 1891), p.233.
73. *Ibid.*, p.234.
74. *Dress and Its Relation to Health and Climate* (London, 1884), p.2.
75. 'The Woodland Gods', *Woman's World*, 1888, p.3, c.i. *As You Like It* had been produced at Coombe in July 1884 and was attended by the Prince and Princess of Wales. *The Faithful Shepherdess* was given seven performances in the summer of 1885 and the Prince and Princess were again present, as they were at the pastoral scenes of Tennyson's *Becket*, produced under the title of *Fair Rosamund* in July 1886. Godwin freely cut and added to his texts. Lady Archibald's leanings were away from archaeological realism. She believed in amateur acting because of its 'freedom of mood'. She makes an explicit comparison between Godwin and Wagner and invariably describes the Coombe productions in terms of music. Godwin, she noted, however, was opposed to cantillation, believing in 'concord-in-discord' where verse-speaking was concerned. The Enthoven Collections at the Victoria and Albert Museum contains much material about Godwin's productions. The extreme of naturalistic presentation at this moment was reached in

the work of another total-artist, Sir Hubert Herkomer (1849–1914). His private theatre was in a deconsecrated chapel in the grounds of his house at Bushey. Herkomer was producer, actor, composer of words and music (which he orchestrated) and state-designer. His first ambitious production, 'An Idyl', was produced in June 1890. Particularly admired were his atmospheric effects achieved by entirely calculated means—a sheet of fine gauze stretched at a certain angle in front of a great canvas on the rear wall on which was painted a graduated blue sky.

76. *Letters to the New Island*, p. 134. Yeats did not actually witness Godwin's production, but report of it seems to have inflamed his imagination. The play was certainly much discussed and illustrated in contemporary magazines, e.g. *The Era*, 22 May 1886; *The Lady*, 23 May 1886 (by Mrs Oscar Wilde); *The Dramatic Review*, III, 6973, 22 May 1886 (by Wilde himself). H.M. Paget, a Bedford Park artist and friend of J.B. Yeats, furnished *The Graphic* with an illustration which shows the chorus and the principal actors. The original watercolour is in the collection of the University of Reading. Lady Archibald Campbell's description closely parallels that of Yeats: 'when, like figures on a marble frieze, the band of white-robed maidens wound through the twilight past the altar of Dionysus, and one by one in slow procession climbed the steps, and passed away, the audience were absolutely stilled in their excitement. All minds were held in strong emotion as by the voice of some God which "when ceased men still stood fixed to hear". The pure keynote of beauty was again struck.' (p. 3, c. 1).

77. See Mallarmé's prose, *passim*.

78. *The Whitehall Review* article had taken particular exception to the Ladies' Discussion Club: 'the female tongue has been publicly unloosed'.

79. *Autobiographies* (London, 1926), pp. 149–51.

80. *The Letters of W. Dixon Scott*, ed. M. McCrossan (London, 1932), pp. 69–70. For Miss Farr, see also Yeats's *Autobiographies, passim*; *Florence Farr, Bernard Shaw, W.B. Yeats*, ed. C. Bax (London, 1947); *The Letters of W.B. Yeats*, ed. A. Wade (London, 1954), *passim.* Miss Farr wrote two occultist plays with Olivia Shakespear, which were privately printed: *The Beloved of Hathor* and *The Shrine of the Golden Hawk*. Her *Dancing Faun* (London, 1894), was published in Lane's 'Keynotes Series' and had a cover-design by Beardsley. Her *Music of Speech* appeared in 1909. She was a member of the Rosicrucian Society of the Golden Dawn, published a volume on *Esoteric Egyptology* and translated Tamil poetry. A 'Mrs Emery' was living in Bedford Park in the early 1880s, but it is by no means likely that this was Florence Farr.

81. *Woman's World*, 1888, p. 94. Other elegaic references to Bedford Park can be found in *The Artist and Journal of Home Culture*, e.g XI (1 December 1890), p. 369: 'Is art deserting Bedford Park and are suburban schools of art becoming impossible owing to the increased facilities of train and "tram" between the outlying districts of the

metropolis? We hear that the Bedford Park School of Art is closed, and that artists cannot be induced to open it.'

82. It consisted of twelve members who 'met in their respective houses every second Sunday at nine, and often did not disperse until three in the morning', John Butler Yeats favoured the club because it was 'without fixed forms or fixed quarters, where all things were discussed in a free spirit'. See John Butler Yeats: *Letters to His Son W.B. Yeats and Others*, ed. J. Hone (London, 1944), p.86. Other members included at different times: R.A.M. Stevenson, Oliver Elton, Moncure Conway, Todhunter, Dr Gordon Hogg, F.H. Orpen, Fox-Bourne, Joseph Nash, Paget and Elkin Mathews and inevitably Jonathon T. Carr. J.B. Yeats persuaded the members to agree to two principles: that just enough wine should be served to loosen people's tongues and that the lights should be turned up so that the members should be able to see one another's faces. See William M. Murphy, *Prodigal Father: The Life of John Butler Yeats (1839–1922)* (1978), pp.167–8. In Lady Gregory's draft autobiography, now in the Berg Collection of the New York Public Library, there is an account of a visit paid in 1897 to the Yeats's house at 3 Blenheim Road. Lady Gregory describes Edward Martyn sitting for Yeats senior, while Susan Mitchell sang to divert the painter. Lily Yeats's ms. journal has information about the Yeats family between August 1895 and December 1898. Susan Mitchell also has a ms. account of her stay at 3 Blenheim Road as a paying guest from late 1897 to late 1899, while W.B. Yeats's collaborator in the three volume edition of the works of Blake with commentary, (1893), Edwin John Ellis, took a house with studio in Bedford Park in 1901.
83. W.P. Ryan, *The Irish Literary Revival* (London, 1894), pp.51–5.
84. W.S. Meadmore, *Lucien Pisarro* (London, 1962), p.82, and nos.1005–9 in C.S. Pisarro and L. Venturi, *Camille Pisarro, son art et son coeuvre* (Paris, 1939), vol.2, Plate 202 shows a Bedford Park scene.
85. See J. Brandon-Jones in *Victorian Architecture*, ed. P. Ferriday (London, 1963), pp.269–87. This includes a bibliographical note. Mr Brandon-Jones refers to an earlier design of 1888 for a house on this site, now in the RIBA. This looks like a more conventional suburban house with a 45-degree tiled roof, rough-cast and ground-floor red-brick exterior. See, for the later design, *The British Architect* for September 1891. A full-length study of the architecture may be found in David Gebhard's *Charles F.A. Voysey Architect* (Los Angeles, 1975). Of the exterior of 14 South Parade, Gebhardt notes its 'purity and severity, its highly disciplined abstraction, and its verticilism' (i.e. the fact that it is urban rather than suburban), p.22.
86. *Autobiography* (London, 1937), p.46. Chesterton would probably have been in one sense delighted had he known that between 1911 and 1914 Francis Herbert Bacon, consecrated Titular Bishop of Durham by Arnold Harris Mathew, frequently administered conditional baptism, confirmation and reordination to Anglican clergymen, 'usually in his domestic oratory at 33 Esmond Road, Bedford Park'. Mathew had obtained his orders from the Old Catholic Archbishop of Utrecht in 1908, and they were therefore valid. See P. Anson, *Bishops at Large:*

Some Autocephalous Churches of the Past Hundred Years and Their Founders (London, 1964), p. 85. Bacon eventually resubmitted to the Anglican Church and became Vicar of St Gabriel's, South Bromley, in the East End of London, where there was a nest of these autocephalous figures.

87. M. Ward, *Return to Chesterton* (London, 1952), pp. 27–8.
88. *Daily Telegraph*, 22 August 1960, p. 11.

3

The White Rose Rebudded: Neo-Jacobitism in the 1890s

On 8 February 1892 a 'demo' took place in Westminster Abbey. The Marquis de Ruvigny et Raineval[1] followed by about 250 people attempted to lay white wreaths on the tomb of Mary Queen of Scots. They were dispersed by the police. This attempted act of loyalty to the most lost of all lost causes is perhaps the most vivid moment in the revival of the Jacobite cause in the 1890s. The revival involved antiquarians, literary figures, painters as well as activists, and makes a story that is not without either amusement or instruction.

The early years of the *fin de siècle* in particular witnessed considerable aggression by the Neo-Jacobites. Their activities were discussed in the House of Commons, while Gilbert Baird Fraser stood unsuccessfully for Parliament in the year 1891 as a Jacobite (though Whittaker is silent about the event). Fraser may be described as a 'Legitimist', one of those who believed that the more direct descendants of the House of Stuart were the legitimate (*de jure*) rulers of Britain. This belief they shared with other partisans of the Jacobite cause, but Fraser and his associates in the Legitimist League also believed that active steps should be taken to restore the House to its own. This involvement with Jacobitism was not, as has been already suggested, confined to political gesture; it is echoed in the poetry and the liturgical literature of the period. There are magazines and occasional publications devoted to the cause, and the cause provoked comment and satire. My purpose is to discuss some of those literary manifestations and to speculate on the reasons for their efflorescence. Although I shall call on some unpublished sources, the usefulness of my piece consists in the fact that the evidence has not been brought together and brought to bear.

The defiance of 1892 is the more odd, for a few years earlier the possibility of any symptom of interest in Jacobitism would have seemed remote. A lost cause must always depend on the adventitious or on the convention of celebrating round numbers: the centenaries of births, deaths, spectacular events. Four years earlier an attempt had been made to organize a solemn Requiem Mass for the repose of the soul of Charles Edward Lewis Casimir Stuart, known among Legitimist circles as Charles III. Charles had died in Rome a century before on 31 January and is remembered by all solid men as the 'Young Pretender' and to most Scotsmen as 'Bonnie Prince Charlie'. His after-life, or legend, begins abruptly with his twenties; the remainder of a sad biography is not suitable for preservation in ballad and song. Re-formed arrangements for the Requiem at the Church of the Carmelites in Kensington had been made by the Earl of Ashburnham, a representative of the Spanish Carlist Party in England and by a newly formed Jacobite Organization. The catafalque had been erected; tickets had been issued, advertisements had been inserted in the press.[2] Whether, in the words of Hilaire Belloc, the middle classes were 'quite prepared' will never be known for at the last moment Cardinal Manning intervened to proscribe the Prior of the Carmelites from holding the proposed celebration.

Manning's motives were touched on by *The Times* in its leader of 31 January 1888:

> It may seem hard that the Church of Rome should refuse a requiem to the chief of a family which threw away three kingdoms for a mass. The design of commemorating his death is likely to have been discountenanced in the Catholic diocese of Westminster from kindness rather than ingratitude. Its ecclesiastical authorities have rightly concluded that the greatest cruelty to this forlorn name is to blazon it and its dismal wreath. By rites they consider to be wanted for the repose of a soul they will solemnly celebrate with pitying reserve. To the most fervid devotee of divine right, to the most romantic visionary the death-bed of a broken-down debauchee cannot appear a martyr's triumphal car.
>
> Some, perhaps, will suspect that the plan of celebrating the centenary of CHARLES EDWARD by a gorgeous scene at the Carmelite Church at Kensington was abandoned in deference to the susceptibilities of the loyal subjects of the House of Hanover. CARDINAL MANNING understands his fellow countrymen too well to suppose that any denomination of them would be offended politically by the offer of ecclesiastical honours to the PRETENDER. Their only feeling is, as it is probably his, that a show of service to an undeserving career is a

> mockery instead of homage. It is to be regretted that an incumbent of a London parish could be found who did not share this feeling.[3]

The leader goes on to interpret the sensibilities of English Protestants. They, no less than the Catholics, were gratified by the beatification of Sir Thomas More, but they deprecated 'the foolish scheme for encircling MARY STUART with a fictitious halo of sanctity, as a burlesque of sacred things', and they felt equally about the Pretender. 'They oppose such an experiment out of compassion for its subject and from no sense that the exaltation of the grandson of James II is an impeachment of the chosen constitution and dynasty'. And with some parting thunders about the worthlessness of Pretenders Old and Young, the wisdom and benevolence of Cardinal Manning and the indiscretion of the English clergyman concerned, *The Times* concluded yet another recording of the Englishman's innate and luminous common sense. The middle classes clearly were *not* prepared, had not been prepared, in fact, since 1688. But *The Times* revealed all its Whiggery in confusing the Prince as private self and the prince as Divine Person. To the Legitimist, its arguments must have appeared irrelevant.

As to *The Times*'s genial interpretation of Manning's motives, a later writer on the subject suggests a more plausible reason for the interdiction. Manning was aware that if Pope Leo XIII could not countenance socialism, he was at least alive to the future importance as well as the present plight of the industrial proletariat. And Manning himself was about to intervene directly between working class and government in the role of honest broker, though he was a follower of Henry George rather than of Hyndman. The Anglican clergyman who so kindled the thunder of *The Times* was the Rev. F.G. Lee, Vicar of All Saints, Lambeth; Bishop of Dorchester in the Order of Corporate Reunion, and a noted Jacobite. Lee indeed furnishes a frail element of continuity in the continuing story, as we may term it, of Neo-Jacobitism. The day before the proposed mass for Charles III, he held what might be termed an Anglican version of the Vespers for the Dead, this main observance permitting any Roman Catholics who might so wish to attend. A number did, and we hear that Lee composed a poem to the memory of Charles Edward which was sold at the church door.[4]

But in 1888 it might indeed have seemed that the Jacobite cause was not so much sleeping as dead. The last member of the House of Stuart in the direct line, Henry IX, the Cardinal York, had died without son or daughter or even nephew, in the year 1807, and the succession descended obliquely through the Sardinian and the Bavarian royal families. The son of the *de jure* queen, Princess Louis of Bavaria, Prince Rupprecht, Duke of Rothesay and of Cornwall, was to visit England in 1897 and be received at Victoria Station by a group of Legitimists, while Lady Helen Mellor, daughter of the 10th Earl of Galloway and wife of one of the more aggressive Neo-Jacobites, presented the prince with white roses.

Pretenders there still were in the nineteenth century. In particular the Stuart brothers, John Sobieski Stolberg (1791?–1872) and Charles Edward (1799?–1880). They were probably grandsons of Admiral John Carter Allen, and their father was a lieutenant in the Royal Navy. In 1811, following their own account, the secret of their Stuart descent was told them and stirred by the news they fought at Dresden and at Leipzig for the 'eagle monarch', in other words the Emperor Napoleon, as they put it in one of their several and not incompetent volumes of poetry. Napoleon himself decorated them for bravery and they fought with the French once more at Waterloo in 'dolmans green, pelisse of crimson dye'. After the war the brothers came to London, learned the Gaelic and proceeded to Scotland, where they attracted distinguished supporters. The Earl of Moray, so the D.N.B. tells us, gave them the full run of Darnaway Forest, but, we gather, at this stage they were still Protestants for 'dressed as always in full Highland garb, they attended the presbyterian worship in the parish kirks' and so of course were not disenabled from succession to the British throne. But from the time of their settling in the year 1838 on Eilean Aigas, 'a lovely islet in the river Beauly, where Lord Lovat built them an antique shooting lodge, they seem to have been devoted Catholics. Eskdale, where they are buried, is two miles above their islet, and every Sunday they used to be rowed up to mass, with a banner flying, which was carried before them from the riverside to the church door'. By the 1840s their claim to Stuart ancestry was open; it depended on a story that the Countess of Albany, Charles III's wife, had been delivered of a son in 1773 but that the infant was handed over to the Allens 'for fear of assassination by Hanoverian emissaries'. Much of this information is not too obscurely rendered in the brothers' poetry. John Sobieski accordingly took the title of Count D'Albanie, and this was, on his death, assumed by his younger brother. Their claim was strongly attacked in the 1840s, but they and their followers remained unshaken. It is not clear whether their supporters believed in their claim to be legitimate heirs of the Stuarts or whether it was simply allowed that they were of the band sinister. In reply to an attack in the *Quarterly Review* John Sobieski accused the author of 'The Heirs of the Stuarts' of being a partisan of a rival claimant: General Charles Edward Stuart, Count Roehenstart, whom the D.N.B. describes as a *soi-disant* grandson of Miss Clementina Walkenshaw, Countess D'Alberstroff, Charles's mistress, and who died in a carriage accident in 1854.[5]

A writer in *Notes and Queries* recalls the brothers in Edinburgh about the year 1846 and the sensation their appearance inevitably excited. They were magnificent looking men and '[my] recollection of them fully agreed with what is said in [the *Life and Letters of Charles Darwin*] regarding Admiral Fitzroy's distinguished aspect'.[6] Did Meredith's Richmond Roy in any way derive from the admiral or from the Stuarts? The brothers attracted attention in the British Museum Reading Room in the 1850s and 1860s. R.E. Francillon, a later and, in this case, sceptical Neo-Jacobite, remembered the elder brother as

> being accustomed to display his air of melancholy dignity—no professional actor could have bettered the part of a dethroned King; his picturesque costume, frogged and furred, the more pathetically effective for the apparent length of its wear; and the Stuart type of his features—though that is by no means uncommon, and quite as capable as other types of being emphasised by a little management of the expression and the hair. With these advantages, and with a literary reputation besides, it is not surprising that he succeeded in impressing the romantically disposed. Of the merit of his contributions to English literature and Scottish history I cannot speak, not being acquainted with them. But he was also a reputed scholar; and I have seen a copy made by him of a Latin life of St Margaret of Scotland so crowded with outrageously ignorant blunders, evidently of a mechanical copyist without the faintest understanding of his original or slightest knowledge of the language he was writing, as to suggest a carriage of his Royal pretences to an equality with those of the autocrat who declared that 'I am the Roman Emperor, and above grammar'.[7]

Earlier, another contributor to *Notes and Queries* commenting on an article devoted to the Sobieski Stuarts by the Neo-Jacobite antiquary and poet Henry Jenner in *The New Genealogical Magazine* of 1897, described how the brothers 'dressed in military style, wore spurs, and I fancy I can remember the jingle of their spurs on the iron gratings on the floor of the old Museum Reading

Room between 1850 and 1860.'[8] And in the entertaining D.N.B. account we are told that 'a table was reserved for them, and their pens, paper-knives, paper-weights, etc., were surmounted with miniature coronets, in gold'. Whether they wore the royal Stuart tartan in England is not known.

That the Sobieski Stuarts should rouse continued attention in the 1870s and 1880s and in the pages of *Notes and Queries* was not fortuitous. The editor of *Notes and Queries* was Dr John Doran, author of *The Jacobites in London*, while his sub-editor for twenty years, James Yeowell (1803?–1875) is intriguingly described by Doran as 'probably the last Non-Juror, if not the last Jacobite in England'.[9]

Pretenders and adherents, *episcopi vagantes* and non-jurors were not the only symptoms of Jacobitism in the nineteenth century. During the eighteenth century a number of Jacobite clubs and societies had been formed, and some of those survived, if vestigially, far into the nineteenth century, though Doran was able to pronounce that by 1877 such institutions had disappeared. Most of them do not belong to our story. We may mention the Cycle Club, of such exclusiveness that it had only as many members as there had been Jacobite pretenders since 1689. In an article by Francillon of 1905 with the title of 'Underground Jacobitism' we are told of John Shaw's Club,[10] held at a punch-house kept by one John Shaw, an ex-dragoon, near the Smithy Door end of the Old Shambles, Manchester. This had been established in 1735 and was still maintaining its convivial though, the author of the article adds, 'presumably not all its political traditions' as late as 1892. 'It had thus honoured its silent toast of "Church and King"—or Queen, "and down with the Rump" with the same unbroken punch-bowl through an unbroken succession of a hundred and fifty-seven years', and maybe for three more. Francillon also alludes to the 'Lord Raglan' in Aldersgate Street, London, which before 1854 had been known as the 'Mourning Bush' for it stood on the site of the inn 'whose host had dared to drape his bush in crepe during the murder of King Charles'. It was in this tavern that the Neo-Jacobites of the 1890s on occasions met. The other party had its own club too directed against not only Charles I but the clubmen who honoured him. The 'Calves' Head Club' was instituted in ridicule of the cult of King and Martyr. Its great annual banquet was held on the King's day 30 January and consisted of a cod's head, to represent the person of Charles Stuart, independent of his kingly office; a pike with little ones in its mouth, an emblem of tyranny; a boar's head with an apple in its mouth, to represent the king preying on his subjects; and calves' heads dressed in various ways, to represent Charles in his royal capacity. After the banquet the *Eikon Basilike* was burnt, and the parting cup was 'To those worthy patriots who killed the tyrant'.[11] The clubs, though, tended to be Tory, higher gentry; but there can be no doubt that Jacobitism was a living minority all through the eighteenth century. Indeed, had the common people been able to vote for their king, it is possible that the Stuarts might have been restored. Boswell, it seems, paid Charles I the doubtful compliment of naming his natural son after the Royal Martyr. Most of the clubs survived either in the Manchester area or in Wales, so confirming the connection of Jacobitism with the Celt and with minorities, in this instance with the Roman Catholics among the Welsh gentry. In a diary entry of Charlotte Williams-Wynn, for 5 December 1843, we find an allusion to the 'Cycle of the White Rose'. This had been founded in 1710 and continued to meet until some time between 1850 and 1860. 'The Sir Watkin of the day', Miss Williams-Wynn tells us, 'was always the president, and his wife the only lady allowed to dine with them. The health of the Pretender was drunk with great solemnities'.[12] That same article alludes to a ballad in Welsh written after 1788, with a South Wales provenance, and called 'Wild Merlin's Prophecy'. Its subject was the Welsh popular hero Owen of the Red Hand, who like Arthur and Charlemagne, no less than Cuculhain and other Celtic heroes, would, it was supposed, one day wake from slumber and work wonders in the world. In the ballad occurs the couplet:

> This Owen is Henry the Ninth,
> Who dwells in a foreign land,

implying not merely familiarity with Cardinal York's royal title, but his identification with the renewal of national glories at the waking of Owen of the Red Hand.[13] Francillon concludes his article by attempting to account for the disappearance of Jacobitism as a continuous factor in popular politics; the popular poetry and the oral tradition of the eighteenth century had contained many references to the 'snow-white rose'. After citing the French Revolution and the transformation of German into British kings, he concludes:

> Among the less obvious are the extinction of the tradition of the Non-jurors for lack of a Bishop to transmit their orders after the death of Bishop Boothe (*sic*) in 1805. None the less it is evident that English Jacobitism stands in need of Charles II's apology for his having been 'such an unconscionable time in dying' ... Unless, like Owen of the Red Hand, it did not die and only waits for a king.[14]

That reference to 'Non-Juring' recalls us to earlier Stuarts than Charles III and in particular to the first Charles. Charles (like his grandmother Mary) arranged his end with a delicate sense of theatre; he did so not only to secure his eldest son's succession but also to save the Anglican Church by a picturesque martyrdom. The rise and fall of this martyrology has been analysed for us by H.W. Randall:[15]

> In an elegant and fulsome Act of Parliament the Lords and Commons decreed that the 29th May (the date of the Restoration and the birthday of Charles II) should be celebrated forever as a day of thanksgiving. In a much less explicit direction, which took only a few sentences in the Act of Attainder for the regicides, they ruled that the 30th January should be observed as a day of fasting and humiliation. Both anniversaries were analogous to one already existing, which had been instituted by Parliament to commemorate the discovery of the Gunpowder Treason, and as on the 5th November, the preachers were expected on the new anniversaries to perform a special office and deliver an appropriate homily or sermon.[16]

Dr Randall observes that 30 January was secretly observed before the Restoration of 1660 by Anglicans who 'immediately humbled themselves under the afflicting hand of God, and kept a true fast on this day for many years before there was any law to authorize it'.[17] In 1661 Convocation approved the 'special liturgical services ... appointed for the day with proper collect, epistle and gospel ... not merely by the insertion in black letter of the king's name in the Kalendar'.[18] The 30 January service, however, was not explicitly ratified by Parliament, though 30 January sermons were preached every year to the House of Commons until 1859, and the service appeared in the Book of Common Prayer of 1662.

Dr Randall's main aim in her article is to trace the manner in which the political and liturgical elements in 30 January sermons diverge. She lists some exceptions to this tendency, but her evidence is culled almost exclusively from the sermons themselves. How it was possible for Charles's death to become both a political and religious myth depended on the king's enemies as much as on his friends. 'The earlier sermons, along with contemporary elegies and pamphlets written very shortly after the King's death, may be said to lay the foundations of a political myth of the Royal Martyr.' But there were also

> serious tactical errors on the part of the regicides. The most egregious blunder was the public character of the execution itself. If Charles's death had been the work of a 'private' assassin, the very claim of martyrdom might have been jeopardized. Instead, the block set up in the sunny street gave the martyrdom a perfect setting. Then, too, the King-killers had grievously overlooked the fact that the second lesson for the 30th January, as appointed in the Book of Common Prayer, was the 27th chapter of St Matthew, on the trial and crucifixion of Christ. To the King himself, when Bishop Juxon read the lesson a few hours earlier, the choice seemed providential; to the myth-makers it held abundant symbolic significance.[19]

In addition, there was the publication, perhaps on that very day, of *Eikon Basilike*: 'Finally, in depriving the king of a funeral and hence of a funeral sermon, they may have prompted unwittingly the choice of the art-form in which the theme of the Martyr was mainly to be developed.' The Sermons of 1649 show how rapidly the myth was elaborated:

> the real character of Charles and most of the tangible circumstances of his life have given way to a stylized representation of an already legendary figure who owes his lineaments more to a sacred than to contemporary history. He is indeed a figure almost allegorical, a personified abstraction not merely of absolute sovereignty but of civil government itself. As such, the outlines of his character are dim enough; he is allowed the same generalized innocence and uprightness that usually obtain with personified virtues; he is given the very slightest degree of individuality in connection with his fortitude in suffering (his own chief virtues are piety and patience); he is called 'the best of Kings'. But the essence of his character is simply that he is *the Royal Martyr*, a term which one is apparently supposed to consider by definition paradoxical. It is construed, in any case, as involving a tissue of paradoxes: the King's death is the paradox of inviolability violated; it is the paradox of the living but beheaded body politic; it was effected at once by a few 'execrable murderers', by the whole nation, by Antichrist, and (that the King should not live to witness divine wrath descending upon his people) by God himself.

And Dr Randall proceeds to tell us how the preachers of the immediate post-1649 period made these paradoxes intelligible: a few concrete details were cited from contemporary history; but the main symbols derived from the Bible where the preachers found parallels to or 'types' of, paradoxically again, the 'unparalleled murder' of their king: Josiah, the upright Jewish king, who died a violent death and was violently mourned: 'the breath of our nostrils, the anointed of the Lord, was taken in their pits'. Charles was also identified with Saul on the single ground of his supposed inviolability. (The texts are I Samuel 24:5–6; 26; 9; and II Samuel 1:4.)

> The theme of inviolability is also at the heart of the bold comparison with Christ (the key words are Pilate's 'Shall I crucify your King?'), but the added support of a sacramental quality in the analogous sufferings of the two men (the sacramental element coming into Charles's story by the analogy only) gave to the legend a religious significance it would not otherwise have had.[20]

Churches were dedicated to the Royal Martyr, particularly between 1660 and 1714: Falmouth; two at Plymouth; Newton on Wem; Peak Forest; Tunbridge Wells; Shelland in Suffolk; and more recently one specially built at Potters Bar. Additionally, there are windows and votive images, while it is not uncommon for Charles to be depicted with a crown of thorns.

Gradually, and particularly after 1688, attention becomes deflected from lamentation over the 'passion' of the Royal Martyr and divine right to specific lessons about civic obedience to properly appointed rulers. Less of the Samuel 24 and more of the Romans 13. Gradually, during the eighteenth century the language of the sermons becomes more 'pallid and innocuous' and the French Revolution with its excesses reduced the significance of the 1649 event: no longer unique, the axe was less prolific than the guillotine.

However, perhaps Dr Randall's equations are a little too neat, though learned and eloquently designed. She notes the foundation of the Society of King Charles the Martyr but rests at quoting its own assertion that it is 'emphatically non-political'. Indeed not so, for a number of its members were Jacobites and belonged to other organizations by means of which they attempted to realize their political ends. And, as we shall see, the Society was included in the activist *Legitimist Kalendar* as an organization with aims analogous to those of the political Neo-Jacobites. Is it possible anyway to divide the political and liturgical elements in the Carolean martyrology so cleanly? As with the Tractarians, the members of the SKCM were reacting to political pressures (for 'dissent' read 'liberalism') on the High Church and resistance therefore necessarily became itself *political* just as the resistance was conditioned by political assumptions about the role of the Anglican Church in society.

The decision of 1859 was not quite so logical and uncontroversial as Dr Randall's account might suggest. There have been four attempts in the present century on the part of the Lower House of Convocation to restore Charles's name to the Kalendar and his office to the Prayer Book. On each occasion the attempt was defeated by politic Bishops.[21] Moreover, Dr Randall leaves the impression that the myth of Charles as martyr and saint was exclusively a creation of learned clergy and poets; but Charles is also an example of popular cult: there were miracles and these miracles were inevitably connected with the notion of the king as sacred body; with divine right.

At this point, it might be as well to glance at elements of continuity in the first part of the nineteenth century. Although the last of the Non-juring Bishops had died in 1805, their 'valid' orders continued through their consecration of Bishop Seabury to the episcopate in the United States. The incidence of Charles churches and Charles services in the United States stems from such a succession. The relation of Church and State in that country might seem to support the argument that the liturgical was by now entirely divorced from the notion of political martyrdom, were it not for the coincidence once more of American High Anglicanism with Jacobitism. As in eighteenth-century Scotland, minority status made the transatlantic Church more extreme in its attitudes; the Americans even have a church dedicated to St William Laud: which is perhaps rather going it.

With the Tractarian Movement, the Charles cult intensified. To the numerous poems about Charles's martyrdom in the seventeenth and eighteenth centuries, we may add John Keble's for 30 January in his famous *Christian Year* of 1827. Keble's offering has all that popular decency and sobriety typical of Anglican poetry, worship and church music—Samuel Sebastian Wesley, for example, and which remind one of the Anglican's response to the Calvinist's statement that man's attitude to God should be abject: 'Oh, no, deferential, but not abject'.

Keble's poem is a useful witness for Dr Randall's case. The poet informs us that 'The Martyr's noble army still is ours/Far in the North our fallen day has seen', and what our fallen day remarkably has witnessed is 'not cottage hearth alone', but 'a monarch from his throne/Springs to his cross and finds his glory there'; the paradox of the Royal Martyr has faded to this. And in lines much visited by the ghost of Walter Scott, but also with some sense of the sanctity of place, of Marston Moor or of Carisbrook Castle, Keble continues:

Yes: whereso'er one trace of thee is found,
  As in the Sacred Land, the shadows fall:
With beating heart we roam the haunted ground,
  Lone battle-field or crumbling prison wall.

And there are aching solitary breasts,
  Whose widowed walk with thought of thee is cheered,
Our own, our royal saint, thy memory rests
  On many a prayer, the more for thee endeared.

True son of our dear Mother, early taught
  With her to worship, and for her to die . . .
  . . .

And well did she thy loyal love repay;
  When all forsook her Angels still were nigh,
Chain'd and bereft, and on thy funeral way,
  Straight to the Cross she turn'd thy dying eye.[22]

And Keble has a note which consists of a quotation from Herbert's memoirs recounting the incident of the king's response to the Chapter 27 of St Matthew when he was told by Juxon that it was the proper lesson for the day: 'so aptly serving as a seasonable preparation for his death that day'. Keble allows that the pattern of individual martyrdom derives from and resembles that of the Lamb of God, but any notion of exact analogy is muted. The political tradition in this poem has indeed given way to the purely ecclesiastical.

Keble's associate Hurrell Froude had a more distinct cult for Charles; but he died young and the conversions to Rome and the drift from Patristic and Carolean theology to the Middle Ages and Ritualism deflected Anglican attention from the cult.[23] Not all High Churchmen were neglectful of Charles, though in the middle years of the century it tended to be the eccentric and schismatic who preserved the cult. To the name of F.G. Lee may be added that of 'Father Ignatius' Abbot of Elm Hill, Norwich and later of Llanthony in Wales. In the *Church of England and Monastic Times* of 25 March 1884, the Father set out the case for an absolute devotion to the cause of the Royal Martyr.

The 1860s probably witnessed the faintest energies of Jacobitism; but in the 1870s interest in Legitimism generally was roused by the Bourbon Pretender to the crown of Spain, Don Carlos and his fluctuating fortunes till the final defeat of March 1876. A Carlist Committee had been founded in England in 1873. This naturally led to consideration of a British claimant in the person of Carlos's uncle, the Duke of Modena. In the previous year the League of Scotland had held an important meeting in St Mary's Hall, Edinburgh, and Scots Nationalism and Neo-Jacobitism were to come together in the 1890s.[24] And in 1877 several members of the Carlist Committee, including some who were later to found Neo-Jacobite societies, established the Thames Valley Legitimist Club. Disraeli, in his novel *Endymion* (1880), with a politician's sense of the topical, has an heir to the Stuart right who is called the Duke of Modena.

The next phase of the story and the one which remains my peculiar concern begins in 1886 with the foundation or rather the refounding of the Order of the White Rose. One of the Order's founders and its first chancellor, Henry Jenner, antiquarian and poet, of the British Museum, wrote a letter to the *St James's Gazette* of 24 April of that same year:

> I learn from the daily newspapers that the Persons who call themselves Liberals intend to adopt the White Rose as an Ensign or Device. If this report be true, in the name of a small but faithful Remnant, I beg to protest against the Desecration.
>
> 'Tis now near two Centuries since the White Rose was first worn by honest Man on the Tenth of June, the birthday of His Majesty King James the Third and Eighth, and there are those that wear it yet. Nay, more, there is already an Order of the White Rose, secret only in that we do not expose the sacred sentiments of our Hearts to the vulgar gaze. We meet, we drink to the Health of the Queen (for it is a Queen now) over the Water, but we do not seek to disturb the Good Princess on the Throne. We are quite harmless, but we feel it hard that the Liberals (as they are call'd), having the exceeding many Flocks and Herds of all Linnaeus open to them, should take our little Ewe-Lamb from us. The words Jacobite and Jacobin may differ as little as those two Greek adjectives concerning at which Mr. Gibbon sneers in his History, but the opinions are divided by the whole of Heaven and would not willingly be confounded.
>
> If I may be permitted to suggest a suitable Flower (if they must needs be Plagiarists and have a Flower) for the Liberals, I would name the

> Trumpet-Flower, or Bignonia Radicans. It comes from North America. It attaches itself as a parasitical growth to some Tree or Building, and flourishes to the Destruction of that on which it fastens. Fixed firmly it blows (and its own trumpet) all over the Place; and the Trumpet of it is blood-red with a centre of guilt, I ask pardon. I mean gilt.
>
> I am, Sir, your obedient Servant,
> A Jacobite.[25]

The humour is heavy; the metaphors somewhat interfibrillated, but the letter has point. The activity of the word 'Jacobite' is so unusual that it becomes vulgarly confused with its opposite 'Jacobin' though the two words are as polar as 'homoiousion' and 'homousion' where the distinction of a vowel resulted in the propagation of that heresy of Arius which had so charmingly begun by drawing away 'seven hundred virgins from the church'.

Jenner's coadjutor in the foundation was the 5th Earl of Ashburnham. According to an unpublished letter of Jenner's, the Order was not yet in existence at the time of the communication to the *Saint James's Gazette*:

> [it] was incorporated at an evening party ... in Campden Hill on 10th June (... called White Rose Day) 1886 ... [at] the house of Mr Henry Wilberforce. Among the other persons in the house was a Mr Ernest Radcliffe Crump,[26] a solicitor ... a member of a Cheshire family, which had been connected with the Cycle of the White Rose.

Having established its valid succession, the letter goes on to distinguish between the Order's actual origin and the gathering on the ideal date. The context of the letter becomes clearer: 'the report in the papers that the Liberals proposed to start a White Rose League in opposition to the then new Primrose League, it being alleged that the white rose was Gladstone's favourite flower', and Jenner describes his letter to the *Saint James's Gazette* as being in 'a rather eighteenth century style of English' with its stiffening of capital letters and how he dated it 'with the double date of Old and New Style, as was not unusual before 1752'.[27] Later, we are told that Francillon, Lady Maidstone, Ruvigny and others joined and that for several years the Order flourished so that at one time there were close on 500 members. Among members not mentioned by Jenner were Whistler, that amazing and amusing rogue Charles Augustus Howell and the poet and translator, Sebastian Evans.[28] In 1888 the Order printed a Stuart Calendar; that year marked the centenary of

Charles III's death, but the purpose also involved pre-empting any celebration of the Glorious Revolution's bicentenary. And in the following year the Order was active behind the scenes in mounting a Stuart Exhibition at the New Gallery in Regent Street, where numerous relics of the family kindled public attention. In 1890, on the anniversary of the Battle of Culloden, the Order founded its own monthly magazine *The Royalist*, which was to survive for fifteen years. *The Royalist* was not merely of genealogical concern or full of sentimental politics, it also contained poems on Stuart topics, some distinguished, and liturgies and offices for Charles the Martyr.

By the early 1890s Jacobitism, or rather Neo-Jacobitism, was assuredly 'in the air'. Queen Victoria herself had acted as patroness of the Stuart Exhibition. In 1891 Henry Irving shrewdly 'judged the state of the atmosphere suitable for a successful revival of W.G. Wills's 'King Charles the First'.[29] The theatre might well find it difficult to compete with the tragic poem personally presided over by the royal victim.[30]

As late as 24 January 1892 we find Ruvigny contributing to the organ of the White Rose, a mere month before the 'demo' at Westminster Abbey. The most elaborate account of this event appears in *The Daily Graphic*:

'A Jacobite Jest'

> February 8th, the anniversary of the execution of Mary Queen of Scots, falling this year upon a Monday, which is one of the days when the Chapels Royal at Westminster are open free to the general public, the occasion was thought by the Legitimist Jacobite League to be a suitable one for laying wreaths upon that sovereign's tomb. Unfortunately the resident Canon appeared to have thought that no occasion could be suitable for anything akin to a demonstration within the walls of a sacred building, and accordingly on the arrival of the Jacobites the Chapels Royal containing the tomb were found to be closed. It subsequently became evident, and was a cause of some acrimony of discussion between the disappointed members of the Legitimist League, that the same announcement of the projected ceremony in certain journals which had been intended to call together the faithful, had also warned the Ecclesiastical authorities at Westminster Abbey. Shortly after the arrival of the Jacobites at about two o'clock (a quarter past two being the hour fixed for the ceremony) a little procession, which included the Marquis de Ruvigny, Mr R.E. Francillon, Mr Stewart Meade, Mr Clifford Mellor,[31] and a local descendant of the Robbie Anderson who 'showed the way to Prince Charlie at the Battle of Prestonpans'—made

their way to the gate of the Royal Chapel. It was closed. After a little time, however, it was resolved that under the circumstances the only thing to be done was to place the wreath of the Legitimist League on the gate which barred the way to the tomb of the dead Queen. This was done in spite of the remonstrance of the attendant verger and the Jacobites politely, but firmly, refused to take it away again. Indeed, whereas the wreath at first had faced the main body of the Abbey, it was afterwards placed so that the arum lilies and other white flowers of which it was composed should face towards the tomb over which the spirit of the 'martyr Queen' might be hovering. The wreath bore the inscription: 'In Memory of the Martyrdom of Mary, then of England, Scotland, Ireland and France, Queen'. There were other wreaths, including one from members of the Order of the White Rose; but these had been taken away as soon as it was found impossible to make use of them. There were some two hundred and fifty persons present, and there was some talk of constituting a deputation to the Resident Dean. It was thought, however, by some of the weaker vessels of the part that this might lead to apprehension on a charge of brawling, and the project was abandoned. There was an unusually large force of police present.[32]

The Daily Graphic's leader was lofty about both Abbey authorities and Legitimists; under the heading of 'Amateur Traitors' it observed:

The only effect of locking the gates ... is to give a ridiculous notoriety to a silly performance, which is just exactly what the latter-day Jacobites most desire. The absurdity of the whole affair reached its climax by permitting the verger, as a proxy, to accept the floral tributes to the memory of this very equivocal saint.[33]

To-Day, however, was able to distinguish between the antiquarian and activist wings of the movement and conveniently lists the *dramatis personae*;

The members of the Legitimist League ... represent the very advanced wing of Jacobitism. Dissatisfied with the purely academic Jacobitism of the Order of the White Rose, to which several of them originally belonged, they formed a more belligerent society of their own. The leader of these would-be revolutionists is the Marquis de Ruvigny et Raineval. His most prominent supporters are Mr Clifford Meller, the Jacobite candidate for the Romsey Division of Huntingdonshire, Mr R.W. Stewart Meade, who yesterday distinguished himself by carrying the wreath, Mr Herbert Vivian and the Hon. Stuart Erskine, the co-editors of that bright but brief-lived periodical the *Whirlwind*, and Mr R.C. Fillingham, a beneficed clergyman of the Church of England.[34]

Ruvigny had already begun to take 'a more extreme line' as

Jenner phrased it; he and his followers attempted to impose a more activist policy on the Order, were defeated, as *The Royalist* reports, by a majority of more than three to one, and a motion was passed that four of the members should be called on to resign. Ruvigny and Vivian accordingly founded the Legitimist Jacobite League on 30 June, 1891, Ruvigny being president, and the vice-presidents including Erskine, Mellor and Theodore Napier,[35] another prominent Scottish Nationalist who had in 1887 instigated a national pilgrimage annually to Culloden. Among those controlling the branches was Christopher Millard, bibliographer of Wilde and one of the principal actors in A.J.A. Symons's *Quest for Corvo.* Millard's area was 'Cambridge, Dorset and Hampshire'; his address is given as 'Lady Cross, Bournemouth', and we may assume connections with Gleeson White and his Christchurch circle. Later Millard emigrated to Woodford Green.[36] It is notable also that the Legitimists had their American branch whose agent general was an Episcopal clergyman.

Relations between the Order and the League continued to be troubled so long as Jenner and E.R. Crump were, in succession, chancellors; but the breach appears to have been healed by 1898 when Francillon, one of the 'advanced' Jacobites, succeeded and the *Legitimist Kalendar* of 1899 admitted the Order to its list of Jacobite institutions. In 1892, however, feelings still ran high, and in April of that year Ruvigny contributed an article, 'The New Jacobitism', to a monthly of somewhat miscellaneous and consumptive tendency, *The Albemarle.* This periodical was edited by W.H. Wilkins, novelist and biographer, and the realist short-story writer and friend of the *fin de siècle* poets, Hubert Crackanthorpe. Ruvigny's title polemically aligns and distinguishes Legitimism from the other 'new' symptoms of a revolutionary moment: *new* journalism; *new* woman; *new* humour, and so on, for he preaches the doctrine of Filmer and divine right, fighting battles about the nature of kingship, savagely outlined already by Dryden in *The Medal.* 'Jacobite candidates' he tells us 'are coming forward for constituencies in England, Scotland and Wales'. Such candidates are not bound by the past, that is the post-1688 past; the Jacobite Party, Ruvigny tells us, believes 'in the law of primogeniture and the right of descent, and utterly repudiates the idea that the people gave and the people can take away'. Liberty and Equality no less than the sovereign will of the people are delusions; the permanent values are devotion, loyalty and chivalry. The Legitimist League is the only true Jacobite movement. Its aim is 'to enlist people's sympathies on behalf of the eldest branch of the Royal Family: to let the nation know that the present occupant of the throne reigns only by Act of Parliament and by no right descent'. The people must be made aware that Princess Louis of Bavaria is by right Mary II of England and Ireland and IV of Scotland. And Ruvigny asks a question that marks this as a *fin de siècle* document: 'what will come to pass when the gracious lady who so long and so well has reigned over us, passes from the world?'.[37] Other aims of the League are the repeal of the Act of Settlement, that 'act which scouts all notions of Divine Right' and of the Septennial Act, which is 'analogous to the act of the Long Parliament in declaring itself indestructible', the removal of the remaining religious disabilities; maintenance of royal prerogatives; the reversal of all attainders against the adherents of the House of Stuart and the repeal of the Royal Marriage Act. The League's proposals, Ruvigny continues rather unrealistically, are of a root and branch character and so should appeal to Radicals no less than Tories. To be sure, this radical of the Right does attack the new plutocracy of Parliament. The divine right of democracy is every day diminishing, but first, schismatics within the Jacobite Movement itself must be contemptuously named and isolated:

> The legitimist League has nothing to do with, and is essentially different from, that body calling itself the Order of the White Rose, for that little society is Jacobite only in name; its sole business is of an antiquarian kind, and at its few public appearances its members only chatter Jacobite folk-lore over their tea-cups, or read dreary papers to each other under the exhilarating influence of watery claret. The Order certainly professes some excellent principles, but it lacks the courage to act up to them, and is avowedly hostile to all who wish to do so. On this account wide is the gulf which divides the Order of the White Rose from the Legitimist Jacobite League.[38]

Ruvigny was making a bid for popular attention. The question of religious disabilities, as Francillon reminds us in his *Mid-Victorian Memories*, was topical. In 1891 Gladstone had introduced a Bill for removing the remaining religious disabilities excepting those attaching to the Royal Family. This was supplemented by Mr John Pope-Hennessey's attempt to extend the Bill's provisions to the Royal Family so that the Stuarts need no longer speculate on whether Buckingham Palace was worth a Mattins. And that very phrase: the 'divine right of Democracy is diminishing every day' had been used by H.D. Traill towards the conclusion of his life of Lord Strafford published in 1889.

The first response to Ruvigny was some limpid satire by Andrew Lang in the *Illustrated London News* of 7 May (Lang had written nostalgic Jacobite verse) and this was followed by a direct reply in the *Albemarle* by R. Duncombe Jewell on behalf of the Order of the White Rose: 'The True Jacobitism: A Survival'. No less fiercely reactionary than Ruvigny, Duncombe Jewell none the less seized on the right-wing Radicalism of the League's programme and accused the League of adopting the 'ardent methods' and postures of a Social Democrat or Anarchist Association. 'It has "propogandists", a "Programme" and, which is its worst feature, it is fond of appealing to the People (distinguished with a capital P) and then to those noble instincts which your Socialist or Fabian Society street-preacher claims that the people possess'.[39] It is a question of tone as well as tactics. The attempt to influence that unconstitutional and plutocratic body Parliament is absurd, but then the very notion of Jacobitism attempting to advance by 'constitutional methods' is in defiance of all Jacobite tradition: 'Our present leaders apparently believe that the Archangels are elected by universal suffrage, that Heaven itself is periodically devastated by a general election, and that entrance thereto will be regulated by competitive examination.'[40] And stung by Ruvigny's blue-blood sneers about 'watery claret' and cosy middle-class antiquarianism, Duncombe Jewell protests that many members of the White Rose are persons in direct descent from those 'out' in 1715 and 1745 or had distinguished themselves on the right side in the Great Rebellion. And appealing to an apostolic succession of Jacobitism, he pointed out that some of the more elderly members had actually belonged to the Cycle of the White Rose, which had continued to meet at Wynnstay, Wrexham, as late as the 1850s.[41] Finally, to counterpoint Ruvigny's programme, those ambitious and—so Lang termed them—'plausible schemes', Jewell printed the *Preface to the Rule of the Order of the White Rose*:

> I. That Sovereign Authority is of Divine Sanction, and existeth not solely by the Will or Consent of them that are subject thereunto; and
> II. That the Murder of Charles I and the Revolution of the year 1688 were national Crimes.
>
> And the purposes of the Order are these:

1. To maintain and to promulgate, both by Precept and by Example, a Belief in True Kingship and its Divine Sanction:
2. To study, and to aid others in studying, the History of the Royal House of Stuart, and of the upholders of its Cause:
3. To keep their Sufferings and their Sacrifices in perpetual Remembrance:
4. To fulfil all Loyal Duties:
5. To refrain from, and to discourage in others, all evil speech concerning lawfully appointed Sovereigns:
6. To oppose all that tendeth to Democracy, whether within this Realm or beyond Sea: and to give good Will and Furtherance to them that anywhere support lawful Authority against its Enemies: and
7. To keep in mind that the White Rose is the token, not only of Honour to the Royal House of Stuart, but of all Faithfulness of Heart, and loyal Obedience; to the end that its Companions may make this Symbol of their Faith the Symbol of their Lives.[42]

Such a ritual gravity of language strongly contrasts with the brisker affirmations of the League. The Order's principles and purposes, Jewell continues, 'are far better calculated to appeal to the only persons worth appealing in these days—men of intellect and letters like Mr Andrew Lang ...; and men of ancestry and position ... but they will not appeal very directly to the wealthy lower orders, to the illiterate and immoral plutocrats who fraternally associate with the Heir Apparent to the Throne', nor to 'the present electorate of colliers, hinds and factory-hands' who have gradually assumed the administration of the country (evidently the extension of the franchise in 1888 still rankled). And with some strong words about the Order's implacable opposition to democracy Jewell ringingly concludes: 'in good hope of final victory have we planted our White Rose. Our watchwords are "Remember" and "Vigilemus"'.[43]

At about this time appeared Allen Upward's two Anti-Jacobite novelettes *This High Treason* and *Mary the Third*; at least one sermon was preached against the Jacobites, and the popular magazine *Black and White* carried an article on the Order of the White Rose with a photograph of Jenner as chancellor. In June 1890 the Hon. Stuart Erskine, who had contributed to the *Albemarle* an article on the related subject of Scottish Nationalism, along with Herbert Vivian (and, according to Jenner, Ruvigny) published the first of twenty-six weekly issues of *The Whirlwind*.[44] Erskine was to cede the editorship to Vivian. Whistler, Sickert and Mallarmé contributed to this brief but lively periodical—its title is clearly programmatic and Jacobitism consorts oddly with advocacy of Impressionism.

On 4 April 1894 the Society of King Charles the Martyr was founded, the principal movers being the Hon. Mrs Ermengarda Greville-Nugent (née Ogilvy) and the Rev. James Leonard Fish.[45] The Society had partly cohered in reaction to Kensit and 'a renewal of Puritan iconoclasm'.[46] By 1896 four churches in New York were keeping the feast of St Charles. The Society's object as stated on its earliest admission forms was simply 'Intercessory Prayer for the Defence of the Church of England against the attacks of her enemies', and these included the Nonconformist campaign for disestablishment and disendowment. One of the Society's early membership leaflets stated that it was 'emphatically non-political', none the less if not explicitly Neo-Jacobite, it was sometimes implicitly so.

In 1893 there began the custom of decorating the king's statue in Whitehall—an attempt made the year before had been prevented by the police. In 1901 permission to decorate and assemble at the statue was again refused as a consequence of certain Jacobites having proclaimed Princess Louis of Bavaria as Queen Mary IV and II on the death of Queen Victoria, which had taken place earlier in that same month. One of the main purposes of the Society was to restore the 30 January service to the Prayer Book and the name to the Kalendar.

Rev. J.L. Fish had been Rector of Saint Margaret Pattens in the City of London since 1866 and had introduced 'Catholic teaching', ceremonial and elaborate music. Dr Fish, with his 'silvery hair and buckled shoes',[47] was Neo-Jacobite, a companion of the Order of the White Rose, and on 31 January 1890 'there was Missa Cantata and Evensong in honour of St Charles' with an appropriate sermon for the day. From 1891 to 1906 when an unsympathetic incumbent succeeded, Evensong took place on 29 January and Missa Cantata on 30 January. In 1896 the Society and the Neo-Jacobites were rewarded with satire in *Punch*, who mocked both at King Charles's last word before execution, Duncombe Jewell's first watchword, and the habit of congregating at Le Sueur's statue in Whitehall.

Remember, remember, each scatterbrain member
  Of Leagues for Legitimist rot,
That now is the season for amateur treason
  And playing at piffle and plot.

At three in the morning, the powers-that-be-scorning,
  Turn up at Whitehall in full force,

And there with doffed hat you must worship the statue,
  And pay your respects to his horse.

With excursions, alarums, bring lilies and arums
  For brutal police to remove;
And for this year's display, lick the record with Gaelic
  Inscriptions, your ardour to prove.

Then, Jacobites, sally from out the Thames Valley
  By sixes and sevens to the Tryst;
White Cockaders, stand ready! St Germain's be steady!
  With danger the cause is well spiced!

For if you're too bold, Sirs, you'll doubtless catch cold, Sirs,
  And people will laugh at your pranks,
And at self-advertising and STUART uprising,
  And freaks of our latterday cranks.

KING CHARLIE THE SECOND, we're sure, would have reckoned
  These tricks as a comedy rare;
Nor will Punch to-day smile less at humours so guileless,
  Shown off in Trafalgar Square![48]

The middle classes were not prepared, but they were not afraid either.

Other allusions, beyond the faithful, to the Jacobite societies may be found. In 1893 'A Hanoverian' impressionistically noted that

> In addition to the Legitimist League in London, there is the White Cockade Jacobite Club in Huntingdonshire, a Jacobite Restoration Club in Brixton of all places, and local branches of the Legitimist League. Jacobites exist, too, in Canada and the States, thanks to the proselytizing efforts of a noble marquis (French creation) who comes of a line of soldiers, of which one member at least died in a Legitimist cause ...
>
> From time to time ... there are held treasonable meetings by night, usually in the old hall of one of the smaller Inns of Court.[49] Then the passenger down Holborn may observe figures suddenly disappear up a narrow and mysterious passage off the main artery.

If he had a ticket, the visitor would find himself in an old-fashioned hall with oaken rafters supporting a vaulted roof and great carved open fireplaces. He was present at a meeting of the Legitimist League. Treason by Ticket!

> Not improbably there would be a bouquet of white roses on the piano ... and the motto *Loyale je serai durant ma vie* would greet the eyes of the intruder. Not improbably, also, a clergyman of the Church of England, ready of tact and humour—as a lively Jacobite meeting at Cambridge once testified—would be in the chair, supported by fierce Carlists and other Legitimist enthusiasts.
>
> As in a dream, the visitor would hear the Act of Settlement, the Septennial acts, and other matters, which were duly settled centuries since, discussed as though they were the burning questions of the day ... this vexed century end with its Home-Rule and Suspensory Bills, would fade from sight ... The flame of loyalty would be fanned by such pathetic songs of the north as 'Wha wadna follow thee?' 'Waes me for Prince Charlie' or 'Will ye no come back again?' Thoughts might crowd upon him ... of the King who as the Puritan poet said, 'nothing common did or mean, upon that memorable scene' wherein he met his death ... and of the bonnie Prince Charlie 'hero of a hundred songs, who flirted so outrageously with the Scottish ladies'. Then our wavering Hanoverian would think of the plain German 'Geordies'; indeed the League would gratuitously supply him with some edifying reading matter ... culled from the pages of Bradlaugh's terrible 'Impeachment of the House of Brunswick' ... and with the lilt of the Jacobite melodies still ringing in this head our Hanoverian friend might cherish a secret sympathy for the League ...
>
> Our modern Jacobites have for the most part no desire to oust Queen Victoria from the throne ... till that day ... when she lays the sceptre down in obedience to that dread monarch that the Charleses First and Second met with so gentlemanly a grace.
>
> But after that, who can foretell what new things may happen. Anarchy, Republicanism, Socialism, have all their fierce apostles. Should any of these forces get the upper hand, and the present dynasty be dethroned, there will be need of a rallying flag for those who cling to monarchical traditions. Then it will come to pass that the legitimist will flock from St Ives and from Brixton, wearing the white rose of loyalty, and do battle with the hydra-headed monsters spawned by Democracy.
>
> If nothing is possible but the improbable, we may yet see these things, and so shall the Stuarts enjoy their own again.
>
> In the meantime we hope the authorities will not see fit to behead any of the excellent and amiable gentlemen who are espousing what we fear we must consider a lost cause.[50]

From the Legitimist League's occasional publication *The Legitimist Kalendar* we may more precisely gather something about the existence and origins of these societies. The Legitimist League was itself to incorporate on 24 February 1898 the Society of the Red Carnation. Of its various branches and clubs, the most important was the White Cockade Club of Huntingdonshire. This had been founded by Gilbert Baird Fraser in 1890 and united with the Huntingdonshire branch of the League on 26 February 1891. The Order of St Germain, formed in September 1893, had as its registrar Clifford Mellor. The Order's principles were (1) deep reverence for religion; (2) deep reverence for the divine right of legitimate princes; (3) deep reverence for ancient precedent. The Thames Valley Legitimists had among their aims the maintenance of the royal prerogatives and by constitutional means the attempt to obtain the removal of the remaining religious disabilities that afflict the Royal Family. By 1899 the *Legitimist Kalendar* included both the Order of the White Rose and the Society of King Charles the Martyr, even though it was 'not strictly Legitimist'. And in *Notes and Queries*, still concerned with the cause, we find eager answers to a Miss Conway-Gordon's enquiry about contemporary Jacobite societies. "R.D. J(ewell)' replies that the OWR is the oldest and probably best known of those, while 'M.H.B.' in his reply describes the League as the largest and principal Jacobite organization in the country. The two organizations were still at odds in 1894. 'M.H.B.' also details the League's branches: The Jacobite Restoration Club of South London (located presumably at Brixton), the Eastern Jacobite Club, the Mary Stuart Club at Wishaw, the Forty-Five Club of Grimsby.[51] And on 27 March 1897, Augustus Lumbye, chairman of the Thames Valley Legitimist Club (based on Chiswick and Hammersmith) answers another query (possibly a bogus one) by listing the four chief London societies, the OWR, the Order of St Germain, the Thames Valley Legitimist Club and the Legitimist Registration Union.[52] Apart from programmes and letters, however, the League and its offshoots appear to have made no mark on the literature of the 1890s. The case is otherwise with the Society of King Charles the Martyr.

Mrs Greville-Nugent was a learned lady, attracted both to poetry and liturgy. In 1897 she devised a *Litany of St Charles, King and Martyr, with a Hymn and Other Devotions*, which the authoress hoped would 'be found useful to Associates of the Society KCM, of the Church Needlework Guild of St Charles; as well to all those members of the Church of England who venerate 'our own, our Royal Saint'.[53] After the Trinity, the king is impetrated in these terms:

St Charles of England
Pray for us [response after each line]
St Charles of England,
Flower of kings,
Worthy successor of St Edward,
Anointed of the Lord with the oil of gladness, …
Who in the white robes of purity wast wedded to thy people,

Pillar of the Church of God,
Restorer of altars,
Pious adorner of churches,
'Princely Pelican' despoiling thyself of thy substance, for the Church,

Mirror of modesty, …
Constant frequenter of the Sacraments of Penance and of the Altar,
Powerful worker of miracles both in life and after death,
Healer of deseased persons,
Enlightener of the blind,
Hater of sacrilege, …
Made strong through suffering,
Patient in anguish,
Meekly submitting to all indignities,
Unjustly tried by cruel and ignorant men,
At whom thy persecutors did spit and scoff,
Who didst suffer many things like to Thy Master,
Who, fortified by the Holy Viaticum, didst go cheerfully to thy passion,
Who, upon the scaffold didst intercede for thy murderers, after the example of St Stephen,
Who, by the shedding of thy 'sacred and innocent blood' wast 'espoused to the Blessed Jesus',
Whose hearse was made white by a sudden fall of snow, as if to declare thy sanctity and innocence,
Who has exchanged a temporal for an eternal crown,
Glorious Martyr 'more than conqueror'.[54]

After versicles and responses and a prayer, there follows a hymn whose first verse may be given:

O Holy King, whose severed head
The Martyr's Crown doth ray
With gems for every blood-drop shed,
St Charles! for England pray.[55]

After the hymn, the Proper Collect for King Charles the Martyr's Day is given from the Prayer Book of 1662, in which the king is described as 'being enabled so cheerfully to follow the steps of his Blessed Master and Saviour, in a constant meek suffering of all barbarous indignities, and at last resisting unto blood; and even then, according to the same pattern, praying for his murderers'.[56] The Litany concludes with a prayer from the Bishop of Salisbury, Dr Duppa's *Private Forms of Prayer* of 1660.

The immediate model for Mrs Greville-Nugent's Litany is clearly the Anglican Prayer Book of 1662. The imagery of the Pelican relates the king once more to Christ: 'soft self-wounding Pelican'. The allusions to Charles as 'the white King'—Charles had been unusually vested in white at his Coronation and was to be buried in St George's, Windsor, in a fierce snowstorm—are frequently made in the 1890s. Holbrook Jackson in his classic study of the *fin de siècle* discusses the acute colour sensibility of the period, isolating the taste for yellow, green and white:

> White gleamed through the most scarlet desires and the most purple ideas of the decade ... In midmost rapture of abandonment the decadents adored innocence, and the frequent use of the idea of whiteness, with its correlatives, silver, moonlight, starlight, ivory, alabaster and marble, was perhaps more than a half conscious symbolism.[57]

And Jackson cites Whistler, Pater, Alice Meynell, Francis Thompson: 'a fair white silence', Dowson 'dominated by a sense of whiteness', Wilde, Lionel Johnson, Crackanthorpe, Le Gallienne and Symons. And he might well have cited Mallarmé and Verlaine, though in the first instance whiteness is less innocence than horror and fascination with the void, the purity of negation. Where Charles is concerned that whiteness is retrospective: martyrdom being, as Pater observes in *Marius the Epicurean*, 'as the church has always said, a kind of sacrament with plenary grace'. Or, as Mrs Greville-Nugent put it: 'he defended unto death the Church's apostolical Hierarchy; for he who suffers death [for] *one vital article of the Faith* as for the whole Faith, dies a Martyr, says Benedict XIV (*De Canon Servorum Dei*, 1746)'.[58] In that light, Charles's dubious politics and his betrayal of Strafford merely highlight the candour of his sacrifice: his sanctity has the equivocal quality, in the last analysis, which appealed in an age of the transvaluation of values; the period of Nietzsche and Huysmans. Similarly, his art connoisseurship and what could be construed as his dandyism made him a martyr of 'the Decadence'.

At broadly the same time as Mrs Greville-Nugent's offering, the Rev. Canon C. L. Broun, a member also of the SKCM composed a somewhat more professional office, on the model of the Sarum breviary: *Officium festi sancti Caroli regis Angliae et martyris.* The office is, excepting the rubrics and the divisions of the day, in English and was subsequently translated into Latin, in part by Ronald Knox, at that time (*c.* 1910) an Anglican still and a member of SKCM.[59] Canon Broun's Office has an epigraph: 'Hic jacet nec Carolus Victor/Nec Carolus Magnus/Sed Carolus Agnus.' The Office is divided into: *Ad primas vesperas, Ad completiorum, Ad Matutinas, In prima nocturna, In seconda nocturna, In tertia nocturna, Ad laudes, Ad secundas vesperas.* I give some excerpts:

Lo, the Feast of Charles the Martyr draweth nigh:
behold a King ariseth to be the martyr of his people.[60]

And here from the *Hympnus* of the *Ad primas vesperas:*

Gathered within this holy place
  Make we memorial due;
Praising the Martyr's two fold grace,
  Crowned and espoused anew ...

White King! Thy vesture whiter gleams
  All bright with dew impearled—
Blood of the Lamb, whose cleansing streams
  Flowed to redeem the world ...[61]

And from *Aria Super Magnificat:*

HAIL, Monarch of the Angels' race,
  Thou soldier of the Angels' king:
Charles, Flower of Martyrs, Thee we sing
  Like rose or lily is thy grace ...[62]

And this from the *Hympnus Ad Matutinas*, which encapsulates the doctrine:

The praise of Charles our martyred King
With heart and voice come let us sing:
Who earthly shame with Christ did bear
The Victor's Laurel now doth wear.

The prison's gloom, the battle sore
Christ's martyr here with gladness bore:
And mounting from the scaffold's shame
To his sure hope in heav'n he came.

For Holy Church his head he bowed,
Upon the axe his lifeblood flowed
And where that kingly seed was sown
New harvest unto Christ hath grown ...[63]

In 1934 the Society of King Charles the Martyr printed a composite Office consisting of the Duppa Collect, Epistle and Gospel taken from the 1662 Prayer Book, Offering and Communion from the Invitatory of the same book. The Alleluya Verse and Offertory also occur in the Office authorized by the bishops in Scotland. The sequence was composed by Henry Jenner, had been first printed in *The Royalist* in 1905 and was designed to be sung to the melody of *Plaesu Chorus Laetabundo*. The note to the Office concludes: 'The Feast ranks with an inferior double (Sarum use) or a double (Roman use). Where the Roman Kalendar is observed, a memorial of St Martina, Virgin and Martyr, may be said'.[64] Jenner's sequence has been twice translated, by Mrs N.P. Noel and by Dr C.B. Moss.

Rex divine, Rector Regum
Juris Auctor, Dator legum,
  Omnem regens populum,
Tibi laudes extollamus
Hodie dum honoramus
  Florem Regum Carolum.

Eheu! Clades et dolores
Generarunt proditores
  Maculati crimine;
Cadunt templa gloriosa,
Cadunt leges, alba rosa
  Rubra fit de sanguine!

Vere dixit rex Bardorum
'Tempus erit miluorum
  Et stragis mirabilis,
Quando regnum amittetur
Et in auram elebetur,
  Albus rex et nobilis'.

Jus divinum, lex celestis
Ab hominibus scelestis
  Arrogantur spurnitur;
Ad tribunal creuntatum,
Ab insanis designatum,
  Rex Anglorum ducitur.

Carae matris fili vere,
Tu servasti persincere
  Precepta fidelia;
Propter illa propugnasti,
Ipse victus superasti
  Caesus pro Ecclesia.

Nihil vile tu fecisti,
Semper digne tu gessisti
  Mirum per spectaculum;
Nil maligne proclamasti;
Pulchrum caput inclinasti,
  Velut super lectulum.

Et corona peritura
Data, bona mercatura,
  Pro incorruptabili,
Tenuisti cursum durum
Per securim ad securum
  Regnum Christi Domini.

Te Precursor, cujus nomen
LAUDEM sonat (felix omen!)
  Ille Praesul inclytus
Expectabat coronatus
Ubi laudet candidatus
  Martyrum exercitus.

Caede Regis venit vita,
Venit lege demolita
  Renovamen patriae;
Sanguis Martyris Regalis,
Facti morte immortalis,
  Semen fit Ecclesiae.

Letum priusquam acerbum
Passus fuit, unum verbum
  Dixit 'Reminiscere';
Tu, Ecclesia sanata
Hujus morte reparata,
  Numquam obliviscere![65]

It is an ingenious conflation of history and literature. Jenner's practice in medieval Latin mode is not uncommon in the 1890s. Lionel Johnson comes readily to mind. However, Jenner wrote much competent English verse. In October 1890, for example, we find him lamenting the fall of Men Amber, a menhir in Cornwall; as long as that stood, so popular repute, a king should reign over

Britain. It was overthrown by the Parliamentarians on the morning of 30 January 1649.

The black cloud bursts, the snowflakes drop,
  They hide the fallen stone;
On moor and down they drift and spread
  And all is white and lone.

Not only on the Druid's rock,
  On Cornish moor they fall,
Solemn and sad they come to weave
  A royal funeral pall.

Ah, well as Landsdowne's fatal field
  Where the loyal Cornish lie,
And well for them they could not live
  To see the White King die.

Then fell that blackest winter night
  The prophet's ban could bring,
Until the May-dawn broke at last,
  With the coming of the King.[66]

Of the literary figures of the 1890s, Crackanthorpe, Dowson, Marmaduke Langdale (a descendant of a famous Civil War royalist), Texeira de Mattos and McGregor Mathers, *soi-distant* Count Glenstrae in the Jacobite peerage and Kabbalist, are all known to have possessed Jacobite sympathies. Lionel Johnson's were the most pronounced and had the most distinguished issue. Four of his finest poems and a short story revolve round Charles and the Civil War, while his most anthologized piece, 'By the Statue of King Charles at Charing Cross', written in 1891, appeared (with some variants from a slightly earlier printing in *The Second Book of The Rhymers' Club*) in *The Royalist*.[67] Johnson's ancestry was Irish and Scots (his parents were 'High and dry' Anglican); he was attracted always to lost causes. In 1884 his family rented a house from relatives at Mold in Flintshire, and here Johnson spent some of his vacations for the next three or four years. It is less than twenty miles as the crow flies from Wynnstay, so that Johnson may well have had local knowledge of the White Rose Cycle. His first recorded sentiments about the Royal Martyr are not favourable, though they occurred in the non-committal context of the Winchester College Debating Society.[68] In 1891 Johnson was received into the Latin Church by the Rosminian, Fr William

Lockhart, who had been a companion of Newman's at Littlemore and had preceded his master in conversion. But Fr Lockhart also had Carlist connections.

Johnson was already in spirit a Latin Catholic by 1889 so that he could barely present Charles convincingly as political martyr except in the sense that the 'crowds' and 'rebels' of the poem have affinities with the Shakespearian mob. A new image of the king is clarified: Charles as martyr not for the state and/or for religion, but for art's sake: 'His death/By beauty made amends'. If Charles possesses sanctity and is the vehicle of grace:

> His soul was of the saints;
> And art to him was joy

and:

> King, tried in fires of woe!
> Men hunger for thy grace.

Grace and sanctity are assimilated to 'comeliness' and 'calm': 'Comely and calm, he rides/Hard by his own Whitehall'. Life operates as Purgatorial fire, which allows his death to be a work of art; indeed, Charles's final triumph is to *become* a work of art; to adapt the words that Professor Richard Ellmann uses of Oscar Wilde's *Intentions*, 'his thin skin has turned' not 'to marble' but to the stonework of Le Sueur's statue. But the image of Charles involves more than the virtuoso art-collector or the perfector of life and death as art. The work of art itself, the statue, displays an image of triumph through tragic acceptance:

> Armoured he rides, his head
> Bared to the stars of doom

for Charles has been, the poem tells us, 'Crowned, and again discrowned'.

But, as in the seventeenth century, Charles has become a glittering abstraction; nothing attaches Charles to contemporary history except perhaps the quotation

> *Speak after sentence*: Yea
> And to the end of time.

That applies to the statue rather than to the man; Charles must put off kingship and humanity to become the work of art which expresses the triumph of beauty more completely than history can. But historical actuality is not so much denied as transcended; the word that Johnson applies to Charles's face, 'austerity', derives from a witness to the king's trial, but now the 'austerity' is 'sweet'. History, chronology, the attempt to reconcile the statue with the living man are all transcended, and this is reflected in the structure of the poem where progression springs solely from mood and circles rounds the words 'still', 'dark', 'stars', and even these are rendered in terms of art, of theatrical setting: 'Sombre and rich, the skies', like a mourning tapestry.

We are finally returned to the speaker confronting the work of art and his distance from that. 'By the Statue of King Charles at Charing Cross' is a poem about London, about loneliness and martyrdom in London; Charles as triumphant artefact becomes an emblem of what the speaker desires to be. The statue inhabits a world cleansed of communication; of contamination by humanity who are merely 'crowds and rebels'

> Yet when the city sleeps;
> When all the cries are still:
> The stars and heavenly deeps
> Work out a perfect will.[69]

It is an Arnoldian ending, perhaps; but with less any sense of Sophoclean law and more the sense of individual dissolution which relates this issue to other poems of Johnson such as 'The Dark Angel' or 'To Morfydd'.

On 7 September 1895, Johnson published in *The Speaker* a poem on 'Cromwell', which is distinctly less known than the verses on Charles. One characteristic Johnson shares with his master, Walter Pater, is an unwillingness to renounce: the main theme of his verse is reconciliation between profane beauty and the beauty of holiness; analogous are the frequent attempts he makes to reconcile the Classic and the Christian in such poems as 'Men of Aquino' (Juvenal and Aquinas) and 'Men of Assisi' (Propertius and Francis). Where Cromwell is posed against the dead of Drogheda and Charles. Johnson responds to the *terribilità*, for him an aesthetic quality, in Cromwell, England's 'mighty mastering son' and to the enigma of the Lord Protector's personality: 'Mystic desire and fierce delight' of battle. Cromwell's personality is tragic, and his destiny remains opaque: Hell, Purgatory or Heaven; the chief witnesses against him will be the women and children of Drogheda and:

> Answer, O fatal King!
>   Whose sad, prophetic eyes
> Foresaw his glory bring
>   Thy death! He also lies
> Dead: hath he peace, O King of sighs?[70]

The king's title suggests the analogy with Christ. At the end of the poem comes the tragi-comic resolution in the context of the great storm of 3 September 1658:

> Nay, peace for ever more!
>   O martyred souls! He comes,
> Your conquered conqueror:
>   No tramplings now, nor drums
>   Are his, who wrought your martyrdoms.
>
> Tragic, triumphant form,
>   He comes to your dim ways.
> Comes upon wings of storm:
>   Greet him, with pardoning praise,
>   With marvelling awe, with equal gaze.[71]

It is the storm of Lear, or of Oedipus, rather than a demonic rite of passage.

'Mystic and Cavalier' is a dramatic monologue, but neither element of the polarity fully involves Johnson: he remains equally inhibited from heroic action as from heroic sanctity. The climax of the poem arrives at the familiar pattern of self-dissolution as the only remedy for self-disgust and pain:

> O rich and sounding voices of the air!
> Interpreters and prophets of despair:
> Priests of a fearful sacrament! I come,
>   To make with you mine home.[72]

The sonnet 'The Age of a Dream' casts light (as does his imaginary portrait 'Mors Janua Vitae') on Johnson's attitude to the Carolean Church and Age: he endorses that Church for its elegance and the beauty of its holiness, but the ideal Church becomes a conflation of Tridentine and Medieval as well as Carolean elements:

Imageries of dreams reveal a gracious age:
Black armour, falling lace, and altar lights at morn.
The courtesy of Saints, their gentleness and scorn,
Lights on an earth more fair, than shone from Plato's page:
The courtesy of knights, fair calm and sacred rage: ...
Vanished, those high conceits! ...
Gone now, the carven work! Ruined, the golden shrine!
No more the glorious organs pour their voice divine

we are now surely well within the Restoration Church;

No more rich frankincense drifts through the Holy Place.[73]

and now in some baroque acre. Johnson's ideal Church can no more be embodied than Plato's dream of another world.

In 1899 a fellow-member of the Rhymers' Club, Victor Plarr, published a poem on John Hampden. Plarr, we may gather from his daughter's fictive biography of Dowson, *Cynara*, was a rationalist, a republican and, though sympathetic to the spirit of the Celt, quite antipathetic to Jacobitism and to Charles. Hampden is represented as a stranger in his own time, isolated by his powers of reason: 'a golden angel' but one powerless to save him from 'a mighty king' and from a disabling melancholy.[74]

Louise Imogen Guiney, an American poet, lived much of her life in England. She was a correspondent and friend (though they met rarely) of Lionel Johnson and like him a convert to Latin Catholicism. Miss Guiney was sympathetic to Jacobitism and to Charles particularly, and was prepared to confer on the king the title of Martyr by analogy. 'The Blessed Martyr Limited is a nice thing and new to me. It had the dearest little old portrait print of "Carolus Agnus" on its fly-leaf, pasted in: did you put it there or did it grow?', she writes to a friend.[75] And again: 'The lines on King Charles I would call Quasi-Beatus, only I fear you might eat me.' This was Herbert Clarke, an Oxford don; but we hear also of a poem on Charles written in youth by Miss Guiney.[76]

That New England followed old England in its Neo-Jacobitism, we may also gather from Miss Guiney's letters. This refers to the distinguished Gothic revival architect Ralph Adams Cram: 'Poor old R. Cram has been making a DONK of himself, since he became Prior of the No. American Cycle of the Order of the White Rose. My kind of Jacobinism [*sic*] is scandalized at his kind of Jacobitism.'[77]

The form that Cram's transmogrification took, we do not know. It can hardly have consisted in his contributing this sonnet to *The Royal Standard* of Boston in 1900:

With all the pomp of splendid majesty
  He comes, anointed King; the word is said,
The crown of kingdoms rests upon his head,
  And he stands clothed with Divinity,
Monarch of men, with sad, grave eyes that see
  Dimly the dusky future, half afraid
Of all the awful power God has laid
  Within his hands for righteous ministry.

With tears and prayers in solemn majesty
  He comes, anointed King; no longer now
An earthly monarch, but upon his brow
  The Crown of martyrdom, and drawing nigh
Men hear the music of the beating wings
  Of mighty armies of the King of Kings.[78]

I have quoted only salient lyrics; the Neo-Jacobite magazines are naturally full of poetry of this order. The poets were responding to a shift of mood, which had made possible the revival of Jacobitism in the 1890s. The long reign of Victoria; the dubieties about her heir (we may recall Yeats's somewhat unfair line written in 1902 'new commonness upon the Throne'; though about Edward's closeness to the plutocracy, there can be no doubt). The immediate comparison is with the last years of Elizabeth I's reign. The *fin de siècle* mood embodied both reverence for the person of the Empress of India—'the divine Victoria', as Oscar Wilde enjoyed referring to her[79]—and a reaction against the materialism, vulgarity, inflexibility and hypocrisy in morals of the age which took its name from her. Neo-Jacobitism can be aligned with the numerous sects of the *fin de siècle*, political, whether radical of the left or the right, Anarchist or Legitimist, the occult and illuminated societies, and with autocephalous Churches. One quality such sects have in common: the pursuit of power, if a strange type of power; a power that is abstract, almost metaphysical, and can only be exercised by leaders over their followers. But the notion lying behind such sects is always that of the remnant, whose real power is to come; they are aristocrats whether of blood,[80] or intellect or by ordeal. With this there goes the fascination with *soi-distant* titles and the power to generate titles for others. The *episcopi vagantes* are merely the flagrant instance; sometimes the same figures may be found in minority Churches and in hidden political sects. And if power is to come, it is necessarily derived from authority, an authority which is more than human: call it mahatmas, divine right or the spirit of history. Of all these groups, Jacobitism is possibly the purest. It appealed to the poets for several reasons. The 'decadent' could find in it a tragic stage on which he could perform his ritual of helplessness in the presence of the *zeitgeist*. For Jacobitism always represented the triumph of an idea over reason, common sense and the tendency of events. And if Jacobitism was Platonic politics, Neo-Jacobitism represented, surely, neo-Platonic politics; politics in its least contingent form, uncontaminated by the possible. Its antiquity, its acute abstraction from the foci of power; its legends; its limpid appeal to those gifted with historical imagination, all assure its presence in the 1890s. But the quiet succession of Edward was its quietus, though it continued to flourish down to 1914 when the about-to-be *de jure* King Robert IV and I of these islands, Rupprecht of Bavaria, was found in arms against his Britain and for her enemies. This event was virtually fatal to political Neo-Jacobitism. After the First World War it tended either to become once more merely nostalgic or became merged in the wider energies of Legitimism. This can be substantiated from the Jacobite magazines published between the wars. A long-lived example was *The Jacobite*, published from Gisborne and announcing itself as 'The only Jacobite paper in New Zealand', between 1919 and 1952, whose antiquarianism now enfolds the middle and later nineteenth century.[81]

The liturgical aspect of Jacobitism preserved with more ease its continuity. The Society of King Charles the Martyr survives in spite of the formation of a rival group, which also survives, the Royal Martyr Church Union and King Charles Memorial League, founded, so *Church and King* somewhat sourly tells us, 'towards the end of 1906' by 'a young man with the romantic name of Baron Montrencie ... better known by his patronym of H.S. Wheatly-Crowe'.[82] So that on 30 January the faithful cluster still to 'remember' at the statue: gentlemen in British warms and bowler-hatted representing the several Jacobite sects, give collusive nods, stand at attention as the chimes 'collect their strength' and the air tingles with the wail of the pipes while in churches, offices are still read and sermons are still given in thankfulness to God and to the 'White King'.[83]

Notes

1. The 9th Marquis (1869–1922), Melville Amadeus, held a number of foreign titles (including a French barony dating from the eleventh century). See obituary in *The Times* and *The Jacobite* I, II (1 May 1922) for a fuller account. Ruvigny compiled *The Jacobite Peerage*, a standard work. *The Times*, 9 February 1892, p. 6, col. 6.
2. See H.R.T. Brandreth, *Dr Lee of Lambeth* (London, 1951), pp. 183–5.
3. *The Times*, 31 January 1888, p. 9, cc. 5–6.
4. The Order of Corporate Reunion was an irenic organization set up in the 1870s against the background of the anti-Ritualist Public Worship Regulation Act of 1876. Lee was an *episcopus vagans*, and legend has it that he was involved with Mar Julius, Patriarch of the revived Ancient British Church in consecrating a perpetual co-adjutor to carry on the true succession obtained from the Syrian Jacobite Church. Lee, like some of his fellow (political) Jacobites, was one of those who, whatever nobler motives may have been at work, enjoyed self-generated titles and honours. See Peter Anson, *Bishops At Large: Some Autocephalous Churches* (London, 1964), p. 46 in particular.
5. There is a brief article on Rohenstart in *The Royalist* IV, 1 (n.s.) (December 1951), p. 4. See also, G. Sherborn, *Rohenstart: A Late Stuart Pretender* (Edinburgh, 1960) and Sir Charles Petrie, *History of the Jacobite Movement, 1688–1867* (Chicago and Toronto, 1933), particularly Ch. 10, 'The Aftermath', pp. 277–87.
6. *Notes and Queries*, 7s., V, (1888), p. 282.
7. *Mid-Victorian Memories* (London, 1914),pp. 284–5. Francillon was sub-editor of *The Globe*.
8. *Notes and Queries*, 8ths, XII (1897), pp. 6–7.
9. D.N.B.
10. *The Monthly Review* 21, 63, p. 20.
11. *Ibid.*, p. 8. For a brief notice of the Calves' Head Club see W.H.K. Wright, 'Clubs: Literary and Whimsical' in *Pleasantries from the 'Blue Box'*, being a selection of papers by Ye Brothers Blue (London and Plymouth, 1891).
12. *Ibid.*, p. 22.
13. *Ibid.*, p. 24.
14. *Ibid.*, p. 30. The Scottish Episcopal Church submitted to the Hanoverians in 1788. Apparently Bishop Low (1768–1855) was its last clergyman who could fairly be described as Jacobite, though his Jacobitism seems to have been sentimental and antiquarian.
15. H.W. Randall, *Huntingdon Library Quarterly* 10, pp. 135–67 (1946–7), pp. 135–67.
16. *Ibid.*, p. 135–6.
17. *Ibid.*, p. 136. Dr Randall is quoting William Lloyd writing in 1697.
18. *The Commemoration of Saints and Heroes of the Faith in the Anglican Communion* (1957), p. 35. Charles is described as a Red Letter saint (the only non-scriptural one).
19. Randall, p. 137.

20. *Ibid.*, pp.138–40.
21. Lord John Russell, anxious to appease the dissenters, persuaded the queen to consent to the removal of the service, and this was effected under the Statute 22 Victoria, c ii of 25 March 1859. The queen's printers, on their own authority, removed the king's name from the Kalendar. The abrogation of the office proved the easier as Parliament had never given it formal ratification. The last attempt at restoration was in 1927. The present ecumenical climate does not appear favourable, though it could be argued that without one saint, the anglicans will 'go naked to the conference table'.
22. *The Christian Year*, n.d. (London, c.1884), pp.388–9. The poem was omitted in some post-1859 editions.
23. Thomas Arnold's comment on the Tractarians is relevant: their 'system ... seems to be leading to a revival of the non-jurors; they are the very non-jurors and high-church clergymen of William's, Anne's and George's time'.
24. Modern Scottish Nationalism is generally considered to date from the agitation of 1853 over the question of a Secretary of State for Scotland being appointed. This prosaic question may have resulted in the movement guttering out in the 1860s. Nevertheless, it attracted the attention of such literary figures as W.E. Aytoun and J.S. Blackie.
25. I quote the text Jenner himself gives in an unpublished letter. Jenner (1848–1934), a Cornishman, returned to his native county and became active in the campaign to revive the Cornish language, which had attracted new interest some years before, see his paper to the Philological Society of 1873. At first his own interest was purely antiquarian, but by 1901 he became active in efforts to restore the Cornish language to use, composing original poems in Cornish and translating English poems into that language. He became the acknowledged leader of the movement: First Grand Bard between 1928 and 1934, and from 1920 on president of the Old Cornwall Society. The movement had political implications, and its origins are connected with the wider Pan-Celtic movement of the 1890s. The best account is to be found in P. Berrisford Ellis, *The Cornish Language and its Literature* (Boston, 1974).
26. Crump had arranged himself to resemble a Van Dyck portrait of Charles the First, a Neo-Jacobite contemporary tells us, while Jenner was of imposing height with a lengthy beard.
27. Letter to Miss Lloyd of 27 February 1932.
28. *Mid-Victorian Memories*, pp.282–3.
29. The subject of King Charles in dramatic literature has only been partially touched. There is a useful brief article by Nigel Foxell, 'The Royal Martyr and Heroic Drama' in *The Royal Martyr Annual* (1966), which dwells on Andreas Gryphius's *Emordete Majestat oder Carolus Stuardus* begun by its author a matter of days after its subject's execution and Alexander Fyfe's *The Royal Martyr King Charles I* of 1705. Among other plays there are Girolamo Gratiani's *Il Cromuele* (1671); William Havard's written in conscious imitation of Shakespeare in about 1770; Browning's *Strafford* (1837) with its

vacillating, uxurious king and the offerings of Shelley and Mary Russell Mitford.

30. It was reported, erroneously, that Francillon, his wife and other Jacobites had attended the first night of the Irving production with white roses in their buttonholes or on their dresses.
31. For Mellor, Papal Count and Knight of the Holy Sepulchre, see the obituary in *The Jacobite* II, 2 (20 March 1927). He appears as Rupert Clifford in W.H. Wilkins' and H. Vivian's novel *The Green Bay Tree*. In his Chelsea house, Mellor was waited on by kilted Gaelic-speaking servants among the gilded and silver candlesticks on chandeliers and the hanging braziers of coals in the great open fireplace.
32. *The Daily Graphic*, 9 February 1892, 657, IX, p.5, c.4.
33. Sixth Leader, *ibid.*, p.7, c.4.
34. *To-Day*, 9 February 1892, p.11, c.3.
35. For Napier's obituary, see *The Jacobite* II, 9 (1 November 1924).
36. For Millard's obituary, see *The Jacobite* IV, I (15 March 1930).
37. *The Albemarle* I, p.122.
38. *The Albemarle* I, pp.123–4.
39. *The Albemarle* II, p.31. Duncombe Jewell was also involved with the antiquarian phase of the Cornish language movement in the 1890s. He published a set of poems entitled *Ballads of the Forty-Five* in 1925.
40. *The Albemarle* II, p.32.
41. Francillon tells us, however, that 'nor was it till nearly so late as 1890 that its last surviving member died', p.271. But Francillon was an activist.
42. P.32. Jenner, in a letter of 5 March 1932 to Miss Lloyd, mentions two leaflets published by the Order in 1886 and 1887. See the *Preface to the Rule of the Order of the White Rose* (n.d.), 4 pp.
43. *The Albemarle* II, p.34.
44. Erskine's later periodical the *Hounhynhym* of 1893 preserves aristocratic principles but has no connection with Neo-Jacobitism.
45. *Church and King*, the Society's organ, has notes on the history of the SKCM at VIII, 3 (29 November 1954); XXIV, 4 (Christmas 1971); and XXV, 1 (May 1972).
46. From Mrs Greville-Nugent's notes on the Order of the White Rose in *The White Cockade*, June 1926.
47. *Church and King* XXIV, 4, 2. John Creasey, 'Some Notes on the History of the Society of King Charles the Martyr'.
48. '"Remember"—A Jacobite Carol. (Sung to a Well-Known Air, 30 January). *Punch*', 8 February 1896. See also for another facetious comment, *The Star*, 29 January 1898, p.3, c.3: 'It's Jacobite cold'. And to prove that current journalism can be as trivial and vulgar as its predecessors, Paul Pickering's 'Squabbling still over the ghost of Charles the Martyr', *The Times* of 28 January, 1983, may be cited, though it does embody some factual data. The recent absurd proposal to celebrate 1688 has roused some protest though it has been defended by that last scion of the Bloomsbury Whigs, Lord Annan.
49. Either Clifford's or Barnard's presumably; Furnivall's had, by this time, been largely demolished.

50. *The Bohemian*, 1893, pp.13–14.
51. *Notes and Queries*, 8ths, V, 24 March 1894, p.234.
52. *Notes and Queries*, 8ths, XI, 27 March 1897, p.250.
53. *A Litany of St Charles, King and Martyr* (privately printed, 1897). *With a Hymn and other Devotions* (p.2).
54. *Ibid.*, pp.3–5.
55. *Ibid.*, p.8. On the unofficial missals published by Anglicans, see J.M.M. Dalby in the *Church Quarterly Review* 168, CLXVIII, 1967, pp.204–16, and S. Morison, *English Prayer Books*, 'Anglican Missals', 2nd revised edition (London, 1949).
56. *A Litany of St Charles*, p.8.
57. *The Eighteen Nineties* (London, 1939), pp.125–8.
58. 'Of the Respect due to King Charles His Day', contributed to Vivian's *The Rambler* III, p.31 (1902). This was a Legitimist magazine which ran from 1901 to 1902.
59. Knox composed a sermon for King Charles's day, and this is republished in his *University and Anglican Sermons* (1963).
60. MS. *Officium festi sancti Caroli* p.(4).
61. *Ibid.*, pp.(4–5.)
62. *Ibid.*, p.(5.)
63. *Ibid.*, pp.(7–8.) Parts of the Office were printed in *Church and King* in 1966, and the whole office had appeared in the same magazine in 1937 and 1938. I follow Canon Broun's manuscript. *Officium festi sancti Caroli*.
64. P.(4).
65. *January 30th Saint Charles King and Martyr*, pp.2–3. The text is taken from Jenner's revise published in *The Guardian* in January 1906.
66. Quoted from *Church and King* VII, 2 (29 May 1954), p.(3).
67. *The Royalist* II, 29 February 1892.
68. *The Wykehamist*.
69. *The Collected Poems of Lionel Johnson*, 2nd revised edition, ed. I. Fletcher (New York, 1982), p.13.
70. *Ibid.*, p.178.
71. *Ibid.*, pp.178–9.
72. *Ibid.*, p.30.
73. *Ibid.*, p.83.
74. See *The Garland of New Poetry by Various Writers* (London, 1899), pp.(3)–4. May Probyn's 'A Jacobite Snatch', *Poems* (London, 1881), p.24, is the merest nostalgia deriving from the Jacobite songs of the eighteenth century.
75. *The Letters of Louise Imogen Guiney*, ed. G. Guiney (London, 1926), Vol.II, p.22. Among relevant poems of Miss Guiney, mention may be made of 'A Jacobite Revival', in *Songs at the Start* (Boston, 1884), and 'Written in Lord Clarendon's *History of the Rebellion*' in *England and Yesterday* (London, 1898).
76. E.M. Tenison, *Louise Imogen Guiney* (London, 1922), p.118.
77. *Letters*, Vol.II, p.4.
78. Quoted from *Church and King* V.3 (29 November 1952), p.(2). The Bostonian Jacobites appear to have been founded by Ruvigny in the

early 1890s; see W.B. Harte, *Meditations in Motley* (Boston, 1894), pp.(45)–102.

79. Wilde also referred to Charles as 'The dreamy, treacherous king'.
80. The Legitimists included a number of genuine aristocrats: Lady Maidstone, Lady Helen Mellor, the Hon. Mrs Greville-Nugent, Ruvigny, and so on. Often they were members of the Jacobite, French or Papal peerage.
81. Other twentieth century Jacobite magazines include *The Fiery Cross*, (1901–12) and *The White Cockade* (1926–9).
82. *Church and King* XXV, 1 (May 1972), p.(5).
83. King Charles is now in the New Alternative Prayer Book, restored to his status as a Black Letter saint. The Royal Martyr Church Union celebrate in the recently built Church of King Charles the Martyr in Potters Bar. The Society of King Charles the Martyr hold an annual service in the banqueting hall and High Mass in St Mary-le-Strand. The rector of St Mary-le-Strand, a High Church vicar, speaks of relics. Apparently the church possesses a few hairs, a piece of his shirt, his glove and a piece of his coffin, which was opened in the early nineteenth century.

PART II

YEATS

4

Rhythm and Pattern in Yeats's *Autobiographies*

I

The title of *Autobiographies* is accurate. The single volume contains approaches to the past made at distinct times in differing modes, ranging from the mosaic of *Trembling of the Veil* to the *journal intime* structure of *Estrangement*, a man talking to himself after the day's work and bitterness with a kind of vivid formality. I want to touch only on *Reveries*, *Trembling of the Veil* and *Dramatis Personae*, not because I believe that *Estrangement*, *The Death of Synge* or the 1930 Diary are less important, but because they are less consciously historical, more disjunct, aphoristic, the raw material for composed autobiography.[1]

Of all Yeats's prose *Autobiographies*, though sometimes occasional and often polemical, are the most sustained. The aphoristic and fragmentary sections were possibly intended as prolegomena to that 'new autobiography—1900 to 1926' which Yeats thought of as 'the final test of my intellect, my last great effort', and which he kept putting off. There are problems about the three parts of *Autobiographies* that are my concern. *Dramatis Personae* was largely composed from Yeats's letters to Lady Gregory, but the history of the composition of *Reveries* is obscure: it probably went through several drafts (one, virtually a fair copy, is at Colby College, Maine). Richard Ellmann informs us that an earlier draft of *Trembling of the Veil* was completed in 1916–17. Comment on *Autobiographies* must be provisional.

The first mention of *Reveries* in Yeats's letters belongs to November 1914. From this it is clear that Yeats had been engaged with the book from about the late summer on. The seven years before this date had been both painful and frustrating, and *Reveries* was composed in their shadow: schisms in the Abbey, the mere success of esteem of his own plays, the *Playboy* controversy of 1907, Synge's death in 1909 and the controversy with the Dublin Council and populace over the proposed Lutyens Gallery for Lane's pictures. In 1908 the appearance of Yeats's *Collected Works* must have seemed to the poet to mark off an era, as though his achievement were already in the past. At this time we find him in letters referring to himself as 'belonging to the fabulous ages' and 'becoming mythical even to myself': we find an increasing identification with the past and with his dead friends of the 1890s in particular. Such backward looking was a symptom of general discouragement. His emotional life had become random, and in his spiritual life there was a void. By 1914 he had broken his connection with the rump of the Golden Dawn that remained after the schisms of Mathers and Waite. We find him resorting to spiritualism and trying somewhat pathetically to verify the historicity of the spirits who 'came to him through mediums'.

The pressures in such circumstances were towards the organization of an attitude; documentation and self-clarification; an attempt to stabilize the present—an aim that makes its first positive appearance in his volume of poems *The Green Helmet* of 1910. It is here that the process of mythologizing himself and his friends begins. Recent history is frozen, stylized. Maud Gonne becomes the emblem of his present despair—a Fatal Woman, still making a traditional appearance as an Irish Helen, but now associated directly with Dublin: 'Was there another Troy for her to burn?'

It is rather in *Poems Written in Discouragement* of 1913 and in *Responsibilities* that the mythologizing becomes explicit, and past and present are consciously poised against one another. Addressing in the opening poem of *Responsibilities* his burgess ancestors of the late eighteenth and early nineteenth centuries, Yeats writes:

> Although I have come close on forty-nine,
> I have no child, I have nothing but a book,
> Nothing but that to prove your blood and mine. (Collected Poems, 113)

In this volume the events of the last seven years are mythologized: the epigrams of the *Green Helmet* edge into dramatic lyric. Synge, Lady Gregory, John O'Leary and Hugh Lane are poised against the Dublin of the present which fumbles in a greasy till by the light of a holy candle. Aristocrat, noble Fenian and poet equally represent a heroic and defeated past.

Placing himself in history and tradition was indeed one of Yeats's 'responsibilities' at this time, but it conflicted with a 'responsibility' to the present: he needed to associate himself with Lady Gregory and Hugh Lane; the enemy being a textbook burgess capitalist such as William Murphy or those petty-burgess Paudeen enemies of Synge and Lane. His own impeccably burgess ancestors have to be dignified with 'the wasteful virtues' that 'earn the sun', credited with spontaneity and 'personality'. But what we can accept in *Responsibilities* as dramatic speech (even so amusingly defiant a line as 'Blood that has not passed through any huckster's loin') will be harder to accept in a prose account; we accuse the historian of self-interest. In the poems the 'personal ego' (J.B. Yeats's phrase) has evaporated, a role in contemporary history can be enforced and acted out.

In the Preface to *Reveries*, dated Christmas 1914, Yeats wrote: 'I have changed nothing to my knowledge; and yet it must be that I have changed many things without my knowledge; for I am writing after many years and have consulted neither friend, nor letter, nor old newspaper, and describe what comes oftenest into my memory.' But the past remains the possession of others, and he fears that 'some surviving friend may remember something in a different shape and be offended with my book'. The frankness is partly ingenuous: he is attempting to transcend his past self by presenting a selective image of that self, and he wishes to trust what has survived by impressing itself most deeply, though he is aware that memory not only shapes the past but actually imposes meanings. And re-enacting the past not only changes the past, it changes the present.

A recently published letter of 20 November 1914 to Lady Gregory indicates how Yeats wished to see himself:

> That is a wonderful letter of my father's. It came at the right moment for I am writing an account of Dowden (I shall wind up with the Rhymers' Club). I think we shall live as a generation as the Young Irelanders did. We shall not be detached figures. I think it is partly with that motive I am trying for instance to improve my sisters' and publish my father's letters. Your biography when it comes will complete the image.

Here Yeats explicitly associates himself with his friends, the tragic actors of *Responsibilities*, as 'a generation', and associates his friends as a group with Young Ireland. As D.J. Gordon has put it, 'an acute, exacerbated sense of his own historicity comprehended the historicity of others, sharpened and nourished by the awareness that he and his friends were part of the history of modern Ireland'. Implicitly he also associates himself with the Rhymers' Club—another 'generation' whose defeat substantiates and extends the defeat of the artists of J.B. Yeats's and Yeats's own 'tragic' generation. The pressure here is towards overcoming a tragic determinism.

Lady Gregory was still very much alive, while the Rhymers (with the exception of Symons, whose career had been broken by madness) were dead and so historically perfect. Poetry demonstrated its classic superiority over history: it could mythologize the living as though they were not themselves still part of an emerging historical process. This mode was not to be abandoned. Yeats continued to write poems, consciously conceived as historical acts, on persons and on the places associated with them. Writing these, he was deliberately creating a version of the modern history of Ireland, 'an Ireland the poets have imagined terrible and gay', a version he wished to transmit as a document to posterity. But as the letter to Lady Gregory shows, Yeats was not averse to documentation of another kind. It is in this light that his father's unfinished and his own achieved autobiography must be seen. And while he was engaged on *Reveries*, Lady Gregory was concluding her chapter of autobiography, *Our Irish Theatre*, with its selective extracts from Yeats's letters and its heroic portraiture of O'Leary and Synge.

Yeats's original plan had been to conclude *Reveries* with an account of the Rhymers' Club; that the Rhymers were much in his mind at this time we know from *Responsibilities*, where Johnson and Dowson are given tragic status. Like the Young Ireland writers, the more prominent Rhymers possessed a much greater historical than aesthetic importance, even though the Rhymers' devotion to art was altogether opposed to Young Ireland's subordination of art to rhetoric and politics.

Young Ireland had been an attempt on the part of a few to realize a nation's soul, in contrast to O'Connell's flattery of the mob. The Rhymers also attempted, in a different way, to realize in themselves the historical spirit, and they rejected popular culture. Both groups survive as groups rather than as individuals: the Rhymers partly because they were to be memorialized by Yeats in much the same way as Gavan Duffy had memorialized the Young Ireland figures in *Young Ireland* and *1845–1849*. Yeats's intention was to follow Duffy as the historian of a generation that had realized itself historically because 'it thought the same thought' and created its own history. And Duffy's historical record had itself been an attempted reshaping of history.

Yeats's portrait of Duffy looks forward to the graceful malice of *Dramatis Personae*. It presents him as the anti-type of O'Leary among the Young Ireland generation, living on like some Latimerian fish to abash the new age. It is one version of history competing actively with another, though the ground disputed is narrowly literary: 'Sir Charles Gavan Duffy arrived. He brought with him much manuscript, the private letters of a Young Irish poetess, a dry but informing unpublished essay by Davis, and an unpublished novel by William Carleton into the middle of which he had dropped a hot coal, so that nothing remained but the borders of every page.' A fussy short sentence is swallowed by a long sentence, whose gyre concludes with the exquisitely emblematic case of the burning coal and so acts out Duffy's dry-fingered antiquarianism; his incapacity to sustain whatever was genuinely creative in Anglo-Irish literature. Yeats's position in the quarrel with Duffy may have owed something to Arnold, but it was immediately influenced by the beliefs of the Rhymers.

The Rhymers—as Yeats saw them—were, unlike Young Ireland, concerned not merely with personal art but with collapse and disintegration, and they wished to enact this in themselves sacrificially. Yeats's association of Young Ireland with the Rhymers, and of J.B. Yeats's generation of artists and poets with his own, is not simply because (contingently or not) they formed part of his own drama. It sprang from the need to find what Yeats termed 'rhythm' in history (a rhythm of heroic failure). As his early interest in Joachim de Flora's Four Ages showed, this had been one of his preoccupations in the 1890s.[2] Such 'rhythm' had to be recognized in the multiplicity of the self before it could be recognized in history; it determines the structure of *Trembling of the Veil* rather than that of *Reveries*.

Reveries is concerned with heroes and sacred places. The book's polarities are Ireland and England: Sligo, Dublin and London. Yeats as child and young man is involved in his father's uneasy shifts between these places: a rootlessness symbolic of the modern imaginative artist (it predicts the rootlessness of Simeon Solomon or Dowson), and also of the decline of true nationalism. Places for Yeats have a quality of *mana* that owes little to patient visual detail (it is hardly 'Pre-Raphaelite'). It is the *interaction* of places and persons that he particularly evokes. He was probably always moved more by the human image than the painter's. Yet he still saw that human image partly in terms of the painter's eye. From his father, he had caught an eye for pose and gesture, for the unselfconscious stance that reveals the intimate self, the ground of this perception being that gathering of the 'moment' in J.B. Yeats's impressionist portraiture.

With Yeats, physical image creates narrative, is both cause and symptom: what actually happens becomes metaphorical. In *Autobiographies* people tend to be arrested in moments that reveal 'a fragment of the divine life', an instant which has the effect of a complete statement, both stylized and spontaneous. Yeats owes this, however, less to his father's portraits than to his letters.

Just as *Dramatis Personae* wins immediacy from the dialogue *outre tombe* with George Moore, *Reveries* wins immediacy from its dialogue with Yeats's father: 'Someone to whom I read [*Reveries*] said to me the other day "If Gosse had not taken the title you should call it 'Father and Son'." I am not going to ask your leave for the bits of your conversation I quote.' Father and son influenced one another, and one of John Butler Yeats's gifts, that of aphorism, was clearly passed on. Between 1912 and 1914 he wrote his son a number of remarkable letters which had much to say on the subject of 'personality', the essential self freed from accidents of time and habit; on the necessary solitude of the artist and the need for dramatizing one's experience to avoid a purely personal art. 'Personality' for J.B. Yeats was 'love': '*neither right nor wrong*—for it transcends intellect and morality, and while it keeps to being pure personality we love for it is *one* with our very selves, and with the all *pervasive* Divine.[3] In precisely these terms the 'personalities' of Yeats's *Autobiographies* are presented as parts of his 'very self'. At a moment of indecision Yeats was using his father as a mentor, as he had previously used other mentors (Johnson, Ricketts, etc.).

Practising his father's advice to dramatize experience, Yeats began with J.B. Yeats himself. His father's crisis, a crisis in romantic art and literature, is presented in *Reveries* through an argument in terms of 'personality' between Pre-Raphaelite imagination, intensity, on the one hand, and Positivism and an Impressionism defined as 'Realism' on the other. J.B. Yeats's betrayal of Pre-Raphaelite principles is associated with the treason of his other friends.

The material here is derived from J.B. Yeats's letters. The elder Yeats's friends were a pathetic rather than a tragic generation. Some, to be sure—Page, Wilson, Potter—die without a choice being offered. They are solitaries, without an audience. Others like Nettleship or Dowden survive by compromise. All are caught in emblematic gestures that lead one from the work to 'personality'. The crippled genius of Nettleship enacts its own mutilation: the enormous cup he drinks from contains—cocoa, so that Edwin Ellis's remark that Nettleship 'drank his genius away' has vibrations the speaker barely intended. Dowden's ironic calm and O'Leary's moral genius, passionate, Roman, Hebraic, confront one another.

Dowden may be taken as characteristic of Yeats's problems. His subject had died only a year before, and J.B. Yeats had been Dowden's 'intimate enemy', but after Dowden's death Yeats was not prepared to adopt his father's gentlemanly attitude. J.B. Yeats wrote that it was better to be illogical than inhuman, and accused his son of presenting Dowden deliberately and exclusively from a personal and didactic point of view; of submitting Dowden to a contrived biographical pattern. After the publication of *Reveries* W.B. Yeats returned to the question, admitting that he was nervous about the Dowden section, but arguing that it could not be omitted, since the book was 'a history of the revolt, which perhaps unconsciously you taught me, against certain Victorian ideals'. And as though admitting his father's accusation of being inhuman, Yeats observed in the following year that 'in my account of Dowden I had to picture him as a little unreal, set up for contrast behind the real image of O'Leary'. The juxtaposition is not really dramatic, but drama enters in the presentation of the divided self common to both Dowden and O'Leary. O'Leary's noble head, his intransigence, his sense of political morality as style and his love of literature are poised against the flatness of the autobiography on which he lavished such effort. Dowden's romantic face and his earlier poetry that hints at passion, though passion renounced, are poised against his over-reliance on intellect.

J.B. Yeats's relationship with Dowden has a subdued parallel in his son's relationship with J.F. Taylor, obscure great orator, ugly, solitary, flashing into high speech; a disappointed though pertinacious lover of women. The image of Taylor is important in several ways. It enacts that opposition between poetry and oratory that J.B. Yeats believed was inevitable; but explains Taylor's greatness by presenting him in *O altitudo* moments as altogether solitary, unaware of the blind crowd, a poet. Taylor is also a man divided in himself—his jealousy of Yeats's friendship with O'Leary is more than a Young Ireland Fenian distrust of the new 'literary' nationalism. The encounter is presented less definitively than it would have been in *Trembling of the Veil*. Taylor's motives, his inner life, remain unpredictable, mysterious. He is viewed from a distance, and this precisely catches the 'point of view' of the young Yeats of the late 1880s and 1890s, a young man who was a late-comer to an Irish scene which he found already peopled by powerful figures. He shows himself here, as always, intensely aware of the difference between his own generation and theirs. The enmity between himself and Taylor is constructive: to choose one's intimate enemies objectifies one's limitations.

Such stringency hardly seems reflected in the record. The prose of *Autobiographies* is often thought of as Paterian, lushly mantic, salted with some good Irish stories. Yet if *Reveries* owes anything to Pater, that influence is less of cadence and vocabulary than attitude, and of an attitude that reinforces the influence of Yeats's father. In *Style*, Pater had distinguished between the debris of fact and the writer's personal sense of fact. Analogously he had distinguished the 'moment' as the unit of experience, isolated, absolute, flexible, in protest against the 'positive' fiction of a stable world. The creative role of contemplation and, particularly, memory in Pater's work and his influence on Proust and Virginia Woolf are well known. For Pater, memory constitutes an identity which can be redeemed from time by re-enacting moments of sensuous significance: 'the finer sort of memory, bringing its object to mind with great clearness, yet, as sometimes happens in dreams, raised a little above its self and above ordinary retrospect' (*The Child in the House*). In Pater's words, this is a substitution of the 'typical' for the 'actual'; memory operates discontinuously, if vividly, and is recognized by the sense of loss. But substitution of 'typical' for 'actual' is distancing, and few of Pater's evocations of childhood have any eager directness of detail or sense of the jaggedness of recall. Similarly, Yeats's account of family, schools, holidays, adolescent awakening to sex and ideals is distanced by a meditative style—as Mr Ellmann has pointed out, anger is 'adroitly excluded'. But the arrangement of *Reveries* with its sharp sections (rather than the 'chapters' Yeats termed them) is intended to enact discontinuousness. The sections vary in length (xviii and xx by contrast with xi) resembling (in intention at least) that lyrical dissolution of event in Romantic historians where rapid sections and sentences echo the pulse of what is re-enacted and the historian's excitement in re-enaction. Yeats's rhythm of anti-climactic reflection in *Reveries* is naturally slow and even. (He uses the Carlylean historic present only for the first page or two of *Reveries*, in Section xv of *Ireland after Parnell* and in Section xx of *Trembling of the Veil* to evoke the 'crack up' of the 1890s.) His early memories leave the impression of being recorded solely because they are remembered; but each 'spot of memory' relates to such themes as: I, the poet, William Yeats, Ireland, romantic past and sordid present.

We have seen that what is acceptable as dramatic speech in *Responsibilities* might become suspect in autobiography. In prose Yeats stresses heroism, nobility of personality rather than aristocratic value connected with property; despite a mild flourish of ancestors in the third section, *Reveries* are surprisingly devoid of social context. What emerges is Yeats's sense of being 'Irish' in the English Babylon.

In *Reveries*, many of the connections, as in *Responsibilities*, are carried by syntax. Style in courage and Platonic courtesy is mediated through asyndeton, punctilious subjunctives,[4] magniloquent 'buts', yet the sentence-structure is rarely overelaborate. Where we find elaboration of rhythm it is, like the imagery, functional, as in this passage on George Eliot where style itself rebukes:

> She seemed to have a distrust or a distaste for all in life that gives one a springing foot. Then, too, she knew so well how to enforce her distaste by the authority of her mid-Victorian science or by some habit of mind of its breeding, that I, who had not escaped the fascination of what I loathed, doubted while the book lay open whatsoever my instinct knew of splendour (p. 88)

The second is an unusually long sentence for *Reveries*. The histrionic pauses, contours almost of the breathing mind, the anxious poise between authority and instinct, the final freed tune with its faint Pauline echo fully realize the inwardness of the experience. (The experience has perhaps little to do finally with George Eliot.)

'Now that I have written it out', Yeats wrote in his preface, 'I may even begin to forget it all.' A middle-aged bore, bowed down with the weight of 'a precious, an incommunicable past', he may stop button-holing strangers. But the deeper meaning suggests the cathartic; final responsibility to the past involves not rejection, but transcendence: liberation from guilt, self-pity, historical necessity, the inescapable folly of art, multiplicity and indirection, that 'wilderness of mirrors', whether of Wilde's competing gifts or magian temptations. Writing is the act of self-criticism that detaches the poet from the composed image, even if the composure issues from anticlimax, 'a preparation for something that never happens'.

In *Reveries* Yeats's past self is realized, painfully encountering and addressing others, socially clumsy, morally naïve. This book ends not with the Rhymers' Club but with Yeats's return to London in 1887, giving the volume a severer shape. He stands at the beginning of his career as an Irish poet, at the moment when he realizes himself as an exile, and in this light the final judgement on himself in 1914 is ironic rather than self-pitying. The title *Reveries* is not an escape into the past, it signifies an attempt to distinguish pattern. At the point of painful disengagement from spoiled aspirations the conditions have been fulfilled for the narrator's 'epiphany': a synthesis, as often in Yeats, has been proclaimed at the point where it is rejected.

II

Writing to his father on 26 December 1914, Yeats indicated that when he carried his memoirs beyond 1887 he would be liable to further difficulties of the type already encountered in treating of Dowden: 'they would have besides to be written in a different way. While I was immature I was a different person and I can stand apart and judge. Later on, I should always, I feel, write of other people. I dare say I shall return to the subject but only in fragments' (Letters, 589). Often one of his best critics, Yeats has defined the limitations of *Trembling of the Veil*. Far more ambitious, eloquent and richly detailed than *Reveries*, *Trembling of the Veil* is tonally and structurally puzzling. The second draft was composed during the period of the Anglo-Irish and Irish civil wars, when Yeats was clarifying the material of *A Vision*. The period described lies between 1887 and 1897, the death in 1891 of the political Messiah

Parnell marking an important division. Formally *Four Years* is the most satisfying section; the remainder was written to contract (60,000 words),and Yeats more than once expressed uneasiness as to whether the years between 1891 and 1897 could be stretched to the agreed length.

Writing to Olivia Shakespear on 22 December 1921, he observed that the book was likely to seem inadequate, since 'I study every man I meet at some moment of crisis—I alone have no crisis'. And in another letter of 28 February 1934 he reveals that the problem of omission was still with him when he came to compose *Dramatis Personae*: 'I am just beginning on Woburn buildings ... alas the most significant image of those years must be left out.' The reference is to the *enménagement* with Mrs Shakespear in 1896 or that of 1903. And since the unrecorded crises are the heart of much of his later poetry, the loss is severe. If there is little sense of the author's presence in *Trembling of the Veil*, little self-criticism and self-clarification, the abstention is clearly deliberate.

In addition to reticence about his deepest emotional experiences, there were other difficulties. 'Whenever I have included a living man I have submitted my words for his correction. This is specially important ... I want to show that though I am being published by Moore's publisher I do not accept Moore's practice.' That he still had doubts is indicated by this passage from a letter to Mrs Shakespear: '[The book] needs the wild mystical part to lift it out of gossip, and the mystical part will not be as clear as it should be for lack of diagrams.' 'Mysticism' was beyond Moore, that 'precious thing' that Moore, like a passing dog, 'defiled'.

It is Moore's version of history which Yeats's autobiographies challenge. In *Trembling of the Veil* Yeats uses something of Moore's approach not to the living but to the dead. The distinction lies between Moore's malice and Yeats's didacticism; the similarity lies in the thematic and apologetic elements. As Arthur Schumaker has pointed out, *Hail and Farewell* uses distinct thematic devices derived from Wagner's *Ring*, all leading to the climax where Moore discovers himself as Siegfried 'given the task of reforging broken weapons of thought and restoring Ireland to thought and responsibility'. His stated intention was to represent the past moment as a passing *now*: 'To take a certain amount of material and model it much as [one] would do in a novel.' The persons in Moore's trilogy become types of human character, representative of a fallen Ireland; transitions are concealed, meditation modulates into speech, chronology is fluid; manipulation of the past is added to selection of event and, as is not the case with *Trembling of the Veil*, there is a high incidence of direct speech. The similarities to Yeats's work, and the contrasts, are plain.

Another passage from a letter to Mrs Shakespear reveals how in *Autobiographies* even energizing hatred of the dead was to be muted. Tenderness to the living can be exemplified by Yeats's treatment of Johnson, who was Mrs Shakespear's cousin and to whom she had been deeply attached: he was to be shown 'as the noble tragic figure that he was ... those who follow me are likely to take their key from what I have written'. But the effect was to puzzle rather than convince. Charles Ricketts found the memoirs in general persuasive, but the presentation of Johnson surprising:

> It is singular that he should have impressed himself on you, doubtless it was the attraction of the *opposite*, he struck me then, and in recollection, as a typical 'Fruit sec' of his class, time and training. I caught him making a lamentable howler in a translation of Baudelaire. He said or did something else which I have forgotten and never created that bogus atmosphere with which he impressed you.[5]

Where *Reveries* had been the record of self-discovery through others, in *Trembling of the Veil* all sequence of cause and effect is fractured by a new teleology, the invasion of the 'supernatural', the most violent force in history. Gossip and mysticism collide, but do not coalesce. Another sophisticated form of determinism results, though not the Positivists' mere aggregation of fact against which the whole structure of *Trembling of the Veil* is a protest. The relatively firm chronology, the questing quality of *Reveries*, is dissolved and the book given a sense of omen fulfilled: the validation of his own insights and those of his generation of poets and occultists, 'the things wild people half scholars and rhapsodical persons wrote about, when you and I were young'. With Parnell's death in 1891 *Four Years* comes to an end; 1892, the year Yeats began from in his *Oxford Book of Modern Verse*, the year of the *First Book of the Rhymers' Club*, ushered in the poetry of what he came to see as the last phase of the historical cycle. The insights of his friends and their rejection of the vulgar dream of progress was to be more violently corroborated than either he or they had anticipated.

Yeats shared with his generation a sense of history that expressed itself as an acute, even exacerbated sense of contemporaneity, of the moment defined only in its relationship to past and future.

Scholarship, revolution and the natural sciences had conspired to induce in late-nineteenth-century artists and intellectuals what was often an anguished sense of the moment as isolable, definable, an unstable ridge between abysses. It is in the nineteenth century that the sense of belonging to a decade, to a generation, was developed. Not until the 1890s could Lord Henry Wootton have said to Dorian Gray 'fin de siècle' and have received the antiphonal answer 'fin du globe'. Such tremors are common to ends of centuries, but the 1890s have more in common with the year 1000—a year of perfect numbers—or with the year 1600, than with the shrugging dismissal of, say, Dryden's *Secular Masque*. As the blank zeros of the calendar figure approached, the temporal uncertainties of the century merged in a diffuse, an irrational chiliasm.

The sense of Apocalypse, of the new age heralded by some terrible annunciation, was substantiated by Madame Blavatsky, Mathers and the Symbolists. Against this was posed the possibility of unity of culture: the symbol, to be achieved like Stalinism in one country, Ireland. But the historical pattern faltered into anticlimax: the 'Tragic Generation' immersed themselves in the flux, dying 'as soon as their constitutions would permit', and the attempt to achieve unity of culture through societies, through the more literate Unionists and landowners, and finally—transcending tragic individualism—through a Symbolist theatre, failed. The Easter Rising forced Yeats to redefine the past, in Morton Zabel's words 'to discover the laws of character, of creative power and of history'. The last three sections of *Trembling of the Veil* break off into a 'bundle of fragments', into the incoherence of an historic present without a future tense, which requires *A Vision* for its clarification.

'In art rhythm is everything', Arthur Symons had declared in a Symbolist manifesto published in *The Dome* of 1898. Yeats assumed Symons's phraseology of 'pattern' and 'rhythm' and applied them (in an article published also in *The Dome*) to the Symbolist designs of Althea Gyles and subsequently to poetry and to Symbolist 'total' theatre and history.[6] The words themselves imply 'image' (rather than naturalist 'subject'), the non-rational, the visionary. The Symbolist reaction towards trance is accompanied by a reaction against the tyranny of fact: a supernatural 'rhythm' against which personality (the individual in tragic passion) defines itself.

The search for both 'rhythm' and 'pattern', recurrence in time and space (the artist's isolation and the dilemma of a generation) manifests itself in the search for a cyclical view of history. This Yeats began to wish to substitute for the notion of history as chaos or as chiliastic. He was already reaching towards this in the 1890s, though the members of the Tragic Generation are without it. When he came to write *Trembling of the Veil* such a view becomes a category for the interpretation of personalities, individualities. The Tragic Generation merely re-enact more violently and self-consciously the experiences of J.B. Yeats and his friends.

Yeats's 1890s are hardly those of history, or of literary history. To the sober historian the imposition of Death Duties in 1894 appears more significant than the trials of Wilde in the following year; the continuous economic depression of 1890–96 than the sputtering history of the Rhymers. Yet Yeats focuses on two of the major characteristics of the decade: Ireland, and the climax of the revolt against Victorianism, the so-called normality that was sick. We get the flavour of a London that was now dominating the provinces, imposing its own centralized cultural pattern; and we even have some vague sense of the brooding, almost iconic figure of Victoria herself, ageless, it seemed, the dignified if dowdy incarnation of a people's dream. But Yeats's 1890s may still seem altogether too narrow, since we now associate the decade's revolt with figures who seem more relevant to the twentieth century, with Ibsen, Zola, Shaw, Butler and Gissing, rather than with the denizens of the Cheshire Cheese. Yet the *fin de siècle* mood was startlingly diffused: in James's *Altar of the Dead*, in Wells's early fables, for example. And the themes of *Trembling of the Veil*, the sense of isolation and alienation and the confrontation of artist and audience, remain valid comment beyond Yeats's circle.

For Yeats the 1890s include (if somewhat obliquely) many pressures common to all schools. There are, for example, the temptations of placating and securing an audience through the new publicity media, 'the interview and letter to the press'; what Yeats calls Moore's 'immediate sensational contact with public opinion'. Again, we find the imperialists' self-destructive energies of aggression realized in the image of Henley and his 'regatta' of young men. Much of Yeats's comment is gossip, but it remains if not actual, typical: his image of Beardsley as Huysmanish saint conforms to the image John Gray gave when he edited Beardsley's letters. Johnson (in *Mors Janua Vitae* and *Mystic and Cavalier*) and Wilde had both mythologized themselves. With Dowson, however, the case was different. Yeats followed Symons, who had presented

Dowson in 1900 as a conventional *poète maudit*, 'a demoralised Keats', though understandably Symons makes little attempt to associate Dowson with his contemporaries. Dowson, however, had also done his mythologizing, and this ran counter to Symons, and to Yeats's association of the Tragic Generation with the protest against Positivism. Submitting to the Huxley–Tindall world-view, Dowson's early ethic of 'drift' was culled from the negative side of Schopenhauer's philosophy: a willed will-lessness.

Yeats had then every excuse for mythologizing his friends, for like all young poets, they mythologized one another, and Yeats was performing a service similar to Gautier's history of Romanticism, where the generation of 1830 is aggrandized by gossip. The Tragic Generation insisted on suffering and dying mythologically: they were always trying to invent themselves, such was their sense of the individual's isolation in history, their distrust of 'generalization'. And Yeats's mythologizing begins as always from physical appearance: Henley, the paralysed viking; Johnson, the suave ambiguous Hellenistic head over the figurine body tapering away to vanishing-point; the uneasily bewigged Davidson; suggesting verdicts on lives and art.

Moreover, the process by which the notion of a 'tragic generation' was elaborated can be studied. Yeats had mythologized Johnson during Johnson's lifetime in a brief essay in Brooke's and Rolleston's *A Treasury of Irish Poetry* (1900).[7] He associated Johnson with Villiers's Axël in his tower, wavering in solitude between two dreams: of Ireland and the Catholic Church. But Johnson was a special case—his life had by that time passed already into a 'mythic' phase, a living death of illness, terror, remorse, whisky and isolation. Yeats had not associated Johnson with a generation. In 1908 Symons suffered the nervous collapse that virtually ended his career, and in 1909 Davidson walked into the sea. In a lecture given at the Memorial Hall, Manchester, on 31 October 1910 Yeats reveals that by this time he was placing his own generation historically, but in a manner that was strictly limited. His account anticipates strikingly the account of the Rhymers' programme given in *Trembling of the Veil*. He begins with the Renaissance discovery of Academic Form (against which Pre-Raphaelitism had rebelled) and proceeds to the rejection of 'subject' in painting and its parallel in poetry. It is the version of 'dissociation of sensibility' which Yeats offers elsewhere. The hero-villain Milton is 'the Raphael of traditional morality', and the expression of classical morality alternately ennobled and dulled Wordsworth's genius and chilled Tennyson's *Idylls*. The 1890s witnessed 'the revolt of my own fiery generation' and 'the man who first proclaimed it was the younger Hallam who invented the phrase "the aesthetic school in poetry"'. The new type of poet was one who did not aspire to teach, eschewing popular morality and easy anecdote, but simply gave one 'his vision'.

Yeats, his lecture goes on, had come to recognize that 'we have thrown away the most powerful of all things in literature—personal utterance'. What he had thought of as a purely personal insight was, he now saw, 'the thought of his generation ... One thing I had not foreseen and that was if you make your art of your personality you will have a very troubled life. Goethe said, "We know ourselves by action only; never by contemplation." The moment you begin the expression of yourself as an artist your life in some mysterious way is full of tumult.' It was a lesson explicit already in Hallam's essay on Tennyson which had been reprinted by one of the Rhymers, Le Gallienne, in 1893. 'To me it meant Irish leagues and movements and all kinds of heterogeneous activities which were not good for my life, as it seemed to me at the time. To the others it meant dissipation; that generation was a doomed generation ... I believe it was that they made their nature passionate by making their art personal.' And of Johnson and Dowson, Yeats spoke in terms that closely resemble those in *Trembling of the Veil*, concluding that when he thought of that 'doomed generation I am not sure whether it was sin or sanctity which was found in their brief lives'.[8]

It is an interpretation which has not been strictly touched by notions of 'personality'. The tone is far more tentative than that of *Trembling of the Veil*, where Yeats is more assured about sin and sanctity, while the doctrine looks back to *Ideas of Good and Evil*. Of Dowson Yeats had written that his art 'was curiously faint and shadowy. I believe that the art of any man who is sincerely seeking for the truth, seeking for beauty, is very likely to be faint and hesitating. The art that is entirely confident, or the speaking and writing ... entirely confident, is the work of the kind of man who is speaking with other men's thoughts.' That hint as to false certainty provides the only crystallization of what the Rhymers—in Yeats's presentation of them—were reacting against; not anecdote but the formalism of English Parnassians such as Gosse, Dobson and Lang. In an article published in the *Providence Journal* of 1892 Yeats had attacked the foreign forms of these Parnassians, though the main target was the false 'objectivity' of attempting to rid a poem of any taint of its author. The attack on exotic forms seems to consort with the church-warden pipes, ale and Dr Johnson's Cheshire Cheese.

Yeats's presentation of himself in *The Tragic Generation* sharply illustrates the process to which his material was being subjected, and perhaps some of the limitations, even the inadequacies, which this treatment resulted in. In the 1910 lecture, as in *Autobiographies*, Yeats claims that he founded the various societies with which he was connected in the 1890s; to make substantive the moral of the artist losing himself in toil that is not sedentary (Yeats's unhappy emotional life at this time had affinities with the passive Dowson's). It remains difficult, however, to determine whether his inaccuracies are due to stylization or simple forgetfulness. But two examples are certainly central. Yeats obscures the origins of the Rhymers' Club, which he claims to have founded with Rhys in 1891 and which, in fact, gradually cohered out of informal readings at 20 Fitzroy Street, 'Whiteladies', the house Arthur Mackmurdo had bought in 1889. For Yeats this process is not sufficiently dramatic. If on the one hand his own account is false to the young man of *Reveries*, feeling his way, on the other it dramatizes, legitimately perhaps, that young man's latent decisiveness: he presided over the moment of coherence. There is little sense in *Trembling of the Veil* of the Rhymers' miscellaneous muster, ranging in age from the fifties down. Consequently, the Rhymers tend to be confused with the 'Tragic Generation'. The 'pattern' that Yeats is distinguishing applies not merely to the Rhymers and to Henley, but to naturalists like Crackanthorpe, whose unhappy love affair and suicide make him severely exemplary.

Similarly, although there was a preliminary meeting of the Irish Literary Society at the Yeats house in Bedford Park, Yeats's assertion that he was the Society's founder was challenged by the secretary, Michael Macdonagh, in an unpublished account of the Society's archives, and Yeats's claim is not supported by the Society's early historian, W.P. Ryan. To be sure, Yeats admits that the Society cohered out of the Southwark Club, but it is clear that he is presenting himself in a way that is not altogether usual in this section of *Autobiographies*.

For other reasons, Yeats's relationships with women in the 1890s are subjected to 'pattern'. The counterpart of the male artist is the 'new' woman who tends to assume male characteristics: Althea Gyles (the red-headed girl in AE's settlement in Dublin and one of

Smithers's repertoire of mistresses), Florence Farr, Maud Gonne. Apart from the luminosity of her first visit to Bedford Park, Maud Gonne scarcely appears as the object of Yeats's 'barren passion'. That she should appear at all is perhaps remarkable, though she is confined to her agitator's role, particularly to the male role of orator (there is no account of her interest in the occult). Metaphor carries a narrative force when she is glimpsed *en passant* with her regalia of bird-cages and canaries (though once with a Donegal hawk) rather as she appears with a more conventional monkey in Sarah Purser's oil. Cruelty and triviality are hinted—Yeats's usual defensive assertion of the Fatal Woman theme.

Yet the very elaboration of *Trembling of the Veil* defeats its own purpose. It muffles the book's climax. What we seem to be fundamentally concerned with is the relation between artist and audience. This is resolved most nakedly by the artist's counter-attack through the theatre. In the theatre the dramatist encounters that audience under conditions of sharp excitement. When he belongs to a generation self-consciously in revolt, the hostility between himself (making a customary first-night appearance) and his audience is almost ritually enacted (the disapprobation of plays was distinctly less inhibited then). Moore in *Ave* tells us that Yeats believed that the author should be present at first nights: only by watching the effect of his play could he learn his trade.

The Tragic Generation opens with a theatrical episode—the staging of Todhunter's *Sicilian Idyll* at the Bedford Park clubhouse.

It was Todhunter's practice that had given Yeats his earliest model for emulation, as we gather from an unpublished letter of 24 April 1885 to Todhunter from J.B. Yeats:

> I am most grateful to you for your kind letter and your interest in Willie—but did not write because I suppose painting devours everything—yet I have been wanting to tell you that Willie on his side watches with an almost breathless interest your course as dramatic poet—and has been doing so for a long time—he has read everything you have written most carefully.
>
> —he finished when at Howth your Rienzi at a single sitting—'the' sitting ending at 2 o'clock in the morning …
>
> That Willie is a poet I have long known—what I am really interested in is seeing the dramatic idea emerge and I think before this present drama … of his has finished, you will see evidence of his dramatic instinct.[9]

The whole account of Todhunter in *Trembling of the Veil* is manipulated with such firm economy that nothing sways the reader from the definitive image of Todhunter sitting in his box at the Avenue Theatre, surrounded by his family, enduring the crass cries of gallery and pit, without gesture though with dull courage, as his *Comedy of Sighs* staggers to its fiasco.

'Petulant and unstable, he was incapable of any emotion that could give life to a cause.' Todhunter refuses to act out the drama of the passionate artist confronting the enemies of art; artistically he dies in his bed. Successful at Bedford Park, Todhunter had been tempted to conquer the commercial theatre, but to conquer the managers he abandoned poetry for Ibsen, or more precisely, Pinero. Of Todhunter's *Helena of Troas* (1886) Yeats wrote that 'I had thought [it] as unactable as unreadable', though in 1892, following second-hand accounts of its production: 'its sonorous verse united to the rhythmical motions of the white-robed chorus, and the solemnity of burning incense, produced a semi-religious effect new to the modern stage'.

Nothing could more firmly relate to the theme of Symbolism triumphing over Positivism and Naturalism. What seems to have struck Yeats most was the 'mood' of E. W. Godwin's production in 1886, 'acting, scenery and verse were all a perfect unity'. But the account of Todhunter has to submit to its climax. His experience at the Avenue Theatre in 1894 predicts that of Synge, though it was Yeats himself and his father who actually faced the audience when the *Playboy* challenged their cosy Puritan clichés. There is a brisk contrast with Wilde (or Shaw) cajoling the audience with the play and mocking them in person. When James was edged before a hostile crowd on the first night of *Guy Domville*, history obliged with an exemplary episode: the solitary artist extending the dramatic ritual by appearing as scapegoat (Dickens's public readings which so shortened his life provide the anti-type).

The most famous of the scapegoats was, of course, Wilde. In Yeats's account of him the artist's life becomes itself a play; though Wilde's genius balked at tragedy, 'that elaborate playing with tragedy was an attempt to escape from emotion by its exaggeration'. The trial is only obliquely mentioned, but for Yeats it was clearly Wilde's last and greatest play. Wilde played it as comedy, but its note turned tragic, and when he was convicted, 'the harlots in the street outside danced upon the pavement', a tousled maenadic parody of the tragic chorus, or the Furies on the roof-top of Agamemnon's palace.

G. S. Fraser has best defined Yeats's attitude to Wilde as one of 'Platonic tolerance':

> Thrasymachus and Protagoras are archetypal figures of intellectual comedy, they are there in the dialogues to be destroyed, yet they represent something in human nature—the bully or the sophist in all of us—that is indestructible. Yeats's Oscar Wilde is (given another scene, another set of weapons) as indestructible an archetype as Plato's Alcibiades. His life should be a great tragedy, or a horrid melodramatic warning; but his temperament is irrepressibly that of what Yeats, in another connection, called 'the great comedian'. And his Mask dominates his Body of Fate.... What should be appalling becomes farcical, and what should be ignoble farce is magnificently lent style.[10]

Of this the brothel episode in Dieppe is the most graphic instance. Dowson and Wilde pool funds to teach Wilde 'a more wholesome taste'. A crowd attends them to the brothel and awaits the event. Wilde appears:

> He said in a low voice to Dowson, 'The first these ten years, and it will be the last. It was like cold mutton'—always, as Henley had said, 'a scholar and a gentleman', he now remembered that the Elizabethan dramatists used the words 'cold mutton'—and then aloud so that the crowd might hear him, 'But tell it in England, for it will entirely restore my character' (*Auto.*, 328).

The episode is conceived dramatically and Wilde disappears with an exit-line that is both pathetic and funny.

The section on *The Tragic Generation* which began with the account of *A Comedy of Sighs* ends with the meeting with Synge and with Yeats and Symons witnessing Jarry's *Ubu Roi*[11] at Lugné Pöe's Symbolist *Theatre de l'oeuvre*. In Jarry's play, from a distance of twenty years, he can see only comedy and the return of the objective cycle. The reduction of human beings to marionettes, where the self-conscious and the primitive come full circle, the point where 'the painter's brush consumes his dreams', provides a faltering finish before the onset of 'the Savage God', confirming the circular and determinist structure of the whole book.

III

On 28 February 1934 Yeats referred to 'the drama I am building up in my Lady Gregory'. The material taken from his own letters was to be transformed into an epitaph on the conflict of personalities that preceded the founding of the Abbey Theatre and into an exaltation of Lady Gregory as aristocrat and prose artist over Moore and Martyn. Himself the only survivor, Yeats approached the past in a manner at once detached and involved: 'things reveal themselves passing away'. The years between 1897 and 1902 assumed coherence: 'It is curious how one's life falls into definite sections—in 1897 a new scene was set, new actors appeared.' But the dramatic metaphor at once pays tribute to the excitement of those years and distances them: Yeats himself, or rather his idea of himself, is a puppet among puppets. If the national theatre is to be judged, he wrote, 'what [Moore] is and what I am will be weighed and very little what we have said and done'.

Yet much of *Dramatis Personae* is concerned with what Moore said and did. Through a pretended auditor, it is a dialogue with Moore. Before composing it, Yeats was reading Moore 'that I may write'; and the writing was designed to overgo Moore in his own art, impressionist autobiography, an art based on Paterian 'style', self-transparency. 'Style' is indivisible, and what one says or does or writes flows from what one is.

Moore's side of the dialogue had begun in 1898 with *Evelyn Innes*, dedicated to Yeats and Symons, 'two writers with whom I am in sympathy'. Moore cast Yeats as the poet and magician Ulick Dean, and a letter to Olivia Shakespear suggests that Yeats was both pleased and amused. *Hail and Farewell* appeared long after the quarrel between the two men. In *Ave* Moore hesitates between two images of Yeats. The poet's operatic appearance suggests an image close to Katharine Tynan's: 'an Irish parody of the poetry I had seen all my life strutting its rhythmic way in the alleys of the Luxembourg gardens, preening its rhymes by the fountains, excessive in habit and gait'.[12] The other image suggests latent strength, and Yeats's slippery dialectic is accorded appreciation. Yeats did not take ridicule kindly, and the breach between himself and Moore was final, though Moore carried his ingenuousness into old age and complained that when Yeats came to London he never visited Ebury Street.

Although *Dramatis Personae* attempts to surpass Moore in his own art, Yeats is no Messiah. Under the relaxed surface, however, the book focuses Yeats's version of history, the game or play which every literary achievement imposes more firmly on the past, even if it is a past that has now a splendid irrelevance.

We begin with the three Galway 'great houses', Coole, Roxborough, Tulyra (and by implication we think of Moore Hall in County Mayo). The relaxed quality of *Dramatis Personae* owes something perhaps to the fact that Yeats had already written the poems that celebrate Lady Gregory and the part she and Coole played in modern Irish history. There is none of the 'spilled poetry' and spilled mythology of parts of *Trembling of the Veil*. Yet *Dramatis Personae* itself clarifies the ground for 'The Municipal Gallery Revisited' and supremely the 'painted stage' of 'The Circus Animals' Desertion'. In *Dramatis Personae*, after judging Moore and Martyn, Yeats implicitly judges himself.

The judgements on Moore and Martyn are full of malicious insight. Yeats proceeds to use them, as Moore had used Martyn and Yeats, for copy. A mutual contempt binds Moore and Martyn and a common self-esteem. Martyn, the saint, warms himself with his own sanctity in the presence of the sinner, Moore, and the sinner feels more self-importantly wicked in the presence of the saint. The judgement is framed through a peasant saying which reduces both men to a very ordinary humanity. Indeed, both Moore and Martyn reduce themselves to the peasant. Yeats's note here is one of malice discovered through the questing rhythms of talk—Martyn's mother is of dubious class and Moore's education was not at Urbino but in the stables. Physical appearance promotes, as usual, mythologizing: Moore's face is carved out of that sour and vulgar vegetable, the turnip. The most inconsequential narrative serves the theme: 'One evening ... I heard a voice resounding as if in a funnel, someone in a hansom cab was denouncing its driver, and Moore drove by.' This is sinewy talk: frustration and aggression are suggested by the simile, and the final resonant anticlimax turns Moore into a one-man juggernaut, 'not a man, but a mob'. Moore's lack of style, of the aristocratic values, is tangentially but convincingly demonstrated by his treatment of cabmen and waiters. Yeats's 'style' emerges simply through talk and once only by reference to 'my great-grandmother Corbet, the mistress of Sandymount', where the resonance is well-manneredly casual. Yeats's values are again obliquely asserted. His insistence on Moore's gross frankness about women recalls his own reticence; the frankness is even dismissed as compensation for ugliness: 'he never kisses and always tells'. His own love for Maud Gonne, Yeats distances as he distances his mystical circus animals, 'which I have discussed too much elsewhere'. His own Platonizing view of one man, one woman, whether wife, mistress or obsession, he treats without pomp. The auditor is invited to distinguish.

There are connections with the method of *Trembling of the Veil*. History assumes a metaphoric role in the account of the emblematic fire at Tulyra, which divides the present from its roots in the past and reinforces the image of Martyn as mule. Indeed, the presentation of Martyn is queerly harsh compared with Moore's genial contempt. Differences in politics and the schism of the Theatre of Ireland in 1907 may have rankled, and Martyn's rather public conscience irritated Yeats as it had irritated Moore.[13] Counterpointing Moore's account in *Ave*, Yeats's account of Gill's dinner to himself and Martyn is conducted through the familiar dialectic of 'images'. Moore speaks first, inaudibly, badly, succeeded by Taylor, who is below his best. But physical description distinguishes the two men. Taylor's body, as the tense phrases record, 'was angular, rigid with suppressed rage, his gaze fixed upon some object, his clothes badly made, his erect attitude suggested a firm base'—a firm base in the Ireland whose provinciality condemned him to obscurity. Moore, the failed cosmopolite, is hit off in one comprehensive sentence: 'Moore's body was insinuating, upflowing, circulative, curvicular, pop-eyed.' The lack of physical definition is brilliantly suggested by the use of near-synonyms, each purporting to catch at the oddity, the absence of style, and after the rise into the mock-pompous 'circulative' and 'curvicular' the word 'pop-eyed' forces its way artlessly out and the image collapses into finality. Both Taylor and Moore are placed by the image of O'Grady, who speaks with such a drunken majestic sweetness that his Unionist opponent applauds the Nationalist sentiments. 'Their torch smoked, their wine had dregs, his element burned or ran pure.' O'Grady's oratory is the purest symbolism, includes but transcends logic.[14]

For both Yeats and Moore final judgement on their respective styles, their respective self-transparency, is a literary judgement. Moore had learned the necessity for style in the later 1880s under the influence of Pater,[15] but the books that most satisfied their author, *Heloise and Abelard* and *The Brook Kerith*, though written after *Hail and Farewell*, had their roots in the trilogy and in *The*

Lake. Yeats's shrewdest stroke is the suggestion that the painful limpidities of the later Moore were based on some 'silly youthful experiments' of his own. (Susan Mitchell's suggestion that Moore owed to Yeats the notion of revising and re-revising his earlier work is instantly plausible.) Yeats does not underestimate Moore's force, but praise is polemical. Moore's work is a triumph of will, not the effect of grace, and the effort shows. Apparent magnanimity is frequent in *Dramatis Personae*. Episode is balanced against episode and Yeats's side of the *Where There Is Nothing* encounter, with its sputter of threats and telegrams, is prepared by the reference to Moore's plagiarism that reveals both shamelessness and courage.

The structure of *Dramatis Personae* moves towards the exaltation of Lady Gregory,[16] and Yeats's own talk is taken up into her translation of Grania's lullaby over Diarmuid in that 'musical caressing English which never goes far from the idiom of the country people she knows so well'. This has been ushered in by the compunction of the last reference to Moore ('I look back with some remorse'), by the brief account of Hyde's ease of style in the Irish language and a reflection on Synge, the inheritor. Our thoughts are swayed deliberately to 'Coole' and 'Coole and Ballylee'; and by the comic sparagmos of the tinkers after the performance of Yeats's and Lady Gregory's *Unicorn from the Stars* to the *Playboy* and its consequences both on stage and off, to riots and the superior fictions that cause them.[17] The subject of the lament, Diarmuid and Grania, indicates that more than a requiem over the episode of the National Theatre is intended, for its subject symphonically associates Lady Gregory with Yeats and with Moore, since all were concerned in writing a play of that title that was finished to no one's satisfaction and whose comic history is recorded in Moore's *Ave*. It remains a final comment on *Dramatis Personae* also, on the fiction that does not deceive its author, but whose unity of tone makes it the most artfully achieved of Yeats's essays in self-transcendence.

Notes

1. The complex relationship between Yeats's poetry and *Autobiographies* lies beyond the confines of this essay. It is, however, a topic that would repay study. An acute reviewer of the 1926 volume commented on the two-way traffic: Section vii of *Hodos Chameliontos* 'touching on the innate nature of ideas drawn from watching caged canaries' suggesting an unwritten poem (possibly sections v and vi of 'Meditations in Time

of Civil War'), while 'certain parts are indeed refashionings of experience already passed through the difficult alembic of the verse'. This can be related to that progressive 'self-transcendence'—Yeats's interpretation of the doctrine of Wilde's *Intentions*—which *Autobiographies* was designed to serve.

2. See also 'The Adoration of the Magi' and G. Melchiori, *The Whole Mystery of Art* (London, 1960), pp.60–63, for documentation.
3. J.B. Yeats's rhetoric is skilfully vague. This seems to point to some rather Emersonian transcendentalism. It is interesting to note that Susan Mitchell defined the older Yeats's portraits of women in terms that may well have been in W.B. Yeats's mind when he made his famous polemical comparison between Strozzi and Sargent: 'John Butler Yeats had the rare quality that he not only made his women pretty, any artist can do that, but he made them lovable, manifesting some interior beauty in their souls. Incomparable executants like Sargent and William Orpen have not this faculty: they exhibit all a woman's character, but no spiritual life looks out of the faces that are so superbly drawn.'
4. George Moore in *Ave* claims to have introduced Yeats to the subjunctive; it is more likely to have been Lionel Johnson.
5. From a letter in the possession of Mrs W.B. Yeats. Yeats seems to have had the impression that Johnson might have admired his work, but did not like him.
6. The terms I have borrowed from Northrop Frye's *Anatomy of Criticism*. For Mr Frye, *Finnegans Wake* is 'a great circular organisation of mutating categories'. Recurrence is generally spoken of as 'rhythm' when it moves along in time and 'pattern' when it is spread out in space. From Mr Frye's criteria, *Autobiographies* might perhaps be judged as overmimetic, not sufficiently mythicized. As an example of rhythm, there is the role of Simeon Solomon. He poignantly associates the two generations by his occasional visits, 'a ragged figure as of some fallen dynasty', to the haunts of the Rhymers. Solomon's poverty and vice foreshadow Dowson's and Wilde's last years and Johnson's vision of himself as reduced to borrowing half-crowns from friends.
7. p.467. But see also p.xxii of the first edition of *A Book of Irish Verse*, edited by Yeats in 1895: 'the arts that consume the personality in solitude ... the immortal [arts], which could but divide him from the hearts of men'.
8. These excerpts from the text of Yeats's lecture I have taken from the occultist magazine *The Path* I, 6, pp.105–10. Yeats's version of Hallam's review of Tennyson is misleading. Yeats suggests here that Pre-Raphaelitism, his own generation and Augustus John, all share a 'rhythm' of revolt against Academic Form.
9. Manuscript in Reading University Library.
10. Yeats employs the phrase in his poem 'Parnell's Funeral'. Tim Healy is reported to have called Parnell 'a tragic comedian' soon after the *débâcle*, probably rememberng Lassalle and Meredith's novel.
11. See A. Symons, *Studies in Seven Arts* (London, 1906), pp.371–7.

12. Katharine Tynan had published without Yeats's permission extracts from his letters of the 1880s and 1890s in her *Twenty-Five Years* (London, 1913).
13. For the Theatre of Ireland, see M. Nic Shiubhlaigh, *The Splendid Years* (Dublin, 1955), pp. 73–107 in particular.
14. The description, like the description of Taylor's oratory in *Reveries*, seems to owe something to J.B. Yeats's account of Isaac Butt *chanting* his sentences when speaking in the Four Courts on some case that appealed to him. See *Passages from the Letters of John Butler Yeats*, ed. Ezra Pound (London, 1917), p. 34.
15. With rather gruesome results in *A Mere Accident* and *Mike Fletcher*, where Aestheticism and Naturalism jostle uneasily.
16. In *Dramatis Personae*, the absence of self-conscious 'rhythm' involves a corresponding absence of omission and distortion. The connections of Sir Robert and Lady Gregory with Egyptian Nationalism are probably casually omitted and Lady Gregory's role as dramatist is muted.
17. The tinkers appear in *Our Irish Theatre*. Lady Gregory recalls that a magistrate called one of them 'Paul Ruttledge', the hero of *Unicorn from the Stars*. Hearing that they had been put in a book, the tinkers reacted in riot.

5

Yeats's Quest for Self-Transparency

Like many poets, Yeats used his gift as a writer of prose in the service of his poetry. It was the instrument of his sharp designs on the audience: to extend, manipulate, redirect, even at times to bamboozle. But however melismatic or oracular or witty an instrument it might be, prose he considered a job for the left hand. Mrs Yeats was once heard to remark: 'W.B. thought nothing of his prose', and Yeats's sense of the role it was designed to play has tended to condition how it should be received and discussed. There was that not precisely satisfactory collection issued under the title *Explorations*. Moreover, Yeats himself went some way towards establishing a canon when he dropped *John Sherman*, *Dhoya* and other prose pieces after the 1908 collection of his work.

It is barely surprising, therefore, that the prose has been little discussed in its own right, though much used by Patristic critics in hushed exegesis of the master's 'ideas'. Yet it is no body of inert doctrine but supple and various. There is one short novel and sizable fragments of another; there are short stories, prose poems, and including the beautiful 'Per Amica Silentia Lunae', snatches of theory and polemic from the pages of *Beltaine*, *The Arrow* and *Samhain*; the nasty oldy of *On the Boiler*, a mask resembling that worn in the more sour passages of *Last Poems*, and there is the cosmic nightmare *A Vision*. But of all the works in prose, the most various, sustained and continuously absorbing are those grouped in 1938, the year immediately preceding their author's death, as *Autobiography*. The title with its change from *Autobiographies* of 1926 appears programmatic. It announces that what Yeats had written he had written: there was to be now no 'final test of his intellect', no carrying through of the account beyond the year 1902.

Recent years, however, have somewhat changed this matter; *John Sherman* and *Dhoya* have been republished and that indispensable collection of early reviews, *Letters to the New Island*, has been reissued. The uncollected early prose has been largely collected by J.P. Frayne, and Jon Stallworthy has continued patiently recording the snarled evolution of Yeats's later poetic manuscripts. *Yeats Studies*, of which several issues have so far appeared, possesses a proper historical bias and devotes many of its pages to the reprinting of manuscript material. A series of editions of the dramatic manuscripts announces itself with the publication of *The Shadowy Waters*, bringing together, from various sources in Ireland and the United States, drafts up to the year 1899. And another work at which Yeats worried sporadically in the late 1890s, *The Speckled Bird*, has also been edited from manuscript. This novel with its cast of poets and magicians should furnish fascinating points of comparison with *The Trembling of the Veil*. The surviving manuscripts of the Yeats–Ellis collaboration on the works of Blake have been described in *The Book Collector* and will presumably be published in turn, while, most resonant of all such pieties, the draft *Autobiography* of 1915–17 and the text of Yeats's journal have been made available for us by Denis Donoghue under the title of *Memoirs*. Another task which is much needed and for which the materials are at last becoming available is an edition of the *Autobiography* with full notes and commentary.

Comparing the draft autobiography with its final form, Professor Donoghue observes rightly that the draft constitutes 'a work of notable candour, remarkable in a poet who found it hard to be candid'. In *Autobiographies* (reverting for convenience to that form) Yeats's lack of candour seems willed. In his poetry, he is often candid against his will. The visionary speaker, for example, in 'Meditations in Time of Civil War' may slam his door on the storm of twentieth-century history, but the poem has already spoken too powerfully for the events of time so that they may not be shut out. If, however, one were to assert flatly that Yeats is more honest in poetry than in *Autobiographies*, it would suggest that the main value of that work is as record of achieved poems or as rendering possible the writing of poems through self-clarification. To be sure, some future poetry floats unprecipitated on the prose of *Autobiographies*. Yeats's design there, though, was to pre-empt an area of the past and to impose a version of historical truth no less than an attempt to affect in Romantic historical mode the future. And Yeats so triumphed that actual and typical truth have become radically and memorably confused. His glittering libels on those sad and stylish friends of his youth are often quoted as though factual or even as representing his own response at the time of encountering them. The record rather applies to figures performing roles in Yeats's continuing self-drama, though such figures could barely perform those roles without his release of potentialities within their failed selves.

Structurally, *Autobiographies* consists of six parts, each a different exercise in achieving autobiography. The parts are unified not so much by form or tone as by worrying at certain themes: the embodiment of Yeats's wavering but persistent insights into the deeper self at different stages of his life, the quest for 'unity of being' and 'unity of culture'. And if we recall the versatility of the life—editor, literary journalist, lover, Decadent poet, senator, philosopher of history, obscure nationalist agitator, mage—it must be apparent how formidable was the quest for self-transparency. We begin with *Reveries over Childhood and Youth* published in 1916, but written in 1914, a quarter of a century after the fact, at a time of dejection and in answer to other versions of that earlier self. Katharine Tynan's *Twenty-Five Years* of 1913 had presented, with its unauthorized publication of old letters, a sucrose dreamer. The witty malice of George Moore's autobiographical fantasias in periodicals between 1910 and 1914, though toned down somewhat for book publication, was equally inopportune.

The second section of *Autobiographies*, *The Trembling of the Veil*, appeared in somewhat reduced form in magazines in 1921 and 1922 and was published in book form in that latter year. In 1926 under the title of *Estrangement* Yeats published fifty-five edited extracts from a diary kept in 1909, while in 1928 there appeared in *The Death of Synge* equally edited extracts from the diary, between 1909 and 1914. In 1935 in *Dramatis Personae* Yeats gave his polemical account of relations between himself and Lady Gregory on the one hand and George Moore and Edward Martyn at the time of the Irish Literary Theatre. In 1938 the definitive edition gathered up *The Bounty of Sweden*, a record of Yeats's visit to Stockholm in 1923 to receive the Nobel Prize. Here Yeats's intention was to assume the role of courtly artist celebrating the patronage of Sweden's Academy and Sweden's king in return for their presentation of the Prize. The mask is that of an Ariosto celebrating duke and courtiers of Ferrara. In spite of the impressionistic diary form, the attempt is made to embody place and patron in the time-defying dignity of high language. But the intention is also polemical and this is made more clear by the inclusion of the lecture Yeats gave on the Irish Dramatic Movement in the inconsistently titled *Autobiographies* of 1955. This forces connections with other areas of the volume. Sweden is what, after the factions and anticlimax of 1922–3, Ireland so conspicuously is not. In Ireland there is no courtly centre. It is Stockholm, not Dublin, that approximates to Ferrara, to Byzantium, just as the Stockholm Town Hall is a modern version of Hagia Sophia, with its mosaics and other works of art by many artists speaking for and to the people. In 1944 *Pages from a Diary*, written in 1930, was privately printed, and some years ago Curtis Bradford edited a somewhat fuller version of parts of the 1908–14 diary. The draft autobiography covers events in Yeats's life until just past the turn of the century (corresponding broadly with the span of *Dramatis Personae*) while the journal with its names, indiscretions and self-rebukes is now printed for the first time and in its entirety.

Essence Rather than Accident

In *Reveries* Yeats did not wish to counteract Tynan and Moore directly. The first word of his title has *symboliste* associations; announces concern with essence rather than accident. Like the other parts of *Autobiographies*, *Reveries* dwells on sacred persons and sacred places (by implication, also on profane persons and places): persons and places as epiphanic. For Professor Donoghue in his terse but illuminating introduction, the draft 'Autobiography', raw and candid though it is, also renders essence rather than accident.

> Yeats appears to move from one life to another according to the easy regulation of memory; but, in fact, the movement is conducted according to his more exacting sense of a time, a decade, a generation, that network of conditions and relationships in which the historical moment is revealed. We call the movement a memoir to indicate that its content is public and historical. Yeats is concerned with a particular person for the pressure he exerts upon his society, and for the pressure, perhaps equal and opposite, exerted by society in return. Such a person is presented in his symbolic moment, as if he were a character in a play, fixed in his characteristic gesture. What such a man is, beyond his nature as a *dramatis persona* Yeats does not presume to say. He is not here a

psychologist, indulging himself in what Yeats regarded as the modern vice of curiosity. A man's life is significant in its bearing on other lives: a memoir is an approach to that significance.

But Yeats does not surrender to history: he creates for himself and his associates a new history out of the mere facts of their lives. A person may be content with mere fact, but a memoirist is not; he is not content until his persons have become personages, surrounded by an aura which is their enacted presence. Yeats's memory reconstitutes these presences, fixes them in space as they were not perhaps fixed in time. The persons so recovered achieve their identities by being placed in relation to their time. Many ... are minor figures ... but a minor figure achieves his identity by finding an enabling role to play ... Identity is a form of transcendence, and a person who achieves it is redeemed from the chances of daily experience. Yeats moves about from one person to another, handing each a script of his part in the play. He does not merely enumerate the events of a plot: behind the several scripts he composes a generation, many lives engaged in a play of history.

Yeats's word for the movement of a mind under these auspices is 'reverie'. 'I have changed nothing to my knowledge; and yet it must be that I have changed many things without my knowledge; for I am writing after many years and have consulted neither friend, nor letter, nor old newspaper, and describe what comes oftenest into my memory.' It may be said that this disclaimer ... is merely Yeats's charming excuse for not bothering to get the facts right. But the passage is more than charming: it is Yeats's tribute to the sinuous ways of memory. His confidence in the ostensibly lawless ways of reverie comes from his confidence in the imagination: it may be wrong in the short run, but in the long run it is right ... Reverie is memory under the sweet sway of intuition. (*Memoirs*, 9–11).

This is ably generalized, but would the description be possible if we had the draft only and no *Reveries* and *The Trembling of the Veil*? Professor Donoghue's answer is Yes: 'Yeats's style in the [draft] autobiography is often rough, his first draft is imperfect, but for most of the way it moves with the freedom of reverie and meditation.' Yeats's apology is prefixed to *Reveries*, but even there Yeats and perhaps Professor Donoghue are being a little disingenuous. Yeats was forced to use his father's letters for documenting oral memories of his father's friends, Nettleship, Potter, and so on. For *The Trembling of the Veil*, his father and Lady Gregory were to furnish their autobiographies though, more perhaps as corroboration than as *aide-mémoire*. But distinctions between draft and finished work remain significant. 'The perceiving subject', to quote Professor Donoghue once more, 'takes himself as object, ponders his own case'. His ponderings are less coherent, but sometimes more vivid and certainly more direct, in the draft. The means that Yeats used to distance his own case in *Autobiographies* are conspicuously absent in the draft. There is no dark muttering about 'out of phase', 'full of the moon', 'mask' and 'image', little elegant mystifying. One perceives him groping towards a difficult insight, not gilding it with obscurity as he does in some of the vaguer passages of *The Trembling of the Veil*. The myth to which Yeats submits in the draft, that of the *poète maudit*, would have been so familiar to him as to be a cliché, as we may gather from this passage on Lionel Johnson and Olivia Shakespear:

> I had found the Rhymer who had introduced me under the influence of drink, speaking vaguely and with vague movements, and while we were speaking this recent memory came back. She spoke of her pagan life in a way that made me believe that she had had many lovers and loathed her life. I thought of that young man so nearly related. Here is the same weakness, I thought; two souls so distinguished and contemplative that the common world seems empty. What is there left but sanctity, or some satisfying affection, or mere dissipation?—'Folly the comforter', some Elizabethan had called it. Her beauty, dark and still, had the nobility of defeated things, and how could it help but wring my heart! I took a fortnight to decide what I should do. (*Memoirs*, 85).

What survived from that passage was the generalization more eloquently and concisely presented but with a vanished particularity. Olivia Shakespear is absent from *The Trembling of the Veil*, and there are only fugitive glimmers of Maud Gonne. Both are vivid presences in the draft and modern vice of curiosity or not, many readers may be forgiven for preferring the women above the system. Yeats was assuming a courtly reticence—Olivia appears under a Walter Scott pseudonym in the draft—a rebuke to the half peasant-blooded Moore for rarely kissing but always telling; but both ladies were very much alive when *The Trembling of the Veil* and the final arrangement of *Autobiographies* were accomplished. As Yeats remarked, only the dead are perfect: their lives have the finished quality of a work of art, can be patterned. It always remains possible, as with Yeats himself, to produce a disturbing last phase.

The draft records plainly and with a realism not found elsewhere in his prose sexual awakening and frustration: brutally put, Maud and masturbation. Like Dowson, Yeats remained inescapably caught between the desire for woman as sexual object and the desire to worship her as physical symbol always just beyond touch. What he writes of Dowson in *The Trembling of the Veil* he writes of himself, but with this distinction. Dowson's search, located in a twelve-year-old girl, failed and was not to be repeated but parodied: sober, Yeats wrote of him, he would look at no other woman, drunk he would look at any. Yeats was sober and his affair with Olivia was an attempt to mediate the obsession: she was beautiful, intelligent, vulnerable, hardly more experienced than he, despite her brave pagan tongue. The shadow of Maud fell; they failed.

While his friends resorted to prostitutes, Yeats preserved what he terms an 'unctuous chastity'. That the sexual and the ideal remained enemies still, we may gather from the terms in which he describes how he was tempted by the sight of a prostitute plying up and down Hammersmith station: he thinks of 'offering himself to her'; the phrase may suggest the humility of inexperience but surely has overtones of sacrifice, some black communion rite. Such sexual demonism resembles the interesting early drafts of *The Shadowy Waters* peopled with supernatural eagle-headed predators who disappeared from the later versions. Human love in the early drafts is a mere image of war between the sons of light and those fallen heirs of darkness in plain Gnostic mode. Two events have iterative force in the draft: the first passionate kiss of love from Olivia which startles, almost frightens him, counterpointed by Maud Gonne's not precisely sisterly kiss after a symbolic marriage on the astral plane: both dangerous sacraments. The account closes movingly with his failure, through physical and psychic exhaustion, to win Maud. There is no self-pity, the more remarkably so since he was still a solitary man; but not so far distant is Maud's marriage to John Macbride and Macbride's letter of triumph with its allusion to 'weeping Willie'. And perhaps still more distantly the consummation with Maud, which was also a failure.

The Encounter with Verlaine

As to documentation, it is amusing to find Yeats asking in the draft when was it that he first met Wilde and half-answering his own question in *Autobiographies*. That is trivial, but on another level we find him relying on documentation, in part admittedly for an event at which he was not present. In the second issue of the *Savoy* of 1896, Yeats had written:

> In the spring of 1894 I received a note in English inviting me to 'coffee and cigarettes plentifully' and signed 'yours quite cheerfully, Paul

> Verlaine'. I found him in a little room at the top of a tenement house in the Rue St Jacques, sitting in an easy chair with his bad leg swaddled in many bandages. He asked me, and in English, for I had explained the poverty of my French, if I knew Paris well, for he knew it well, 'well, too well' and 'lived in it like a "fly in a pot of marmalade"'; and taking up an English dictionary, one of the very few books in his room, began searching for the name of the disease, selecting, after much labour, and with, I understand, imperfect accuracy, 'erysipilas'.

This is repeated with improvements, the most notable being 'comparative' for 'imperfect'. And the certainty of 'the spring of 1894' becomes now the consciously vague question 'In what month was it I received a note?' Before this passage, Yeats inserted in 1922: 'Paul Verlaine alternated between the two halves of his nature with so little apparent resistance that he seemed like a bad child, though to read his sacred poems is to remember perhaps that the Holy Infant shared His first home among the beasts.' (*Autobiographies*, 341)

Later, in both versions, we are referred to Verlaine's 'homely' middle-aged mistress and her homely *mis-en-scène*, including the caricatures of himself as monkey, which Verlaine had torn out of the newspapers. Then in 1896 we read: 'a singular visitor, a man, who was nicknamed Louis XI, M. Verlaine explained, because of a close resemblance, and who had not shaved for a week, and kept his trousers on with a belt of string or thin rope, and wore an opera hat which he set upon his knee, and kept shoving up and down continually while M. Verlaine talked.' The ripple of copulas is effective: the old man goes on shoving his opera hat up and down like a concertina and all the time and all the while Verlaine talks and talks and talks. The passage is given speed. Editorial comment goes in *The Trembling of the Veil*; Louis XI enacts his own singularity; Yeats knows now that it is rope and not string and the comment on Louis XI—Bibi-la-Purée, Verlaine's worshipper, pimp, odd-job man—is put in Verlaine's direct speech while the sentence about the opera hat by casual modulation of tenses suggests the distance between 1894 and now, 1921: 'He sat down holding his opera hat upon his knees, and I think he must have acquired it very lately.' That 'think' could be either simple or historic present or both. In the later version, a short paragraph puts all before it into a further key: 'At Verlaine's burial, but a few months after, his mistress quarrelled with a publisher at the graveside as to who owned the sheet by which the body had been covered, and Louis XI stole fourteen umbrellas that he had found leaning against a tree.' (*Autobiographies*, 342). Such a passage would barely have been possible in 1896: that article was something of an *éloge*, even if a faintly dry one, over the dead master. Fiction or not, it is typical truth and emblematic of Verlaine's whole life and the image of that life presented in the poet's work, and of its meaning for Yeats and his generation and for the Yeats of a quarter of a century on. And it defines what is often present in *The Trembling of the Veil* and rarely in the draft. Physical image, acts and *agrapha* are synthesized at more than one level. The final scene suggests first a conflation of the Passion and the interment: the soldiers who part Christ's garment at the crucifixion. Verlaine appears not as Christ but as his parodic double in a grotesque *pietà* scene with his elderly mistress doubling also as *mater dolorosa* and Mary Magdalen. Verlaine's mistresses were mother figures: he liked coddling and scolding. The image has been prepared for by the opening sentence that insists on the doubleness (and works forward to the famous sentence: 'After us, the Savage God.'): Verlaine's nature comically alienated from itself, wavering between sin and sanctity, Godhead and bestiality. Verlaine had parodied with perfect seriousness the sinner's role in his confessional verse, but even in death he refuses to lie down and be respectable, for he is not precisely tragic as are Yeats's friends of 'The Tragic Generation', he is a tragic clown. Louis XI acts a supporting role in Verlaine's garret, playing on his opera hat as though trapped in a Marx Brothers' film. The precision of *fourteen* umbrellas reminds us that those belonged to Verlaine's fellow poets who were making suave, embarrassed orations over the grave. Louis XI parodies and protects Verlaine. But the passage also parodies the worship of Verlaine by the young Yeats and his earnest contemporaries.

'The Tragic Generation'

'The Tragic Generation': that phrase is at the heart of *The Trembling of the Veil*, though there is little sense of it in the draft. No metahistorical coherences were needed. Such studies as those of Focillon and Vulliaud have shown us how the last decades of centuries acquire their irrational chiliastic awareness—in the 1890s the analogue was with the French revolutionary Terror. The shaping of time into the unit of the 'generation' is not purely notional—a decade is a small fraction of the conventional century—but properly organic; it corresponds to human rhythms. The origin is presumably Romantic, German perhaps, while the French certainly refined it down to a year, speaking of the generation of 1830, and Yeats would have had the 'Young Ireland' generation of 1848 well in mind, no less than the generation of his gifted but not conspicuously successful father and his father's less gifted and equally unsuccessful friends. In 1920, when Yeats was rewriting his autobiography, the First World War was of very recent memory. Was it from that year or probably later that there emerged the phrase 'The Lost Generation'—those who died sacrificially at the Dardanelles, on the Somme, at Passchendaele?—while the draft itself was composed precisely during the years in which those 'bloody frivolities' had occurred. And the phrase embraced also the drifting survivors of that war. What 'tragic' suggests can be gathered from a phrase used by Yeats's father of the writers and artists of the 1890s: 'a generation of Hamlets'.

Whatever view is taken of Hamlet and his notorious delays, the interpretation Yeats seems to favour is of one who is at once the most innocent and yet the most conscious of evil in that state and prison of Denmark. One whose revenge is, at the last, less willed and personal than a matter of 'accidental judgments, casual slaughters'. The consummation comes when Hamlet ceases to will, when he accepts that what will be will be, accepts the sum of guilt and dies as a scapegoat so that life can continue and yet dies with dance music sounding behind that 'absent thee from felicity awhile'. Once the 'sacred' has been expelled, the tribe can survive: for the sacred by definition brings violence with it. Ritual victims who maximize, embody and finally remove evil, that is how Yeats views his Tragic Generation, and he is the survivor. Their vocation was will-less suffering; they were short of time and space—as one of them remarked at a Rhymers' Club meeting, 'only one thing is certain, we are too many'. But Yeats's play was accomplished from sources. Wilde and Verlaine both flouted society and were imprisoned, but the record of others is dramatic. If one takes the Registrar General's view, it was a bad risk to write verse if one was born between 1854 and 1867.

William Watson hardly qualifies for membership of this gloomy club (Yeats tells us he joined but never came to the Rhymers' meetings), but obliged with exemplary madness. In 1892 walking through Windsor Park he met a royal coach containing the then

Duke of Edinburgh and his family, stopped and tried to enter it. He was clapped into jail. During the hearing he announced that Milton was Samson reincarnated, that he was Milton reincarnated, that Delilah had been reincarnated to tempt him but that he had kept himself pure. John Barlas, who wrote under the name of 'Evelyn Douglas', fired a revolver in the House of Lords and was shut up for the rest of life in an asylum. Arthur Symons went mad in Italy. He picked up a cheap plaster cast and declared that he had discovered a hitherto unknown master work of Cellini, writing an excited letter to his wife which began, 'Dear Beloved Dodo Dumpty Delicious Darling Dolis'. Her name was Rhoda. Symons is treated somewhat more amply, though with reticence still, in the draft and his madness is only glancingly alluded to in the journal. Dowson was not imprisoned, but well might have been after his famous fight with the French baker. In both draft and finished work, Yeats, depending presumably on oral sources, has a falsely heroic end to the story. The French magistrate on hearing that Dowson is a famous English poet declares 'quite right to remind me' and imprisons the baker. The *procès-verbal*, alas, merely informs us that Dowson was let off with an insultingly low fine.

The profane version of another actor, William Sharp, is that he invented a female double of himself, publishing many books under the name 'Fiona Macleod', who, he informed the curious, was his cousin and lived in the remote Highlands of Scotland. Convinced of her reality, he developed a second handwriting for her and was accustomed to dress up in woman's clothes when he was writing as Fiona: 'does he—the bitch!', a contemporary observed. Sharp died exhausted by his double life well before the draft was written; but he appears only as visionary and that again glancingly in *Autobiographies*. His role is a little more substantial in the draft (where Yeats's visionary experiences are recorded more fully but also more tentatively). One clinical Ursula Le Guinish episode is a tale told after dinner to two highly unsympathetic listeners: 'He had been somewhere abroad when he saw the sideral body of Fiona enter the room as a beautiful young man, and became aware that he was a woman to the spiritual sight. She lay with him, he said, as a man with a woman, and for days after his breasts swelled so that he had almost the physical likeness of a woman.' (*Memoirs*, 129) That 'almost' is masterly. No one apparently thought to ask Sharp if his braces were too tight. If campy stories are in, more relevant truths about Sharp are not.

He had been an early historian of the Belgian Literary Movement, which had problems—that of a dual language. How much of a model it furnished is arguable, but the tactics of the writers and artists involved must surely have influenced Yeats, and Sharp's own activities in the abortive Scots Renaissance of the 1890s must also have seemed relevant. Sharp, like Symons, was close to Yeats, particularly in the later 1890s, when all three were in process of associating 'magick' and international symbolism. Even Sharp's appearance, high-coloured face and Viking beard allied with frail health, suitably suggested the instability Yeats found in the physical appearance of his actors. But Sharp's symbolic appearance had been pre-empted by Henley, who was more picturesque: alternative Viking face, heroic chest and one leg, but an eloquent crutch. Probably Yeats simply despised Sharp's actual literary productions. And Henley had the additional convenience of serving the sub-plot: Imperialism was no less a dream, though a more widely shared dream than the fantasies of the Decadents. And the extremes define one another at the point of tragedy. Where they believe themselves most distinct, Yeats's Decadents and his Imperialists, exalters of the will, are virtually identical: Henley's little daughter 'the Empress' dies and he is broken.

The most vivid presence of *The Trembling of the Veil* is Lionel Johnson: the head of a Hellenistic figurine, the tiny body, the sexlessness. The draft account of him is brief but adds one anecdote which so obviously should have been applied to Enoch Soames that Yeats dropped it: 'Somebody said, "Johnson is, I am told, a neo-Catholic", and when I asked what that was said, "There is no God and Mary is his mother".' This can be placed in context of *fin de siècle/fin du globe* by a more recent graffito on an inner wall of the Library of Congress: 'God is dead, but beware, Mary is pregnant once again.' Unlike Dowson and Yeats, Johnson did not locate his ideal in woman but in minority institutions: at school he had been a Blavatskyite; later he was briefly associated with a more marginal group still, the White Rose League, supporters of the House of Stuart; and finally there was the Catholic Church and Irish Nationalism.

The account of Johnson's imaginary conversations of such informal splendour with the high and the brilliant also appears in the draft. It raises a further question of source and documentation. Lady Gregory did not complete her memoir, but substantial fragments are located in the Berg Collection of the New York

Library. It appears that she began her work in 1914, a year before Yeats's draft autobiography had its commencement. One passage in Lady Gregory's work closely corresponds to the passage on Johnson's fantasies in the draft; but which parts of the draft were first composed, as Curtis Bradford observes, it remains difficult to establish. The scene is a dinner party in February, 1897. Lady Gregory tells us that Yeats himself was the source of the information. Additionally, Lady Gregory has an amusing description of Yeats himself at a meeting of the Irish Literary Society confronting J.F. Taylor, which is quite in Yeats's own manner.

What applies to the draft applies to the full journals, though these, underpinned by chronology, are less raw but no less candid. Yeats here is a man 'in crisis', subject to accident, searching for essence, found in daily living. The most testing episode involves Edmund Gosse's attempt to secure for Yeats a Civil List pension, the matter being mediated through Lady Gregory, at Gosse's request. In the middle of the negotiations Gosse wrote to Lady Gregory an apparently unmotivated insulting letter. Yeats needed the money; but he owed much (including money) to Lady Gregory. The solution was adroit and faintly comic. Yeats wrote stern letters, more or less breaking off relations with Gosse and gave them to Lady Gregory to post. That shrewd, admirable and gifted person let them lie. The pension was granted but Yeats argues anxiously with his conscience in the journal.

It is surely no vulgar curiosity that moves us to be acquainted with great authors in their slippers. The unique value of both draft autobiography and journal is that they bring us nearer to the human, the vulnerable Yeats, a man stripped of pose and gesture, of like weakness with ourselves. And this surely is the Yeats of the greater poems.

6

Poet and Designer: W. B. Yeats and Althea Gyles

Up to 1929 the book by which Yeats was best known to the general public was *Poems* (1899), which had run through a number of reprints, the last in 1927. The cover of that book was by Althea Gyles. When the book appeared once more in 1929, her cover had disappeared. At the time of her invitation to replace that insipid angel on Granville Fenn's cover for *Poems* (1895), Miss Gyles had already designed for Yeats *The Secret Rose* of 1897 and had devised a portrait of Yeats as mage with attendant roses for *The Wind among the Reeds*, another of Miss Gyles's designs (the roses, though not the head, were to be used for *The Shadowy Waters* of 1900). And in 1906 the spine of *The Secret Rose*, with its emblem half spear, half caduceus, was to be used for *Poems, 1899–1905*. Visually, the entrance to the popular Yeats lay through the imagery of Althea Gyles, though that imagery was actually a collaboration between artist and poet. Their connection, lasting for a few years only, was important, if puzzling. Yeats had his reservations about her talent from the beginning. But Miss Gyles's broken relationship with him owes something to her voluntary abstention from work in design and something to a deflection of Yeat's own interest—theatre business and the founding of the Dun Emer Press in 1903 which involved a new approach to the presentation of his work. It also owed not a little to the difficult personality of the lady herself.

What tenuous fame Miss Gyles possesses she owes to Yeats, and naturally enough comments on her have been strictly in terms of Yeats. The present essay attempts to treat her as a subject in her own right: Yeats was not the only, though he was the most important, episode in her life. We shall place that episode more securely by giving it context. Yet, after all, it is through Yeats that we must approach her. True, in the prose he devotes to her she becomes the servant of his rhetoric, of his image-making rage, of his propagandizing for his own poetry and for the literary movement. But she emerges there with more energy, with more clarity even, than in her own letters and poems. First, in the essay entitled 'A Symbolist Artist and the Coming of Symbolic Art', which he contributed to *The Dome* in 1898, Miss Gyles emerges as a sojourner among the Dublin Theosophists, that eager society of apprentices and clerks, some living, some attending merely, at Number 3 Upper Ely Place, seeing dreams and visions, now a little Christian, now very Irish, now altogether Celtic. Such a syncretism appears in Miss Gyles's designs, though the Christian Kabbala is more in evidence than any Oriental vision:

> I know that Miss Althea Gyles, in whose work I find so visionary a beauty, does not mind my saying that she lived long with this little company, who had once a kind of conventual house, and that she will not think I am taking from her originality when I say that the beautiful lithe figures of her art, quivering with a life half mortal tragedy, half immortal ecstasy, owe something of their inspiration to this little company.[1]

Quivering litheness! How well it describes the art of George William Russell. The conventual house had been established by E.J. Dick, the 'bearded Manichaean Engineer' of Yeats's *Autobiographies*, in April 1891, and Russell was an early inmate. From the *Irish Theosophist*, the community magazine, we gather that a visitor would 'have been struck by the extraordinary and weirdly fantastic and Blake-like frescoes adorning the walls of an otherwise commonplace room'.[2] This was Russell's work, and from a further source we gather that he would often put designs or charcoal portraits on the walls, an activity disconcertingly reminiscent of Balzac. Life at Ely Place was frugal and chaste, but odd enough to provide a more or less natural setting for Miss Gyles. Her contemporaries, so to speak, were D.N. Dunlop, H.M. Magee, Magee's brother 'John Eglinton' and Edmund J. King. When H.M. Magee left in 1894, his room was taken over by A.W. Dyer, while Dunlop left as early as December 1892 to marry, and the small community had moved to 13 Eustace Street, Dublin, by January 1897. Neither these dates nor the details given in the group's magazine assist in defining when Miss Gyles was taken in and the circumstances of her arrival and departure. We know that she arrived in Dublin in 1889 and that she was in London probably by 1892, so her connection with the community must have been early on in its life. For further information we have to turn once more to the 'typical' truth of Yeats. Miss Gyles is that red-headed girl who makes a brief appearance in *Autobiographies*. She was living, he tells us, on a lower floor, and all her thoughts

> were set upon painting and poetry, conceived as abstract images like Love and Penury in the *Symposium*; and to these images she sacrificed herself with Asiatic fanaticism. The engineer had discovered her starving somewhere in an unfurnished or half-furnished room, and she said that she had lived for many weeks upon bread and shell-cocoa, so that her food never cost her more than a penny a day. Born into a county family, who were so haughty that their neighbours called them the Royal Family, she had quarrelled with a mad father, who had never, his tenants declared, 'unscrewed the top of his flask with any man', because she wished to study art, had run away from home, had lived for a time by selling her watch, and then by occasional stories in an Irish paper. For some weeks she had paid half-a-crown a week to some poor woman to see her to the art schools, for she considered it wrong for a woman to show herself in public places unattended; but of late she had been unable to afford the school fees. The engineer engaged her as a companion for his wife, and gave her money enough to begin her studies once more. She had talent and imagination, a gift for style; but though ready to face death for painting and poetry, conceived as allegorical figures, she hated her own genius, and had not met praise and sympathy early enough to overcome the hatred. Face to face with paint and canvas, pen and paper, she saw nothing of her genius but its cruelty, and would have scarce arrived before she would find some excuse to leave the schools for the day, if indeed she had not mentioned over her breakfast some occupation so laborious that she could call it a duty, and so not go at all. Most watched her in mockery, but I watched in sympathy; composition strained my nerves and spoiled my sleep; and yet, for generations ... my paternal ancestors had worked at some intellectual pursuit, while hers had shot and hunted. She could, at any time, have given up her profession, which her father raged against, not because it was art, but because it was a profession, have returned to the common comfortable life of women. When, a little later, she had quarrelled with the engineer or his wife, and had gone back to the bread and shell-cocoa I brought her an offer from Dublin of some fairly well-paid advertisement work, which would have been less laborious than artistic creation; but she said that to draw advertisements was to degrade art, thanked me elaborately, and did not disguise her indignation. She had, I believed, returned to starvation with joy, for constant anaemia would shortly give her an argument strong enough to silence her conscience when the allegorical images glared upon her, and, apart from that, starvation and misery had a large share in her ritual of worship.[3]

Althea Gyles was born in 1868 and, as Yeats had indicated, of an old, distinguished family from Kilmurry, County Waterford. The Gyleses had originally come from Minehead, Somerset, and settled in Ireland at Youghal about the year 1649.[4] Her father, George Gyles, had married in 1862 Alithea Emma, daughter of the Hon. and Rev. Edward Grey, Bishop of Hereford, one of the Greys of Northumberland. On her maternal side Miss Gyles was connected with the English aristocracy; yet she belonged to the same generation as Maud Gonne and the Gore-Booth sisters, and like them was to become in her own eccentric manner a 'new woman'. As with Constance Gore-Booth, painting represented the way out of 'big house' society and the approved marriage. With her family, she came to Dublin to attend an art school 'on Stephen's Green'. Her appearance was striking: very tall, with dusky red-gold hair and a voice of commanding music. By late 1891 or early 1892 we find her in London, alone, still pursuing art, first at Pedders, then at the Slade School, where her expenses were paid for by one of her Grey relatives. In those years she seems to have moved in literary society: Wilde, shuddering at her rustic surname, is reported to have paused and then anagrammatically remarked: 'You must call yourself "Alethea Le Gys"'. In October 1894 she published 'Dew-Time', some verses somewhat in the vein of AE's earlier work, in the *Pall Mall Magazine*:

Life gives us many spirits thro' the day
To laugh and fling fair flowers upon our way,
But at the end she gives us one to grieve
With our tired hearts that tears will not relieve—At Eve.

Slowly the colours fade, the world grows grey,
And hopes and fears lie faded by the way.
Her soft tears all the meadows dew-drenched leave,
Shed from her heart for tearless hearts that heave—At Eve.

And when the mystic dew-time fades away,
Dying with the last light, I hear her say
'Until dead hopes and flowers new life receive,
I will return and weep with you who grieve—At Eve'.[5]

The capitals of the title are in Gothic. A weeping female angel at bottom right kneels in a wood of mildly stylized trees with long stalked flowers beneath them. The roots of the flowers (a favourite motif of Miss Gyles), shown in a border at base, are more like hands.

A border at the right drips petals. The poem is written in capitals contained by a panel broken at lower left by the flowers and the figure of the weeper.

Miss Gyles did not become a member of the Golden Dawn. Though familiar with some of its symbolism, if not an adept—'Her occultism' Clifford Bax remarked to me, 'was skin deep'—its rites had some influence on her designs and earlier verse. The transition from Ely Place to the Isis–Urania temple of the Rosicrucian Golden Dawn had already been made by Yeats. It represented a move to a more elaborate, but more pragmatic mode of mysticism, that word so often occurring in late-nineteenth-century England and France. We find it in the 'dedication' to Yeats of Arthur Symons's *Symbolist Movement in Literature* and in George Moore's *Evelyn Innes*, again dedicated to Yeats, where the poet appears as the mage-musician Alick and where the word is associated with the arts. Broadly, 'mysticism' signifies the belief that the universe has a supernatural ground; that there is an esoteric body of knowledge resuming the secrets of this ground or order and that by participation in ritual, religious but not Christian, the Mysteries in fact, the adept may achieve mastery of this wisdom and thereby mastery of himself and of the world. The circumstances of Yeats's secession from Madame Blavatsky's Theosophists are familiar: the Golden Dawn provided a more propitious context for experimental magic. The instrument of that magic is the symbol of the universe posited by the mystics in a universe of hieroglyphs: the world of correspondences of Neo-platonic tradition. An object from the world of the senses is a sign of a divine essence and is, in this meaning, *symbolic*. Of this essence it also partakes. Natural objects are not simply signs that point to something at a distance: they participate in the supernatural reality they signify. By contemplation and manipulation of certain symbols, the mystic can move into the spiritual world for which they stand. It was in the technique for evocation of visions taught by the Golden Dawn that Yeats was chiefly interested. For him, the symbol as it appears in poetry or in the visual arts is not distinguished from the symbol as it appears in religion or in magic, and it is the function of the artist in any field to mediate symbols. 'All art', he declares in 'Symbolism in Painting' of 1898, 'that is not mere story-telling, or mere portraiture, is symbolic, and has the purpose of those symbolic talismans which medieval magicians made with complex colours and forms, and bade their patients ponder over daily, and guard with holy secrecy; for it entangles, in complex colours and forms, a part of the Divine Essence.'[6] This passage is important. The art that is rejected is not merely the anecdotal Victorian painting or Impressionist portraiture, it is all art that denies the imagination and transcribes from 'life'. The passage is also a prescription for Miss Gyles's cover designs.

How Yeats reacted against what he saw as his father's betrayal of allegiance to imaginative art, by turning from the Pre-Raphaelites to Impressionist portraiture (conceived of by the early Impressionists as naturalist) is another familiar story. It had been through the Pre-Raphaelites that both John Butler Yeats and his son had come to admire Blake. Rossetti and Morris practised literature, painting and the applied arts, but what Yeats was in search of in the 1890s was what he called the 'great procession of symbols'. The artists and poets whom he cared for in the past had provided him with fragmentary words, what he now required was a language of symbols that could function in all or any of the arts. This he found in the syncretism of the Golden Dawn, a syncretism carried further than that of the Theosophists: the order admitted all gods, Egyptian, Irish, Greek or Christian, in to the one pantheon as images from the divine ground. And through its rituals it gave the adept mastery over images and the power to evoke them, but Yeats's main interest naturally lay in seeing how the symbols could be mediated in poetry. He was fortunate in finding an example in William Blake, whose designs he had admired as a schoolboy. At the time when he was passing from Madame Blavatsky to the Golden Dawn, he had been working in collaboration with his father's friend Edwin J. Ellis on an elaborate commentary on Blake's system. Yeats found in Blake a poet who had made an order out of his symbols and found, also, that the symbols of Blake were related to those he was finding in Theosophy and Rosicrucianism. And, furthermore, Blake had accomplished a union of the arts of poetry and design in terms of the symbol.

It is precisely through the symbol that the arts are united. And Yeats, like his contemporaries in France and England, was much concerned with union of the arts. Originating in the 'great memory', appealing to something deeper than reason or environment, the symbol can transcend the fragmentation of cultures and classes, the isolation of the artist from his society, even from the groups to which he belonged and the consequent alienation from himself that his failure to communicate involved. All this underlies Yeats's essays of the 1890s and in particular his 1898 essay on 'A Symbolic

Artist and the Coming of Symbolic Art', an essay he did not reprint. It also underlies his use of Miss Gyles's talent for design. The account of Miss Gyles in *Autobiographies* makes use of two words cardinal in Yeats's vocabulary, 'abstract' and 'allegory', and by 'allegory' Yeats means what Blake meant by that word: it is sharply distinguished from 'symbol': it implies one-to-one equations, pedantry and the will. What 'abstract' suggests, I will try to show later. Miss Gyles was still living when Yeats was writing *Autobiographies*, and like a number of his protégées, she had failed to serve his version of history: immediately, the triumph of the symbol in art. I shall want to suggest that the failure lay as much in Yeats's limited intentions as in any failure of her talent.

In 1898 Miss Gyles's art is described in terms of a vocabulary designed to escape from the polarization of Yeats's earlier ideas about art and imagination. The words are 'pattern' and 'rhythm', and an earlier word 'subject' is displaced. What is being displaced is not naturalism merely, but precisely the fragmentariness, the inadequacy of Pre-Raphaelitism. 'Pattern' suggests Morris, of course; 'rhythm' perhaps suggests the wiry line of Blake, the organic rhythms Yeats aspired to in the poetry of this moment; it also suggests Poe. The word 'subject', however, recalls not merely anecdotal painting but Pre-Raphaelite literary painting. However, Yeats's position now and later seems to me close to the main theorist in the 1880s of a late Pre-Raphaelitism, Selwyn Image. In an essay of 1884 Image had declared: 'Art though it is based on Nature, and is forever returning to Nature for inspiration, is not an imitation of Nature, but a co-existent world ... Art is one creation and Nature is another.'[7] By 1886 Image's aesthetics had become polemically formulated in response to Francis Bate's manifesto on behalf of the Impressionist New English Art Club. Essentially, Image's distinction is between 'truth' and 'appearance'. For the Impressionist, beauty consists in *first* impressions: 'In the accurate representation of Nature is represented also all the beauty and poetry of Art ... that without such actual and truthful representation, the highest form of beauty is lost, and the poetry remaining can only be such as is contained in the symbolical.'[8] Impressionist art, Image implies, then, is *only* a reflection of appearances. But this is precisely what art is *not*. It is not in mere observation, but in the imagination that art's source of energy lies: to art, nature remains 'a storehouse of raw materials, of symbols'. But in Rossetti, the Pre-Raphaelite master, naturalism persists in a curious way: Rossetti was careful to collect the bric-à-brac which provided symbolic support for his 'female heads with floral adjuncts'. By 1898 'subject' has been opted as a mandatory word. It is only possible, Yeats declares in his 1898 essay, to the cynicism of a Degas, repeating a medieval *contemptus feminae* in a 'wearied world'. Degas is implicitly associated with Baudelaire and with Decadence. But a new type of art responds to the mood of *fin de siècle*, one that is not decadent, not tied to naturalism, but 'symbolical', one that represents nature, but in order to find entanglements of the divine essence. Yeats's synthesis recalls that of his friend Arthur Symons, who in 1893 equates Symbolism with Decadence, but by 1898 sharply distinguishes the two. The allusion to Degas is explained by the row over *Au Café* or—the literary, and anecdotal title wished on it—'L'Absinthe'. Degas' painting had been shown at the Grafton Galley in 1893 and the correspondence columns of the press had been inflamed for a month or more. It represents Degas' friend, the painter and etcher Marcellin Desboutin, and Ellen Andrée, actress and model at the Elysée Montmartre, seated at tables at the Nouvelles Athenes. D.S. MacColl gives the English avant-garde view: 'the subject was repulsive, if you like, before Degas made it his'. MacColl's attempt to meet the philistine halfway deceived no one. J.A. Spender retorted that for MacColl 'subject is nothing, the sense of paint, the handling everything'. Sir W.B. Richmond cleverly suggested that like *L'Assomoir*, *Au Café* was a novella in paint, a treatise against drink; but Sickert insisted that too much had been made of 'drink' and 'lessons'; the title ought surely to read *Un homme et une femme assis dans un café*. A collector added the final irony: he pointed out that the 'strong drink' before Desboutin was *black coffee*. Admirers of Degas saw the fundamental issue as the freedom of the artist to choose his own subject: 'that the dignity of the performance does not depend on the dignity of the subject, but on that of him who treats it, is surely indisputable'.[9] Indisputable it should have been by 1893: it was a cliché of the Parisian ateliers; it had been argued over, this 'subject'—'handling' formulaic contrast—since the earlier 1880s in England, and the *Pall Mall Gazette* of 1892 had been full of it.

Yeats's remains the literary reading; 'subject' and literary painting must go: naturalism and imaginative art were no longer sufficiently polarized. The new vocabulary was reinvoked nearly twenty years later when abstract and Cubist art forced on Yeats another dilemma. On 5 March 1916, to his father, Yeats was to write:

> You spoke of all art as imitation, meaning, I conclude, imitation of something in the outer world. To me it seems that it often uses the outer world as a symbolism to express subjective moods. The greater the subjectivity, the less the imitation ... The element of pattern in every art, is, I think, the part that is not imitative, for in the last analysis there will always be somewhere an intensity of pattern that we have never seen with our eyes. In fact, imitation seems to me to create a language in which we say things which are not imitation.
>
> At the present moment, after a long period during which all the arts have put aside almost everything but imitation, there is a tendency to over-emphasize pattern, and a too great anxiety to see that these patterns themselves have novelty.[10]

This seems to take us little further than Image. Yeats returns to the topic nine days later in another letter to his father:

> I feel in Wyndham Lewis's Cubist pictures an element corresponding to rhetoric arising from his confusion of the abstract with the rhythmical. Rhythm implies a living body, a breast to rise and fall, or limbs that dance, while the abstract is incompatible with life. The Cubist is abstract. At the same time you must not leave out rhythm and this rhythm is not imitation. Impressionism by leaving it out brought all this rhetoric of the abstract upon us. I have just been turning over a book of Japanese paintings. Everywhere there is delight in form, repeated yet varied, in curious patterns of lines, but these lines are all an ordering of natural objects though they are certainly not imitation. In every case the artist one feels has had to *consciously* and deliberately arrange his subject. It was the impressionists' belief that this arrangement should be only unconscious and instinctive that brought this violent reaction. They are right in believing that this should be conscious, but wrong in substituting abstract scientific thought for conscious feeling. If I delight in rhythm I love nature though she is not rhythmical. I express my love in rhythm. The more I express it the less can I forget her.[11]

It redefines what in 1898 Yeats had said of Whistler and of Beardsley in his middle period: 'they had thought so greatly of these patterns and rhythms, the road to open symbolism' that 'the images of human life have faded almost perfectly'; 'the arts have learned the denials, but not the fervours of the cloister'. 'A vigorous and visionary beauty' is what Yeats discovered in Althea Gyles, 'the contrary of what is called decadent'. But the second letter of 1916 also takes us to *Autobiographies*. The Love and Penury of the *Symposium* lead to the word 'allegory'; the crude polarizations of one who hates her gift, as Maud Gonne hates her own beauty, lead to the word 'abstraction'.

But it is time to relate Yeats's formulations to Miss Gyles's actual work. He describes her own favourite drawing, *The Rose of God*, which sounds more interesting than the four drawings actually illustrating his *Dome* article, as a 'personification of the beauty which cannot be seen with the bodily eyes, or pictured otherwise than by symbols', in the form of 'a naked woman, whose hands are stretched against the clouds, as upon a cross, in the traditional attitude of the Bride, the symbol of the microcosm in the Kabala; while two winds, the one full of white, the other full of red rose petals, personifying all passion whirl about her and descend upon the fleet of ships and a walled city, personifying the wavering and the fixed powers, the masters of the world in the alchemical symbolism'.[12] Some imperfect but beautiful verses which accompany the drawing describe her as for 'living man's delight and his eternal reverie when dead'.[13] The poem was preserved by Yeats and is heavily revised both by Yeats and Miss Gyles:

When the rose opened its leaves in paradise,
When long expected beauty flowered at length,
They softly sighing set Thee in men's eyes
To waste the strong and bring the weak to strength.

O will that sigh of God with which He made
My garment be a spirit of sighs in Thee,
The hands that tore the purple and betrayed
Will they too rend the rose's mystery?

And wilt Thou shiver standing by the flood
Of the earth's sin, O priestess of the Rose,
When round Thy feet the red leaves fall as blood
And on Thy head the white are shed as snows?

Wilt Thou grow pale with pain when night winds blow
The white leaves deep into the trodden dust,
Wilt Thou burn red with shame when mornings show
Thy red leaves bound about the brows of lust?

With two swift winds, the winds of life and love,
Thou wast blown worldwards from the Rose's heart;
Dark was the Earth below, the sky above,
Save where those winds had swept the clouds apart.

They showered about Thy forehead rose leaves white
They showered about Thy bosom rose leaves red

At Thy eternal majesty the light
Broke as a path for living and for dead.

God made one wind for love eternal white
He made another for love's passion red.
Wrapt Thee round him for living men's delight
And his eternal reverie when dead.

Thou shalt be lonely in the midst of praise,
Unknown, cast-out, with heart that understands
All pain and sorrow. And at the end of days
Be changed into a sceptre in God's hands.[14]

Yeats must have found the rhythms 'inorganic', the inversions ugly. His comments on the four drawings actually illustrated in *The Dome* and those on *The Rose of God* are based on Miss Gyles's letters to him. The first of these letters appears to have been lost; the second, undated, gives in its tone a foretaste of the difficulties she was to impose on him:

> I have just received your telegram asking for the meaning of '*Noah's* Raven' ... it is really but the vaguest idea I once had as part of a romance of the world under the sea. I first did the study for the 'Romance of the Red Sea' with the Queen enthroned on Pharaoh's chariot. But I suppose that this mermaid tempted the Raven with the ring that had belonged to his Master, a magician (or perhaps a magician turned himself into the Raven? but perhaps Mr Oldmeadow would think that if this latter were the case Jehovah would not have let him into the Ark)—pray do not try Mr Oldmeadow any further. I have been very angry with him about my 'Rose' but I cannot help seeing how good he has been all through, he has taken such a lot of trouble and is really wonderful for a parson—you will see the hands of the other sea people have [?] on the treasures of the mighty Earth. I do not think there was any genuine emotion or romantic passion in the sea before they beheld the Rose. (*This* is the rose of the world.) It caused entire revoltion! Perhaps it was lucky for Mr Oldmeadow's feelings I did not choose a later period for illustration. I have written something about them which I will show you sometime.
>
> Is it not dreadful about the Rose of God? I suppose Mr Oldmeadow told you he had rejected it on the grounds—oh I can't go into it now, but it's supposed to ruin the Dome to print it. You hate the only three other finished ones I have. I don't know that he'll like 'Pan' or 'Lilith' but I have another study (if I can get it back in time) it too is deeply religious. It is the study of two figures for a drawing of Pan and his nymphs [illegible] the image of the Star of Bethlehem is seen in the waters at their feet. The Real Star they did not see ... Write a few words about the Star one that can be left out if not wanted. If they use the *other* I will wire

> particulars. You have the Knight; do please speak of the hearts of the bulbs. I needn't explain that they are the symbols of resurrection. People are given to calling this drawing morbid which annoys me. It is a pity about the rose as it is the best bit of *fine* work I have yet done.[15]

Miss Gyles describes the origin of 'The Raven of Noah' in off-hand terms: it might really be a dream, a vision, where Yeats relates his interpretation to Blake and controlled symbolism: 'the story is woven out of as many old symbols as if it were a mystical story in "The Prophetic Books"'. He sharpens the moral of the emblem: if Rosicrucianism tolerates the flesh, man may well 'seek for the ideal in the flesh, and the flesh will be full of illusive beauty, and the spiritual beauty will be far away'. The reading of 'The Knight Upon the Grave of His Lady' is near to Miss Gyles's notes.

The second Pan drawing has not survived. The first is probably identical with the 'The Offering of Pan', which had appeared in the *Commonwealth* in June 1896.[16] Of many versions of the relationship between Pan and Christ—Pan slain by Christ; Pan *as* Christ; Pan living on as a sinister border to the world of civility; Pan as *genius loci* of the Home Counties or Pan within—Miss Gyles plumps for a sentimental reconciliation: Pan offers his pipes to a child who is all head and nimbus. The drawing space is smothered in detail. The central rondel surrounded by a border of stars, foliage and flowers is emblematic presumably of natural and supernatural. Above the rondel, a band shows the Father beneath the Dove with warriors kneeling on the Father's left and angels to his right, corresponding to the three wise men walking out of the left base and mourning fauns and nymphs moving out of the right. At the extreme left and right top of the drawing space are representations of sun and moon with stars. The composition moves away from the trend in the middle 1890s of using white space positively.

A year before the appearance of Yeats's piece in *The Dome*, Miss Gyles had designed the first of his book covers, *The Secret Rose*. This was designed to give the impression of a *grimoire*. In pristine state its appearance is striking if not precisely pleasing. The iconography is related to Golden Dawn rituals and the Tarot; and has been explained in detail by Professor Allen R. Grossman. The only point in his analysis which I would question is his absolute identification of the object on the spine with the spear of Lug 'symbol of everlasting and uncontrollable desire'. Without denying this symbol's presence, the object to my eye suggests a generalized sacred cone and particularly the caduceus, a resonant emblem, relating to Hermes, Thoth and, through its flowering, to Moses and so to a familiar secret wisdom tradition. Symbols concealed as well as revealed. A certain ambiguousness would be appropriate. The caduceus involves hermaphroditism (the kissing heads in the tree of life seem androgynous rather than male and female) and its touch turns to gold.[17] (We have similar forms in other books of the Pan-Celtic Movement: the cover design of Fiona Macleod's *Washer of the Ford* of 1896, for example.) The flowers wreathed round the cone might well be fritillary, a spotted snake flower, elegant, sinister, white-purple-red touched with green and with a drooping cup.

The ambiguity, or rather inconsistency, appears in the lettering. That on the spine is hand-drawn. The 'T' and 'H' are traditional Irish, the 'B' (of 'Butler') is not. Irish makes no distinction in the 'b' (nor with later founts in the 'r' or 's') between upper- and lower-case. 'W' and 'y' do not occur in Irish, so that they have to be mocked-up: 'w' is done as a 'u'. The lettering is condensed. The publisher's imprint is clear and may be in type. On the front cover, the lettering of the title is eccentric (and mediocre) and does not altogether match the lettering of the title on the spine. This is particularly true of the 'r', where the tail is snapped off. The 'a' of Yeats is ordinary English. The form of the 'e' is tenuously nearer to Gaelic script; Miss Gyles's lettering improves as she persists.

To preserve the secret wisdom of the Golden Dawn, Yeats presumably devised the programme for the cover. The Tree of Life there is heavily stylized 'into an intricately twined love-knot, the thorny branches twisting in a complicated imitation of Celtic strap work', as Peter Stansky puts it.[18]

Mr Grossman rightly connects Yeats's cult of the talismanic book with Blake:

> Like Blake, whose dissatisfaction with the existing image of the book led him to reject the conventional modes of printing, Yeats attempted to express his revolt against the imposed image of the sacramental and artistic vehicle and against the paternal image of him by composing a new book and a new self. The talismanic book thus constructed proved to be neither truly sacred nor artistic, but it symbolised like the typographical experimentation which became popular two decades later, the deeply felt necessity to reform the tradition in the direction of a newly found subjective organicism.[19]

Here, I must confess to losing Grossman. The reference to typographical experimentation is presumably to the Continent. But what surely should be insisted on is the radical distinction between Yeats and Blake. In Yeats's books, experimentation stops at the cover. That experimentation should stop at the cover was perhaps inevitable: it was the images of the verse that carried the symbolic weight, and perhaps with commercial publishers no attempt to unite illustrations, borders, initials and text could be attempted (though had Yeats chosen Ricketts at this time or Laurence Housman the tale might have run differently). And had not his collaborator in the Blake edition, Edwin J. Ellis, in his *Seen in Three Days* (1893), attempted to unite the arts in terms of a handwritten text and an image on each page? though he made no attempt to integrate letter and image so that lettering did not become part of the decoration.

The publishers of *Poems, 1899–1905* were to take over Miss Gyles's design for the spine of *The Secret Rose* but altered its dimensions. The spine of *The Secret Rose* is repeated for the augmented reprint of *The Celtic Twilight* published by Bullen in 1902 (Wade 35). On the front cover, bottom right, a moon at its first quarter is pierced by three downward arrows. It is uncertain whether this design is by Miss Gyles.

Of *Poems* (1899), J. W. Gleeson White commented on the uneven and marginal quality of her talent, though he conceded it to be 'remarkable': 'The name of Althea Giles (*sic*) belongs properly to the neo-Celtic school and her cover ... is highly characteristic of a sombre, mystical and weird imaginative power expressing itself through a talent still vagrant and diffuse.'[20] In her use of gold on dark blue ground and the total drawing space, Miss Gyles was far from modern. Designers were indeed now applying two or more colours, but generally in the flat manner of the poster, such as Beardsley's design for *The Dream and the Business* of 'John Oliver Hobbes', or the design for the translation of Sudermann's *Regina* published by Lane in 1898.

The lettering of *Poems* is as eclectic and capricious as that of *The Secret Rose*. The 'm' is not Irish, a blown-up version of the lower-case. The 'a' in 'Yeats' does not turn up in any traditional fount but it does turn up in such nineteenth-century founts as were attempting to emulate traditional formal scripts (e.g. the productions of the Irish Archaeological Society). This again may be the effect of a necessary compression. There are odd variations in thickness of lettering in the author's name. In 'Fisher Unwin' there is a proper version of the 'n' but not of 'f' or of 'h'.

The Wind among the Reeds is Miss Gyles's most accomplished design. Grossman has sufficiently analysed the relation of the book's cover with its content. The cover expresses the origin of inspiration and the posture 'is that of the poet in Coleridge's *Dejection* who seeks to recover a lost harmony between mind and nature through the mediation of emotion symbolized by the wind rising in the strings of the Aeolian lute, like the "rushing of a host in rout", a "self-image as the overthrown artist, the reed bowed by the wind"'. The reeds on the front and back cover look more like bamboos; they are jointed and mixed up with long ribbon-like leaves (Papyrus, perhaps, probably too broad a head for bulrushes). On both front and back there is a well-defined base panel and on the front an equally well-defined top panel. This top panel contains the title in an almost consistent Celtic lettering, while the author's name on the front base panel, again in Celtic, is surrounded by some Beardsleyish *japonaiserie*. The base panel on the back cover presents formalized water. In this design there is greater use of the dark blue base colour, while the back cover with its whip-lash leaves is nearer to the prevalent *art nouveau* idiom. Asymmetry renders it more visually exciting than the front cover. It is less symbolic than decorative in treatment. In its rare, pristine condition this is a distinguished book.

The lettering on the spine of *The Wind among the Reeds* is academically accurate with the exception of the 'e' which has no extended crossbar. This is an English capital 'B' which is not found in Gaelic founts until they began to be aligned to international use. The author's name is vertically compressed. The imprint is in roman. On the front cover the lettering is again accurate with the exception once more of the 'B'. The composition here is less firm than on the spine, but we can trace a continuous evolution from *The Secret Rose*.

Miss Gyles's other cover design of this period, for Matthew Russell's *The Idyls of Killowen* (1898), has some dully formalized patterned shamrocks, a theme not of her own choice. The lettering here is more effortless than that of *The Secret Rose* and pleasantly spaced on the spine. It is not academic but has an Irish flavour. The 't' on the spine is uncial but not peculiar to Irish; there is also a mixing of lower- and upper-case, but this is diffused practice in the 1890s. The 'l' curls up here, and in Irish, but also elsewhere. The 'M' is an uncial form.

At about this time Miss Gyles made a pen drawing of Yeats in profile stylized as Rosicrucian mage blowing a rose petal with rose petals on the top right and left base. As Stansky puts it: 'for Althea Gyles, Yeats was the reality, these symbols merely images'. Above the mage's head is a haloed rose, outlined in dots, employed by the mystical draughtsman, another protégé of Yeats, W.T. Horton, as indicating souls or, according to Stansky, 'inner beings surrounding and emanating from his worldly beings'. Beardsley, on the other hand, uses delicate dots for ironic purposes. This roseal design was used with the petal for the eloquently simple cover of *The Shadowy Waters* (1901). It was, according to a note by Yeats in the New York Public Library, intended as a portrait for *The Wind among the Reeds*, but the plate was, Yeats believed, lost and only one copy of the drawing survived.

Why did Althea Gyles do no more designs for Yeats? His letters of this time give an oblique answer. On 20 November 1899 he tells Lady Gregory that the brokers are to be put in Miss Gyles's rooms: 'she took the brokers quite cheerfully and seemed rather to enjoy the sensation'. And on the 28th of the same month to the same correspondent he wrote:

> A very unpleasant thing has happened but it is so notorious that there is no use in hiding it. Althea Gyles, after despising Symons and Moore for years because of their morals, has ostentatiously taken up with Smithers, a person of so immoral a life that people like Symons and Moore despise him. She gave an at home the other day and poured out tea with his arm round her waist and even kissed him at intervals. I told her that she might come to my at homes as much as she liked but that I absolutely forbade her to bring Smithers ... Last night she came, and afterwards Smithers, and now I am writing to repeat more emphatically my refusal to have Smithers come. This may, and probably will, make her quarrel with me, for which I shall be sorry as I imagine I am about the only person who belongs to the orderly world she is likely to meet from this out. She seems to be perfectly mad, but is doing beautiful work. I did my best last week to make her see the necessity for some kind of disguise, but it seems to be a point of pride with her to observe none. It is all made the more amazing because she knows all about Smithers's past. She is in love, and because she has some genius to make her thirst for realities and not enough of intellect to see the temporal use of unreal things she is throwing off every remnant of respectability with an almost religious enthusiasm. Certainly the spirit 'blows where it listeth', and the best one can give its victims is charity.[21]

It was all rather difficult. Dublin malice, a poet's insight, a touch of middle-class virtue and Yeats's hieratic sense of his own occasions combine. And about the spring of 1900, that *agon* on the astral plane between Aleister Crowley and Yeats had taken place with the Golden Dawn of London as prize. The *agon* was without quarter: it involved Crowley's burglarizing of the Order's rooms dressed in black mask, Scottish kilt and golden dagger, his ejection by Yeats and others followed by a law suit. From Crowley's short story 'At the Fork of the Road' published in his magazine, the *Equinox*, in 1909, we gather than Althea Gyles acted as Yeats's agent. In the tale she appears at 'Hypatia Gay'. Crowley himself makes the identification in a holograph marginal note in a copy of the *Equinox* now at the Warburg Institute. As a consequence of Crowley's counter-magic, which was sexually based, Miss Gyles unpredictably succumbed to Leonard Smithers, publisher of erotica and collector of first editions of women: Althea may well have been a virgin in 1899. It appears that eight years later Yeats and Crowley were still contending astrally for Althea's soul.

While Yeats was writing about Miss Gyles to Lady Gregory, the subject was writing to him:

> Smithers is being *awfully* nice both about the work itself and paying and now at last I shall be able to start with the proceeds. It will be finished by August and I mean to return to the country and write the play and do my own beloved pictures. I have no more of the little play done but when I have I will send it to you to show Mr Symons—please thank him for me in advance. I have 'a few words' for both you and him which are that it is very wrong to slander so *excellent* a man as Mr Smithers.
>
> I think the best design you can have for the bookplate would be a simple square filled with the 'dust of the Dead'.
>
> I should not take more than
> three months to do this.
> I have written a good
> many short things chiefly
> about Angus and the Red
> Hound.[22]

Four of the short things survive among Yeats's papers: parodies of *The Wind among the Reeds* mode. The first is addressed to 'Angus the Beautiful', subtitled 'The Prayer of Gervaise the Hunter Who Slew Himself':

> Thro' dust my ears have listened for the tread
> Of Thy fair feet, O Waker of the dead.

For sign of Thee mine eyes have wearied long
Thro' bare boughs gazing upwards. For Thy song
My heart hath longed so that it might not sleep
Tho' quiet is my bed and dark and deep.
Waiting the Red Hound lies, and in his side
My spear is bright as on the day he died.
O Angus, 'Lord of Day' and all Delight,
Come quickly I am weary of the night.

The second piece is a sonnet, written in rapid pencil and concluding with two unrhymed lines, 'The Bard Alathor in Heaven':

I dwell in the white Dunes of God a guest.
I hear no more the murmuring of the sea.
I see no more the Island of the Blest
To whom I gave my life for victory.
I sing no more the glorious deeds of Kings.
Now no more echoes of old Battles wake
My lips to song—I am gone past these things
Into a peace they have no power to break.
The Dunes of God with peace are walled about,
Far up above the stars that shine for men,
Listlessly wandering by them, I lean out,
Bending far forward over them—ah then
I feel my Heart—grown hot—against them beat—
And they as barriers of Death grown cold.

There can be no doubt about who is hidden behind the *wortspiel* of the Outlaw's name: 'The Prayer of Oona for her Lover Horemon the Outlaw':

O quivering voice pray on, O pray,
Cease not your passionate prayer for me,

Miss Gyles begins in mellow Tennysonian chime; but soon modulates into a twilight echo:

The seven hounds chase me night and day.
No refuge holds the earth or sea.
Only your prayers God's angels hold
As flaming swords they may not pass.
Your prayers unbar the gates of gold
And bar the gates of brass.
O steadfast Heart pray on, O pray;
Cease not your crying night or day.

And in another poem she refers to that symbol of male sexuality once more:

> Fling wide your gates, let me in honour depart.
> I hear the Red Hound calling to my heart.

Yeats did indeed fling wide the gates. But if he did not take the message of the poems too seriously, he was serious enough about the odd 'dust of the Dead' proposal, for once more we find him, on 21 December 1899, keeping Lady Gregory informed about the goings-on of Horemon, surrogate of the Red Hound:

> I am afraid it will be some time before Althea Gyles does that bookplate. I have heard or seen nothing of her since I wrote her that letter, and expect, or rather Symons suspects, that Smithers has forbid[den] her to come near me. In which case I shall hardly see her until Smithers is a lost illusion. I wish I could have postponed the quarrel until the plate was done but it was not possible, for I could not have permitted my guests to meet Smithers, who would have come drunk as likely as not. Althea Gyles hardly means a final quarrel as she has left a number of her books with me including some in a loose brown paper which she asked me not to look at—I conclude they have affectionate inscriptions. I keep all these to evade the bailiffs but refused some improper Japanese ivories which are probably loans from the admirable Smithers.[23]

And in Faith Compton Mackenzie's novel *Tatting* where Althea Gyles emblematically appears as Ariadne Berden, the outcome of the Smithers business is transpicuously summarized:

> after treating reasonable admirers with prudish contempt, [she] had fallen into the arms of an abominable creature of high intelligence, no morals and the vivid imagination which was perhaps what she had been waiting for ... Ariadne lost caste, and when the affair ended after more than a year of heady intoxication, and with a certain amount of inspired work, she collapsed.[24]

The inspired work possibly consisted in the illustrations to *The Song of Songs* (which I have not been able to trace) and to Wilde's poem 'The Harlot's House', both published by Smithers.

The cover design for Dowson's *Decorations in Verse and Prose*, issued by Smithers in 1899, is not particularly inspired; or, if inspired, more by Selwyn Image than any unexpected Muse. The cover is in vellum and consists of a squat rectangle enclosing a smaller rectangle, and so looking back to the consistent use of this

Italian idiom by the Century Guild designers. There is a small formalized pattern at the corners within the space created by the two rectangles. This includes the dots that one finds on Rossetti's designs for his sister's poems, a witty reference to designer's tools. The main design on the front cover is floral and formalized. The lettering again recalls Image, but is rather more eccentrically styled, and on the back on the bottom right there is a pattern of thorns and foliage which strongly recalls the cover design of the *Century Guild Hobby Horse*. The illustrations for Wilde's *Harlot's House* are her most achieved work and represent a move from a debased 1890s black-and-white idiom to a tonal fantasy. They are distinctly nearer to Beardsley than to the average W.T. Horton image. *Art nouveau* curvilinear waverings have mostly vanished, and so too has the Celtic detail.

Miss Gyles collapsed certainly and did no more book designing. That field was presumably associated in her mind too strongly with Smithers.

By the year 1900 the closest phase of Miss Gyles's association with Yeats was over. In that year he selected her poem 'Sympathy', already published in *The Dome*, for an anthology edited by Stopford Brooke and T.W. Rolleston, adding a prefatory note to the effect that she might 'come to be one of the most important of the little group of Irish poets who seek to express indirectly through myths and symbols, or directly in little lyrics full of prayers and lamentations, the desire of the soul for spiritual beauty and happiness. She has done, besides the lyric I quote, which is charming in form and substance, a small number of poems full of original symbolism and spiritual ardour, though as yet lacking in rhythmical subtlety. Her drawings and book-covers, in which precise symbolism never interferes with beauty of design, are as yet her most satisfactory expression of herself'.[25] Miss Gyles was now his rather than AE's disciple and he seems to have been prepared, if not to approve, at least to condone her stammering imitations of himself. 'Sympathy' is neat, but distinctly finite:

The colour gladdens all your heart;
   You call it Heaven, dear, but I—
Now Hope and I are far apart—
   Call it the sky.

I know that Nature's tears have wet
   The world with sympathy; but you,

Who know not any sorrow yet,
  Call it the dew.

The next episode in Miss Gyles's story may be gathered from a letter of Arthur Symons to his future wife, postmarked 15 September 1900.

> Rhoda, shall I tell you about a sad little story which has just come under my eyes? A woman knocked at my door late last night with a letter and parcel from a girl I know called Althea Gyles, an artist and poet of uncertain but really remarkable talent ... It was a landlady from a side street in Hampstead Road, and she brought a bundle of MSS poems. The girl wrote to say she was ill in bed, had been ill for a year, thought she was going to die, and was to be moved into hospital on Monday, and before it was too late she wanted to put together a little book of her best poems. She asked me to go over them and decide; and asked if I would come and see her. I called to-day and found her lying in bed in a bare room without a thing in the place, except five books (one a presentation copy from Oscar Wilde) and one or two fantastic gold ornaments which she used to wear, chloral by her side, and the bed strewn with MSS. She was very white, with her red hair all over the pillow. I stayed a couple of hours, going over all her poems with her (some are full of a queer, genuine kind of poetry). As I was going to go I said 'Can I lend you any books?' She said: 'I've been in bed for three weeks and I've had nothing but these old books of mine. I wish you would lend me Wm. Morris's first volume of poems'. Then she asked me to let her see my Dowson article (she used to know him) and said, quaintly: 'When I meet him I'll tell him all about it!' Then, as if she were letting out a secret she had not meant to tell, she said: 'All my friends have deserted me: I've not seen a creature but the doctor ever since I've been ill. Look (she waved her hand towards the wall) I've taken down all their photographs. I've only left my own now. I don't know anyone else now.' I sent her up some of the books she needed, by special messenger, as soon as I got home, and on Monday I am going to get something else from the London Library. I have carried off a poem (really fine) to try if I can get it into the *Saturday* [*Review*]. I'm awfully sorry for her, though I found her a very trying person when she was well, and she used to rather hate me, I thought. I can't imagine how she came to send for me. I'm afraid she hasn't a penny. Lady Colin Campbell used to be a great friend of hers, but now she has left her like all the rest. I can't possibly do anything for her, beyond going to see her sometimes and lending her books. Her people are rich, but she has the pride of the devil, and won't take a penny from them. I may get £2 from the *Saturday*, if they take her poem.[26]

Lady Colin had been mixed up in a particularly notorious divorce case and had earned her living since with her pen. By birth she was also Irish, spontaneous, high-spirited. She would not have been likely to drop Althea simply for taking up with Smithers, though she may well have warned Althea off. But Althea's shrill reaction to the end of her affair may well have exhausted Lady Colin's patience. A memorial of their friendship remains in Lady Colin's portrait of Althea.

The *Saturday Review* duly published on 22 September 'For a Sepulchre', one of Miss Gyles's better poems. Here, two millennia after Catullus, 85, she discovers the antinomies of sexual encounter:

Between the hands, between the breasts,
Down the white body twixt the thighs,
The sword is laid, until it rests
Upon the once-kissed feet. Men's eyes
Read 'Odi et Amo' graven there.

Behind cold eyelids now fast sealed,
Behind cold breasts that rose and fell
With passion, what has Life revealed?
The great sword guards her secret well
With 'Odi et Amo' graven there.

O was it Love that conquered Hate?
Or was it hate that set her free?—
To Death all questioners come late.
The sword and the woman all may see
And 'Odi et Amo' graven there.

But oddly if this is the poem Symons carried off, it radiates strong echoes of the phrasing of Dowson's 'Extreme Unction' and the use of the refrain is also suggestive. 'The Sword', a less happy version of the same poem, ends:

the high sun thrust
A golden ray deep down into the dust
That was the woman's body and found there
A great sword, all rust-eaten saving where
It has lain on her heart.—O heart's desire!
It turned the word 'Amo' to flaming fire.

In the *Candid Friend*, a scurrilous paper run by Frank Harris, Miss Gyles published on 1 May 1901 'The Song of the Seine: To the Court of Kings', which deals with the same set of experiences:

My silver ripples wash away
All madness from the brain of man,

In my cold darkness, you shall surely say,
  'Oh, but Death's arms are tenderer than
My lover's arms, wherein I lay'.
  Those arms from which you fled at last,
Shuddering through the night and day,
  With maddened hands, that strove to cast
From out your life the fires that cling,
  My depth can quench and heal, and low,
Long lullabies my sedges sing
  To a heart that, beating upon a heart,
Slowly heard awful echoes there
  I will draw you to silence, so far apart,
Memory comes not, nor despair.

And you poor body, who once joyed so
  In my city, and found it fond and fair
(Not even yet a year ago)
  In royal state I will take you there;
Deaf to man's laughter and man's lies,
  That is the royal way to go;
Cold to man's kisses, and with eyes
  Too calm for tears and triumphs. Low
My courtier willows shall bow the head,
  And proud, white clouds their shadows throw
Before the cold, triumphant dead.
  O! Death is a royal road to go.
And men in the city of your delight—
  Glad city that once your laughter heard,
And the beat of your heart in the hush of the night,
  Shall do your bidding without a word.
Without command they shall carry you where
  Kings—conquerors of the world—keep state,
Whose courtiers do not even dare
  To speak to them—they are far too great,
With a conquered world beneath their feet,
  Serene, indifferent, cold, they wait,
No voices can make those calm hearts beat
  Not even the voices of Love and Hate.
'O Silver Singer!' the woman said,
  'Would that you held me cold and dead;
But to do your bidding—then must I
  Cast out Ivoe ere I could die'.

Two other poems of this period may be quoted. The first is 'The Garden at Dusk':

As colours at the shrouding of the day,
So dim, remote, so very far away

Seem supreme joy and sorrow which I fled,
But bending close I see the rose is red.

O kind, concealing darkness for the sake
Of all thou hidest, let not bound love wake
For I have called him—still would call him dead.
Ah yet, beneath day's shroud, the rose burns red.

To the *Kensington* of 1901, Miss Gyles contributed two poems. One, a sentimental Nativity offering, need not concern us; the other belongs to the group of poems connected with Smithers, but is in a mode more Yeatsian than the 'Odi et Amo' poems.

O Heart-shaped rose-filled space between
  The Trees of Knowledge and of Life,
In that delirious moment seen
  When passionless peace is turned to strife,
How fair before those eager eyes
  The rose-bowered path from Paradise!

O Heart-shaped, thorn-filled space between
  The Trees of Sacrifice and Pain,
So from the higher side is seen
  The old Land whereof our hearts are fain,
How hard before those tear-blind eyes
  The thorn-sharp path to Paradise!

Yeats himself may well have had something to do with placing these contributions. The *Kensington* dealt with all the arts in high dilettante fashion, had art-work competitions in the manner of the *Studio*, and there was some accent on women contributors. Yeats himself contributed and of his circle, Olivia Shakespear and Pamela Colman-Smith.

Yeats's increasing involvement with the Irish Dramatic Movement probably accounts as much as anything else for his dwindling relationship with Miss Gyles after 1901. In an undated letter, probably of 1899, she had written:

> I meant to write to you long ago and congratulate you on your success with the Celtic Theatre. I hope it really was as successful as I heard and then again to answer your other letter but I have been and am still so busy. Of course I will do the block plate with much pleasure but you will have to wait a bit as I must finish this job and then get poor Sir Vincent's and Stephen Gwynn's brother's done any way if not before at the same time.

> I am doing a book for Smithers. It is by Oscar Wilde & is called 'The Harlot's House'.[27] It is most interesting and I am supposed to be doing it very well. It's chiefly shadows on a blind.
>
> I hope the drawings won't shock Mr Symons. He won't see them in a crude state but modified by Mr Smithers!
>
> People are being horrid to me about it so please listen to this, don't say anything to any of my personal acquaintances about it such as the Coopers or Gore Booths etc. if you chance to come across them. They can do what they like when the book comes out but I cannot endure any more lectures on the subject this hot weather. They are most impertinent. Nothing will alter my determination to do it. I have two most excellent motives & I cannot have my best moods betrayed for no object. Mr Colvin is horribly shocked. Dear Lady Colin of course sympathises.[28]

How revealing, the arch formalities and breathlessness of the style, the mild tinges of paranoia; but what were the two excellent motives? Aesthetic hunger, perhaps, and, I would hazard, her loyalty to Wilde. It was this admirable sentiment that in 1904 prevented the publication of a volume of her poems. Symons had now succeeded Yeats as her principal patron, and a letter of his to Thomas B. Mosher of 5 July 1904 invites the famous pirate of Portland, Maine, to publish her 'slight, fantastic' verses with 'their genuine touch of lyric quality'. The comic pathos of her dealings with the publisher follow:

> [He] accepted her book, and was having it set up, when he discovered that she absolutely insisted on dedicating it 'to the beautiful memory of Oscar Wilde'. He would have passed everything but the word 'beautiful', but there he stuck, and she also, and the MS was returned. The point is ridiculous on both sides, but she is quite unmanageable and unpractical.[29]

Four years earlier, with a shrewd eloquence, Yeats had written of her response to Wilde's death:

> 'He was so kind, nobody ever lived who was so kind'. As she said it I thought of Homer's description of the captive women weeping in seeming for Patroclus yet each weeping for her own sorrow because he was ever kind.[30]

And in a letter to Rowland Strong of 29 July, Symons alludes to Laurence Binyon knowing more about Althea than himself, to her having a touch of madness or genius or both and suggesting that two or three of her designs could go in the volume of poems he was asking Strong to press on Duckworth the publishers. The letter also informs us that Miss Gyles was at this time in deplorable health and utter poverty.

What *was* wrong with her? Anaemia? Consumption? Or did she, like Ralph Touchett, make consumption her career, a position she had taken up and worked hard at? Symons's letters indicate a pattern. From now on Miss Gyles was to be passed from patron to patron, from friend to friend, intermittently in hospital or in nursing home, gradually receding into obscurity and squalor. Symons did his best for her until his breakdown in 1908. To the second issue of the *Venture* in 1905, Miss Gyles contributed a poem on the highly ninetyish topic of Pierrot. (The magazine is itself the last of those sumptuous annuals of the previous decade such as the *Pageant* or the *Parade*. Yeats and his circle contribute; nineties figures, such as John Gray and Vincent O'Sullivan, are in evidence, while Cecil French, who had appeared in the *Kensington* and was to be one of Miss Gyles's firmest patrons, writes on a late, late Pre-Raphaelite painter.)

O some there are who bury deep
Lost joy in a grave far out of sight,
Saying 'O trouble me not, but sleep
In silence by day and night.'

But I have left my joy to stray
Alive in the wood of my Delight,
Where the thrush and the linnet sing by day
And the nightingale by night.

But I—I wander away, away
Far down where the high road stretches white,
And I laugh and sing for the crowd by day
And weep for my heart by night.

I wait for the Hour when Death shall say:
'O come to the wood of my Delight,
Where thy Love shall sing to thee all the day
And lie on thy breast all night.'

And in the *Academy* of December 1906, she returns to the days of 1899 and 1900 for the last time in a poem entitled 'From Rosamor Dead to Favonius for Whom She Died'.

You loved my rounded cheeks!
They have grown thin and white,
You loved my carmine lips!
They give no more delight.

You loved my flame-bright hair!
Quenched now its gleaming gold.
You loved my fragrant flesh!
'Tis waxen stark and cold.

But ah! the one thing, Dear,
You did not love in me,
Blooms soft, and red, and gold,
Fragrant immortally.

Not you, nor Time, nor Death,
Have any power to move
One crimson petal from
My perfect rose of Love.

Yet when Death calls to you
The breath of Love shall part
The petals of my rose
And bare its burning heart.

In a letter probably of September 1908, Yeats tells Florence Farr 'a fine tale of Althea Gyles. She brought a prosperous love-affair to an end by reading Browning to the poor man in the middle of the night. She collects the necessities of life from her friends and spends her own money on flowers'.[31] About 1910 Miss Gyles met Clifford Bax and contributed a number of poems to his occultist magazine *Orpheus*. One of these which appeared in the January issue of 1912 (p.27), 'Freedom (Summer Afternoon)', represents a return to the manner of AE:

Here where each moment transubstantiating
  With Beauty's alchemy celestial fire
For the gross senses, leaves us rapt, awaiting
  The longed-for vision of the soul's desire,

Hailing the dawn the Earth yields up her treasure
  From out the shadowy empire of the Moon:
Colour on colour, beauty none can measure,
  Glowing and flaming to the golden noon!

In halcyon pause that bids the body slumber
  When Beauty burns a clear unshaken flame;

To joy beyond all joys that man can number,
  To knowledge past all knowledge man can name,

Goes the free soul, soaring beyond the voices
  Of the loud world, beyond the dust that clings
To dust, into the land where love rejoices
  In unity, nor hopes, nor fears but sings!

And when the joy of that celestial singing
  Shall echo poignantly through lips of clay
We shall be even as torch-bearers bringing
  Into the night the message of the day.

The diction is tired, but Miss Gyles's technical adroitness in the handling of enjambment is notable. This increased technical facility marks 'De Profundis', though the Tennyson and Alice Meynell echoes and the sibilants of the fifth line limit its achievement:

Out of the deeps, O voice, out of the deeps
You call the long unwept; and my heart weeps.

You call the long unprayed; and my heart prays,
And the long years seem only as short days.

O marvellous voice, cease singing, cease, O cease!
Lest my will—overcome at last—release

My Conqueror Captive—Lest I run to greet
The heart I have forbidden my heart to meet.

In 1957 I discussed Miss Gyles with Bax, and he recalled that when first they met her hair was already verging on grey and that she was living at that time in Paradise Walk, a slum quarter of Chelsea, where she had a draggled bed-sitting room. Bax was unncessarily sharp: 'She would lie in her grubby bed till noon ... a born dependent, a parasite, emotional and mental'. He passed her on to Eleanor Farjeon, who passed her on to Cecil French, though French indeed had been concerned with her affairs as early as 1899. French speaks of her as 'a noble difficult being who invariably became the despair of those who had helped her'. At some time after 1910 she moved to Folkestone where she lived in a small cottage overlooking the harbour, cultivating a garden which was much admired by her friends. At Folkestone six carols—a kind practised by Herbert Horne, Selwyn Image and John Gray among nineties poets—were privately printed for the Order of the Holy Mount.

Perhaps Miss Gyles sympathized with A.E. Waite's Christian Party when the Golden Dawn had its second schism. At all events her interests were now extended to vegetarianism, anti-vivisection, Buddhism and the casting of horoscopes. In 1914 she published a children's book, letters on art under the pseudonym of 'John Meade', and at this period was contributing to the *Vineyard*, the organ of the Peasant Art Guild and connected with the John Ruskin school at Haslemere: AE was another contributor.

Faith Compton Mackenzie's *Tatting* is a *roman à clef*. It is placed in 1909 and describes a visit that Althea made to the Rev. Sandys Wason (editor of the *Spirit Lamp* before Alfred Douglas), writer of elegant nonsense verse and a very advanced Anglo-Catholic who held the two Cornish parishes of Cury and Gunwalloe. Two friends of Wason's (the author and her husband) rescue Ariadne Berden (Althea) from fading away in Chelsea:

> Those blazing feverish eyes, that cavernous mouth, lacking teeth that she could not afford, that wild faded hair: so proud and poor, her purse still yawning exhausted on the chimney-piece, with the dead rose for company, her rent in arrears, and only one poem accepted by a literary weekly in six months. In justice to the enlightened weekly, it must be conceded that it was the only poem she had sent in. Inspiration was drying up. She lay on her camp-bed without even her pencil poised, gazing on her precious Beardsley, solitary on the whitewashed wall. Aubrey himself had given it to her and it had never been published. A delicious riot of fauns and satyrs ... But oh! she had said that long ago. Now it didn't inspire. Aubrey was dead. Life was surely over.

So with the frail smile, famous black cape and saffron scarf she comes to Cornwall and almost completes a fresco for Wason's church. But that Beardsleyish Madonna fades when she unexpectedly returns to Ireland, having been invited by an aunt who had sold the big house in London to join her in a new home. Faith Compton Mackenzie's husband is less charitable and less amused, if more amusing, in his memoirs. He places the episode in 1908 and describes Miss Gyles as looking on arrival rather like part of the decorations of a harvest festival which had been caught up unwittingly by the congregation and dropped ouside. 'Her large-brimmed black straw hat was wreathed with poppies; her green silk dress hung upon her, not in graceful folds, but in the depressions one may see in a field of hay-grass beaten down by heavy rains'. Althea's physical appearance was no better: cheeks once perhaps youthfully blooming were now pale; her hair 'no doubt once autumn gold' was now 'as dead as a faded rug; her pale blue eyes lacked lustre'. To life in a small cottage, she was hardly adapted, always bringing in 'armfuls of flowers, grasses which she stuck into any receptacle she could find; in the course of arranging these armfuls she used to throw on the floor whatever vegetation she did not need for her vases'. The lady who 'did' remarked that she would like to sweep Miss Gyles herself into the dustbin. The Mackenzies were glad to project an excuse to be rid of this dim latter-day Meg Merrilees.[32]

If the aunt was not fictive, the arrangement was brief, or perhaps Miss Gyles simply refused to take it up. Her later years were to be spent in those dreary bed-sitting suburbs of South London, moving from Tulse Hill to Sydenham, casting horoscopes, collecting antiques of a shadowy value. Her family were anxious to help; she refused all offers. The final room contained no furniture, only a chaise-longue and a mass of valueless trinkets and china. After several falls, she died in a nursing home near the Crystal Palace in the January of 1949.

Aubrey was indeed dead and so too was Yeats. In those years when a Second great war had been lately consummated, burying even more irrevocably the world she had known, the last stragglers from the nineties, Symons and M.P. Shiel, Conal O'Riordan, Rhys and Arthur Machen, were all 'experiencing the last curiosity'. Althea had outlived them all; but she too belonged to the Beardsley period; she too had died long before.[33]

Notes

1. *Dome*, n.s., I (1898), p.233.
2. *Irish Theosophist* III, 86. I have not been able to identify Miss Gyles's contributions to this periodical or indeed the contributions she is presumed to have made to other Irish periodicals in the 1890s.
3. *Autobiographies* (London, 1955), pp.237–8.
4. See *Aegydiana: Gleanings among the Gyles's* (privately printed, 1910). In Faith Compton Mackenzie's *Tatting* (London, 1957), p.31, Althea's farewell note appears as 'I am going away and will never come back. *I am called*'. Called, that is, to the vocation of art.
5. *Pall Mall Magazine* IV, p.161.
6. *Essays and Introductions* (London, 1961), p.148.
7. The essay was based on a lecture of 1882 and published in *Century Guild Hobby Horse* I (1884), p.48.
8. *Century Guild Hobby Horse* III (1888), p.118.

9. For a useful summary of the controversy, see R. Pickvance, 'L'Absinthe in England', *Apollo* LXXVII, 15, p.395 (col. 1), p.398 (col. 3).
10. *The Letters of W.B. Yeats*, ed. Allan Wade (London, 1954), p.607.
11. *Ibid.*, p.608.
12. *Dome*, n.s. I, p.234.
13. *Ibid.*, p.235.
14. From the collection of Senator Michael Yeats.
15. *Ibid.* Ernest Oldmeadow was the editor of *The Dome*, where the drawings and Yeats's article appeared.
16. *Commonwealth*, I, 6 (1896), p.221.
17. The caduceus is much discussed in one of Yeats's sources, Goblet D'Alviella, *The Migration of Symbols*. The English version was published in 1894; see pp.225, 237 and *passim*.
18. I am indebted to a sight of Dr Stansky's unpublished work on some of the minor artists of the 1890s.
19. Allen R. Grossman, *Poetic Knowledge in the Early Yeats* (Charlottesville, Va., 1969), pp.47–8.
20. *Studio*, special winter number, 1899–1900, p.32.
21. *Letters*, p.330.
22. From the collection of Senator Michael Yeats.
23. *Letters*, p.332.
24. MacKenzie, *Tatting*, (London, 1957), p.12.
25. Stopford A. Brooke and T.W. Rolleston (eds), *A Treasury of Irish Poetry in the English Tongue* (London, 1900), p.475.
26. From the collection of Symons papers at Princeton University.
27. Published by Smithers under the imprint of the Mathurin Press, probably in 1904. The name of the press may allude to Wilde's ancestor and object of his admiration, the author of *Melmoth the Wanderer*.
28. From the collection of Senator Michael Yeats.
29. Symons papers, Princeton University.
30. *Letters*, p.347. In a letter of 24 February 1900, Wilde asks after Althea: 'has she still the green wand?' and he refers to her in one of his last letters as 'an artist of great ability'. See *The Letters of Oscar Wilde*, ed. Rupert Hart-Davis (London, 1962), pp.817, 843.
31. *Letters*, p.511.
32. Mackenzie, *Tatting*, pp.8, 97–8; and Compton Mackenzie, *My Life and Times*, Octave 4 (London, 1965), pp.36, 38–9.
33. In 1957 I was privileged to meet Mrs Lena Barrington, Miss Gyles's surviving sister, a memorable lady of memorable age. Mrs Barrington with great generosity presented to Reading University Library such papers of Miss Gyles as were in her possession, securing the equally generous permission of her daughter, Mrs Joyce Cazalet. Among these were a typescript of the greater number of Miss Gyles's poems; the first chapters of two novels—*Mrs Campion's Campaign* and *Pilgrimage*; a number of miscellaneous essays; two children's stories and several drafts of the play which Miss Gyles mentions in her letters to W.B. Yeats.

7

Yeats and Lissadell

I

Sacred persons; sacred places. One definition, that, of the principal subject, the principal itself perhaps, of Yeats's poetry. It was precisely in the years, around 1912, which witnessed his sense of acute alienation from Ireland; of failure in love and fear of age; failure in the Abbey Theatre; of the need for new directions in verse as in the spiritual life, that the poems about his friends and the places connected with them began to appear; a mode never to be abandoned; persons and places. John O'Leary, Easter 1916, Coole Park and Lady Gregory, poems deliberately conceived as historical acts. Writing them, Yeats was deliberately creating a version of the history of modern Ireland that he wished to transmit as document to posterity: 'an Ireland the poets have imagined, terrible and gay'. A poem has many lives and their number cannot be limited by the fiat of the literary critic: trouble comes only when we are confused in our minds about which life, which mode of existence or operation we are describing. This mode, the historical mode, of the projection and creation of history, is entirely valid, and concern with it is entirely valid. The poem is an act embracing the objects of concern: the house of Lissadell, the bust of Maud Gonne, the churchyard at Drumcliffe.

Sacred persons: people, that is what most interested Yeats. No poet in the English tradition since Pope—not even Browning—has been more consistently, more continuously, more obviously moved and excited by human personality. It is not Plato, it is not pictures, that rivals that ardent achievement. He found his stimulus and material for his poetry in men and women. He sees them in time, as he saw himself, caught in a moment that reveals the self, by action or gesture or by stance and appearance. He was probably always more moved by the living image than by the painter's. And ruthless, self-contained, though he may seem to be, and indeed was, a marked susceptibility to the impact of personality is present throughout his life. It was through people that he found his way to ideas, whether through dialectic, submission or plain curiosity. His father, or Madame Blavatsky, or Macgregor Mathers, or Charles Shannon, Arthur Symons, Lionel Johnson, Ezra Pound or Synge, or W.T. Horton. The process continued to the end of his life: F.R. Higgins, Dorothy Wellesley, or the Shri Purohit. The list is endless.

Stephen Spender has a good remark about Yeats:

> The Symbolists, and Rilke, are content for the most part to translate their experiences into terms of their own inner life, and create symbols which the reader can only understand by entering their closed-up intellectual spheres. Yeats is consumed by a passion to project his metaphors into an external framework which supports and affirms them, giving them as it were a life or super-life of their own, outside his own subjectivity.[1]

That external framework includes, as I have suggested, Hindu metaphysics, Rosicrucianism and, most rewardingly, Irish history at some dramatic moments in its mostly dramatic development. The political and sectarian divisions of Ulster and the South remain witnesses to the voraciousness of a past that always tends to engulf the present. It is a record which has often memorably, often sentimentally merely, fallen into the diagrams of historians and the passionate oral history of the people themselves; a history which is fluid, open, self-generating. The ease with which Yeats mythologized his present owes much to that.

Yeats's elegy on the Gore-Booth sisters was written in 1927 at a period of gross anticlimax after the heroics of 1916 and 1919. Heroism now seemed irrelevant. And the Kathleen Ni Houlihan of the poets could be described by C.P. Curran as 'a vampire hag of Beare ... We lie in mortmain. The words of dead men, the reliques of bogus tradition hold us in fetters'. Denis Johnston in his Expressionist 'The Old Lady Says No!' (1926) shares this climate and mocks impartially at past and present.

Yeats was in a happier position. Where the facts contradicted insight, where the agents of those values in history he most cherished turned betrayers, the poet was ready with a justification that asserted tragedy against pathos; singularity against mediocrity; individuality against mob, though always with a sense of the frailty of his own myth-making.

'In Memory of Eva Gore-Booth and Constance Markiewicz' began from a visual image of two girls met in earlier life, an image that had haunted the poet for thirty years and which had been betrayed by subsequent history. To recapture that image in its validity, the poet had to work dialectically; to embrace a number of alien objects and to reject these in order that the image might be reaffirmed, but in the course of such reaffirmation the inadequacy of the image to the present is recognized and becomes the ground of another image. The poem then is a conscious act of history, a conscious reinterpretation that attempts to change history.

II

I am tempted to begin analysing the opening lines of 'In Memory of Eva Gore-Booth and Constance Markiewicz' in musical terms. This is necessarily to be subjective. The opening is legato, light, even-fingered with resonant silence between words. These caesuras of recollection do not snatch into focus or even stroke in detail with a musing economy. They are distinctly 'won'; etched with a refiner's art: 'Light of evening/Lissadell/Great Windows.' That first line seems to accomplish what Pound in his essay on Arnaut Daniel terms 'clear sounds', though there is a momentary sensuous break of s-noises in 'Lissadell'. The rhyme of Lissadell/Gazelle is again light, glancing, associating the solidity of the great house with the fragility of the girls, qualities suggested by the rising tune of 'Lissadell' and the falling tune of 'gazelle'. The poet himself in his own evening stands outside the house looking in, and house and girls are poised in an elegaic twilight. The solidity of the house is melting already perhaps in the fluid darkness of history, but that the way of life emblematized by the house was already vanishing is only now apparent in the act of recollection. The half-rhymes 'south' and 'both' present perhaps a muted dissonance and suggest the pathos of distance, innocence, strangeness, though this too-subjective response might lead one to qualify the claim; they might equally distinguish (both ... but one). Thomas Parkinson remarks that the off-rhyme is predictable by the antecedent 'two girls', and when the full rhyme comes it does not clang heavily because the carry-over of the preceding line holds the gazelle in its web.[2] The rhymes are not to be unnoticed, but they are to be seen as part of the line. Insistence on linear form rather than periodic. The rhyme of recall–gazelle merely fortifies the resigned imperfection of life so far presented. The imperfect rhyme is consonant with the imperfections of experience that have led from the recollection to this hesitation to bring back to mind what had once occurred without conscious thought. The fourth line modulates into dactyls: the past life of the girls enters the poem, vibrates; 'both/beautiful, one a gazelle': the girls' beauty is a double flower on a single stem.

Musical idiom seems appropriate to structure no less than to texture and tone. The structure is circular, and all through the elegy, rhyme, half-rhyme and syntax, like nagging voices, work against rhythm. The poem itself is won out of the conflict between the initial visual image and the insights of the present.

Those 'great' windows, grandiosely colloquial, suggest the young Yeats's wonder, through rhythm partly, but the 'great' acts antithetically against the girls. The windows are open, but only to the light, warmth, colour, opulence of the south and the promised future: security in a rooted order. That this is a political and economic falsity; that the 'Ascendancy' had been for twenty years or more the West British equivalent of the Algerian French, is irrelevant. The master of Lissadell was a fine representative of his class, and Yeats had particular reasons, at the time when he first met the girls, for believing that that class had a crucial role to play in the rehabilitation of Ireland. Through those windows we, excluded by time, glimpse the girls dressed with rich informality, in Peter Ure's phrase 'a silken ambience' of leisure. Rhythm in the third line recoils faintly from sense so that a flicker of hesitance checks the voice between 'both' and 'beautiful'. Like the half-rhymes, such hesitance lingers on the girls' beauty and also on its fragility, as does the more glancing pause between 'one' and 'a gazelle'. The gazelle is already being hunted by time and does not yet know that it has enemies. The pause at the end of the fourth line is substantiated by rhythm: syntax and rhythm act together to announce that a movement is over.

The lines quicken. Autumn comes with shears, rather like Atropos, to 'slit the thin-spun life', but what is shorn is not life, but more poignantly, beauty. The shears clash together with the somewhat brutal rhyme of 'shears' and 'years'. Contrasting as they do with the previous four lines, these have an almost melodramatic shrillness, and it is difficult not to believe that these half-rhymes are designed—like those of Owen's *Strange Meeting*—'to set', in William Empson's phrase 'your teeth on edge'. The 'wreath' suggests the formal achievement of the Great House: ordered garden, leisured civility. The wreath is beauty's tribute, the hair itself, perhaps. The texture has turned harsh and generates a harshness of tone: syntax and rhythm ride impatiently over the line-ending: 'Lonely years/Conspiring among the ignorant': aristocratic formality is not set against, it is in vulgar collision, collusion almost, with mob-ignorance. The poet mimes his contempt: 'Pardoned, drags out lonely years', dragging, the vowels deny the heroic; enact Constance Markiewicz's later futilities.

At this point the poet himself enters the poem and comments on his own narrative: 'I know not what the younger dreams.' Was the betrayal already consummated? One sister is isolated by futile action, among the ignorant; the other by futile dreams, 'some vague Utopia'. The poet—Yeats recalls perhaps the distinction in Keats's *Fall of Hyperion*—neither dreamer nor agent, judges both dreams and actions. 'I know not'—although Yeats is fond of the construction 'I know', the phrase seems to have an evasive formality matching its object's evasiveness: Eva's gazelle quality is a quality of mind no less than of personality and physical beauty. 'Withered old' asks for hyphenation by the reading voice and like 'skeleton-gaunt' the compound word suggests the logic of the sisters' self-reduction: the body becomes almost Platonically an emblem of the soul.

> Many a time I think to seek
> One or the other out and speak
> Of that old Georgian mansion, mix
> Pictures of the mind, recall
> That table and the talk of youth,
> Two girls in silk kimonos, both
> Beautiful, one a gazelle.

And yet the poet is both speaking and reliving *that* table and *that* old Georgian house: the 'thats' are at once distancing and definitive, the old poet looking through the window as though he were looking at a picture. The enjambed appeal to 'mix' memories suggests, besides communion, an actual painting of pictures together. But for that mutual re-enactment it is now too late. 'One or the other' leans back to 'one a gazelle' and 'older' and 'younger'. The girls are no longer distinguishable but associated merely in the context of the great house: the flowering of an order. Eva 'the other' is also 'the one' (Constance's beauty was bolder) but 'one or the other' now associates the two girls in a judging indifference. The memories are more important than the persons who have betrayed them.

Once more rhyme and syntax have worked against rhythm with the decision of the full stop after 'politics'.

An image of such politics.
Many a time I think to seek
One or the other out and speak

But the 'music' of memory carries over, a music of deprivation. Still, it remains that the poet did not meet and talk over the past with the two women and that fixes the visual image 'Two girls in silk kimonos' the more firmly, as a picture simply, as something composed, final. The pictures in the mind, the mansion, the table, the talk, the clauses in as yet uncomposed apposition, mount up to the restatement, fugal, ritual, authoritative, achieved by the music alone, the essentials of the case:

Two girls in silk kimonos, both
Beautiful, one a gazelle.

Yet at this point the visual image can hardly be valid. The return to the beginning has left too much unsaid; presents perhaps too facile a balance between the autonomy of the visual image and condemnation of the autumn of these beautiful bodies, a mere:

Dis, qu'as-tu fait, toi que voilà,
    De ta jeunesse.

Another elegist might have rested there. But memory, for Yeats, is not sufficing, is precisely that 'mere translation' into the terms of the inner life of the pure symbolist. To seal off, to preserve the bloom of recollection, is the poet's treason. Intruding events must be transformed: the dream must envelop reality. The dead shall listen for themselves, and here the poet leaves off his passive role as memorialist and assumes the active role of mage. But first he pronounces the judgement which that easy musical finality of the first stanza had attempted to transcend: the definitive rhymes that follow 'fight' and 'right'; the marching definitive rhythm of the two lines they clinch, enact the necessary judgement. But while the rhythm spills us over to the fourth line, the syntax, the full stop, arrests us. And rhythm here works other ends. The pause enforced by syntax and by the frank rhymes precisely gives the two following lines their gnomic force. The ear must forget the syntax and return to 'the dear shadows'. The judgement condones. The 'shadows' pick up faintly that 'light of evening' at the poem's beginning so that the instant perfection of the 'two girls' is associated with 'shadows' in fuller recreation. The justified rhythmical coarseness, the mechanical iambic:

> All the folly of a fight
> With a common wrong or right

distinguishes the 'all' of the first line from what they now merely negatively 'know': what they know is what the poet knew all along; the poem informs them.

'Arise' might seem to promote some suggestion of a Lazarus come back from the grave at the command of one who has power over life and death: the poet is omnipotence in his own poem. (The comparison would be with the magian poet of 'All Souls Night'. There the poet begins as pupil and ends as teacher, summoning dead friends in their desolate wisdom). Yet in Yeats the ghostly is much more potent to arise than the resurrected human.

The change from condemnation to collusion is reinforced by the change from imperative to impetrative, to prayer: 'Bid me'. The poet's claims, though, are bounded by the prosaic 'match' rather than (say) the more vaguely impressive 'spark'. Thomas R. Whitaker quotes the Gospel utterance 'I come to cast fire on the earth, and would that it was already kindled' (Luke, 12, 49), and he continues:

> But the tone quite consciously mingles proud declaration, courtly fealty, sly conspiracy, Castiglione's 'recklessness', an absurdly child-like make-believe. The actual conflagration or apocalypse with which the poem concludes in 'The Last Judgement' of self-knowledge and self-revelation. Consequently his own yearning can include the other exhilarating moment when 'the images from *Anima Mundi* ... would, like a country drunkard who has thrown a wisp into his own thatch, burn up time'.[3]

A subdued circular movement is working again: light of evening, shadows, match, suggesting that it is the world rather than the tomb, which is dark. Wisdom is the property of the dead, though 'match' may at first suggest 'fuse', the sordor surrounding the conspiracies, crazy pieties and politics that gnarled the later years of Constance and Eva. The dead are summoned into life not in the silky languor of their first appearance but in the passion of their aberrations, the 'folly' of their fight. Syntax runs opaque here. Does the 'run' refer to the fire (it will run) or is it a renewed imperative to the girls? The pointing would suggest the first, but logic suggests the second sense: the girls and their foolish, passionate dreams and acts are indistinguishable. The word 'sages' does not suggest the religious sages of Byzantium as Jon Stallworthy proposes in his *Between the Lines*; for there is no absolute guarantee that a word in Yeats preserves the same meaning in all contexts. Rather 'sages' here suggests prudential wise men, wiseacres: those who from *their* prosaic security would condemn these wrecked lives. Syntax and rhythm again conflict: the violent rhythmical pause after 'know' dramatizes the change from 'you' to 'we'. In his own reading of the poem, Yeats would markedly stress 'we' and 'they'.

The word 'gazebo'[4] has caused much trouble. It has several richly associated ranges of meaning. First, it means 'folly' in the architectural sense, a kind of conspicuously wasteful joke, a sham ruin often of fantastic elaboration that was not unusual in aristocratic grounds so representing those 'wasteful virtues' that 'earn the sun'. Another meaning is summer-house and this possibly has its place in the seasonal curve of the poem. In an autobiographical prose fragment (quoted in the Preface to the collected edition of her poems) Eva Gore-Booth refers to a summer-house in the grounds of Lissadell: 'In the wonderful transition time between winter and spring ... the child came alone ... appalled by the sudden thrill of the first touch of the world's mystery.'[5] And the third meaning, still current in Anglo-Irish, is something to look *at* rather than look from and can be metaphorically used of a ridiculous person: 'to make a gazebo of yourself'. There is a further meaning: a place to look *from*. There was, to be sure, a look-out place at Lissadell on the shore and this sense might seem to glance at Constance's conspiracies to change history and Eva's Utopian politics and shrill feminism. Who *can* glimpse the future?

But by now both poets and girls are seen as those who are not concerned with the future, never really were concerned with it. Common sense would have marked out a conventional, secure, uneventful future for the girls, and poetry itself is a kind of desperate wager. Poet and girls equally made gazebos of themselves in the eyes of the sages. Indeed, Constance and Eva made architectural follies of greater grandeur than usual, not of their bodies, but of their lives, when they left the security of the great house, betrayed their order and their beauty, and made their gestures towards the mob. The poet too made a gazebo of himself by his early romantic dreams—'the talk of youth'—of a unified Irish culture and of the part he and the girls were to play in that. He can mock now at *that* table and *that* talk: though memory may cling to them, time is always betraying them. Yet the poet has perhaps betrayed those early dreams and so provides a counterpart of the girls' betrayal. Only the last supreme folly, the madness of art, can preserve dreams, but paradoxically preserves by burning up, for the image belongs to time and time corrupts: time must be consumed with all the opportunist sages who submit to time by exploiting it.

The *great* gazebo: the word qualifies and is qualified by the *great* house, which history has shown to be folly also. And the energetic liturgical process continues with 'Arise and bid me strike a match ... Bid me strike a match ...' The last conjuration picks up the earlier line and rests in it, resolving the conflict between syntax and rhythm, between logic and feeling, between 'know' and 'we'. 'Blow' has a rising tune, so that it can hardly be ambiguous. The poem concludes with the poet inspiring, breathing life into shadows and subsumes the image of the two girls in their haunting first appearance by appealing to the crooked logic, that irresponsibility that can make the case against the girls and triumphantly justify them in the same breath. Syntax, prose-sense, is finally consumed and mastered. Yet in punning terms, the poet like Constance turns anarchist, destroying his poem and its pretensions. It is absurd for a poem to kill time as it is for a match to gut the universe.

III

> Dear Miss Gore-Booth: I thank you very much for your most interesting account of Casements purpose. I had all ready written strongly to the Home Sec. & sent a copy of my letter to Mr Asquith. I feel that the argument for clemency is so strong that the government cannot disregard this argument, and I believe also from all I have heard that Asquith is himself humane. Will you permit me to say how much I

> sorrow over the misfortune that has fallen upon your family? Your sister & yourself, two beautiful figures among the great trees of Lisadell, [*sic*] are among the dear memories of my youth.[6]

So Yeats wrote on 23 July 1916. His correspondent was Eva Gore-Booth. Constance had, on account of her sex, recently been reprieved from the death-penalty and had been sentenced to a long term of imprisonment. Casement's fate was still not finally decided. The other leaders of the 1916 rebellion had been executed in small groups of two and three so that no one knew when the shootings were going to stop.

In that letter, the visual image of Constance and Eva is already operant. The occasion, the catalyst of Yeats's poem, was the death of Constance in August 1927. Eva had died the year before. What remained in the old man's mind was the contrast between their lives and that visual memory, a memory of the year 1894.

From the early years of the century on, partly as a result of his friendship with Lady Gregory and the hospitality of Coole, Yeats had developed firm notions about the role of women, particularly aristocratic women, in society, and of the responsibility they owed to their traditions of birth. *Adam's Curse* is too solemnly dogmatic about the topic, but remains the clearest statement of their social role as ritualizers of passion and inspirers of art.

Yeats's Irish friends, Lady Gregory, Synge, O'Leary and Hugh Lane were all amenable to mythologizing in their own lifetimes. They formed part of the history of modern Ireland that Yeats's poetry and prose laboured to transmit as a document to posterity. Constance and Eva, because of their political activities, resisted myth-making, and the poet's relationship with them was too distant for either to be transformed, as Maud Gonne was transformed, into a Fatal Woman.

Their roles had been cast for them by Yeats in the 1890s. From the beginning, the activity of Yeats and his friends in Ireland had been a consciously historical activity. After the death of Parnell in 1891, Yeats and his friends turned to an attempt at creating or, rather, recreating the culture of Ireland. That there was no Irish nation, Parnell's betrayal, and the schisms that followed it, had revealed. Yeats's aim was to unify the nation through culture: cultural independence was to be the first stage of independence from England. This was an historical task because the problem as Yeats and his friends saw it was finally neither one of creation nor of recreation but of allowing the *potentialities* of the true culture of Ireland, defined historically through language, literature, heroic stories, national character, to free themselves after the long corruption of alien domination by the English. Appeals to the blood of the martyrs are intrinsic to any nationalist movement, but this went further. The movement was to end in both success and failure. Ireland was liberated, but by persons who used methods and were inspired by notions of which Yeats did not approve: violence, appeal to mob hatred, sectarianism. It was a success in that from small Ireland emerged in a matter of two decades a world literature: Synge, Joyce, Lady Gregory, O'Casey, Johnston.

Yeats began by helping to found literary societies in London and Dublin for the study and promulgation of Irish letters. He then cast round for support beyond the men of letters, journalists, minor politicians and liberal churchmen who provided the membership of such societies. There was one element in Irish society to whom in particular he began to look: the Protestant Anglo-Irish landowning aristocracy—the Ascendancy.

At the same period Yeats became concerned with a new ancestry for modern Irish poetry as part of his programme for 'unity of culture'. His aim was to purify the tradition of the *Nation*, that organ of the Young Ireland Movement of the 1840s. Because of its overt political rhetoric, that tradition was likely to make little appeal to the educated. In 1895 Yeats published an anthology of Irish verse[7] that was designedly polemical, a substitute for that other anthology *The Spirit of the Nation*. And in his preface (the aspirations and polemics are largely omitted in later editions) Yeats wrote that his literary movement was directed towards 'our more leisured classes [who] read little about any country, and nothing about Ireland. We cannot move these classes from an apathy, come from their separation from the land they live in, by writing about politics or about Gaelic, but we may move them by becoming men of letters and expressing primary emotions and truths appropriate to the country.'[8]

It was in pursuit of such an ideal that Yeats visited Lissadell for the first time in November 1894. The importance of this visit has been somewhat overlooked; for Yeats went to Lissadell before he went to Lady Gregory's Coole: it was the first great house to receive him as a poet.

Lissadell is a plain house in neo-Grec mode built to the design of Francis Goodwin in 1832 and standing among woods that go down to the sands of Lissadell Bay. At this time it was the home of Sir Henry Gore-Booth, an enlightened Protestant landlord.

Writing to his sister a day or so after the visit was over Yeats remarked:

> I have been staying at Lissadell for a couple of days and have enjoyed myself greatly. They are delightful people. I am to lecture to the parishioners of their clergyman ... on Irish fairy lore. All the while I was at Lissadell I was busy telling stories—old Irish stories—first to one then another [sister?] and then telling them over again to the sick Miss Gore upstairs. Miss Eva Gore-Booth shows some promise as a writer of verse. Her work is very formless as yet but it is full of telling little phrases. Lissadell is an exceedingly impressive house inside with a great sitting room as high as a church and all things in good taste ... But outside it is grey, square and bare yet set amid delightful grounds.[9]

Yeats went to Lissadell in his own eyes as mentor. Eva was to be brought into the Irish literary movement. In 1898 she published her first volume of poems, full of vague late Romantic themes, but not of *Irish* themes. On 26 December 1898 Yeats wrote to her:

> Your gift is for putting very serious delicate emotions, into fragile rhythms. Avoid every touch of rhetoric, every tendency to teach. Keep before you the idea of doing a little book of delicate poems full of a feeling that nobody will know whether to call romantic or religeous [*sic*]. I think too that if you would read our people Miss Macleod, A.E., Miss Hopper & the like it would gradually help by uniting with your own feeling for Irish scenery and Irish needs to give you a new & rich kind of symbol & metaphor. I in fact agree with what Russell said in his review, of your book in *The Express* except that I think your power is wholly lyrical, that you would do well with lyrics made out of old celtic legends. Miss Hopper has done just such lyrics except that your feeling would be more deep and serious.[10]

This is consciously programmatic advice, and the doctrine is close to that of *Ideas of Good and Evil*. Already in this letter Yeats was criticizing Eva in terms that begin to take one forward to the elegy: 'The defect of your work is that your thought, as apart from your feeling, is still too slight, too pretty, too phantastical.'

Up to a point, Eva was a willing hearer. Her next volume *Unseen Kings* (1904) contains much Irish material. The process of conversion had begun soon after Yeats's visit of 1894. In a letter dated 25 March 1895 to Katharine Tynan, another of Yeats's people, he talks of the creation of a public for the new Irish writers and of Miss Tynan's copy of Norah Hopper's poems 'crusading at

Lady Gore-Booth's and the whole family have taken to Irish things. They are now busy with [Standish] O'Grady, and were a little while ago on the hunt for folklore among their tenants.' That last touch is not without comedy. Yeats continues: 'These people are much better educated than our own people, and have a better instinct for excellence. It is very curious how the dying out of party feeling has nationalized the more thoughtful Unionists.'[11] To Olivia Shakespear on 13 April 1895 Yeats wrote referring with his usual faintly mandarin condescension to Eva and associating Eva with Mrs Shakespear:

> I am delighted at your liking 'The Two Trees' ... you and one other person are the only people who have said they like it. The other person ... a Miss Eva Gore-Booth, daughter of Lady Gore-Booth ... She has some literary talent, and much literary ambition and has met no literary people. I have told her about you and, if the chance arise, would like you to meet her. I am always ransacking Ireland for people to set writing at Irish things. She does not know that she is the latest victim—but is deep in some books of Irish legends I sent her—and may take fire.[12]

Eva indeed, was to take fire but not in poetry and not in activities that interested Yeats.[13] For Eva, literature provided something of an escape from her present, rather richly confined life. The same was probably true of Constance's essays in painting. The two girls when Yeats first met them, so beautiful and yet so different in their beauty, must have seemed the very embodiments of the order to which they belonged: the aristocratic tradition expressed equally in architecture as in life. A family album which covers the years from 1886 to 1888 substantiates Yeats's image. One photograph shows them posed together dressed up in the clothes worn by their father's tenants. Eva is nearly always caught looking timidly down or away. Other photographs show Constance in an enormous hat, catching moths or taking part in family theatricals.

The lives of the two girls ranged predictably between Lissadell, Dublin and the country houses of their parents' friends, for this was the golden phase of the aristocratic and political house party. Their future seemed predetermined then: coming out at eighteen; presentation at Court—there is a striking photograph of Constance in her first ball dress; the suitable marriage. Their gentle enthusiasms and amiable eccentricities over, they would conform to and continue a given pattern of life.

The most documentary of those early photographs shows us the room facing south that the sisters shared for their painting, drawing, reading, the scene of their keen and pantheistic chatter—'the glory hole' as they called it. What emerges from the photograph is the genially choked mid-Victorian aspect. The two sisters practised all the accomplishments of the mid-Victorian young lady, but London intellectual fashions have intervened. There is much Pre-Raphaelite and Japanese disarray. Two Pre-Raphaelite paintings (knights and phthisical ladies—Constance's work?) rest on easels and not the kimonos merely but the fire-screen with its slender crane motif assert the Japanese mania of the 1880s. A reproduction of *Hope*, that famous allegorical painting of Watts, hangs on the wall (Yeats admired Watts in what he called his 'Symbolist' vein, a vein to which, he declared, this painting belonged). There is what looks like a Morris tapestry and a bad cast from a reproduction of the head of the famous Hellenistic statue, the Apollo Belvedere. The taste is eclectic, English, fashionable. Emphatically it is not in the least Irish.

But if these were Victorian young ladies, they belonged also to the new generation of 'new women' who forced their way into public life and who if necessary would commit adultery on principle, like Florence Farr, as a gesture against the double standard of morality. The very eagerness with which the two girls listened to Yeats in that bay-windowed room—full of the apparatus of their leisure—must have been an index of their restlessness. Constance painted and later was to write plays full of revolutionary propaganda. Eva, as we have seen, wrote verse and in spite of short-sight was a fearless rider. But Constance was famous and reckless as a horse-woman, said to be the finest in the Ireland of her time, and it is in this role that Yeats celebrates her in 'On a Political Prisoner'.[14]

In Eva, restlessness may have been latent, but it somehow emerges positively in those early photographs of Constance. They seem to reveal some element of wilfulness. She always, through gesture and expression, seems quite deliberately to isolate herself from the carefully posed and smiling group (both girls stand out from the others in a house-party photograph with its fine splay of guns and deerstalkers).

To these girls, Yeats came as a reminder of the world outside, of a freedom which their class and their security denied them. Yet it is ironic that by leaving the great house, as both girls did by the turn of the century, they cut themselves away, in a manner of which Yeats could not approve, from that aristocratic order 'growing like a tree'.

Eva went in 1897 to do social work at Manchester and became more and more deeply involved in the organization of women workers in textile factories, struggling to unite them in trade unions and to fix conditions and hours for them, running papers, interviewing Members of Parliament and taxing the frailty of her health. She also did work of great importance for the women's suffrage movement, that final explosion of the 'new woman'. At this time 'Votes for Women' was moving towards its militant phase in the troubled context of the weak Liberal government of 'All the Talents' between 1908 and 1914. Delicately nurtured ladies went on hunger-strike in prison and Lady Constance Lytton, daughter of a Viceroy of India, threw a stone at an anti-suffrage mayor (unfortunately, it is reported, the stone hit another mayor who happened to be a supporter of women's suffrage). And during the period between Casement's trial and his appeal and execution, Eva wrote numerous and cogent letters to members of the Cabinet in an attempt to save that mad patriot's life.

Action in Eva's case was accompanied by an intense cultivation of the inner life. She studied neo-Platonism and Indian mysticism, but like her poetry such studies became increasingly didactic. Her poetry like her beauty was withered by the abstract: there is no sense of provisional solutions, solutions that are recognized as fictions such as one finds in Yeats's system-making and in his later poems. That gazelle quality was one of sensibility no less than physical appearance (one thinks of 'The Two Trees') and perhaps ambivalently in his draft autobiography (*Memoirs*) Yeats speaks of Olivia Shakespear as having 'the same sensitive look of destruction I had admired in Eva Gore-Booth.'[15]

It is both to the history and the legend of Ireland that the life of Constance belongs. In 1898 she left Lissadell for Paris, where she studied painting and met and married another painter, Count Casimir de Markiewicz, an honest adventurer of great talent and greater charm. Returning to Dublin, where she and her husband settled, their social life—and it was varied and entertaining—failed to give her what she needed. Like Maud Gonne, whose marriage also failed, she found satisfaction in the excitement of revolutionary politics. She founded the Fianna Scouts, boys who played a useful role five or six years later when in 1916 the moment for action came. Photographs of her at this time show her in the Fianna uniform, her sash pinned with appropriate Celtic metalwork. In 1914 she joined the left-wing Citizen Army, another revolutionary organization which had been formed by James Connolly to protect workers from the police brutality that had accompanied the great Dublin lock-out and strike of 1913. Connolly, indeed, a martyr of 1916, was a kind of embryonic Irish Lenin, and had he lived the subsequent history of Ireland might have been strikingly different. Connolly became Constance's leader, and her own politics became increasingly left-wing. Two photographs survive of her in Citizen Army uniform. Of the first image it has been said, 'there is something at once absurd and touching, the face is fragile, the cheeks, sunken, the bravura of youth has vanished and has been replaced by what seems an almost factitious bravura of uniform and intended action'.[16] Yet another and flatly comic photograph shows her sitting on the ground again with the rather absently menacing revolver while a painted cloth representing an ideal landscape serves as background.

She was to become the deputy-leader of the group which held Stephens Green in Dublin during the Easter Rising. After the surrender, she suffered a term of imprisonment, and returning to Ireland continued for a few years to play a prominent part in Irish politics, always as an extremist. Only in the last year of her life did the range for action desert her. It was at this time that Eva died. Constance seemed to change: for the first time she discovered the resources of the inner life. There is a sad story of her in these last years speaking to a small audience in her native Sligo with a sling round the arm she had broken while cranking her small car. In the rather diminished Ireland of the 1920s she had become irrelevant. At this time she was living in the slums of Dublin, working for the humblest poor not as great lady or as politician but as one who had identified herself with them in a spirit of quiet humility. She had long since rejected the manners of her caste, even the care of her physical appearance.

Though converted in middle-life to a creed that was altogether alien to her heredity and upbringing, Constance preserved the dashing qualities of the aristocrat in politics, following her 'star' intuitively. Aristocrats in England nineteenth-century democracy allied themselves on occasion with the working against the middle classes, and in 'Madame's' case we have her alliance with James Connolly against the 'soft' Dublin Nationalists with capital interests. 'Madame's' part in the 1913 strike is exemplary: from out-door relief at Lissadell to the Dublin soup-kitchen. Aristocratic noble opportunism was crossed by passionate attachment to men as much as to causes—Bulmer Hobson, James Connolly, De Valera:

the men were ultimately incompatibles. The cogent comparison remains with another 'new woman' from an upper-middle-class British military background, Maud Gonne. Both women were tall and beautiful; both disappointed in their marriages, though 'Madame' and Casimir remained affectionate down to the time of her death in 1927. Both women found compensatory excitement in conspiracy, the histrionic gesture, the sensual response to group-emotion. Of the politician's gifts, 'Madame' had one: she was splendid on stage; but her upbringing had made her too ingenuous for real success. The love of dressing-up which began with amateur theatricals at Lissadell continued logically with the time-travelling fancy dresses which she and Casimir incessantly donned: she was Joan of Arc, the Empress Josephine, a Russian peasant woman. She wrote plays, acted in them, was prominent in the explosion of little theatre in the Dublin of the 1900s. It was only one small step to the uniforms of the national struggle: the Fianna or the Cymann nd mBar, commemorated in various carefully posed studio photographs against ideal backgrounds in which the preferred gesture was a revolver being pointed at some invisible Tommy. And then, there were the occasional disguises. About her career, as about much of Irish politics, a tragi-farcical halo clings, though the same halo sulphurates round the English 'new woman': poor Eleanor Marx. Both Maud Gonne and Constance Markiewicz possessed a rage for action; both, by and large, were unintelligent women—it has been said that had Constance been more intelligent Connolly's doctrines might have had more effect in post-Treaty Ireland: she translated them into compassion for the poor. And yet her career has its own logic; she persisted in moving roles to the end; and she remains, therefore, as exasperating, but a far more haunting and sympathetic figure than Maud Gonne. Her biographers remain faintly puzzled by Yeats's bitter and regretful comments on her, but in the elegy he wrote after her own and her sister's death there is a finer perspective, a final justice to one whose fire could now be seen as no longer fanatically self-destructive, but purificatory.

Yeats's lines: 'Dragging our lonely years/Conspiring among the ignorant' may do her mythical violence, though the poem finally subdues its own injustice. For years, Yeats's elegy was her only memorial (if we except Sean O'Faolain's splendid biography). The Irish Office of Works commissioned the sculptor Seamus Murphy of Cork to commemorate her in another art. In Murphy's statue on Stephens Green, unveiled on 2 April 1956 Constance has been translated into myth: that apotheosis that Yeats in 'Easter 1916' rather ambiguously grants to her fellow-leaders executed after the failure of the rebellion. Yet the image is blandly trivialized. The sculptor's emphasis falls on the hair and the details of the uniform, and though the features are strongly marked, they are vapidly ideal. The image finally suggests a brisk young nurse or a YWCA worker cheerfully carrying on after a heavy bombing raid, impersonally and intemperately cheerful, full of the soft answers that augment wrath.

Subsequent history is more true to Yeats than to official Ireland. It has the trick of authenticating his prophecies. The most dramatic instance is Coole, where indeed the rooms and passages that welcomed Irish genius are gone and nettles wave upon a shapeless mound and saplings root among the broken stone. Lissadell, unlike Coole, still stands; those windows still look out over the bay past Rosses point to the hill of Knocknarea crowned by the supposed cairn of Queen Maeve, a beautiful violent woman from older legend. Yeats's mythologizing forces Maeve and Constance into apposition. Inside the house, Casimir de Markiewicz's immense humorous fresco in the breakfast room recalls earlier days. Outside in the demesne trees are being felled.

Such observations made originally in 1963 were more pointed than I had imagined. Seven years later, an article appeared in a Sunday newspaper that accented the sense of elegy and the decline of a family that shared a common ancestry with the Earl of Arran and the Barons Harlech, and had been lords lieutenant, high sheriffs, justices of the peace, soldiers, sailors and civil servants. The sons, so Ms Anne Robinson's article reminded us, went to Eton and Rugby, Oxford and Cambridge, and served with the Royal Irish Fusiliers, the Dragoons, the Irish Guards, the Scots Fusilier Guards and the Royal Navy. A very breviary of the Ascendancy.

Lord Gore-Booth rose to head the English civil service, and on the other side there was Constance and Sir Josslyn Gore-Booth, the sixth baronet, who like his father was an excellent landlord. It was Sir Josslyn's death in 1944 that began the decline. Ms Robinson, in her piece, gives this account of Lissadell:

> The avenue to the once-magnificent Georgian house is lined with potholes. The garden is overgrown. The greenhouses are shattered and empty, the stables beyond repair. The roof of the main block leaks badly and the paintings show patches of mildew. In two tiny bedrooms and a cramped kitchen live Angus Jocelyn, the heir presumptive to the family

baronetcy, and his sister, Miss Gabrielle and Miss Aideen. They scratch a living showing visitors over the estate at 3s a head. In winter they sit around the kitchen stove because they cannot afford a coal fire.

The Gore-Booths claim that the trouble they are now in is not of their own making. They tell an alarming story of a 14-year battle against the Irish legal establishment, of political pressures, mismanaged accounts, vanishing forests, unusual business practices, missing funds, and threats of prison, as in front of their eyes, their father's legacy was allowed to be whittled away by the very people appointed in law to protect it.

Their account sounds like a 19th-century melodrama, yet in Sligo few doubt that it is true. 'The Gore-Booth business', a neighbour said last week, 'is one of the great Irish scandals of the century'.

The decline in the fortunes of the Gore-Booth family began with the death in 1944 of the sixth baronet, Sir Josslyn. Sir Josslyn, one of the founders of co-operative dairy societies throughout Ireland and a man with a strong social conscience, had steadily built up the 2,670-acre estate, concentrating on commercial timber. His idea was that forests coming progressively into production would take care of his death duties without ruining his family and without the need for dismissing any of the estate workers.

Sir Josslyn had eight children, four boys and four girls. Two sons, Hugh, the second, and Brian, the third, were killed in action during the war. The youngest, Angus, has had periods of absent-mindedness. The eldest, Sir Michael Savile, seventh baronet, is in a Yorkshire nursing home suffering from a mental illness. Sir Michael was already ill when his father died, and incapable therefore of managing the estate.

Accordingly, the Irish Government, through the Solicitor-General for wards of court (the Irish equivalent of the official solicitor) stepped in and made Sir Michael a ward. The Solicitor-General thus became responsible for administering the financial affairs and the property of Sir Michael. As well, three trustees were appointed and were to be consulted on any major issues concerning the estate.

The day-to-day management was left in the hands of Miss Gabrielle, and under her care, during the early years of this arrangement, the estate ran profitably. Then, in 1952, trouble began.

In that year Mr Gerald Maguire became the new Solicitor-General for wards of court. Mr Maguire, who came from a family of lawyers (his brother is former Irish Chief Justice Conor Maguire) had his own ideas of how the estate should be run. They did not coincide with those of Miss Gabrielle and by 1955 the family had a bank overdraft of some £20,000. There are two versions of how this occurred. Mr Maguire said that Miss Gabrielle had no idea of how to manage Lissadell and her incompetence had caused the loss.

Miss Gabrielle says that although the timber trade went through a depressed period at this time, the real reason for the loss was that Mr Maguire would not allow her enough money from the family funds to pay reasonable wages, and that Mr Maguire's unusual accounting methods made it hard to keep track of the progress of the business. She says, for example, that in September 1954, the timber firm of McAinsh and Company paid £5,750 for timber it had felled on the estate. When Miss Gabrielle received the 1954 accounts there was no sign of this amount. After representations to Mr Maguire the figure was inserted and the accounts altered accordingly.

This incident led to a further deterioration in relations and Miss Gabrielle was not surprised when Mr Maguire sacked her and appointed a new manager. However, when the new man turned up at Lissadell to take charge, 41 out of the 53 workers on the estate refused to serve under him unless the Gore-Booths ordered them to do so. Mr Maguire replied by dismissing them.

Miss Gabrielle announced that she was not going to let loyal workers be sacked in this manner and that if Mr Maguire would not pay their wages then she would. She began selling props and timber from the estate to raise the money. Mr Maguire took to the law. He appealed to the High Court in Dublin and succeeded in obtaining an injunction restraining the Gore-Booths 'from selling, removing, or disposing' of any of the property at Lissadell.

This produced a stalemate, interest was mounting on the £20,000 overdraft (it has now reached £40,000) and the estate began to deteriorate. Miss Gabrielle's idea of how to solve the problem was that Mr Maguire should release enough of her brother's capital to pay off the overdraft and start afresh. Mr Maguire saw another, more direct solution and on October 5, 1956, moved to apply the coup de grace. He applied to the High Court for an order to allow him to sell Lissadell to the Land Commissioner.[17]

Mr Justice Davitt, son of one of Ireland's great national leaders, Michael Davitt, founder of the Land League that in the nineteenth century broke the power of the landlords and enabled tenant farmers to become owners of their own holdings, granted the solicitor-general's application in which it was stated that the three trustees had approved the sale. The trustees had not approved and said so and the order was rescinded. Part of the policy of the new, potato republic was to break up the large estates, and no one wanted to assume a cause which, as Ms Robinson aptly observes, was a 'political hot potato'. Mr Maguire took over the management of the estate himself and secured an order evicting the Gore-Booths from their own house, suspended just so long as they kept quiet. He then began felling large areas of woodland on the estate and, instead of asking timber merchants to offer a bid, gave the exclusive right in the timber to a now defunct firm who, in an improved version of felling and selling, first measured and then made an offer. The inventive Mr Maguire went to a well-earned rest in 1960 and the new solicitor-general for wards of court gave the family permission to receive revenue statements for the sale of timber for the previous five years. A figure on a piece of paper, no more, was all that actually proceeded from the solicitor-general's office. Miss Gabrielle Gore-Booth, a lady of splendid energy, measured the stumps and came up with a figure of about twenty times more than the cryptic arithmetic of those charged with the affairs of wards of court; on a conservative estimate at least five times more would have been minimally just, so the Gore-Booths had recourse yet again to the justice of the republic and that ever-active land agent Cahir Davitt ruled against them once more. By now they had run out of money and soon another obliging justice made another order for the sale of the Lissadell estate to the Land Commission. Lord Mountbatten (and we know what happened to him) owned a nearby estate and employed Miss Gabrielle as manager, and with takings from visitors the Gore-Booths survived until such time as the attorney-general could make a decision. His comment was not encouraging: 'little can happen unless a claim is put through the courts, and that has already been done'. Still, the Gore-Booths were hanging on to the house when I was last at Lissadell.

New ironies develop in Irish history. For sixty years, Southern Irish politicians made a living out of demanding unity. Personally I doubt if they really want it: it is yet another hot potato. And the North has become steadily less prosperous as the prosperity of the South has temporarily prospered, *vive* the EEC, the potato and German and Japanese factories, and with mild prosperity has come vulgarity (down with Georgian Dublin, it was all built by the Saxon anyway); come, dwarf the Liffey and skyscrapers that show that Ireland counts in the world. Discrimination, of course, is a matter exclusively of the North: how many people have read De Valera's black constitution which ties Southern Protestants to Catholic puritanism? Myths and icons persist: Fenian oaths and Unionist covenants of passionate memory, persist. The Unionist parody of the State Irishman, an impractical, comically melodramatic boyo: *Punch*'s 'eternal knee-breeched pipe-in-Caubeen travesty', hot wax in the shifty hands of priests and ever gargling and ullulating archaically what Edmund Gosse called 'the eternal snivel of Ireland', but which a later generation more vividly perhaps terms 'whinging'.

Yet as one stands there is it not anticlimax that one feels: only the generous emotions remain. One can only murmur 'mana! mana!', that power over the living that belongs to non-human objects and the dead. We stand on haunted ground, ground where objects are spiritually active: the dead are vivid here. It is not the elegaic pause over the end of the Ascendancy way of life, or the history of the Gore-Booth family. It is that art has affected life; that history as Yeats intended has been stylized. The ghosts with whom Yeats conversed have indeed arisen and have here a permanent habitation, here and not in Manchester or on Stephens Green; here and in Yeats's poem.

Notes

1. Stephen Spender, 'Hammered Gold and Gold Enamelling of Humanity', in *The Creative Element* (New York, 1954), p. 113.
2. *W.B. Yeats: The Later Poetry* (Berkeley, 1964), pp. 195–6.
3. Thomas R. Whittaker, *Swan and Shadow: Yeats's Dialogue with History* (Chapel Hill, 1964), p. 275.
4. *The New English Dictionary* suggests that 'gazebo' was formed by a waggish imitation of a Latin future, e.g. 'lavabo', a kind of hedge-schoolmastering process. The word appears first in 1752 and its meanings range from turret or lantern on a house-roof to belvedere or look-out in a garden. Sir Reginald Bloomfield observes: 'Banqueting-houses, gazebos and garden houses, all mean pretty much the same thing in an English garden. The origin of the word "gazebo" is obscure. It was used in the last century [i.e. the eighteenth] for the garden-house built at the corner of the terrace at the further end of the garden' (*The Formal Garden in England*, 3rd edn, 1901), p. 189. Both *OED* and Bloomfield, however, are concerned with *English* rather than Anglo-Irish contexts.
5. *Poems of Eva Gore-Booth* (London, 1929), p. 52.
6. From a manuscript in the possession of the late Professor D. J. Gordon of Reading University.
7. *A Book of Irish Verse*, Selected from Modern Writers with an Introduction and Notes by W. B. Yeats (London, 1895); (2nd edn, rev., 1906; 3rd edn, 1911).
8. *Ibid.*, (1911 edn), p. xiv.
9. *The Letters of W.B. Yeats*, ed. by Alan Wade (London, 1954), pp. 239–40.
10. From a manuscript in the possession of the late Professor D. J. Gordon.
11. *Letters*, p. 254.
12. *Letters*, pp. 256–57.
13. See the account of Constance and Eva in S. O'Faolin *Constance Markievicz* (London, 1934); W.B. Yeats, *Images of a Poet* (Manchester, 1962). Two recent biographies: Anne Marreco, *The Rebel Countess* (Philadelphia, 1967), excellent on the family and the personal life; Jacqueline Van Voris, detailed on the political life in her

Constance de Markievicz (Amherst, 1967), though she takes a Boston-Irish line.

14. *The Collected Poems* (London, 1958), pp.206–7.
15. In a manuscript version, not, so far as I know, published, the line 'an image of such politics' reads 'the mirror of such politics'. This recalls 'The Two Trees' and the admiration for that poem which Eva and Mrs Shakespear shared.
16. *W.B. Yeats: Images of a Poet*, p.42.
17. Anne Robinson, *Sunday Times*, 25 October 1970, p.13, cc.1–8.

8

Yeats's 'Leda and the Swan' as Iconic Poem

'One more word on "Leda and the Swan" is three too many' has been apologetically or defiantly intoned by critics about to commit three thousand. The brevity, force, ambiguousness, of Yeats's poem continously challenge, so I too join their number. I shall not rehearse the names of this Asian horde: are they not written in the bibliographies and in the footnotes even unto the third generation? Yet it would be arrogant not to allude to those critics who have decisively shaped my own response.[1] 'Leda and the Swan' has been read in context of *A Vision*, of whose text it is indeed part; it has been read, sometimes exclusively, as parable of the poet and his *daimon* as though Yeats were an overseas agent of the Hartford insurance business; a poem about to be born and thrown aside by the poet as in Mallarmé's *Don du poème*; as a species of Lawrentian sexual encounter; it has been discussed as part of the dramatic structure of the volume of poems in which it made a third and more public appearance; its sources in visual and plastic art have been deployed with rigour by Giorgio Melchiori who displays for us the complex forces that entered into the poem's making, while Leo Spitzer has given us sensitive close reading and elegant generalization.[2] The best criticism has been that which does not attempt to limit the significance of the sonnet by *fiat*. My aim here is modest: to proffer some possible additional sources both in literature and art and return the poem to its iconic genre.

A strong reason why the poem will not let us rest are those questions: rhetorical? expecting the answer Yes, No or Don't know? Can one, there, or in Blake's 'The Tyger', resist answers, even ones that *do* limit by *fiat*?

Leda, Helen, Mythology

It would be dangerous to assume that there is only one form of the Leda story, or that Yeats knew only one. Some commentators indeed seem to take their account from the incongruously reverend Lemprière, whose enlightenment paraphrase reduces the matter to Olympian bedroom farce: nothing so radical as rape occurs, and Jove suavely nestling in Leda's bosom, 'avails himself of his situation'. Lemprière succeeds the *prisca theolgia* versions of the Renaissance allegorists; the scholiasts; the tragic and the cyclic poets, let alone the living days of myth. The matter is difficult because there are so many strata.

When myth was still alive (by 400 B.C., in round figures, one might say it was dead) it was almost amorphous; a great seed-bed of narrative material set down in no handbooks but existing polymorphously in the popular imagination and taken up by the poets in almost any way they chose. When myth died there were those, like Apollodorus of the *Library* (usefully available to Yeats in the two 1921 Loeb volumes) who tried simply to catalogue it, not specially looking for 'meanings'. And there were the allegorists, of various stamps, such as the perhaps first century A.D. Stoic Heraclitus (called sometimes Heraclides) whose *Homeric Allegories* Milton possessed.

All sorts of combinations had been arrived at: there were versions both of the narrative, its actors, and the generation of the children of the rape. Yeats, if not precisely learned in the mythographers, was capable of getting behind the sardonic and business-like account of Helen's origins in Euripides' *Helen*, lines 17–21. Other literary sources were accessible to the poet in translation. In Homer (if not in the cyclic poem *Cypria*) Helen's mother was said to be not Leda but Nemesis (whose shifting shape and bird flight through the air probably explains the notion that Helen was born from an egg). Nemesis, a nymph-goddess, flees from Zeus; both undergo various transformations until Zeus as a white swan violates Nemesis as a wild goose: Nemesis lays a hyacinth-coloured egg in Sparta, which Leda finds and fosters. And according to Robert Graves there is a pre-Hellenic myth in which Nemesis pursues the Sacred King Zeus, who suffers seasonal transformation. Nemesis, embodiment of female aggression, counters each transformation with one of her own, and finally devours Zeus at the summer solstice. Then another story runs of Zeus-Swan embracing Leda, and the egg of Nemesis being brought to Leda. Nemesis as mother foreshadows Helen's role as destroyer of cities, and at a later stage Helen becomes the authentic daughter of Zeus-Swan and Leda. Apollodorus rationalizes the multiple births by recounting how the night after the Zeus-Leda copulation, Tyndareos takes his rights as husband. So Leda bears Polydeukes and Helen to Zeus, and Kaistor and Klytemnestra to her husband. But Apollodorus adds: 'Some say that Helen was a daughter of Nemesis and Zeus. She, fleeing from Zeus's embraces, changed herself into a goose, but Zeus then took the likeness of a swan and mated with her and from this copulation Leda laid an egg.' In other versions, Helen becomes the daughter of Tyndareos; Kaistor and Polydeukes are sometimes both sons of Zeus; sometimes Polydeukes only; sometimes Klytemnestra is born of Tyndareos; Nemesis is sometimes the mother of the Twins; and a late attempt to make sense of the situation asserts that Leda after death was deified as Nemesis (Lactantius 1.21.3).[3] Nemesis, we gather, became connected with death, the Underworld, irresistible Fate. The tradition that connects Leda with Leto and so with Night, I shall touch on later. As a final illustration of the confusion, one may quote the scholia on Pindar's *Nemean* (10.80). Polydeukes has appealed to Zeus on behalf of his brother Kaistor, who lies mortally wounded, and Zeus says to him: 'you are my son—and so I will grant your request.' The scholion reads:

> Hesiod traces the descent of both brothers to Zeus while Pindar, following other authorities, says that Polydeukes was the son of Zeus, and Kaistor the son of Tyndareos—just as Herakles was the son of Alkmena and Zeus, (his brother) Iphikles the son of Amphitryon. For it is said that Polydeukes and Helen were the children of Zeus and Leda, while Kaistor's father was Tyndareos. Hesiod, however, holds that Helen was the daughter neither of Leda nor of Nemesis but of a daughter of Ocean and Zeus.

Such is the highly fluid state of Greek myth, and of that fluidity I suggest that Yeats was aware. It is therefore perhaps too summary for Edgar Wind to suggest that the closing questions of Yeats's sonnet indicate the birth of the demi-gods is in doubt.[4]

But source-material is to be used primarily to indicate the non-derivable extra:

> A shudder in the loins engenders there
> The broken wall, the burning roof and tower
> And Agamemnon dead (*Variorum Poems*, p.441)

Yeats certainly associates the conception of Helen with the destruction of Troy; the broken wall actually *engenders* a mythological connection between entry into the labyrinthine city and entry into the woman: rape of woman is equated with rape of city; female genitalia with the city's labyrinthine entrance. Yeats's sources pose problems; could he have been familiar, given his interests in dance, with the labyrinthine dance and Troy; with the idea of the breaking of the 'sacred veil' of the city, of civilization? of 'the labyrinth of another's being'? And a further 'non-derivable extra', is Yeats's stress on rape rather than seduction. Rape is found in the remoter myths and in post-Yeatsian art, but not in the sources that were probably available to the poet.

Myth and Intuition

'Leda and the Swan' belongs, it is well known, to a small group of 'Annunciation' poems in Yeats's *oeuvre* celebrating objective or subjective incarnations: 'The Magi', 'Two Songs from a Play', 'The Mother of God', 'The Second Coming'. All four stress the violence and terror of annunciation: three through the onset of bird or beast gods, what is both above and below the rational and human, animal vitality and supernatural energy being required to energize a declining civilization. Each of these poems stresses the trance state of the speaker: 'I saw a staring virgin stand', 'In the mind's eye', 'A vast image out of Spiritus Mundi': each involves a gratuitous act of mind. 'The Second Coming' describes a future incarnation from the point of view of a seer in an objective phase of culture hungering for 'subjective' renewal, and in familiar terms, but who instead discovers a horrifying projection of what he himself is nurturing. In 'The Magi' the tone remains more detached. The Magi prefer 'subjective' incarnation, not merely because history's rhythm leads to subjective incarnation; like Saki's imaginary Bishop, the Magi are out for blood, being 'older than the rocks' and distinctly Draculaish.

Trance here is vision with overtones of occult spirit-journey; and vision, Yeats tells us, 'is myth in action',[5] intuiting; recovering what scholia and mythographers rationalized or attenuated; is living presence (though still requiring the gratuitous act of mind) in which essences are unnamed. Leda is not named, nor Zeus; all is immediate. Myth is also identity-making, as Robert Langbaum reminds us:

> for Yeats identity-making goes on not only in this life but between lives ... individual identities merge into archetypal or communal identities.... In the course of one life and many lives, our individuality frees itself from, then returns to, a communal matrix; and the historical periods chart in their varying characteristics the phases of this cyclical movement ... We may in the process of identity-making be unconsciously looking toward a new civilization for the saving image.[6]

Both actors perform their exemplary roles and within the constriction of the sonnet form the tone of the visionary moves from feeling primarily with the girl to subdued feeling with the Swan, creating a middle area of union only to recede from that syntactical 'present' into a future which is also a 'past'—a 'there'—detached both temporarily and spatially. And 'Leda and the Swan' agrees with 'Two Songs' by insistence not merely on violence and horror but on fruitfulness, though that fruitfulness may remain ironic: was there metaphysical, no less than carnal knowledge?

The Iconic Tradition of the Sonnet

These are familiar general reflections. What may be less familiar is another area of source material which casts distinct light on Yeats's proceedings. 'Leda and the Swan', I suggest, relates to a genre popular throughout the ninteenth century, the sonnet descriptive and interpretive of a work of art, a development of the Renaissance iconic poem. Not all such, of course, are sonnets. The epigrams of the Palatine Anthology in the Renaissance mutated into madrigal and sonnet (the epigram was mainly utilized for emblem books). The nineteenth-century tradition is associated primarily with the Pre-Raphaelite 'literary' painters. But examples can be found earlier, connected with the expressive role of the work of art and its reinterpretation in subjective terms, whether by poet or art critic, such as Hazlitt or Wainewright. Minor Romantic poets such as Charles and Mary Lamb, J.H. Reynolds, Bowles, Southey and Leigh Hunt all furnish poems for pictures. The popularity of the type continued to the close of the century, culminating in a whole volume of poems about works of art, the *Sight and Song* (1892) of that 'double-headed nightingale', the two maiden ladies who composed under the pseudonym of 'Michael Field'. *Sight and Song* consists of thirty-one poems, four of them sonnets, devoted to works of art extending in date from the Renaissance to the Rococo.[7] Essentially, *Sight and Song* belongs to the 'imaginary museum' genre of Marino's *Galeria*, since the paintings themselves are located in different sites but the volume is interrelated by a symbolic pattern: 'the tenuous balances between the forces of life and death'. The mode is to 'translate into verse ... not so much what these pictures are to the poet, but rather what poetry they objectively incarnate'.[8] Reviewing this volume for the *Bookman* of July 1892, Yeats was sour about the genre. The Fields were accused of making the critical faculty perform the work of the creative mind and of producing an unmitigated 'guidebook'.[9] Certainly the poems of *Sight and Song* correspond to Rossetti's 'pictorial' early sonnets, passively rendering visual detail and colour and making no attempt at imaginative re-interpretation.

The general tradition involves the *ut pictura poesis* of antiquity. The fourteenth book of the Anthology, devoted to works of art, painting, and sculpture, stresses with epigrammatic point, art as the rival of nature through mimesis: '"When did Praxiteles see me naked", Venus said', or those lines in praise of Myron's Cow, which remark that calves were deceived into nuzzling at its udders. Like the Greek epigrams, the sonnets and madrigals of the sixteenth century and earlier seventeenth century frequently praise the work of art for being more vivid than nature itself, in terms of *enargia*, naturalistic gesture which proclaims identity and motive.

By the end of the 1880s, however, Yeats was trying his hand at the genre. 'On Mr Nettleship's Picture at the Royal Hibernian Academy' was originally contributed to *The Wanderings of Oisin* of 1889, but it was excluded from the poet's first set of revisions for the *Poems* of 1895. It is an unrhymed piece of sixteen lines. J.T. Nettleship (1841–1902) began as a 'visionary' painter working in what Yeats saw as the symbolist tradition of Blake. In his later years, as a consequence of hostile criticism, Nettleship turned to animal painting, particularly of lions, and achieved moderate success. The organization of the poem recalls the Petrarchan-derived Victorian sonnet. First, the painting is described with considerable attention to *enargia*, presenting the topic of lions and a forest fire vividly and minutely before concluding in an allegorical general statement of five and a half lines which are clearly analogous to the sestet of many a Victorian sonnet:

So ever moves
The flaming circle of the outer Law,
Nor heeds the old, dim protest and the cry
The orb of the most inner living heart
Gives forth. He, the Eternal, works His will. (*Variorum Poems* p. 689)

Rossetti's 'Ruggiero and Angelica'

The master of the sonnet for the work of art in the nineteenth century is D. G. Rossetti. Rossetti was also a professional painter, and for him the two arts were associated in especially intimate mode. He wrote sonnets for both his own and others' paintings, sometimes assuming the sonnet into the actual frame of the painting itself, which was indeed itself often of Rossetti's own design and related to the painting it enclosed, so provoking Whistler's well-known gibe: 'Why not simply frame the sonnet?' Rossetti refreshed the poem for picture tradition, though preserving its inscriptional and votive elements: 'a moment's monument'; a moment, that is, sublimed, out of time, rendered permanent, insensible to flux. Rejecting the mere representation of pictorial effects or the enumeration of detail as a means for the iconic sonnet, he aimed at establishing image as *tertium quid*, refined out of the dialectic of picture and word. Rossetti's innovation was popular with poets from 1860 on: more and more sonnets for paintings were written as a consequence of the general Pre-Raphaelite fusion of poetry and painting, though Rossetti's formula was not always followed; for example, Swinburne's *The White Girl* and his *Laus Veneris* originating in paintings by Whistler and Burne-Jones, respectively. Examples could be multiplied well beyond necessity.

It is to the more strict Rossettian tradition of the sonnet for a work of art that Yeats's poem belongs. The relation is loose, but here I want to generalize affinities rather than distinctions. One of the curiosities of Yeats criticism has been that the source materials most accessible to the master, most likely to become a permanent part of his mental history, poems and paintings of the middle and late nineteenth century, have been generally ignored for more modish zones.

The Leda sonnet depicts pagan annunciation, and annunciation is the subject of a well-known early painting of Rossetti's and of a sonnet related to that painting, which takes a received iconography and treats it subjectively. In the sestet of Rossetti's annunciation sonnet there is an intimate foreground that leads to vistas beyond, temporal no less than spatial. A similar effect occurs in some of Rossetti's other sonnets for pictures. We have, as Spitzer pointed out, a spatial and temporal recession in 'Leda and the Swan': 'A shudder in the loins engenders *there*/The broken wall'; the speaker after empathizing with Leda (and subduedly with Zeus) recedes from the action: time flows once more.

A sharp feature of 'Leda and the Swan' is the modulation of the tenses and the contraction of syntax. On the simplest level this represents the arrest of time by the onset of the eternal (the swan); the constriction of space. Similarly in several of Rossetti's sonnets for pictures the intractable present is used and the syntax truncated, and probably for the same reasons; the enactment of psychological chaos, since Rossetti's poems as Pater suggested are essentially records of crisis. The shift from given symbol to private image of personal hopes and fears quite implictly involves a pictorial solution to the speaker's psychological crisis and such could be related to the strict reading of 'Leda and the Swan' as a wrestling with Muse or Daimon or to the praise of a Daimonic intelligence 'transcending the events it initiates through its animal (or humanised) physical incarnations': rather as the poem disconcertingly talks back to the poet in the last stanza of 'Among School Children'.

In the early annunciation sonnet, Rossetti's Virgin represents a type of fulfilled knowledge beyond thought; the same typology emerges from Rossetti's two sonnets for Ingres's *Ruggiero and Angelica*. In Rossetti's sonnet for Leonardo's *Madonna of the Rocks* there are dark questions, while in other sonnets for pictures verbless sentences are present. The effect of such syntax is of a timeless inclusive moment in no sequential context. Ingres's painting is a tableau from Ariosto who describes the sea monster as something beyond the frontier of human and animal, an emblem of chaos. It seems that Ingres departs from Ariosto by depicting Ruggiero as killing the sea monster, while Rossetti certainly varies Ariosto's narrative. The only moment of excitement in the painting is the faintly pornographic 'woman in bondage' motif. Violator and hero bifurcate. Angelica, that distinctly volatile heroine, is quite convincing in her fear; it is the condition of that 'extreme' knowledge with which Rossetti invests her; there is no suggestion, as there may well be in 'Leda and the Swan', that her attitude is ambiguous. Ironically enough in the *Orlando Furioso* as soon as Ruggiero has rescued Angelica he attempts to seduce her.

In 'Leda and the Swan' violator and hero are identical and the heroine's attitude must be correspondingly more complex. The two sonnets on Ingres, Rossetti later dismissed as 'pictorial', rendering the instant through listing the painting's detail, set linguistically in apposition. In the octave of the first sonnet there is no active verb, the noun phrases are clausally qualified. Only in the last line does the poet become truly interpretative: she does not hear or see, she *knows*; knowledge gained not physically or intellectually but through extreme experience; stated not questioned; an intensity of extra-sensory knowledge; life roused to a pitch of *ek-stasis* which suggests the religio-sexual so that the experience of death is, as in Elizabethan conceit, imminent orgasm.

I

A remote sky, prolonged to the sea's brim:
  One rock-point standing buffeted alone,
  Vexed at its base with a foul beast unknown,
Hell-birth of geomaunt and teraphim:
A knight, and a winged creature bearing him,
  Reared at the rock: a woman fettered there,
  Leaning into the hollow with loose hair
And throat let back and heartsick trail of limb.

The sky is harsh, and the sea shrewd and salt:
  Under his lord the griffin-horse ramps blind
    With rigid wings and tail. The spear's lithe stem
  Thrills in the roaring of those jaws: behind,
That evil length of body chafes at fault.
    She doth not hear nor see—she knows of them.

II

Clench thine eyes now,—'tis the last instant, girl:
  Draw in thy senses, set thy knees, and take
  One breath for all: thy life is keen awake,—
Thou mayst not swoon. Was that the scattered whirl
Of its foam drenched thee?—or the waves that curl
  And split, bleak spray wherein thy temples ache?
  Or was it his the champion's blood to flake
Thy flesh?—or thine own blood's anointing, girl?

Now silence: for the sea's is such a sound
  As irks not silence; and except the sea,
    All now is still. Now the dead thing doth cease

To writhe, and drifts. He turns to her: and she,
Cast from the jaws of Death, remains there, bound,
Again a woman in her nakedness.[10]

In the second sonnet that religio-sexual intensity ebbs. There is synaesthesic metaphor 'clench thine eyes'—the girl's sensations are analogous to Leda's confusion of identity, the *vague* fingers, and so on; 'trail of hair' suggests fracture, while metal and vegetation are assimilated: the spear's *stem*. And unlike Rossetti's later sonnets for pictures which constitute a monument to a significant 'moment', but in a sense resembling 'Leda and the Swan', the future perspective of the two Ingres sonnets is not projected as a moment charged with significance; rather, the monument is unimportant in itself because literally anticlimatic. Angelica in the last line is 'again a woman in her nakedness': she has lost the condition achieved through metamorphosis at the 'moment' of death itself; that final instant when one's death, here graphically imaged as Angelica's 'own blood's anointing', initiation, is viewed as spurious eternality, disingenuous, counterfeit. Moreover, as in Yeats's poem there is much sexual periphrasis and the coarser Freudian might have his amusement with the rock-point and the roving knight's stem-like spear. 'One breath for all': the breaking of the hymen or the knight's blood (semen) perhaps? so that the rhetorical question conflates foam, blood and semen; but the rescue amounts to a rejection. Angelica is merely a woman, naked, defenceless, fallen, shamed.

As in 'Leda and the Swan' the narrative of Rossetti's sonnets dramatizes the destruction of a significant moment; a failure of metamorphosis from accidental self to essence. The moment cannot be truly eternalized and the observer recedes from the image, from empathy, in a mode similar to that in Yeats's sonnet. In Rossetti's sonnets, the male and the monstrous are separate (though one might remember that Ruggiero is mounted on the hippogriff) and unable to obscure themselves in material representation and then free themselves once more and so achieve through metamorphosis enhanced identity. With the monster, Rossetti is distinctly less successful than Yeats; after 'geomaunt' and 'teraphim' with its homophone on 'terrible' we hardly need the 'foul beast unknown'. Neither Rossetti nor Yeats names the actors; the names of the God, we are told, 'belong to them by nature ... correctly analysed they must reveal something of the essence of the divinity they signify.'[11] And over the page from the Ingres sonnet we find this line from another sonnet, on Memling's marriage of Saint Catharine with the infant Christ: 'Her life is hushed and mild,/*Laid* in God's knowledge.'[12] The tone is different, but describes a sacred marriage, not a sacred rape.

The Visual and Plastic Sources

If Yeats's sonnet is obliquely connected with the Rossetti sonnets on Ingres's *Angelica and Ruggiero*, is it connected also with the general tradition of the sonnet descriptive of a work of art? The congress of Zeus and Leda was a constant theme in art from the fourth century B.C. to the late nineteenth century; more popular certainly than analogous events such as Zeus and Ganymede or Zeus and Olympia and in the Renaissance probably for reasons of formal elegance.

The most influential single image is furnished by Michelangelo's painting, lost but surviving through a corpus of copies and assumed relevantly into literature by Pater's essay on the master. Yeats's poem has been connected with Michelangelo's version by T.R. Henn and with more elaboration by Giorgio Melchiori, for the poet worked with a photograph of one of the copies before him, and Michelangelo becomes a presence in his last works.

Michelangelo's *Leda* itself was indirectly inspired by an antique prototype preserved in Renaissance drawings of Roman sarcophagi; but Elfriede Knauer has persuasively argued that there are more obvious antecedents: gems, terracottas, lamps, scarabs; small objects, that is, which more readily survived the Dark Ages than art works of a larger scale.[13] One of the latest discoveries of a copy of Michelangelo's *Leda*, that by Rubens, was originally—so an X-ray shows—an elliptical, that is a gem-shaped painting. In antiquity two types of the image of Leda and Zeus as swan emerged. One, a more narrative tradition, shows the nude Leda standing, both repelled and charmed by a swan of god-like proportions; she gently presses it into her thighs, or caresses its neck. The other cult image shows her horizontal and clothed, warding off the eagle and pressing the swan to her bosom. Both types of image remained extremely popular through late antiquity. Renaissance artists preferred the reclining type, a Leda nude and no longer indecisive but passively submitting to the swan-god, heated or in orgasmic swoon: 'the private apotheosis'.

A few examples survive in which Leda kneels, including one sardonyx at the British Museum, while there is a group in which she sits upright, adapted, we may suppose, to the exigencies of material, gems and vases; but the standing and reclining or half-reclining images remain by far the more frequent. That the standing image did survive into the Middle Ages is shown from a drawing of 1374 now in a private collection in London.

In the High Renaissance and Baroque periods, we find the swan and Leda assumed into interior decoration, fresco, stucco, and so on, and shown therefore off the ground, recalling the analogous Ganymede story with the inner meaning of the sacred rapture that unites the two themes, though most, if not all, the examples remain trivial, as in Aeneas Vico's engraving at Berlin or B. Peruzzi's rather aerial vista in the Farnesina at Rome or, perhaps more relevant, stucco examples in country houses near Dublin (Russborough, for example).

Leda's popularity derives not merely from the erotic and dramatic possibilities of the image: 'two forms intertwined in a closed shape'. She becomes the type of other annunciations, as with Michelangelo or Yeats. Zeus's visitation in serpent form to Olympias in the sala of the Arazzi in Rome has close iconographical resemblance to the usual iconography: both the reclining Olympias and the upper parts of the serpent recall the curving neck of the swan and the reclining Leda.

CORREGGIO, LEONARDO, TINTORETTO

Renaissance artists may have preferred the reclining image, but there are prominent examples of the standing image, though these barely represent struggle. Correggio's oil at Berlin presents a *locus amoenus*: trees, streams, some nymphs having a bathing party. A flock of wild swans alight among them, and one of these is Zeus in disguise. He advances on Leda who receives him, as one amused sophisticated critic observes, with a mixture of sophistication and amusement. Another swan attacks a nymph, picture right, who defends herself, while in the air above a swan can be seen flying away.

Correggio intended perhaps to represent three stages in the myth: Leda startled by the bird, accepting his love and the flight of the god; this, though sharply different in tone, corresponds to the three stages of Yeats's sonnet: blow and lock, shudder and release. Cupid, playing on a minuscule harp, presides; there is virtually a tinge of genre in the nymph replacing her garments in the centre background.

In the Borghese gallery at Rome is a Leda long attributed to Leonardo and as such accepted by Pater in his essay on the master ('and as Leda was the mother of Helen of Troy') but which is sometimes attributed now to Leonardo's disciple, Sodoma. The face is that which obsessed Leonardo with muted, mocking smile, smooth brows and centrally parted hair. Leda stands, elaborately coiffured, presumably bewigged (as in the Cesare de Sesto copy at Wilton), turning to caress the swan at her side. One wing of the bird is extended and wrapped about Leda in such a way that the edge of the wing corresponds in contour to Leda's hip and thigh, suggesting possibly a sculptural, presumably antique, source. This produces a graceful, if stylized line. The scene appears to be domesticated: Castor and Pollux play at their mother's feet while a little further off we may see the egg from which they have emerged. All the detail seduces: it is spring-like, 'thick grasses writhe out of the earth' and a thrush, a snail and a dove appear, an allegory of the mystery of sexual intercourse and its connections with the creative processes of nature; the subject being treated, as Kenneth Clark observes, with a detachment that is altogether disquieting. The 'mystery' of Yeats's sonnet is here, but all violence is subdued: 'there may well have been a level on which Leda and the Virgin coalesced in Leonardo's imagination and demanded similar forms'.[14]

Tintoretto's Leda is a Venetian matron with much bust and hip and bejewelment and clearly of the city. Zeus appears to have penetrated, or perhaps like Goosey Goosey Gander in the nursery rhyme has been procured, into Leda's bedchamber. Leda herself reclines on a couch in a half-slanting position. The swan on her left is opening a cage in which a duck—or is it a drake?—can be distinguished while another small cage on the wall suggests that the affair is taking place in a bird fancier's establishment. Or it could be that this Leda is kinky about birds in general? Or is there some allusion to the alternative tradition of Zeus as goose? Leda's head here is Venetian rather than classic and indicates the general movement away from art models.

LEDA IN THE POST-RENAISSANCE PERIOD

Knauer observes that the Leda image becomes less popular after the Renaissance period, evanescing from 'mystery' into 'naturalistic' representation. Certainly we can trace the progressive emptying out of the theme through the elegant marble of Jean Thierry and the graceful erotic bronze of Raymond Sabourand (where the swan mounts from the back), both in the Louvre, though J.D. Draper claims that the mid-seventeenth-century version of Michael Auguier, in *pierre de tonerre*, combines the stately and the mysterious.[15] The lady's hair and the swan's wing wrapped round Leda, both recall Leonardo's version. Knauer (like most critics of Yeats), however, curiously omits one nineteenth-century painter whose whole artistic effort was directed against Naturalism and whose early philosophy was a neo-platonism pressed almost to an absolute dualism. Gustave Moreau described his own images as 'mysterious'. Of Michelangelo, whose 'grandiose dreams' haunted him, Moreau wrote that his figures seemed 'asleep—their movements unconscious. They seem absorbed in a dream world and inhabit a divine and non-material realm quite different from our own. They do not enact clearly recognisable dreams, and in some inexplicable way their actual movements often seem in contradiction to the meaning we attach to them'.[16] Such contradiction makes the image suggestive beyond the allegorical level on which the specific images are totally comprehensible. In this sense, Moreau's paintings are strictly symbolic. One of Moreau's earliest compositions was on the subject of Leda and, as was his custom, he returned to the theme at various times. It is, with Salome, Oedipus and Sphinx, Sappho and Orpheus, one of his obsessive subjects. Where most painters have stressed the eroticism of the theme, Moreau, 'by a process of syncretism, assimilated it to the Annunciation, the flexible arabesque of the swan's neck, surrounded with a halo of light above the head of Leda, taking the place of the dove'.[17] The analysis of Pierre-Louis Mathieu continues:

> the very pure, idealized outline of Leda's face answers to the canon of Greek sculpture, eliminating the accidental and individual; her full-bodied, intensely feminine body is coiled up in a position recalling that of Michaelangelo's *Night* on the tomb of Giuiliano de'Medici.... The cult of the Virgin, implying the birth of the Divine Logos, is emphasised by the presence of angels bringing in a crown, as in a picture by Van Eyck.[18]

Moreau (like Munch) was in the habit of producing prose-poems to indicate the programme of his paintings:

> Le Sacre.
> Le Dieu se manifeste, la foudre éclate, l'Amour
> terrestre fuit au loin. Le Cygne—roi, auréolé,
> au regard sombre, pose sa tête, sur celle de la
> blanche figure, toute repliée en elle-même dans sa
> pose hiératique d'initiée, humble sur ce sacre divin.
> L'immaculée blancheur sous la blancheur divine.
> L'incantation se manifeste, le Dieu pénètre, s'incarne
> dans cette beauté pure.
> Le mystère s'accomplit.
> Et devant ce groupe sacré et religieux, se dressent
> deux génies accompagnés de l'aigle porteur des
> attributs divins, le tiare et la foudre. Ils
> tiennent devant Léda cette offrande divine, officiante
> de ce Dieu, s'oubliant dans son rêve.[19]

Immaculately blanched! In 1854 the dogma of the Immaculate Conception was promulgated and the lily is the symbol of annunciation to Mary. Pierre-Louis Mathieu quotes another commentary which may be given in translation:

> The Swan-King, his head laid against the chosen woman, in his sovereign attitude incarnates in her his whiteness and divinity. Attentive, living out her dream, she remains motionless in its divine spell. Hers is the august slumber that goes before a transformation. She is all grace in her very power and strength. A white camelia beneath the white lily. Two spirits bear the diadem and the thunderbolt, living caryatids presenting Leda with the emblems of power. Farther off, its hands outstretched and open in token of possession, victorious and triumphant love soars away to the conquest of the world. The intermediate divinities, fauns, satyrs, dryads, hamadryads, nymphs of the woods and waters, come to commune at this altar of whiteness. And out towards the horizon, kneeling in an attitude of worship, the great Pan takes part, sancifying with all nature this apotheosis of eternal beauty.[20]

Moreau's Ledas differ from his ritual temptresses: Salome, the Chimera, the Sphinx, in particular, where woman functions as an aggressor and where the painter appears to fear that the fluid feminine principle will overcome male rationality.

Moreau's suite of images appealed particularly to the *fin de siècle*. Moreau himself was part of the pantheon of John Gray's and Sturge Moore's friend, Charles Ricketts, and was prominent in Charles Shannon's and Rickett's periodicals, the *Dial* and the *Pageant* and Gray and Moore both have poems on the Leda theme. Ricketts was also one of Yeats's mentors, and another of his mentors, Arthur

Symons, devoted an essay to the French painter. However, in Moreau's images, sacred marriage rather than rape is prominent; Leda achieves apotheosis; creature is mystically united with creator. She is 'all grace in her very power and strength' and receives 'the emblems of power', while the figure of love suggests future perspectives. Yeats could hardly have evaded Moreau's images, yet their feeling is quite polar from the violence and sensuality in the sonnet. For a time the poet reacted against the painter. In the second series of *Discoveries*, Yeats remarks: 'I find myself at moments desiring a more modern, a more aggressive art—an art of my own day. I am not happy in this mood unless I can see precisely how each poem or play goes to build up an image of myself, of my likes and dislikes, as a man alive today.' The context is actually painting, and Yeats is recalling his early intuition that one day he would come to admire Manet. Now, at a time when the energy of his repudiations is leading him towards *Responsibilities*,

> those pictures that now delight me most are the least meditative, most animal, active, living, triumphant: more even than Renoir ... the other day when I wandered about the room in Paris where there is nothing but Moreau, I could not sink myself to the dream of kings and queens, witches and unicorns, and strange jewels [undecipherable] of good and evil luck—the mythologies of a thousand poets.[21]

'The room' must surely allude to the Museé Moreau. But this was before 1914, 1916, 1919 and 1921–22. Far from being frozen as 'circus animals' of Pre-Raphaelite youth, Moreau's Salomes and ladies on unicorns were to return in power; and the last section of 'Meditations in Time of Civil War' is presumed to derive from a reproduction of a Moreau painting in Yeats's possession (*Les Licornes*).

None the less, the 'staggering', 'beating' and 'rush', even allowing for translation of visual image into language, have an immediacy that Moreau with his *belle inertie* conspicuously evades, for conflict in Moreau is internalized absolutely; is conducted by a confrontation of glance and profile. Moreau cannot suggest, as the Michelangelesque *furia* can, the energy both internal and external that so awed Michelangelo's contemporaries. Yeats, we might add, rectifies Moreau's passive vision by viewing him through Michelangelo. Criticism, however, has noted that the violence of Yeats's octet leads to a tableau effect in which syntactically and physically Leda remains 'locked' within a situation where she is unable to move, where her identity collapses. Moreover, the 'feathered glory' of the swan besides representing a synecdoche of strong motion, and a telescoping of Leda's impressions could have originated in reminiscence of Moreau's haloed swans. In an earlier draft of the sonnet, Yeats has the line: 'Did nothing pass before her in the air' (*Memoirs*, p.274), which connotes the divine (or the demonic) and may well relate to one of Moreau's more dramatic images, *L'Apparition*; the severed head of John the Baptist not so much haloed as bristling with a blaze of sanctity, appearing in mid-air to a horrified Salome.

Sculptural Sources

Spitzer tells us that Leda in Yeats's sonnet is confined no less temporally than spatially: time is arrested when eternity irrupts into history. Being fixed physically, the only movement granted to Leda is that of 'loosening thighs', almost involuntary and analogous certainly to the quasi-mechanical nature of the 'shudder' and the final, post-orgasmic 'Before the indifferent beak could let her drop.' That tableau effect suggested to Melchiori and Charles Madge sculptural sources. Salomon Reinach's *Apollo* was among Yeats's books, and he may well have looked through Reinach's *Répertoire de Reliefs grecs et romains* of 1912, which contains a number of images of Leda and would have clarified the two iconic modes in the ancient world: erect and receptive; recumbent and possessed. It was a free-standing sculpture belonging to the former category that Melchiori produced, a Roman sculpture based on Hellenistic models that Yeats might have seen when he visited Venice in 1907. The work is far from attractive and Madge's suggestion that the primary source was a bas-relief exhibited until 1939 in the Etruscan Room at the British Museum was more plausible.[23] This dates from about the first century A.D., but the motif goes back to the fourth century B.C. and, Madge suggested, corresponds minutely with the first six lines of Yeats's sonnet: the nape is being forced down by the swan's bill, a habit of the male bird when mating. Yeats was always a haunter of the British Museum and between 1895 and 1917 lived in Woburn Buildings, a few minutes walk from this work of 'exquisite violence'.

However, Charles B. Gullans observed that the position of

Leda's hands suggested that she was assisting at her own seduction.[24] More plausible, Gullans considered, was a woodcut bookplate designed for A. G. B. Russell by Yeats's old friend Sturge Moore and published in *Modern Woodcutters No. 3 T. Sturge Moore* (1921). The swan's neck in this image coils round Leda's, and the webbed foot, virtually edged with claws, is wounding the girl's thigh.

The British Museum bas-relief is given more authority by the fact that it appears as the first illustration to the chapter on the last Greek period in the first volume of Elie Faure's *History of Art*, devoted to the ancient world. The English translation amenably appeared in 1920, and Henn lists the book as among those in Yeats's library, starred to indicate that it would repay further study. None the less, Faure was ignored both by the assiduous Melchiori and by Madge. Even more significant perhaps than the illustration of the bas-relief cited by Madge is the substance of the chapter on late Greek art entitled 'The Dusk of Mankind'. Faure describes with warm Latin rhetoric the decline of Greek art from the heroic period to the Hellenistic often in terms that recall *A Vision*, 'The Statues' and *Autobiographies*. Cultures are defined in terms of art works in a manner that takes one both to Spengler and to the omitted final section of the 1925 *Vision*, where the future is adumbrated in terms of contemporary art. The Hellenistic period, Faure tells us, was one when 'sensibility increased at the expense of moral energy, reason overflowed faith, enthusiasm was dulled through contact; no human power, no miracle could have re-established it'.[25] Here there is space only to cite the passage that describes the bas-relief itself, beginning with Praxiteles who initiates decline:

> To express the inner life he seeks to make it external.... Little by little, the deep structure is forgotten.... He has taught us that the feminine body, by its rise into the light and the affecting frailty of the belly, the sides, and the breasts in which our whole future sleeps, sums up human effort in the unconquerable idealism with which it faces so many storms. It is impossible to see certain of these broken statues where only the young torso and the long thighs survive, without being torn by a tenderness that is sacred.... Look, after seeing the 'Victories', after the 'Dancers' of Delphi—so natural in their grace that they make one think of a tuft of reeds—look at the 'Leda' as she stands to receive the great swan with the beating wings, letting the beak seize her neck, the foot tighten on her thigh—the trembling woman subjected to the fatal force which reveals to her the whole of life, even while penetrating her with voluptuousness and pain. And that is still religious, grave, barely

> infected by heady agitation, barely turning towards the slope of sensual abandon—it is like the adieu of Greece to the noble life of the pagans. The heroic era of paganism begins its death struggle with a smile that is a little melancholy, but tender and resigned. It seems as if this admirable race had had a feeling of the relativity of our knowledge and as if it had accepted the beginning of decline as simply as it had accepted its dawn.[26]

However, though some of the terms of this description accord with Yeats's poem, there are two differences, one radical, the other more apparent that real. Faure defines the Swan–Leda congress not as annunciation but as apocalypse of decline; the bas-relief is a witness to its century, the fifth before Christ, not to the fluid beginnings of Greek civilization. Secondly, the accent falls, if not unequivocally, on Leda's acquiescence, certainly on her ambiguous attitude to the swan: 'standing to receive'.

In Moreau's principal image of Leda, the god incarnates himself within her mortal beauty and by this act divinizes her. The crown furnished by the *putti* is Leda's by grace, and she acquires all the divine attributes which we may assume include 'power' and 'knowledge'. The subject then is apotheosis, brought about through being loved by a god. The bas-relief in the British Museum may or may not have originated as a cult image, but of the connection between reclining images of Leda and the Swan with death and apotheosis there can be no doubt. There is the sarcophagus of Lucinia Magna at Arles, while on another sarcophagus at Aix-en-Provence 'Leda repulses the swan', which would seem to indicate a struggle against apotheosis through physical death. It was this iconography that inspired Michelangelo's lost Leda.

Leda, Michelangelo and Amor as Death

Henn does not tell us which copy of Michelangelo's *Leda* Yeats had before him as he worked. If it were the Rosso in the National Gallery then the contrast between Michelangelo's image and the images of the other painters as well as the affinities between his *Leda* and his *Night* in the Medici Chapel would have been attenuated. But Yeats might just conceivably have come across an illustration of the Rubens copy which Edgar Wind describes as nearer to the heroic proportions of the Michelangelo than the more accessible and elegant version of Rosso. In Michelangelo's image, Leda appears as muscular, heroic in proportion, profoundly asleep, even more than the 'languor of her late sweet toil' might appear to demand; and it is Wind's argument that both the *Leda* and the *Night* are variations of the single theme: Amor as Death. Michelangelo's source for both painting and sculpture was the figure of Leda on a sarcophagus, and he was versed in the neo-Platonic 'mysteries' present in Lorenzo de'Medici's court which would read the love of a god for a mortal in a funerary context as apotheosis, the partaking of eternal bliss through 'death'. The Florentine neo-Platonists made use of fantastic etymologies, random consonances of words: thus the notion of Leda 'being generally associated with Leto and explained as Night, the mother of luminary gods'. And in their syncretizing of pagan and Christian, they discovered this 'love' and 'death' in the Bible no less than in Plato; whether those kisses so lavishly strewn in the Song of Solomon or those of the delicious Agathon in Plato. It is St Paul's *cupio dissolvi et esse cum Christo*, and the Cabbalists termed this desire to be united with God as the *mors osculi*, the kiss of death. Some of the patriarchs of the Old Testament died in such a rapture. This union is experienced as initiation into death; death as communion with God (or a god) through 'love'. The Renaissance then identified Eros with Death, stressing the painful no less than the joyous aspects of union (though the pain was transitory if the union were complete), summed up by the phrase *dulce amarum*. The Florentine neo-Platonists would have distinguished between a 'first' death in which union is constrained by the 'prison' of the body and that 'second death' when 'the soul in the embrace of God would abandon the body altogether, remaining in supreme bliss, conjoined with the Godhead'. Michelangelo's *terribilita*, Wind suggests, was able to divest the bittersweet mysteries of their gentleness. In the *Leda* and the *Night* 'the gloom of death which the idyllic image on the sarcophagus was designed to lighten seems now condensed into a euphoric stupor'. As to the *Leda*, without

> removing the image from its sepulchral context, Michelangelo could not have produced such a ruthless picture. Conversely, when he retained the figure for a tomb, he transformed the Leda into an allegory of Night. Thus the funerary symbolism and the pagan myth, which he had found combined on the Roman sarcophagus, were split by him into separate images, of which each retained some traits of the other, although the attributes and the meaning were changed.

In place of the swan, *Night* has other emblems: owl, mask and poppies signifying Death and Sleep. Michelangelo moves then from the celebration of 'death and the love of a god', to the figure of Leda—Night mourning death 'as the work of destructive Time, in which she laments her own part.... In poetic theology, Leda and Night were one, and their figures represented two aspects of a theory of death in which sorrow and joy coincide'.[27] And Wind reminds us that though Leonardo's design of Leda 'is conceived in the style of a joyful idyll', diverging from the gloom with which Michelangelo invested her presence, the four children, nonetheless, issuing by pairs from the eggs in Leonardo's design, 'would seem to confirm an ambivalent interpretation of the theme: *concors* represented by Castor and Pollux, *discordia* by Helen and Clytemnestra. As they break through the shells, the two amiable and the two obstreperous infants appear as antithetical twins.'[28]

Wind alludes to Yeats's sonnet in a footnote, describing it as 'mythologically accurate'. In spite of Yeats's ferocious reading, one may doubt this, for the poet was more troubled by the Fall of Babel than most; but he had that knack of poets for finding precisely what he needed to support his arbitrary splendours, and he was as facile a syncretizer as his fifteenth-century predecessors. Moreover, his occult sources frequently repeated the neo-Platonists in vulgarized form. Wind tells us that Helen and Klytemnestra are born first from one egg, but that in Yeats's sonnet the birth of the demi-gods is left in doubt: 'Did she put on his knowledge with his power?' referring, so Melchiori suggests, to the superhuman vision and force bestowed by the god, but actually alluding, according to Wind, to the demi-gods. However, Wind is forced to engage with the fact that in *A Vision* (where 'Leda and the Swan' in its final revision first appeared) a variant is adopted. Kaistor being born with Klytemnestra and Polydeukes, with Helen. This variant appears in Gyraldus, whom Yeats is unlikely to have read.

The notion of Amor as death, Yeats could have derived from translations of Cabbalistic literature and from one of his favoured sources, the translation by Hoby of Castiglione's *le Libro del Cortegiano*, where, in the fourth book, Bembo hymns Platonic Love and discusses the kiss as a spiritual mingling of souls in context of the Ladder of Love. Franz Cumont, another of Yeats's known sources, recognizes the symbolic mood of many of those winged funerary figures that flank the central panels of Roman sarcophagi: 'les jambes croisées, et tristement appuyés sur sa torche renversée ... sa tête fatiguée se penche sur son epaule, les yeux clos, la bouche, entr'ouverte, souvent, il tient en main la couronne d'immortalité,[29] though elsewhere Cumont consistently interprets the mortuary Eros figure as connected with 'astral topography of the Beyond', an interpretation equally sympathetic to Yeats. We may agree that *concors* and *discordia* are implied by Yeats, since all things go by antithesis; but whether knowledge and power *can* be concordant, or indeed should be, is another matter; for their junction might well be far from concordant.

Wind has undoubtedly opened up an enriched reading of the sonnet. Two of the phrases in the sestet, 'put on' and 'caught up', work presumably in the *mors osculi–dulce amarum* tradition. Anne Hatcher some years ago noted without pursuing that 'put on' echoed a famous, triumphal passage in I Corinthians v.51–4:

> Behold I show you a mystery, we shall not all sleep, but we shall all be changed … for the trumpet shall sound and the dead shall be raised incorruptible, and we shall be changed. For this corruption must *put on* incorruption and this mortal must *put on* immortality. So when the corruptible shall have put on incorruption and when this mortal shall have put on immortality, then shall be brought to pass the saying that is written: Death is swallowed up in victory, O Death, where is thy sting? O grave where is thy victory?

St Paul concludes with two rhetorical questions while a species of initiation through death is described, but that death is without *amarum* as if the first and second deaths were anachronistically conflated. 'Caught up': Ganymede and Eros are joined through that phrase to Enoch and Elijah, but there would seem to be difficulties as the central Christian tradition insists on bodily resurrection, developed as typological reassurance as to the assumption of the Madonna living into Heaven: for who is without sin must escape the penalty of physical death. The 'caught up' distinctly affords then a junction of the two annunciations, casting a dubious light on the possible 'taking up' of both Mary and Leda. In a contribution to the *Savoy* of 1896 Yeats had written that 'He who sees Jehovah dies',[30] being always able to utilize the 'hidden' tradition by indirect means. The note that we should perhaps stress is one of possible apotheosis, in a domestic as much as a historical context.

In 'Among School Children', Yeats speculates as to whether images may exist independently of the minds that experience them; expressing themselves through such minds and issuing in embodiments that participate in the autonomous reality of that which they image. During the nineteenth century, bird and woman are conditioned by cultural pressures, finding always a mind, a situation, in which they will be counterpointed and joined, though not necessarily under their cult names. For the swan, with its traditional association with poets and poetry in a century when poetry begins to talk more and more of itself, and the Romantic projection of 'mystery' onto women provide an altogether hospitable context. Given the Romantic recovery of myth, we might expect a return of power to the image: Delacroix's fresco decoration at Valmont Abbey shows a recumbent Leda in Michelangelesque posture, *figura serpentinata*, caressing the swan's neck, while Gericault's splendid version (pencil, ink, watercolour and white gouache washed on bistre paper) is both voluptuous and faintly sinister. The drapery has fallen from the recumbent Leda and lies beneath her in an undulant spiral. The composition is hinged on abrupt contrasts of light and dark in relation to the solidity of the two protagonists, while more relevantly, the swan aggressively thrusts its head and beak at Leda, who rather ineffectually attempts to stem the bird's ebullience. The swan is frequent in *jugendstil* art and poetry; its arabesque of neck is the very idiom of *art nouveau* and it becomes a presence in French *symboliste* and English Decadent writings. In the 1890s, John Gray, Sturge Moore, Charles Dalmon wrote poems on the Leda theme, but Leda remains passively possessed. Leda and the Swan is rarely a declared theme among the Parnassians and the Symbolists: Leconte de Lisle renders the scene as *ballet de cour*:

> … sous ton poids charmant se dérobe à dessein,
> Et le Cygne attentif, qui chante et qui supplie,
> Voit resplendir parfois l'albâtre de son sein

while Tyndareos like the husband in a Restoration Comedy

> sceptre en main, songe, l'âme jalouse,

as well he might be, for

> O pudeur sainte, adieu!
> Et l'amante du Cygne et la mère d'Hélène,
> Hélène a vu le jour sous les baisers d'un Dieu![31]

Her birth, the swan's will and Leda's assent are as inevitable as formal dance; the poem is designed as a species of cantata. Henri de

Régnier has a trivial ekphrastic sonnet on the Leda and the Swan fountain at Versailles, but the more distinguished French and German poems and paintings (like the body of Yeats's sonnet) allude only to swan and/or girl. Pierre Louÿs was a friend of both Wilde and John Gray and known to the Ricketts circle. In his *Léda* (1898) he conflates Leda with Night and describes the swan as 'L'idée même du ciel de midi'; and it is the beak that engenders: 'Le bec l'avait brusquement penetrée et la tête du cygne se mourant en elle avec lenteur, comme s'il naigeait ses entrailles délicieusement.' The beak is 'ensanglanté' and 'bientôt il sembla reculer et ses caresses s'altérènt'.[32] Leda is left with a blue egg from which Helen alone, Beauty herself, is born. Of that same year 1898, Max Klinger's small relief (with electric bulbs behind the foliage evocatively lighting up Leda's limbs) presents the girl as crouching down, grasping the swan's neck and thrusting his beak between her thighs. The implied comment on female sexuality becomes explicit in Feliciën Rops's image, where the swan's beak and neck are actually shown as a phallus that Leda devoutly kisses, and the coarseness of Rops's image is analogous to the bawdy puns in Yeats's version of the image: 'laid', 'burning roof and tower', and 'white rush'. By the turn of the century, woman's sexual appetite is recognized, feared and mocked as spurious intensity.

In the twentieth century, the heightening of women's consciousness, the politicization of sexuality, the heightened awareness of the psychological no less than the physical violence to which women are frequently subject, and the diffusion of the Freudian mythology have all tinged the image of Leda and the Swan. Near the turn of the century, Zeus tends to fade from manifestations of the story and the encounter tends to be polarized between Leda as active agent and the swan now as a more generalized symbol (in Yeats appearing as index of the 'soul' and of subjectivity).[33] In Munch's images, woman is represented in her new complexity: swan and woman become conflated, as we may gather from the prose poem connected with Munch's painting *A Vision* (achieved actually in the early 1890s). Woman has become pluralistic: vampire and Madonna—still caught in the traditional *symboliste* and Decadent antinomies—but also swan-woman, Apollo's surrogate, a species of muse so that she acts creatively both in the sexual and imaginative domains and comes to represent the art that momentarily transforms reality and stems the fear of death, of which woman also becomes the symbol. Her role in the sexual mystery becomes increasingly accentuated. In Rilke's sonnet, Zeus puts off godhead and puts true swanhood on only through Leda's mediation. For the Freudian, the myth becomes a vortex of the sexual integer, entertainingly caught for us in a recent article that stresses the neck and beak of the swan as possessing that displaced sexual significance that Rops and others had divined. Indeed there can be few orifices and few fulfilments that the myth cannot sustain.

R.W. Medlicott lists for us the numerous twentieth-century artists who have touched the theme: Leda appears as dream-like, frankly orgasmic, and in some instances unable to distinguish between dream and orgasm. There is a virtually unanimous evasion of rape, but sado-masochistic and more sinister elements are often present, as in Sidney Nolan's image where the swan treads a bloodied vulva. In the mid-nineteenth century (and among Yeats's business friends), the horror of bestiality had tended to drive visual and plastic representations of the Leda story into the closed world of pornography or restrict them to the merely decorative convention. In the twentieth century it was on occasion the very animal energy of the story that incited a response, though the focus on the woman's role could conduce to a reduction of the god-swan to pet-like scale (as in the Veronese) or to the size of the swan in nature, or to the treatment of the situation—examples are offered by *The New Yorker* and *Punch*—as merely comic: 'I don't know what you're doing in that get up, George', says a bikinied Leda on the beach to a vast swan, 'but the answer is still "no".' More recently, the Australians with unflinching seriousness have mounted an exhibition entitled 'Leda and the Emu'.

Excepting Nolan's version (a bloody union not a rape) and Winderlich's, the paintings Medlicott lists seem far from Yeats. Far too is the insight that the Leda and Swan image represents a reversion to a very primitive congress owing to the rudimentary penis of the male swan. This leads to polymorphous diffusion: the head and beak as primary sexual members (here we can recall the egg and yolk *Symposium* image in 'Among School Children'.)

Leda as Aggressor

The Freudian reading permits us to cast Leda as androgynous. It was not until 1970 that Bernard Levine suggested that Leda was as much aggressor as victim, the swan, victim as much as aggressor.

This reading depends on interpreting lines in an opposite sense and on an argument drawn from lack of punctuation which allows more than one sense (though punctuation in 'Leda and the Swan' as elsewhere may owe more to Messrs. Macmillan than to the master).

In such a reading, the sonnet remains dominated by 'the reflexive opposition of concrete and abstract imagery'. Here: 'Leda is identified through concrete detail', but 'the swan ... is never referred to in the poem as "a swan".' Rather, it is described 'as an overpowering abstraction—"the great wings", "the dark webs", "that white rush", "the brute blood", "the indifferent beak". It may be the purely mechanical simplicity of the grammar that finally requires pronominal identification of the "swan", in the third, fourth and thirteenth lines of the poem. But at these points the use of pronouns tends to humanise the essential action.' Lines five to twelve are conspicuously void of pronominal forms and consequently 'the distinction between the concrete (or personal) and the abstract gives way to a profound ambiguity': the swan's will or imagination is 'staggered' by Leda; it is she who arranges for the swan's bill to be 'caught' by her nape; omitted commas permit 'helpless' to allude to swan no less than girl, while the 'vague' (root meaning 'wandering') fingers can apply to Leda as actively, not passively, submissive to the swan, to the webs, and to an archaic sense of 'terrified' as tormented, irritated or teased. The breaking of sexual tension in lines nine to eleven—the ejaculation scene—reveals not necessarily and only 'portents of disaster' but 'release from the feeling of fear or alienation'. As to the word 'there', this now indicates not the temporal or spatial fixity or the detachment of a speaker empathizing almost exclusively with the swan, but pluralized empathy also. 'There' involves five possible loci: Priam's or Agamemnon's house; Leda's womb; 'the supernal consciousness of the swan'; 'the consciousness of a given culture'; 'a confrontation of the physical and the mental event'.[34]

In 1977 W. C. Barnwell elaborated such insights: Leda represents generic man; the swan, generic god. If in the first instance, the swan is the rapist, man's role in the cosmic drama is modest and passive; if, secondly, Leda, man plays a major role; but if some third party, then both man and god are victims. In Barnwell's view, the reader is, in the last analysis, the rapist; himself engendering time and again the blast of sexual union and the subsequent enervation. Both man and god are forced into such a union for the sake of a history that must itself move in prescribed grooves for a destined teleology.

If Zeus is victim no less than Leda, then the answer to the final question of lines eleven to fourteen of the sonnet must be: No, why *should* Zeus have any knowledge to impart? Gods may have knowledge of history's inward rhythms but may be unable to act upon that knowledge, so that man endures violation since that is all he knows.

If the reader is rapist rather than voyeur, then man's role is active. Barnwell proceeds to cite Cassirer's notion that *symbolic* reality is all that man may know; he cannot know something unless he can in some way symbolize it. The act of reading a poem then recreates a specific reality in symbolic space and time within which the great wings are beating still above the staggering girl (the sons of god still seduce the daughters of men): human history is repeated again and again, rehearsed as it is within the specific arenas of the mind. Man's very ability to create a symbolic reality literally isolates him from everything else. It is the reader of the poem who manipulates bird and woman from the onset to the conclusion of their encounter through countless shudders, blows, burnings and deaths; through countless conjectures and questions about life and death and their ultimate meaning. Man lives darkly in and through history, but he also understands its nature and so may hope to affect its rhythms.

I hope I have not myself violated this elegant argument for the reader, in the best modern way, creating the text. That argument and the assurance of man as moral agent leans on Yeats's notion of the thirteenth sphere, which has been described as the 'system' generating its own antithetical 'mask'. But this is perhaps dangerous, for allusions to the thirteenth sphere in the 1925 version of *A Vision* are parsimonious indeed: it is very curtly offered as the abode of daimons and of the perfected human; and when accessible to those in the body it appears at the fifteenth (unembodied) phase. Can two scattered sentences in an elaborate system really be thought of as establishing a heavy antithesis to the cycles of history?

Iconic criticism, as we have seen, has tended to concentrate on the Renaissance, though why the European phase 15 should generate the saving image is not clear: an actual 'shift in the world' insight derived from a later phase would surely be more logical, even if we allow Michelangelo as a special case from his involvement with notions of time, death and resurrection. Moreau and Hellenistic sculpture and the iconic genre; Rossetti's sonnet dramatizing a failed apotheosis, Elie Faure's description of decline of Greek sculpture, are prime sources, and like the 'imaginary museum' of

Marino's *Galeria*, the tableau is, we may agree with Barnwell, endlessly imagined; but with an *enargia* that is circular, not cathartic.

The Questions

In relation to the image, Richard Ellmann declares that Yeats allows both views of the subject (naturalist and idealist) to coalesce, while Kermode takes the view that the reconciliation of opposites is the purpose of the Yeatsian symbol. However, it remains possible that Yeats's 'blast of union' in 'Leda and the Swan' is not Hegelian, but something closer to the Sartrian 'upsurge of being'. Sartre differs from Hegel in thinking that, after the moment when consciousness is born, essence and existence can no longer be re-united; that essence is by definition evanescent (and this in itself constitutes a useful insight into Yeats's early poetry).[35] Hegel, on the other hand, would hold that through the dialectical development of reason in history, and its attendant expansion of self-consciousness, true unity *can* be achieved. Spirit alienates itself into history and recovers itself by completing the knowledge of its contradictory nature in death; or in Platonic terms, the Form is not finally itself till it has obscured itself in material representation and then become free once more; or in Yeats's own terms, 'all life longs for the last day' (Variorum Poems, p. 306). Most critics, indeed, would agree that, in one way or another, Yeats exalts the imagination as the source of such a unity in an almost Coleridgean manner. But this view neglects the fact that Yeats has his roots in the Decadence and that the primary vision of the Decadence involves an aesthetics of failure. In Yeats's later poetry that is aggrandized into the tragic vision, but throughout his career, there is a constant self-distance, a consciousness of failure.

'Leda and the Swan' poses the most compelling image of unity possible, and it does so through the blurring of identities in the act of the rape. And yet within this apparent union lie the seeds of its eventual disintegration, and it is here that those self-indicting questions come into play. The two questions in the second stanza are asked, in the poem's dramatic time, at the very moment of the rape, of the pumping of the eschaton into history. They are poised between the Keatsian ('beating still') moment of the first quatrain and the disintegration of the sestet, obvious both in form and in content. But they *are* questions and they do direct themselves towards the possibility of an ideal intersubjectivity (how can she-he but feel the strange heart, etc.) or to the ontology of the act itself (how can she separate?), asked we may suppose, in a spirit both of fascinated enquiry and of outrage.

That the final question should be answered in the negative, should be self-indicting, would then seem to be established both by the very fact of questioning, following the opening certainty, and by the disintegration of the sestet. 'Leda and the Swan' not merely argues failure, it demonstrates it.

Notes

1. I have profited from conversations with Professors D.S. Carne-Ross, J. Lucas and Christopher Morris, and from correspondence with Dr C. Ligota of the Warburg Institute, University of London. Of the numerous articles on 'Leda and the Swan', I may mention John B. Vickery, 'Three Modes and a Myth', *Western Humanities Review* 12, 4 (Autumn 1958), pp. 371–8; Joseph Margolis in *The Explicator* 12, 6 (April 1955), pp. 4–5; Bernard Levine, *The Dissolving Image: The Spiritual-Esthetic Development of W.B. Yeats* (Detroit, 1970); and W.C. Barnwell, 'The Rapist in "Leda and the Swan"', *South Atlantic Bulletin* 42, 1 (January 1977), pp. 62–8. R.W. Medlicott's 'Leda and the Swan: An Analysis of the Theme in Myth and Art', *The Australian and New Zealand Journal of Psychiatry* 4, 15 (1970), pp. 15–23, is an amusing and informative piece. There are some tersely suggestive remarks in Lillian Feder, *Ancient Myth in Modern Poetry* (Princeton: 1971), pp. 193–4. The articles which compare the poem with the work of others I have not found helpful, with the exception of Jane Davidson Reid's 'Leda Twice Assaulted', *Journal of Aesthetics and Art Criticism* 11, 4 (June 1953), pp. 378–88. However, Reid's piece tends to type and then dismiss visual sources too arbitrarily, describing Leonardo's image as 'familial' (Kenneth Clark's more just description is to be found in his *Leonardo da Vinci*, Cambridge 1939, pp. 126–7); and with some naïveté states that 'Yeats and Rilke do not depart from the myth as it has been retold from antiquity'. James Hepburn in 'Leda and the Bumbledore', *Sewanee Review* 88, 1 (Winter 1980), barely establishes confidence in his confrontation of Hardy and Yeats when he asserts that the line 'I spit into the fact of time' is present in *The Countess Kathleen and Various Legends and Lyrics* (1892). Hepburn typically gives this date as 1893.

   I offer this essay in spite of A.D. Hope's contempt for the 'literary dustmen' who engage in source and parellel studies, his examples being Henn and Melchiori on 'Leda and the Swan'. *The New Cratylus: Notes on the Craft of Poetry* (Melbourne, London, Wellington, New York, 1979), p. 114.

2. Giorgio Melchiori, *The Whole Mystery of Art* (London: 1959), pp. 156–60, particularly for Moreau's Ledas and the excursus on Renaissance versions, pp. 280–83; Leo Spitzer, 'On Yeats's Poem "Leda and the Swan"', *Modern Philology* 51, 4 (1954), pp. 271–6. T.R. Henn, *The Lonely Tower*, 2nd edn (London, 1965), prepared the ground for the study of visual sources in Yeats, though he alludes only briefly to Moreau, mentioning Yeats's possession of a reproduction of the painter's *Women and Unicorns* (p. 255).
3. *Divinarum Institutionum*, I, in Jacques Paul Migne, *Patrologiae Cursus Completus* VI, col. 236 (Paris, 1844): 'Nam et Romulus post mortem Quirinus factus est; et Leda, Nemesis.' For the most convenient study of the fortunes of Leda and Helen, see Jack Lindsay, *Helen of Troy* (London, 1974), esp. pp. 107–8.
4. Edgar Wind, *Pagan Mysteries of the Renaissance* (Harmondsworth: Penguin, 1967), p. 167.
5. As recalled by James H. Cousins in the Introduction to Abinash Chandra Bose, *Three Mystic Poets: A Study of W.B. Yeats, A.E. and Rabindranath Tagore* (Kolhapur: School and College Bookstall, 1945), p. v.
6. Robert Langbaum, *The Mysteries of Identity* (New York: Oxford University Press, 1977), pp. 150–1. Pearse and Cuchulain, for example; *An Ri* and the life of Cuchulain as pattern for the children of St Enda's: 'assimilation into the archetype of the hero'.
7. *Sight and Song* (London: Elkin Mathews and John Lane, 1892). See Jean H. Hagstrum, *The Sister Arts: The Tradition of Literary Pictorialism and English Poetry from Dryden to Gray* (Chicago: University of Chicago Press, 1958), for the iconic poem.
8. *Sight and Song*, p. v.
9. Yeats's review is reprinted in *The Uncollected Prose* of W.B. Yeats, ed. J.P. Frayn (London, 1972), pp. 225–7; see p. 225 for the quotation. Frayne notes (p. 227) the Fields' poem on 'A Pen Drawing of Leda, by Sodoma', which is found in *Sight and Song*, p. 81.
10. W.M. Rossetti (ed.), *The Works of Dante Gabriel Rossetti* (London: Ellis, 1911), p. 189. My graduate student Simon Puxley, in his thesis, 'An Arduous Fullness: Rossetti and the Sonnet Tradition', (University of Reading, 1971), has useful comment on the sonnets for pictures.
11. E.H. Gombrich, '*Icones Symbolicae:* The Visual Image in Neo-Platonic Thought', *The Journal of the Warburg and Courtauld Institute* II (1948), p. 170. This piece has been revised and extended in *Studies in the Art of the Renaissance* (London: Phaidon, 1972), pp. 123–5.
12. *Works of Dante Gabriel Rossetti*, p. 190.
13. 'Leda', *Jahrbuch Der Berliner Museen. Jahrbuch der Preussischen Kuntsammlungen, Neue Folge* (Berlin: 1969), esp. pp. 21ff. There is an excellent bibliography, which involves both literature and art, in Reinhold Heller's 'Edvard Munch's *Vision* and the Symbolist Swan', *Art Quarterly* 36, 3 (Autumn 1973), pp. 209–49. For the Leda myth, its

variants and antique depictions, see W.H. Roscher (ed.), *Ausfürhliches Lexikon der griechischen und römischen Mythologie* (Leipzig, 1884–1937), II, pp. 1922–31. See also A. Piglet, *Barockthemen: eine Auswahl vor Verzeichnissen zue Ikonographie des 17. und 18. Jahrhunderts*, 2nd edn (Budapest, 1974), II, pp. 107–156–60; and A. de Hevesy, 'Léda et le Cygne', *L'Amour de L'Art* 22 (1931), pp. 469–80. A Klockourström's *Leda och svanen* (Stockholm, 1924) furnishes a history concerned mostly with piquancy of subject matter. For the swan in poetry since the Renaissance, see Edgar Lehner, 'Das Bild des Schwans in der neueren Lyrik', in Egon Schwarz, *et al.* (eds), *Festschrift für Bernhard Blume: Aufsatze zur deutschen und europäischen Literatur* (Gottingen, 1967), pp. 297–322. I have not alluded to Mallarmé's famous 'Le vierge, le vivace et le bel aujourd'hui', which also begins with a beating of great wings, but here indicating no species of triumph, but rather a last effort to evade 'otherness', an 'otherness' that is seductive.

14. Clark, p. 127.
15. 'For the love of Leda', *Metropolitan Museum Bulletin* 30 (October 1971), pp. 50–58. In Antoine Coypel's image, the swan engages Leda from the front, while a Zeus altogether prepared moves in from behind (Plate II). Aubrey Beardsley parodies the iconography of Leda and the Swan in two of his illustrations to Juvenal's Sixth Satire: *Bathyllus in the Swan Dance* and *Bathyllus posturing*.
16. Julius Kaplan, *Gustave Moreau* (Los Angeles, 1974), p. 23.
17. Pierre-Louis Mathieu, *Gustave Moreau* (Oxford, 1977), p. 121.
18. Mathieu, p. 119.
19. *Catalogue sommaire des peintures, dessins, cartons et aquarelles exposés dans les galeries du Musée Gustave Moreau* (Paris: Musée Gustave Moreau, 1926), p. 13.
20. Mathieu, p. 119.
21. See Robin Skelton and David R. Clark (eds.), *Irish Renaissance: A Gathering of Essays, Memoirs and Letters from the Massachusetts Review* (Dublin, 1965), pp. 84–5.
22. See Salomon Reinach, *Répertoire de Reliefs grecs et romains*, 3 vols (Paris, 1909–12), and Melchiori, pp. 158–9.
23. *Times Literary Supplement*, 20 July 1962, p. 532. See the issue for 3 August 1962, p. 557, for Melchiori's response.
24. *Times Literary Supplement*, 9 November 1962, p. 864.
25. Elie Faure, *History of Art* (London, 1921–4) 1, p. 187. Like Henn, Melchiori, Madge, *et al.*, I too would have missed this had it not been for the guidance of my graduate student Michael Shaw.
26. Faure, I, pp. 194–200.
27. Wind, 'Amor as a God of Death', pp. 165–6. 'Euphoric stupor' seems less appropriate to Yeats (or even perhaps to Michelangelo) than 'a curiously heroic quality of sleep' which Feder (p. 193) distinguishes in Yeats's 'Lullaby'. There, Leda's sleep, no less than Zeus's, is more 'golden' than that of Paris and Helen, Tristam and Iseult. Yeats would also be familiar with 'mindless ecstasy' distinguished from Christian ecstasy in Erasmus. He certainly knew the *Moriae Encoriun*, as he knew

Plato's *Phaedrus*. The most elaborate treatment of the *mors osculi* is to be found in Nicolas James Perella, *The Kiss: Sacred and Profane* (Berkeley and Los Angeles, 1969), esp. pp. 172, 179–181. According to Perella, Pico della Mirandola was the first to use the range of this imagery.

28. Wind, p. 167.
29. Franz Valéry Marie Cumont, *Recherches sur le symbolisme funéraire des romains* (Paris, 1942), pp. 409–10.
30. *Uncollected Prose*, p. 399, described by Yeats as a 'Hebrew saying'. The article is devoted to Paul Verlaine's visit to London in 1894.
31. *Poèmes Antiques* (Paris, n.d.), pp. 84–5.
32. *Léda, ou la louange des bienheureuses tenebres* ... (Paris, 1898), p. 5.
33. In his notes to *Calvary* Yeats, as Heller points out (p. 215), records that 'certain birds, especially as I see things, such lonely birds as the heron, hawk, eagle, and swan, are natural symbols of subiectivity' (*Variorum Plays* p. 789).
34. *See Dissolving Image*, pp. 114–19. But 'there' is also iconic, corresponding to Marino's 'Ecce'.
35. A passage from Hazel E. Barnes's introduction to Jean-Paul Sartre's *Being and Nothingness* (New York: Philosophical Library, 1956), pp. xli–xlii, may make the point: 'sexual desire is not merely or primarily the desire of physical "satisfaction". It is rather the deep-seated impulse of the For-itself to capture the Other's subjectivity. It tries to achieve this goal by, so to speak "incarnating" in its own consciousness, letting itself feel itself almost wholly flesh and so inducing the Other to do the same. But this appeal of the flesh to the flesh ultimately fails, not only because satisfied desire ceases to be desire, but because in physical possession the lover still knows only his own pleasure and the body of the Other. The Other's subjectivity can become part of my experience only in two ways—either as I know myself to be the object of it or as I look upon it as an object; but in neither case do I as subject know him as subject. The reason why I want to get hold of his subjectivity is, of course, to protect myself against the possibility of his making an object of me. The fact that both lover and beloved feel this same need accounts for the instability and ultimate failure of love.' Ellmann's view can be found in *The Identity of Yeats* (London, 2nd ed, 1968), *passim*. For Kermode's see *Romantic Image* (London and Glasgow, 1971), esp. pp. 56–61.

9

Symons, Yeats and the Demonic Dance

In the early 1920s, in one of his autobiographical fantasias, Ford Madox Ford made this high claim for the influence of Arthur Symons on what was then the 'forward' movement in English poetry: 'Consider the gap there would be in a whole *genre*, if Mr Symons had never written. I might call him, rather than myself, the doyen of free verse.' Ford is always a dubious oracle; but, as the former editor of the influential *English Review*, and as a man who had himself lived through the gap he was talking of, the gap in English poetry between late Pre-Raphaelitism and early Imagism, he could speak, in this instance, with some authority. Like all men who live through such a gap, Ford could feel it, but not explain it; though he instinctively, and rightly, felt that Symons's influence supplied a hidden continuity. We on the other hand have not lived through the gap, but, historically distant from it, feel we can explain it. But such a feeling of objective historical understanding is to some extent illusory, for we are still under the influence of two very powerfully charged versions of the story. In an essay on *Baudelaire in Our Own Time*, Eliot pays generous tribute to Symons's understanding of French symbolism, but he suggests that Symons was unable to profit, in his own poetic practice, by that critical insight. Eliot's early vigorous propaganda for the metaphysicals also disguised the degree in which, both in his poetry and criticism, he was interpreting the metaphysicals in a Symbolist manner, almost in Symons's own manner; his early poems in quatrains are not, like metaphysical poems, imitations of argument, even sophistical argument; their manner of procedure is Symbolist; and in later, more unbuttoned pieces, Eliot had admitted his strong personal debt as a young poet to Symons and other quasi-Symbolist and Impressionist poets of the 1890s. Eliot has misled us in one way; Yeats misleads us in another.

Our present interest in the 1890s is largely due to the fact that Yeats, a very great poet indeed, was in a sense formed by that decade, survived it and beautifully commemorated it. We treat the sections in the *Autobiographies* on the 1890s not merely as great art in prose, as aesthetic modulation of history, but as document; in a sense we are right to do so, for Yeats, unlike many authors of literary memoirs, was not a deliberate liar and factually the *Autobiographies* are surprisingly accurate. Yet two quotations give the essential clue to his method: 'It needs the wild mystical parts to lift it out of gossip': and, 'I study every man I meet at some point of crisis—I alone have no crisis.' He shows, for instance, Wilde and Henley, Beardsley, Johnson and Dowson, Aesthetes or activists, saints *manqués* or crippled Imperialists, mock-aristocrats and mock-tramps, held at a moment of intolerable tension. Symons was still alive when he wrote; Symons's life was not obviously dramatic and is given muted treatment. Yeats does, however, full justice to the dialogue of ideas and personalities between him and Symons in the five years when they were closely associated; yet he appreciated Symons because Symons was, for him, a feminine, receptive personality; a conductor of ideas. He never quite treats Symons as a person or a poet in his own right; if he praises anything, it is Symons's translations from the French, which he saw as extensions of Symons's great gift for making immediately current the latest forces in other European literatures. So Yeats gives us, at the best, a partial version of Symons, as he gives us a partial version of the other actors of the 'Tragic Generation'; though no one will ever give us versions that are more vivid. We will probably go on quoting the *Autobiographies* to clinch a point: not seeing that they themselves have figmented the point we are clinching.

Eliot and Yeats between them have contrived to create a 'set picture' of the 1890s as a whole, and of the role of Symons in that decade; they unconsciously conspire together to remove Symons from the centre of the picture, except in so far as he was a critic, and especially except in so far as his *Symbolist Movement in Literature* had a formative effect on Yeats and Eliot; it underlies Yeats's *Ideas of Good and Evil* (1903), and if Eliot had not read it round about 1909, when he was a student at Harvard, he would not have gone into Boston to buy Laforgue. It would be easy to counteract the fashionable view of the 1890s as an unhealthy egg, out of which

Yeats managed to burst, with some equally hollow generalization; but the best way to disturb this lazy attitude, to reduce Ford's 'gap', is by producing some local and modest but (I hope) suggestive evidence.

What I want to do in this essay is to exemplify three things. There is a fourth thing beyond my particular scope, which I shall mention and let go. The first thing is that Symons bridges the gap between Browning and Eliot, by having written at least one poem which owes a great deal to Browning's dramatic monologues but also something to the manner of procedure of Laforgue; it is a poem half-way between *Bishop Bloughram's Apology*, say, and *Portrait of a Lady*. The second point is a movement in Symons's poetic work from Naturalism through a poetic equivalent of French Impressionism in painting to something that faintly begins to suggest the Imagism of Hulme and the Ezra Pound of *Lustra*. (The fourth thing is that in the 1890s Symons attempts to use Donne, Donne's sexual frankness and Donne's conversational ease, but without any real success.) More broadly, I want to suggest that the dialogue between Symons and Yeats was not restricted to critical doctrines and attitudes, but that they had an equally fruitful effect on one another's poetry. I shall examine this relationship rather narrowly in terms of the symbol of the dancer, and in particular of the fable of the conjunct *persona* Salome-Herodias and St John the Baptist's head, suggesting that it is in one of Symons's poems that we find the main source of Yeats's preoccupation with the image.

Between Symons and Yeats there are certain plain biographical affinities. Like Yeats, his exact contemporary, Symons was a largely self-educated Celt who revolted against his father's beliefs; but where Yeats reacted from positivism into occultism, Symons found another variety of 'literary' faith: the Impressionism of Pater's *Renaissance*. Symons's father, a minister, had been on circuit in Cornwall and Wales, and Symons himself grew up in a hectic atmosphere of religious revivalism and sentimental nationalism. But, unlike Yeats, Symons was never to find in nationalism a creative force: he was essentially a rootless man, at home in any part of the world because he belonged to none; but more at home certainly in London and Paris than in a Celtic world of political histrionics. If Yeats's career can be seen as the successful attempt to control a successive set of identities, Symons is a poet who failed in the search for a single identity.

Much of Symons's work can be grasped in terms of tensions

between his early revivalism (vividly depicted in *Seaward Lackland*, one of the exercises in autobiographical exploration contained in *Spiritual Adventures*, that were themselves part of his search for an identity) and Impressionism; between Naturalism and the occultism of Yeats and in the years when they particularly associated. Symons rejected revivalism, for its group fervours were related to that 'metaphysics' Pater had taught him to distrust. This rejection marked the first stage of his alienation: Seaward Lackland, the young Methodist lay preacher in *Spiritual Adventure* never actually dedicates himself to God in the sight of the community, but oppressed by the sense of sin determines to cut himself off from man and God by committing the unnamed sin against the Holy Ghost, through insisting that his action is determined by love of God: a parable of the poet as rebel mystic.

Basing his life on Pater's *Renaissance* was to intensify Symons's isolation and self-consciousness. The Impressionist pays a high price for the freedom of aesthetic intensity: all sense of neighbourliness, of life beyond the veil, is dissolved: 'each mind keeping as a solitary prisoner its own dream of a world'. For Pater, the only vehicle of communication lay in the senses, for they were all that men possessed in common, and it was finally through Anglo-Catholic ritual that he had attempted to redeem himself from the 'flux'. Symons was not attracted to high ecclesiastical gestures: the 'flux' with its evasive glitter absorbed him, and the dance, stylized, self-conscious, provocative, came to represent for him the perfect emblem of life in the modern city, for it dramatized his own isolation. Yet through his association with Yeats, the dance later became for Symons not spectacle merely, but participation, and, in some sense, religious.

It was towards Naturalism that Symons first reacted and this note dominates his first book of poems, *Days and Nights* (1889). The themes here are mainly contemporary and urban. Symons enjoys extreme situations and his experience of Nonconformity provides material that is treated in the melodramatic spirit of Henry Arthur Jones. Elsewhere, he indulges in the religious pornography his Nonconformist background made voluptuous for him: a woman pleads before the crucifix and then resigns herself to her lover's embraces; in *Red Bradbury's End*, a dying man is anxious to see a minister, but his son will not allow it, for that would involve the confession of a murder in which both father and son are implicated.

That Symons should turn to prose because of such psychological casuistries, was one of Pater's suggestions in a review of *Days and Nights* largely through doubts about the capacity of modern poets to control contemporary data. *Vie de Bohème*, however, is one of Symons's successes in precisely that field.

> The pink light flickered, and a shadow ran
> Along the ground as couples came and went;
> The waltzing fiddles sounded from the tent,
> And *Giroflée* began.
> They sauntered arm in arm, these two; the smiles
> Grew chilly, as the best spring evenings do.
> The words were warmer, but the words came few,
> And pauses fell at whiles.
> But she yawned prettily. 'Come then,' said he.
> He found a chair, Veuve Clicquot, some cigars.
> They emptied glasses and admired the stars,
> The lanterns, night, the sea.
> Nature, the newest opera, the dog
> (So clever) who could shoulder arms and dance;
> He mentioned Alphonse Daudet's last romance,
> Last Sunday's river-fog,
> Love, Immortality; the talk ran down
> To these mere lees; they wearied each of each,
> And tortured ennui into hollow speech,
> And yawned, to hide a frown.
> She jarred his nerves: he bored her—and so soon.
> Both were polite, and neither cared to say
> The word that mars a perfect night of May.
> They watched the rising moon.

The shrug in the voice: 'the smiles/grew chilly as the best spring evenings do', the confidence of tone, the suggestion of nuances, the ease of the topical references, all suggest the 'new' poetry of twenty years later, *Vie de Bohème* stands half-way between Browning and Eliot, and like the early Eliot owes something to Laforgue's *Complaintes* (1886). Still, though one admits all this, sentimentalized irony remains the note rather than Laforgue's cold frivolity: the values are not superbly mocked, other values are not suggested in Eliot's manner by trenchant omission.

In a prevalent Naturalist context, another poem, *Flos Florum* (1887), strikingly prefigures Yeats's Rose poems of the 1890s. Rhythm and vocabulary here are Yeatsian, though there is no symbolism and the moral is a Paterian *carpe diem*:

Poor Flower of Flowers, hoar Time is harsh with us
Time that has made all Edens ruinous ...
Child, if thy mirror warns thee, heed it well ...
One sighs, For I have seen the privet pale,
The roses perish and the lilies fail.
Sigh not at all, but say (if worst be worst),
In these last things shall men recall my first,
Wondering,.and as old age breaks down and bows
The comely walls of my life's crumbling house ...

In 1889 Symons paid his first visit to Paris and his second book *Silhouettes* (1892), as its title indicates, reveals a new approach to contemporary life: the black and white of poetry. By 1891 he had become a member of the Rhymers' Club and was on familiar terms with Yeats. Yeats's *Autobiographies* record one of Symons's remarks at this time: 'we are concerned only with impressions'; but the word is ambiguous. It looks back to Pater's *Conclusion* to the *Renaissance*; but when the poet applies the criteria of Pater's *Preface* the range of the word extends to something that suggests analogues from painting: 'analyse, and separate from its adjuncts, the virtue by which a picture, a fair personality in life, or a book, produces this impression ... [the] end is reached when he has disengaged that virtue and noted it as a chemist notes some natural element.' Much of *Silhouettes* can be read as a delicate set of Paterian exercises in distinguishing appearance from reality; reality consisting simply in these 'beautiful changes', the chance integrities of light, colour and mood. What survive from *Silhouettes* are the images:

A bright train flashed with all its squares
Of warm light where the bridge lay mistily.

Yet Symons cannot maintain this role of impassive recorder, like an Imagist poet; he must comment, often banally, on the order invoked. It is only later that acute visual effects cohere with the creation of mood indirectly through rhythm, so that the poet can be present indirectly and can set up a silent ironic disparity between the 'I' of the poem and the 'eye' of the voyeur. For, by this time, Symons had begun to come under the influence of Symbolism, in the sweeter and scaled-down version of Verlaine, Verlaine's somnambulistic rhythms which promised the lyrical dissolution of that 'discourse' the Rhymers so detested. *Dieppe—Grey and Green* is one of the successful silhouettes and, dedicated to Sickert, attempts to reproduce that master's muted palette:

The grey-green stretch of sandy grass,
Indefinitely desolate;
A sea of lead, a sky of slate;
Already autumn in the air, alas!

One stark monotony of stone,
The long hotel, acutely white,
Against the after-sunset light
Withers grey-green, and takes the grass's tone.

Listless and endless it outlies,
And means, to you and me, no more
Than any pebble on the shore,
Or this indifferent moment as it dies.

Still, as Wilbur Urban remarked, Symons's grey 'epiphanies', though sensed through a variety of scenes and actions, remain fatally subdued to the 'achromatic thinness of a mood'. The divination of beauty in odd places is limited by the narrowness of the temperament that divines.

London Nights (1895) is unified as a volume by the capital itself established as a fugitive set of aspects, made and remade every night and morning. Effect of civilized corruption, fog collaborates vividly with gaslamps hanging 'like rotting fruit' to produce a momentary illusion of the beautiful. With this world, Symons searches for identity:

My life is like a music-hall ...
'Tis I that smoke this cigarette,
Lounge here, and laugh for vacancy,
And watch the dancers turn; and yet
It is my very self I see
Across the cloudy cigarette ...

His life was artificial enough at this time, with its constant play-going, visits to music halls, circular discussions of literature under the coved ceilings of smoky-crocketed public-houses. And the beauty of artifice and illusion out of doors had its counterparts within, for it is in *London Nights* that Symons's obsession with dancers and the dance begins. Yet the dance here is essentially a spectacle for solitary enjoyment, on the level of the 'fatal art of the acrobat'. *Javanese Dancers*, his first poem on this central topic, was written as early as 1889, after his first visit to Paris. The hypnotism of the dance is cleverly evoked through the metre:

Still, with fixed eyes, monotonously still,
Mysteriously, with smiles, inanimate,
With lingering feet that undulate,
With sinuous fingers, spectral hands that thrill
In measure while the gnats of music whirr,
The little amber-coloured dancers move,
Like painted idols seen to stir
By the idolators in a magic grove.

Though some sinister sacerdotalism is hinted at, it is with the routine coolness of the anthropologist.

It was during Symons's visit to Paris in 1892 that he discovered the European equivalents of these ritual dancers: Nini-Patte-en-l'Air, La Goulue and La Mèlinite, with their ominous solipsist quality:

Enigmatically smiling
Back to a shadow in the night.

But they are also valued for their 'science of concupiscence' and this excitingly contrasts with a self-analysing gravity. As a contemporary remarked: 'Apparently [Symons] set out quite early in life to shock himself; and I cannot believe that he has ever failed. Indeed, I have seen him walking about Saint Martin's Lane in a mackintosh, shuddering at the depths he has discovered in his soul: a soul as deep as a soup-plate.' Symons was always trailing himself round corners to catch himself at some trivial vice, trying to assimilate himself to his own myth of the 1890s, and he preserves a naïvely caressing attitude to the image of himself established at this time: a nocturnal beast let loose in the Strand. His real position is rather the inverted sacramentalist's (he often writes on the theme of Amor as God of Death, 'the kiss of the spouse, gustation of God, and ingression into the divine shadow' equated ironically or blasphemously with 'the little death' of physical love: there is perhaps some influence of Wagner's *Tristan*). This can be modulated whimsically:

Why is it, child, you choose to wear
That artful 1830 air
Of artfullness made artifice?
To lure all lips to long to kiss

The saint-like halo of your hair ...
If those calm eyes, if that pure cheek,
If this soft haloed hair could speak
The false, fantastic, final truth,
In some remote remembered youth
I loved Gavarni for a week.

Yet is it not merely mock-innocence with lubricious gestures that excites Symons. In an article written in 1897, he associates his Parisian dancers with the Decadent myth of *chute* and *finis latinorum.* Nini Patte-en-l'Air's cold art transforms her into 'a Maenad of the Decadence', as she dances with 'a sort of learned fury'. Yet she is hardly a Maenad, for her art is painfully erudite, it is not 'free' in the same sense as the dancing of Jane Avril or Loie Fuller. Although he refers to Jane Avril, Symons shows little interest in Loie Fuller (for Yeats the representative dancer of the poetic image); he prefers ballet with its cross-flare of gaslights and footlights, its painted figures and its diaphanous but somewhat mechanical order (the dancers of Degas rather than those of Moreau). Ballet's illusion mimics the illusion of life. But the 'free' dancer does not depend on scenery, music, dramatic interest; she depends merely on her own body, and her dance can be readily associated with possession by god or demon. To admire the 'free' dance is to pass from 'decadent' admiration of artifice to Symbolist recognition of Mallarmé's 'l'incorporation visuelle de l'idée.'[1] From a frivolous spectacle, the dance was transformed for Symons into something quasi-religious. Forces other than Symbolism tended in this direction.

In England, Symons was a devotee of the Alhambra and the empire Music Halls, and like several of his fellow Rhymers fell in love with various ballet-girls (Symons's love-affairs were generally conducted on strict Baudelarian principles: the girl was cast according to type as Infernal or the Uranian Venus). The ballet-girls' custom was to meet the Rhymers at the Crown public-house after their performance and somewhat incongruously the group would include the Rev. Stewart Headlam, Fabian, Anglo-Catholic, and founder of the Church and Stage Guild. The Guild's purpose was to study theatrical dancing and publicize it as a moral and religious activity. As a sacramentalist, Headlam insisted on the sacredness and antiquity of the dance, regarding the art as a form of union with God and appealing to the danced liturgies of the primitive church. For Headlam, dance

> perhaps more than all other arts is an outward and visible sign of an inward and spiritual grace, ordained by the Word of God himself [he is referring to Matthew xi. 17: 'We have piped unto ye, and ye have not danced'], which has suffered more than all the other arts from the utter-anti-sacramentalism of British philistia. ... Your Manichaean Protestant, your superfine Rationalist, reject the dance as worldly, frivolous, sensual.... Your Sacramentalist knows something worth more than both of these. What perhaps the Dancer herself may be partially unconscious of, that we live now by faith and not by sight, and that the poetry of motion is the expression of an unseen spiritual grace.

And Headlam continues by quoting two lines from T.G. Hake: 'She all her being flings into the dance' and 'None dare interpret all her limbs express'. Here is a clear parallel with the Symbolist 'free' dance: but the parallels with twentieth-century versions of Symbolism are as clear. The Church and Stage Guild regarded ballet and Music Hall as social no less than religious art. In John Todhunter's *A Comedy of Sighs* (1894), a Church and Stage Guild Curate remarks: 'It's out of the Music Hall the drama of the future must come ... the drama of the working man.' All this Eliot was to remember, and in the 1920s he was to refer to 'dance at its finest, by which I mean High Mass at the Madeleine'. Dance and Music Hall both perform something of the function of the image in Symbolist aesthetic: they unite classes, if not races and creeds.

In the ambiance of these ideas and his close association with Yeats in the later 1890s, Symons came to describe the dance as 'the natural madness ... men were once wise enough to include ... in religion. It began with the worship of the disturbing deities, the gods of ecstasy for whom energy passing into excess is sacred.' And in *The Turning Dervish* (1902) he writes:

> I turn until my sense,
> Dizzied with waves of air,
> Swims to a point intense
> And spires and centres there ...
> Till with excessive love,
> I drown, and am in God.

The dialogue between Yeats and Symons became intense in the years between 1895 and 1900: the two were never to see as much of each other again. These are the years of *The Savoy* (in which Yeats collaborated), of *The Symbolist Movement*, of Symons's visit to Ireland in Yeats's company. Some of Symons's poems of this period show clear traces of his friend's manner; but the relationship was a dialogue; and in others we catch evident tones of what was to be Yeats's later voice, in his middle years:

O, why is it that a curl
Or the eyelash of a girl,
Or a ribbon from her hair,
Or a glove she used to wear,
Weighed with all a man has done,
With a thought or with a throne,
Drops the balance like a stone?

That dates from 1905. But in 1896, in *Perfect Grief*, Symons anticipates the Yeatsian technique of the dramatized quarrel with the self:

The wandering, wise, outcast sons
Of Pharaoh, the dark roofless ones,
Taught me this wisdom: If Death come,
And take thy dear one, be thou dumb,
Nor gratify with suppliant breath
The attentive insolence of Death.
Suffer thy dear one to depart
In silence; silent in thy heart,
From this forth, by thy dear one's name.
So I, that would not put to shame
So dear a memory dead, repeat
No more the sweet name once too sweet,
Nor from that buried name, remove
The haughty silence of my love.

The epithets are those Yeats was to use when he wished to express approval of artistocratic excess; words like 'haughty' and 'insolent'. We are once more with the poet of *Responsibilities*.

It cannot be proved that Yeats was influenced by such poems. (Their existence, however, is further reason for casting doubt on current views about Yeats's 'transformation' into a modern poet.) But in Symons's *Dance of the Daughters of Herodias*, written in 1897, we can watch the relationship at work; and the conjunction is very significant. In this poem, Symons's dancers are transfigured: he passes from Music Hall or simple spectacle of the ritual dance. We now have an ambitious attempt to present the Dance as a composite image: of the poet's situation; of the predicament of a society which had rejected his wisdom; of the dancer as at once fascinating and terrible; warning and epiphany at once. (Symons was the more ready to reject his previous image of the dancer as cheery girl from the chorus: one of his love affairs with a ballet-girl had proved more self-involving than expected.)

The step could surely not have been made without Yeats. Symons's poem depends on notions that he must have learned from his friend. For while Symons was familiarizing Yeats with French Symbolist texts, he was himself being instructed by his friend in 'mysticism'—that occult tradition that underlies Symbolism (a letter of Yeats in this same year refers to Symons's interest in the subject). And from unpublished correspondence between the two of them we gather that the Preface to *The Symbolist Movement* contains the substance of their discussion of 'mysticism'. Yeats had come to believe that all the gods were masks of the one truth (an ancient idea expressed in the syncretistic rituals of the Golden Dawn) and at the same time Symons was confirming this in another way by placing the Irish Literary Movement as part of an international movement for the recovery of the Symbol that was to unite a fallen and divided world. It can only have been through Yeats that Symons, working in such a vein, learned of the daughters of Herodias. He knew of Salome—who did not—though he had not before seen his various dancers as versions of this most familiar dance: favoured by Moreau, Flaubert, Wilde, Beardsley and others. But in this poem, Salome's dance has the terrible general significance, the note of a move in the world, apocalypse, that can only be given by conflating Salome or her mother with more powerful creatures. In 1893 Yeats had published *The Hosting of the Sidhe*, which he was to use as the opening poem of *The Wind Among the Reeds* (1899) and which expresses that sense of omen pervading the volume, both in connection with personal and general situations. In 1899 he states that these beautiful destructive spirits of the wind are associated with Herodias and her dance:[2] in a note he refers to 'Herodias doubtless taking the place of some old Goddess'. At a time when his occult studies were impressing on him that all the Gods were one, it is not unlikely that Yeats read Grimm's *Teutonic Mythology*, which appeared in English in the 1880s. Grimm traces the story of these destructive angels of the air in the folk lore of many nations, including the Irish, and gives sources for the conflation of the patristic tradition of Herodias with folklore; the legend of Herodias's love for John being transferred to her daughter. Grimm refers to Salome (Herodias) attempting to kiss the Baptist's mouth, while the saint's disembodied head blows her back and whirls her round the sky. And Herodias is associated by Grimm with Diana as Hecate, in her virginal malignant aspects, as huntress of souls and with tree-worship, 'haunting the oaks by night' like an aerial Lamia.

Yeats must have told Symons of this. And through the symbolic extensions that Yeats made available, the history of Symons's concern with the dance achieves its widest reference. But it is in turn through this poem that Salome, and all that accompanies her, enters Yeats's own work. It is in this poem for the first time that we meet the dancer with the severed head associated with the tree: the epiphany shown as rooted in life. Its opening relates it to the eschatological Rose poems Yeats was writing in the 1890s to indicate the first trembling of the Veil of the Temple.

> Is it the petals falling from the rose?
> For in the silence I can hear the sound
> Nearer than mine own heart-beat, such a word
> As roses murmur, blown by a great wind.
> I see a pale and windy multitude
> Beaten about the air, as if the smoke
> Of incense kindled into visible life
> Shadowy and invisible presences;
> And, in the cloudy darkness, I can see
> The thin white feet of many women dancing,
> And in their hands ... I see it is the dance
> Of the daughters of Herodias; each of them
> Carries a beautiful platter in her hand,
> Smiling, because she holds against her heart
> The secret lips and the unresting brow
> Some John the Baptist's head makes lamentable;
> Smiling, as innocently as if she carried
> A wet, red quartered melon on a dish ...
> Here is Salome ... She is a young tree
> Swaying in the wind; her arms are slender branches ...
> Her narrow feet are rooted in the ground.
> But, when the dim wind passes over her,
> Rustlingly she awakens, as if life
> Thrilled in her body to its finger tips.
> ... And she leans
> Forward as if she followed, her wide eyes
> Swim open, her lips seek ...

The poet ends with the same prayer as Yeats in *The Rose*: that the eternal beauty will not come too near, lest he grow mad, drowning in its excess.

Dance in the desolate air,
Dance always, daughters of Herodias,
With your eternal, white, unfaltering feet.
But dance, I pray you, so that I from far
May hear your dancing fainter than the drift
Of the last petals falling from the rose.

It is to this eschatological aspect of the dancer, Yeats returns in *1919*:

Herodias' daughters have returned again,
A sudden blast of dusty wind, and after
Thunder of feet, tumult of images,
Their purpose in the labyrinth of the wind:
And should some crazy hand dare touch a daughter
All turn with amorous cries, or angry cries,
According to the wind, for all are blind.

In Symons's poem, tree mutates into dancer; her eyes open dreamily, but cannot flare with the incandescence of 'that brightening glance' in *Among Schoolchildren* that triumphantly consumes all deceiving truths. *The Daughters of Herodias* ends in nostalgic inconclusion: for Symons the dancer was always distinguished from the dance. He could get no farther than this: it was left to Yeats to absorb and recreate the image. Yet Symons's influence on Yeats extended beyond the 1890s, and the more we examine Symons's work, the more we realize that the 1890s are not, as they are commonly supposed to be, a self-enclosed period, but a continuum which must be re-enacted if we are to 'distance' the 'modern' movement in English poetry.

The sad later history of Symons is the sad iteration of old themes: he could never get beyond what he had learned in the 1890s. In the autumn of 1908 he suffered his own 'crack-up', so identifying himself with the 'Tragic Generation', whose legend he had helped to create, and all development was at an end. That delicate mechanism, so long engaged in distinguishing reality from appearance, now helplessly confused them. His account of his amnesia and flight, *Confessions*, is one of the classics of madness (particularly as it appeared in *Life and Letters*, purified by Desmond MacCarthy of its literary incrustations). Even in the labyrinths of madness, as Yeats remarks in one of his letters, Symons talked sanely of literature. And in the mental hospital, he was hounded still by his dancers: a learned Greek professor confined there would exhaust himself with Dionysiac leaps and monotonous stamping, which he insisted was the rhythm of the angels. When Symons emerged, after a year and a half's confinement, only his past was left to him; his work became a protracted parasitism on that past, and in 1920 he reverted to the theme of the dancer for the last time in faded tones. Yet though criticism will have its icy points against his work, the wreckage is full of glittering hints.

1960

Notes

1. Professor F. Kermode's fundamental essay *Romantic Image* provides the context of these remarks. I should like also to thank Professor J.B. Trapp of the Warburg Institute for help with the biography of Salome.
2. In 1893 Lionel Johnson wrote a poem on this topic, *The Red Wind.*

PART III

CONTEMPORARIES

10

The Poetry of John Gray

'A somewhat beautiful oddity', so Lionel Johnson's phrase for John Gray in that set of luminous and incisive notes he sent to the American poet Louise Imogen Guiney in 1897. Johnson was, it is to be presumed, describing the poetry; but he can hardly not have been sensible of Gray's physical beauty, about which there was nothing odd, or of his working-class origins or of his being devoid of formal education and yet Dandyish in both life and art. Gray's talent as a poet was odd certainly, and it remains unlikely that he would have succeeded in creating a career in letters. His verse plays and musicals are hardly striking, and his short stories and his novel *Park* have as much, perhaps rather more, talent than his poetry. But the novel was written late in life and belongs less to the 'time travelling' genre than to the distinctively Catholic and metaphysical genre of Bernanos and Greene.

Gray, though, had ambitions. His oddity was not confined to what in the years round about 1890 were very much minority enthusiasms: French Symbolist poetry, Huysmans, the Latin Church and the more florid devotional poets of Europe. His poetry was difficult to classify, and so was the man himself: his protectors, Wilde and Raffalovich, could barely regard him as a 'slum chum'. This exquisite may have come of a working-class family and in the 1890s at least retained a cockney accent; may have left school at the age of thirteen and begun work as a metal-turner in Woolwich Arsenal, where his father, a dourish Scot, had a job; but his ready adaptation both to people and ambiance made it impossible to regard him as louche or endearingly naïve or an object of ready patronage. For this he may have been indebted to his mother to whom he was closer than to his other parent. Of his mother, he gives an idealized account in 'Light', a short story contributed to *The Pageant* in 1897. The story centres on a humble woman who is married to a blacksmith (the autobiographical resonance is clear) and who in middle life has a vision of light to which she essays to remain faithful. The force of her sanctity breaks her body, and she dies tended by the women of the neighbourhood, who believe her mad, though the smith declares her sane. In this piece, the father no less than the mother is idealized, but in a brief holograph prose piece a different image of home life at the Grays is given; the drunkenness and sexual voracity of the father:

> home is of a necessary accompaniment to the daily debasement of two bodies. The prospect of family is at first kept out of thought, then hated. The wife is hated, for this man does not accuse himself as the cause of his wretchedness. It is not from lack of affection, for this man is never so soulless but he has some vibration of warmth, however low, towards the men he sees every day, by the mere fact of seeing them: but with his wife, not at all; meekly or fiercely she takes his bread, she breeds mouths. It is conduct minutely parallel to his sexual conduct if this man should drink one third of his earnings; it is the same conduct expressed in two different sets of terms. Approximations to Natural Love are bestial and degrading, and more so as the modifying elements stop short of reason. If they were not, the tie as in this case would not hold; the rotten threads can only bind the feeblest. The interest of the mere sexual act can only continue to the debased. Unanswerable evidence stands that in this instance, brute irrational sexuality is persisted in to the end. If the absolute truth on this subject is of interest, this man never denies himself sexually, in season and out of season, never.[1]

Never denies himself presumably even when his wife is menstruating. However, Gray seems to admit if only implicitly that it is not only a question of the wife's body being debased by the husband, difficult though it must have been to admit her connivance: 'fiercely' might seem to hint at the complexities of sexual relationships. This note was probably written in the middle 1890s and the detached language suggests distancing or the influence of that scientific student of Uranian sexuality—Marc Andre Raffalovich.

Gray's gifts both physical and mental could barely be contained within the narrow ambiance of the dockyard or the crowded family home where observation of one's parents' sexual lives was almost unavoidable. Still, it seems probable that John remained in the family home until his translation to the Foreign Office. While still in adolescence he mastered several languages, at least to the extent of reading them with moderate efficiency. He passed several examinations and found himself in 1884 a clerk in the General Post Office and by 1888 a librarian at the Foreign Office.

His first extant poem had been written at the age of sixteen, but it was not until 1890 that his first published piece appeared in Charles Kains Jackson's *The Artist and Journal of Home Culture*. This was a periodical of slender visual distinction and considerable tepidness of content. From 1890, though, in response to the *Zeitgeist*, it became hospitable to decadent and homoerotic themes. Kains Jackson indeed may be described as the Ombudsman of the Uranian world. A man of alarmingly wide interests, he wrote prolifically on art and published numerous poems. Most of the younger writers were personally known to him, and he counted Max Beerbohm, Hubert Crackanthorpe, Phil May, J.W. Gleeson White, Percy Addleshaw, Corvo and Ernest Dowson among his friends. For four years *The Artist* steered a delicate course between an audience composed largely of minor professional or amateur artists and rather more 'advanced' figures. Finally, in 1894 the editor overstepped the mark with an article defending Uranian Love under the title of 'The New Chivalry', which all too readily lent itself to association with the New Hedonism, the 'new woman' and other sinister symptoms of the love of new things for their own sake. Kains Jackson argued that Uranian Love was more spiritual; would prevent overpopulation and reflected more precisely that higher stage of civilization at which the Western World had now arrived. The next appearance of *The Artist* was with a new format and a new editor. The tepidness was now without alloy, and it quietly died a year or so later. This was the context of Gray's rather feeble version of Verlaine's sonnet in *Sagesse* (1881) 'Beauté des femmes, leur faiblesse, et ces mains pâles', otherwise 'Beauty, the fickleness of women, their hands pale'. All that is notable is the transposition of the French alexandrine at about the same moment as Lionel Johnson and Ernest Dowson were independently exploiting the metre.

The years from 1890 to 1892 were for Gray prolific though a number of the poems dating from that time were either unpublished or if published were not collected by their author. By 1890 Gray was reviewing occasionally for *The Academy*, and in the following year he established himself as the brightest of young men with his shrugging lecture on 'The Modern Actor' at the Playgoers Club and by the private theatre production of his version of Thèodore de

Banville's *Le Baiser* at the Royalty Theatre. This playlet had a Platonized Pierrot motif and was to be translated also by Dowson's friend, the American William Theodore Peters.

By 1890 he had also been converted to the Latin Church. At this time he was acquainted with a Catholic family, the Langdales, and their quiet piety no doubt had its effect on him. But the immediate cause of his conversion was a visit to a remote moorland church in Brittany, where a slovenly Mass was being accomplished by an unshaven priest. 'This is the real thing, John Gray', he reports himself as having said. Such an attitude has a Graham Greene or Bernanos tinge to it and one may perhaps guess that he sensed how the Mystery needed no ornate or decorous accompaniments; indeed, its radiance was the more pungent for its seedy context.

But his conversion seems to have had little immediate effect on his life: his literary ambitions continued to predominate and by the late January of 1891 Gray was well established in the Oscar Wilde circle and had become an occasional attender at the 'Crown' public-house and the meetings of the Rhymers' Club. In either October or November of 1892 he was introduced to the man who was to become his second protector, Marc Andre Raffalovich, a poet of the fourth class, an idealizing Uranian, a pioneer in studies of sexual inversion, and one of the most ugly persons of his generation. He was also a person of high generosity and in him, it has been suggested, Gray 'saw Christ': a moving notion, but one that has some touch of a heresy of the North African Church. Gray probably made the break with Wilde soon after meeting Raffalovich, but he did not attack 'poor Oscar' after the great aesthete's downfall while Wilde himself in *Epistola in Carcere in Vinculis* looked back on his friendship with Gray agreeably. The story that Wilde was responsible for underwriting Gray's first volume of poems *Silverpoints* has been disproved, though certainly Wilde offered to do so and indeed acted as go-between for the author and the publishers.

Silverpoints was published by John Lane and Elkin Mathews in March 1893. Designed by Charles Ricketts, it is perhaps the most delicately evocative of the decade's book productions, with its green boards, wavering *art nouveau* vertical lines hatched with golden fronds or drifts of *fleurs de lys*, and slender cheque-book shape, founded, so the designer himself informs us, on 'one of those rare Aldus italic volumes with its margins uncut'.[1] though it derives also from the Persian saddlebooks. Similar shapes were indeed not infrequent in the 1890s: the Pseudonym Library of Fisher Unwin and to come down market the Little Books on Religion series. The italic of *Silverpoints* carries Gautier's *coquetteries typographiques* to the verge of the exquisitely unreadable. According with Lane and Mathews' economic policy for 'advanced' books of verse, *Silverpoints* appeared in an edition deluxe of twenty-five copies in vellum and an ordinary edition of 250 copies. There are also a few unnumbered copies. The title alludes to a style of drawing by means of gold or silver wire on prepared paper, popular in the fifteenth and sixteenth century, but since abandoned. The characteristics of this style were durability and a cautious line: 'This particularly subtle and shadowy form of art', as James G. Nelson felicitously defines it—shadowy but durable. All Gray's volumes with the exception of *The Long Road* were to be published in limited issues, and such contempt for a wider audience (or modesty perhaps in Gray's later years) is related to the philosophy of Dandyism he inherited from Baudelaire and Barbey D'Aurevilly.

For such a philosophy, the natural is the bad; all that is good is acquired and artificial. Life and art are one; the self becomes an icon, expressing its self-sufficiency, but also its inner vulnerability, through trenchant silences, muted gestures and a tart elegance of clothing. The dandy will have no disciple: his genius is for obscurity. But in the 1890s, with the opportunity and danger of the popular media, these 'golden boys' might well violate their own theorems by using the instruments of the vulgar, by shocking, as when Beerbohm at the age of twenty-four produced his *Works*; or when with an irony rather beyond his audience he praised the prevalence of rouge. Gray was not an Oxford man and has less confidence or impudence than 'Max' (if we distinguish between Beerbohm's real self and his mask at this period) so that his dandyism is more discreet. Where Max and Wilde had ambitions to conquer the philistine city, Gray suggests that he has a severely confined audience in mind by his habit, taken over from Verlaine and Maurice Rollinat, of addressing particular poems to friends: Verlaine, Wilde, the translator Texeira de Mattos, Ellen Terry, the Princesse de Monaco, R.H. Sherard (Wilde's friend and biographer), Pierre Louÿs, famous for his luscious pastiche of Sappho *Les Chansons de Bilitis* and Ernest Dowson: the circle is reduced to a few poets, a painter, an actress whom Gray may well not have personally known, a Firbankian princess. About half the poems of *Silverpoints* are translations from such French poets as Baudelaire, Mallarmé, Verlaine and Rimbaud.

It would not be correct to say that the original poems celebrate Dandyism, the triumph of art over nature: if anything, nature triumphs over art, but nature is presented as indifferent or even hostile to man, and there is no suggestion that Gray anywhere subscribes to the Pathetic Fallacy or to Pantheism, both of which may be termed the opium of the sentimental nineteenth-century intellectual. Jonathan C. Tutor has recently suggested that the poems are closely interlocked and that the secular pieces progress in a dramatically unfolding order, resembling in their minor key the middle and later volumes of W.B. Yeats.[2] It is certainly true that the juxtaposition of art and nature is presented in a variety of modes, but the close organization that Tutor suggests does not seem to me to be present.

Art at its most insolent is in conflict with the natural world in *Les Demoiselles de Sauve*, Sauve being a district in southern France. The title seems innocent of punning.

Beautiful ladies through the orchard pass;
Bend under crutched-up branches,forked and low;
Trailing their samet palls o'er dew-drenched grass.

Pale blossoms, looking on proud Jacqueline,
Blush to the colour of her finger tips,
And rosy knuckles, laced with yellow lace.

High-crested Berthe discerns, with slant, clinched eyes,
Amid the leaves pink faces of the skies;
She locks her plaintive hands Sainte-Margot-wise.

Ysabeau follows last, with languorous pace;
Presses, voluptuous, to her bursting lips,
With backward stoop, a bunch of eglantine.

Courtly ladies through the orchard pass;
Bend low, as in lords' halls; and springtime grass
Tangles a snare to catch the tapering toe.[3]

The connection between the courtly ladies and the natural world is close; it also has faintly ominous overtones: the pun on the word 'palls' and the sequence of 'forked', 'crutched-up', 'snare' along with the assimilation of Ysabeau's lips to an almost blowing rose. As to Berthe, she, like the others, seems to be playing like Marie Antoinette at shepherdesses; her high crest may be her insolent hat, splayed out, horned like a Beardsley virago or, perhaps, it alludes to her youthful majesty of bosom and her slant, clinched eyes *á la japonaise* are also from Beardsley's repertoire though anticipating the artist's images by a year or two. As Tutor points out, 'dew-drenched' grass returns as 'springtime': nature is a continuously renewed process, but human individuals embody a principle of decay. The humorously ironic 'tapering' toe becomes a graceful synecdoche anticipating the ladies' 'Fall'. As in Marvell's 'Garden': 'ensnared with flowers' we may 'fall' but only on 'grass'. The light miming of the 'Fall' is a well-mannered way of enforcing the hard moral.

In 'Heart's Demesne', tripping in *terza rima*, the speaker discovers traces of his impassible lady in the natural scene dashed as it is by touches of omen:

> I love to tell when Daisy stars peep out,
> And hear the music of my garden dell,
> Hollyhock's laughter and the Sunflower's shout
> And many whisper things I dare not tell.[4]

Like the 'bursting lips' of the previous poem, the 'poutmouthed pink' in this is the emblem of a new type of sensual beauty that Beardsley was to make familiar in his middle phase, while the last line recalls the icons of initiation into forbidden mysteries of Beardsley's 'The Mysterious Rose Garden' or of the frontispiece to *Salome*. The diminuendo of stars to daisies is not so much rococo as uncomfortable. This conclusion has indeed a mutedly surreal quality that Gray brilliantly exploits in 'Mishka' and 'The Barber'.

'Lady Evelyn' is sugared pastiche of the routine Elizabethan love sonnet and with a muster of sexual puns that emphasize the underlying sensuality of the persons that Gray presents in *Silverpoints*. 'Complaint', as Tutor points out, is ambiguous, lament and illness. The devotee of the lady here learns of his own subjection, but this leads to no further insight:

> Men, women, call thee so or so:
> I do not know.
> Thou hast no name
> For me, but in my heart a flame
>
> Burns tireless, neath a silver vine
> And round entwine
> Its purple girth
> All things of fragrance and of worth.

Thou shout! thou burst of light! thou throb
    Of pain! thou sob!
    Thou like a bar
Of some sonata, heard from afar

Through blue-hue'd veils …
My aching hands are full of tears.[5]

The last line may well be literal: the speaker catches the tears as they fall from his eyes, the object of cult is perhaps less a person than a personification, perhaps of heterosexual love itself, and the speaker represents himself as aware of its power but unable to find that power redemptive, unable to relate to it because it is nameless, unlike the sonnet Gray addresses to Ellen Terry.

'Wings in the Dark' anticipates W.S. Graham's vivid reportage in *Night Fishing* by more than fifty years. It appealed to that sailor-poet John Masefield, who included it in his anthology *A Sailor's Garland* and reads as if, like Graham, Gray had witnessed and been imaginatively involved in the rituals of the catch, though there is a shift from the first to the third person. We begin with a description of the fishing boat seen both as racehorse or hunting steed and a kestrel or a hawk, ready to pursue and kill at its master's will.

Full-winged and stealthy like a bird of prey,
All tense the muscles of her seemly flanks

and the charged energy contrasts with the dour routines of the men. Flapping her wings, the fishing boat

Backward and forth, over the chosen ground,
Like a young horse, she drags the heavy trawl
Content; or speeds her rapturous course unbound,
And passing fishers through the darkness call,

Deep greeting in the jargon of the sea.
Haul upon haul, flounders and soles and dabs,
And phosphorescent animalculae,
Sand, sea drift, weeds, thousands of worthless crabs.

Darkling upon the mud the fishes grope,
Cautious to stir, staring with jewel eyes;
Dogs of the sea, the savage congers mope,
Winding their sulky march meander-wise.

It is a world that is alien to man, though not without its own order, which can only be disrupted by the intrusion of the fishers:

Suddenly all is light and life and flight,
Upon the sandy bottom, agate strewn.
The fishers mumble, waiting till the night
Urge on the clouds, and cover up the moon.[6]

We return to the extreme world of 'decadence' in the 'The Barber' which invokes another form of alienation. The poem reminds us of Aubrey Beardsley's 'Ballad of Carrousel' and his drawing, both in the third issue of *The Savoy* (1896). The situation is the opposite of that in 'Complaint': the speaker begins by dominating the objects of his desire and ends by being subjected to them, a parable we may take it of an artist's lawless imagination.

I dreamed I was a barber; and there went
Beneath my hand, oh! manes extravagant.
Beneath my trembling fingers.... It was my task
To paint their eyebrows with a timid hand;
To draw a bodkin, from a vase of kohl,
Through the closed lashes....
The dream grew vague. I moulded with my hands
The mobile breasts, the valley and the waist
I touched; and pigments reverently placed
Upon their thighs in sapient spots and stains,
Beryls and crysolites and diaphanes,
And gems whose hot harsh names are never said.
I was a masseur; and my fingers bled
With wonder as I touched their awful limbs.

The use of exotic gems recalls Huysmans *A Rebours*, the manic catalogues of *Salome* and Gustave Moreau's versions of the Princess of Judea. It also recalls Gray's own poem 'Sound', a catalogue of musical instruments, mysteriously dropped from the contents of *Silverpoints*. His fingers bleed as he violates the girls, but the speaker himself also bleeds, indicating power but also pain.

Suddenly, in the marble trough, there seems,
O, last of my pale mistresses, Sweetness!
A twylipped scarlet pansie.

the 'trough' suggests a sarcophagus but taken in conjunction with the twylipped pansie, it extends the feeling from disgust to necrophilia: 'the temple built over the sewer'. And with an absolute creepiness the dead body responds to its lover's ministrations: after 'the pit-a-pat of treatment':

At the sound, the blood of me stood cold.
Thy chaste hair ripened into sullen gold.
The throat, the shoulders, swelled and were uncouth.
The breasts rose up and offered each a mouth.
And on the belly pallid blushes crept,
That maddened me, until I laughed and wept.[7]

This is profounder than the mere fetishism of Beardsley's *Carrousel*, though without Beardsley's usual double entendres for male and female genitals.

'Mishka' offers a similar parable. The name is Russian for a bear but where the Barber is aggressive and attempts to dominate the objects of desire, the other surrogate for the poet Mishka is passively voluptuous. His Fatal Woman is embodied as a honey-child:

Mishka! there screamed a far bird-note,
Deep in the sky, when round his throat
The triple coil of her hair she wound.
And stroked his limbs with a humming sound.

Mishka is white like a hunter's son;
For he knows no more of the ancient south
When the honey-child's lips are on his mouth,
When all her kisses are joined in one,
And her body is bathed in grass and sun.

The honey-child is an olive tree,
The voice of birds and the voice of flowers,
Each of them all and all the hours,
The honey-child is a wingèd bee,
Her touch is a perfume, a melody.[8]

The imagery suggests that his hibernation is permanent, a winter sleep in his white coat, and also that he has become bloodless, though after his copulation with the honey-child he is surrounded by phantoms of summer. As with the Barber, the surrogate poet has been betrayed into sensual madness. The honey-child's kisses are the dew of bees, traditionally dulcifying the lips of infant poets. This transformation of animal into insect into woman, is highly analogous to Beardsley's borders for the *Morte d'Arthur*, which appeared a year later. Linda Dowling transposes Gray's opening line 'Mishka is poet among the beasts' to 'beast among the poets'. He is unlikely to return to the waking world.

While we may grant that the secular poems are unified by the themes of nature, art and love as failed redemption, the order of the poems is not altogether cogent. 'The Song of the Seedling' would appear more fittingly at this point; did we take 'Les Demoiselles de Sauve' as a prologue or programme poem. 'The Song' is a remarkable example of empathy rather in the manner of Blake and when placed beside the *poèmes noires* suggests some counterpoint of innocence and experience. It has the directness and animism of the best songs for children:

Rain drops patter above my head—
    Drip, drip, drip.
To moisten the mould where my roots are fed—
    Sip, sip, sip.
No thought have I of the legged thing,
    Of the worm no fear,
    When the goal is so near;
Every moment my life has run,
The livelong day I've not ceased to sing:
    I must reach the sun, the sun.[9]

What the song suggests is a rejection of the Pathetic Fallacy: the seed is concerned only with the manic thrust towards the light, an innocent egotism. In 'The Vines' we enter a world of grotesque floral eroticism where the bramble husband's fears of 'the mottled snake' cause him to strangle his wife the woodbine.

Bramble clutches for his bride,
Woodbine, with her gummy hands,
All his horny claws expands;
She has withered in his grasp ...
Half-born tendrils, grasping, gasp.[10]

As in 'The Barber' love, whether cruel or tender, becomes its own torment.

'On a Picture' is a sonnet is the iconic tradition, established by Dante Gabriel Rossetti. The lady is clearly Ophelia, and her description recalls Millais' painting:

Not pale, as one in sleep or holier death,
Nor illcontent the lady seems, nor loth
To lie in shadow of shrill river growth,
So steadfast are the river's arms beneath.

Pale petals follow her in very faith,
Unmixt with pleasure or regret, and both
Her maidly hands look up, in noble sloth
To take the blossoms of her scattered wreath.

No weakest ripple lives to kiss her throat,
Nor dies in meshes of untangled hair;
No movement stirs the floor of velvet moss.

Until some furtive glimmer gleam across
Voluptuous mouth, where even teeth are bare,
And gild the broidery of her petticoat.[11]

The poem is about a painting which is about a scene in a poetic play which is now condensed into a poem. The picture (like the play) requires the spectator for its fullest life, but the spectator (or speaker) transforms stationary peace into dangerous process, sensual music. Once more, the note is balanced: reluctant involvement, critical detachment.

The tone, though, is not precisely that of Millais. The 'shrill' river growth points to the hallucinatory brilliant greens of early Pre-Raphaelite painting, but the synaesthesia is of the 1890s, accenting the paradox of 'maidly hands' that 'take', the words seems to assume the meaning of those daffodils that 'take' the winds of March. Here there are no winds, but the Romantic notion of a nereid melting into her 'liquid rest' is confused by hints of artifice and sexuality in the final tercet.

Gray dedicated a poem to Oscar Wilde in which he assumes the posture of a neophyte poet before the Apollonian rather than Neronian Wilde, and Tutor points to the parallel between the speaker's self-diminishment and the masochistic tinges in the love poems. The images of ripeness and fruition would suggest that Wilde has found a way to renew the Romantic imagination as well as acting as patron of the young writers mostly of his circle. However, to see the whole of *Silverpoints* as a Bloomian exercise in which the neophyte poet finally escapes both the Romanticism of the past and the new pagan Romanticism of the present, is perhaps transposing theme into structure rather too schematically.

'Did we not darling' appears to deal with 'forbidden love' and in spite of the reference to the 'bonnie eyne' of the child appears to be addressed to a muse figure and most likely to a male rather than a female lover in view of 'Our melancholy is a thing/At last our own', and the sick synecdoche 'None esteem/How our black lips are blackening' referring, so Tutor suggests, not only to their corpse-like state but also 'to their social, sexual disgrace'. The self-subverting *fin de siècle* line 'How very pale your pallor is' seems more of a comment on the epicene poetry produced by the artifice of a male relationship than merely indicating 'his lover's weakness in her pregnancy', as Tutor suggests, and I find his reading of 'Poem' as a critique of Romanticism ingenious but suspect. Does the gardener's cropping the heads of daisies (line 4) really refer to the Romantic rejection of the extreme neoclassical Rationalism? A gardener, particularly in the period after William Robinson and while Miss Jekyll was active, can hardly be seen as a cropper of daisies. Burns and Wordsworth both wrote rather warmly of these tiresome flowers. And if the daisies thwart the gardener by refusing to die how does this connect with extreme neoclassical Rationalism? The explanation is more baffling than the poem. What does seem to be involved is some species of Decadent reversion to Primitivism: 'the strait allure of simple things' rather as a *faute de mieux*.

If nature and art, whether of the Romantic tradition, or in its later 'Decadent' manifestation in poetry or in person, is presented as inadequate in these secular poems, the only alternative is Grace; and Grace perfects nature it does not abolish it. But Gray, as he was to put it in a review of two of Huysmans' novels is 'only at the beginning of the purgative life'. It is the poems translated from others that carry the deeper commitment. The poet's self-disgust emerges sharply in the versions of such emetic pieces as Baudelaire's 'Femmes Damnées' with its sapphic analogue perhaps to his own sins and the 'Voyage à Cythere' where the translator may perhaps have been moved by the necessity of rejecting any absolute Gnostic contempt of the flesh. In the exasperated baroque 'Madonna (Ex Voto)' of the same poet, the Madonna's icon is reduced to the role of a lay figure in an incompetent juggler's performance at the circus. The Madonna's wounds are many and they are caused by the knowing persistence in sin of the poet of *Silverpoints*. Baudelaire's original has an almost Mexican violence, and this is distinctly muted in the translation. Verlaine's 'Parsifal' is rendered *con amore*, achieving such felicities of equivalence as 'And oh! the chime of children's voices in the dome'. Here his alexandrine avoids the rather broken backed rhythm that sometimes infects the poets of the 1890s when they use that metre, attempting to suggest a wavering eeriness of mood. With Verlaine, though, he is generally less successful than his contemporary

Arthur Symons. He mistranslates from time to time and sometimes fails in tact. Verlaine's conjunction of colloquial language with hesitating metre he generally transposes into the merely hieratic, the merely tuneful. In 'Green', for example, after a good opening stanza where Verlaine's loose, uninsistent but still neat rhythms are agreeably mimicked, in the sixth line for 'le vent du matin vient glacer à mon front' Gray gives us: 'the morning breeze has pearled upon my face'. By retreating into the rococo, the physical resonance of 'glacer' is lost. For 'Et que je donne un peu, puisque vous reposer' in the last line, Gray gives us 'And soothe my senses with a little rest' so that the sense of a warm and shared fatigue is perfectly lost.

The translation of Rimbaud's 'A la Musique' dedicated to Frank Harris represents Gray at his most accomplished:

> The square, with gravel paths and shabby lawns.
> Correct, the trees and flowers repress their yawns.
> The tradesman brings his favourite conceit,
> To air it, while he stifles with the heat.
>
> In the kiosk, the military band,
> The shakos nod the time of the quadrilles.
> The flaunting dandy strolls about the stand.
> The notary half unconscious of his seals.
>
> On the green seats, small groups of grocermen,
> Absorbed, their sticks scooping a little hole
> Upon the path, talk market prices; then
> Take up a cue: I think, upon the whole …
>
> The loutish toughs are larking on the grass.
> The sentimental trooper, with a rose
> Between his teeth, seeing a baby, grows
> More tender, with an eye upon the nurse.
>
> Unbuttoned, like a student, I follow
> A couple of girls along the chestnut row.
> They know I am following, for they turn and laugh,
> Half impudent, half shy, inviting chaff.
>
> I do not say a word. I only stare
> At their round, fluffy necks, I follow where
> The shoulders drop; I struggle to define
> The subtle torso's hesitating line.
>
> Only my rustling tread, deliberate, slow;
> The rippled silence from the still leaves drips.

They think I am an idiot, they speak low;
—I feel faint kisses creeping on my lips.

The casual way in which song has been accomplished from talk is remarkable. Even so, Gray still dilutes the concrete and brutal into the rococo; Rimbaud's bourgeois 'portent ... leur bêtises jalouses', into the vagueness of 'favourite conceit'. And 'the trooper with a rose between his teeth' is a figure out of Opera Bouffe; Rimbaud's trooper is smoking 'des Roses', a brand of tobacco. For the adolescently ecstatic 'le dos divin' Gray substitutes the more concrete but less intense 'torso's hesitating line', finically brilliant but a betrayal of the original.

What remains rather odd is that these deviations are willed. In the Princeton manuscript of *Silverpoints* Gray has:

Flattering in the seat his round haunch
A bourgeois with bright buttons Flemish paunch
Fondles his overstuffed tobacco pouch
Probably contraband one cannot vouch.[12]

Clumsy, perhaps; but a tinge nearer to what Rimbaud actually wrote. The shrugging colloquial note trembles on the verge of better things. Frank Harris was, rather uncharacteristically, responsible for toning down the first and more faithful version of Rimbaud's final stanza:

Only my rustling tread, deliberate, slow,
The rippled silence from the still leaves drips:
I have stripped off the boots, the stockings now
Naked they stand my eyes embrace their hips.[13]

In the published version the speaker retreats into passivity. The theme of 'A la Musique' amounts to a denial of idealism in adolescent sexuality. Like nature and art, sexual love is deeply corrupt, though in the unpretentious translation of Rimbaud's 'Sensation' the speaker commits himself to belief in an innocent voluptuousness.

Silverpoints represents a portion only of the uncollected or unpublished work of the first phase of Gray's career. Two of these poems—'Sound', a piece of acute virtuosity, and 'Song of Stars', with its unambiguous submission to sexual love and the natural cycle—were omitted at John Lane's request. 'Sound' is a catalogue of instruments in which music is resolved into sinister noise; instruments pollute the air:

Bring cruel Bells that scream with lips of jade;
Bring wooden Bells that bark and make afraid;
And Dulcimers that tinkle in their grade:
        Zombomba's monophonous hum;
        That laughter of the copper Drum;

ending with a hysterical dialectic between art and nature:

Come, whistling of the fretted steeple, where
The wind grows frightened in the iron stair.[14]

The gross question of space may have determined the omission of the two poems, though such lines as these from 'Song of Stars' may have passed the frontiers of the permissible even in a limited edition:

Joy of gathering, apples blush.
Women are swollen; men are born.

Bind me about in death
With a garland of twisted wheat.[15]

Other poems are part of the wide experimentation of the early 1890s: besides plays in verse and prose, Gray translated Banville's *Le Baiser*, wrote the libretto of a one-act musical and contributed some rather arcane criticism to *The Academy*. 'Vauxhall 17—' is a tired Austin Dobsonish piece written for an illustration by Charles Ricketts. The title of 'Passing the Love of Women' (of which Gray in his later years had no recollection of writing, but did not specifically deny his authorship) sufficiently indicates its topic—the exaltation of the Uranian over the heterosexual or popular Venus:

Priest nor ceremony
  Or of Orient or Rome
Bound me to my love, mine honey
  In the honeycomb,

Who, albeit of human
  Things the most sublime he knew,
Left me, to espouse a woman
  As the people do ...[16]

The obscure but interesting 'Variations on one subject' with its free metres reinforces the impression that the unpublished poems are superior to what was fugitively published in the period between 1890 and 1904. Before Cranmer-Byng, Waley and Soame Jenyns, Gray translated from the Chinese and with much enterprise. A Han poem 'Couplets Written by the lady Su Ouii' ends with this legato tune:

> And now to creep
> moon of the sea is my deep desire;
> And then the cloud
> the mountain brow
> doth touch, a wing of fire ...
>
> By stone
> and sward
> along
> the mount-
> ain pass,
> (such fate dividing!)
>
> I moan
> my Lord
> so long
> unfound,
> (alas!)
> absent abiding.
>
> . . .
>
> You left, and when
> we said goodbye, the bamboo leaves were green.
> Ah, who would then
> have thought the soft
> Almond trees had flowered so oft
> before we met again?

'The Flowers in Eden' begins in Pre-Raphaelite mode but Gray's diction soon becomes deliberately mixed:

> Eden garden was very fair,
> When sin came not hereby,
> For never any cloud did fare
> Across the iridiscent air
> Or blotch the happy sky.

The poem recreates the 'Fall' of nature and the change produced in animals, birds and flowers. In the unfallen world:

The birds went zig-zag, in and out,
On flower-coloured plats ...

The dandy-coated honey bee
Came by and hummed his prayer:
And for the suppliant's honey fee
The flowers opened prettily
And laid their pockets bare.

Somewhat they kept, in certain cells,
For moths and butterflies
To feed on timorously;—else
How could they keep their downy fells,
And wings like angels' eyes?

But after the 'Fall':

The iris heralds came and went;
All their speech was piercing scent
. . .
Each beast looked up with solemn eyes
That dwelt in Eden park.

The Garden where, as in Milton's Paradise, art and nature are indistinguishable has become a 'Park' with its overtones of eighteenth-century and later municipal gardening and finally as in Milton's epic it becomes a desert. The grass now tastes 'harsh and sour' but flowers, birds and animals all retain on their markings 'a little gate/Of ancient paradise', are living emblems.

'Battledore' and 'Shuttlecock', twin poems published in Ricketts' and Shannon's *Dial* allude to medieval games revived in the Victorian period. Both are the subject of charming oils by Albert Moore. Gray's sister Beatrice was being educated in the late 1890s at a convent near Regensberg; Gray was himself at that time studying for the priesthood and visited his sister on a number of occasions. His observation of the life of the nuns and the girls informs both poems. In 'Battledore' we read:

lazy chaplets told,
Weeds plucked, and garden calvaries visited.

'Shuttlecock' owes a good deal to Browning's 'Count Gismond' and to the Morris of *The Defence of Guenevere* but substitutes whimsy for drama. The reported speech is modern and colloquial, though the setting is medieval. 'Ducks and Drakes', an unpublished lyric, belongs to this same sequence and like 'Battledore' has a teasingly affectionate though too whimsical tone: Reverend Mother has both real ducks and figurative doves, postulants or the children perhaps. The detachment that the tone enforces is deliberate but again not altogether successful.

'The Forge', published in *The Savoy* (1896) is more interesting. It draws on Gray's experience as a metal-turner at Woolwich Arsenal with its pungent description of the processes for working metal:

From its long-embowelled dream,
To uses brought flame-licked and torture-bathed.

The smithy, 'a Chinese Hell', a prison, filled with 'Flame-flesh-shapes, sweat-swamped clinging cotton swathed' might be a fragment of Hopkins. If the metal is bruised and screams 'in the fire and scaling the trough', so too the men themselves are tortured in this decreation process. Presiding over the underworld is the smith, a Vulcan figure, the chief sufferer, who also suggests Prometheus:

Maimed in his poor hands, wry, with crooked back,
Great-armed, bow-legged, and narrow in the chest.
It bends a man to make no matter what.

And the final note is pity for those who (unlike the speaker perhaps) have never and will never escape this determinist Hell:

And this day is the type of many days.

Type will never ripen in antitype. In a larger sense, 'The Forge' is Gray's version of the Immortality Ode: the speaker's escape or his ability to look back in pity and detachment is stroked in so obliquely and is so unlocated, that the poem could amount to a critique as well as a restatement of the 'Fall': from the maternal garden into the gross male world of the Father and competitive economics that Gray had himself experienced.

In the unpublished 'The Wheel' the techniques of the wheelwright are precisely followed:

Oak, elm and ash; these
Are the three greatest trees.

The curious arts of man reveal
No braver engine than the wheel
. . .

Slowly, and many winters film on film
And tortuous fibre tangling, grows the elm.

Its texture many qualities combines;
The strength of ash persists in crooked lines.

The ash makes music when its branches stir,
Because its leaf is like a dulcimer.

Strong and elastic for the slender spoke,
In strength for weight no wood surpasses oak.

(Iron, required to answer the same ends,
Would fail; for iron either breaks or bends.)

The diction is mixed, in the 'Decadent' mode, veering from the seventeenth-century uses of 'curious' and 'brave' to the couplet beginning 'Strong and elastic for the slender spoke', which might have been torn from an Augustan didactic poem on the uses of wood. The poem resolves itself in its last section by typology: wheels are not only useful and indeed the condition of civil advance but are types of man's spiritual advancement: Ezekiel's wheels express the spirit of man who is taught to mock 'the loadstone earth'. It is only retrospectively that the poem evades the didactic, the versified textbook produced by a poet who had considerable skill of hand and practical experience of the other kind of making.

The use of a relaxed prosaic diction is unusual in the 1890s if we discount humour and satire, though it can be found in Davidson, Henley and even in the simple if refined diction of Dowson. The 1890s are also, though, subject to Naturalist idiom and to the seedy Realism of Gissing, Morrison and others.

The topic of 'Leda and the Swan' (*The Dial*, 1897) is common as part of the anti-positivist programme of Symbolists and others in the twilit end-of-century phase; in the incrusted symbolic machines of Gustave Moreau, Ricketts and others. But Gray's treatment is not successful; like the many coitions in the verse of Arthur Symons this is more of a 'shiver' than the 'shudder' of Yeats's famous sonnet. The renewal of an etiolated civilization by bestial energies should be more brutally expressed; Gray can only manage:

Till sudden lightnings split
The burning sky, and empty it;
And raucously as eagles cry
An eagle screamed across the sky.

A menagerie of numinous birds: Zeus and Aphrodite.

'The Flying Fish' is the most distinguished of the poems of this phase that Gray published in periodicals. It was revised for John Masefield's anthology *The Sailor's Garland* (1904) and again when it appeared in *The Long Road.* It is a long, accomplished and not altogether transpicuous piece that Geoffrey Grigson determined as being the equivalent in Gray's work to 'The Waste Land' in the work of T. S. Eliot. A few stanzas from its second section radiate a lean and rapid energy typical of the poem as a whole. After cataloguing some of the strange fish that inhabit the central figure Hang the Sailor's sea, we hear that

The great-faced dolphin is first of fish;
he is devil-eyed and devilish;
of all the fishes is he most brave,
he walks the sea like an angry wave.

The second the fishes call their lord;
himself a bow, his face is a sword;
his sword is armed with a hundred teeth,
fifty above and fifty beneath.

The third hath a scarlet suit of mail;
the fourth is naught but a feeble tail;
the fifth is a whip with a hundred strands,
and every arm hath a hundred hands.

The last strange fish is the last strange bird;
of him no sage hath ever heard;
he roams the sea in a gleaming horde
in fear of the dolphin and him of the sword.

He leaps from the sea with a silken swish;
he beats the air does the flying fish.
His eyes are round with excess of fright,
bright as the drops of his pinions' flight.

In sea and sky he hath no peace;
for the five strange fish are his enemies;
and the five strange fowls keep watch for him;
they know him well by his crystal gleam.

Oftwhiles, sir Sage, on my junk's white deck
have I seen this fish-bird come to wreck,
oftwhiles (fair deck) 'twixt bow and poop
have I seen the piteous sky-fish stoop.

Scaled bird, how his snout and gills dilate,
all quivering and roseate:
he pants in crystal and mother-of-pearl
while his body shrinks and his pinions furl.

His beauty passes like bubbles blown;
the white bright bird is a fish of stone;
the bird so fair, for its putrid sake,
is flung to the dogs in the junk's white wake.[17]

It has been suggested that the fishes and birds are allegorical versions of some of the thaumaturgic figures whom Gray knew in the 1890s.

Of Gray's commitment to the Latin Church, it is not for me to speak, except in so far as it bears on his poetic development. It seems from manuscript evidence that some of the poems of *Silverpoints* and *Spiritual Poems* were written simultaneously in 1891 and 1892. *The Person in Question*, a short story on the doppelgänger theme clearly relates to *The Picture of Dorian Gray*. The person, a young *boulevardier*, is haunted by an older man with a self-indulgent face that seems queerly familiar. The narrator develops pity for the apparition, mingled with a sense of omen. It is his future self, the image of the dandy grown old, when that habit of self-assertion and self-concealment which Dandyism involves has become a prison. The figure disappears finally when the narrator experiences an epiphany on the road to the Cafe Royal. In a review of two novels that may be said to represent Huysmans' 'way down and out', down to Satanism and out into the possibility of Grace, Gray does not romanticize the literary hero and his practice of detachment: it is no more than 'the lethargy of decay'. Huysmans' *persona* experiences, in Gray's words, 'the anxieties of a living growth' after a violent despair, a 'Sickness unto Death', Kierkegaardian almost, Grace ravaging and healing the least attractive of sinners. For Gray, Huysmans makes his case with 'elaborate information, pitiless visual deliberation; a rare sensibility under the play of an obstinate method, which advances upon the longest category, ready at each shift with a more exacerbated epithet, lacerates every scene, makes vibrant each foot of the panorama before which the haggard, despicable hero is ever hounded.' Gray mimes Huysmans' own clinical language. He praises the French novelist's tact in exhibiting the conversion of this representative of the *genus scriptor* through external and aesthetic means: the only means indeed to which the corroded spirit could respond: the Church grants Durtal, that pusillanimous pilgrim, a period of spiritual convalescence. But Gray is aware of the danger of resting in an aesthetic Christianity where the dead clothes of the redeemer are worshipped in place of the disquieting Godhead: 'At the point of utmost progress in *En Route* he is at the beginning of the purgative life. In a very long time he will still be at the beginning.'

Such insights, however, are hardly present in the first of the *Blue Calendars* twelve devotional poems assigned to each month of the year, privately issued from Gray's address at 43 Park Lane, in December 1894. Though written later, the first two *Calendars* precede the publication of *Spiritual Poems*, which more candidly represent Gray's spiritual agonies and exaltations. The *Calendars* indeed strike one as required exercises to a greater degree than the translations that form the major part of *Spiritual Poems* and which, we may suggest, fulfil the same cautious function as the translations in *Silverpoints*. The pervasive influence on the 1895 *Calendar* is the medieval religious lyric and the traditional carol, revived by such seventeenth-century poets as Herrick and Lluelyn, and among Gray's contemporaries by Selwyn Image, Herbert Horne and Lionel Johnson. Deliberately, elegantly playful, sophisticatedly naïve, the poems submit to rather than criticize their models, contrasting with the tensity of dialogue in the better poems of *Silverpoints*. The abdication of poetic personality issues in pastiche.

Hobbinol a gentle riot
Waked upon his several reeds.
Colin singeth, when he heeds
How the pipe is loud and quiet:

Yon is not a common star
Like the other stars in Heaven.
Lo, it walks among the seven
Stars to north which make the share.

... I divine this very hour,
That a famous shepherd lives.[18]

This is neatly done Elizabethany pastoral, but the resemblance to a successful *New Statesman* competition is disturbing. The second *Calendar* published at the close of 1895 develops the same note:

Sit, Apollo-like afoot
  Of the tree of knowledge;
To the chorals tune Thy flute
  Of the angel college.[19]

But in the verses for April, 'The True Vine', calling traditionally on the imagery of the *Song of Songs* as well as John's Gospel, Gray achieves a sparkling rhythm that physically rehearses the Dionysiac joy of the priest and victim.

    Another quells,
Another reins the leopards.
    My portent tells
My story to the shepherds
    Beside the wells.

    My face is tan.
My hair, my hair is golden.
    None brighter than
My eyes were e'er beholden
    By eyes of men.

    I am the vine.
The cup is chiselled garnet
    For garnet wine.
I am the vine incarnate.
    The grape is mine.

    With crown of bright
Green leaf and tender clusters
    My head is dight;
Even as the starry musters
    Adorn the night.

    I am the vine:
The stock, the grape, the dresser;
    In deed and sign,
The purple-footed presser
    Of purple wine.[20]

A more personal flavour returns with the third and fourth *Blue Calendars*. These consist of sonnets addressed to various saints; the topics are now specifically Latin Catholic; are less 'gothick' than baroque. The source material derives from the offices or for the narrative allusions from Charles Butler's *Lives of the Saints*.

Like Lionel Johnson and Pater, Gray often uses Latin words in their root meaning:

Thou didst *advene* where men lay chained and dark ...
Against thy knee his tongue began to speak
Who spoke *stupendously* the living Word.[21]

Happily baroque is the sonnet addressed to Saint John of the Cross:

Thou art, O flame of Carmel, thou art a wing
Thyself of contemplation, thou dost fling
All pediments aside; thy wealth is loss.
Thine ecstasy demands the utmost night,
Wherein to espy thy Lover's glimmering light,
Thy dearest hope abandonment of men.[22]

What is remarkable here is the quick mutation of the Saint from flame to wing and then into a violent architecture of contemplation, along with the lean authority of such a statement as 'Thine ecstasy demands the utmost night', while the last line is dry enough to evade anticlimax.

The sonnet addressed to Saint Agnes stresses through syntax the delicious agonies of martyrdom: Agnes was a virgin martyr obtaining the double crown at the age of thirteen. Gray follows the saint's office closely, and it is profitable to compare the Anglo-Catholic poet Gerard Moultrie in his *Hymns and Lyrics* of 1867:

R. His surpassing love doth deck
With diamond light mine arms, my neck;
In mine ears for love of me
Pearls of great price placeth he,
And with many a sparkling gem
Hath he set my diadem.

V. He hath set a sign to show
Whose I am upon my brow,
That no lover I should own
But himself, himself alone:
And with many a sparkling gem
Hath he set my diadem.

Gray's version syntactically and rhythmically moves away from liturgical monotone:

My Lord has set his seal upon my face,
Engaging all my love to make me sure;
He has set the ring of faith upon my hand,
Upon my neck the necklace of His grace.

Chaste in His love, and having touched Him, pure.
Receiving Him, His Virgin still I stand.[23]

Occasionally Gray flashes into a line of majestically assured rhetoric:

A soul unconquerable clad in flesh
To swell the arena's foul magnificence.[24]

One is tempted to align these sonnets with those of other Catholic sonneteers: William Alabaster—presumably still unknown to Gray—and Henry Constable, whom Gray edited. Yet what remains absent from the mnemonic mode of the *Calendars* is any sense of the many bittersweet 'conflicts between God and the soul' that energize the finer Carolean devotional verse. Gray is the psalmist, the celebrator of moral order rather than the poet of the obedience that tests the moral order. Little of his religious poetry explores the nature of spiritual experience. In such later collections as *Ad Matrem* (1904), *Verses for Tableaux Vivants* (1905) and *Saint Peter's Hymns* (1925) he follows the same pattern with a diminished success, though the last volume contains several mild successes. Perhaps *Christmas 1904* which appeared as a broadside for friends may be cited as a favourable example of the mode:

Dear Mother of the blessed One;
O gate of their return
Who look to heaven, whence the Sun
Shone forth, O star that dost upon the waste of waters burn!

Thy fainting people, else undone,
Through thee aspire to rise
To Him thou bearest, Source and Son,
Thy Holy Child; while nature wonders from a million eyes.

O Mother-maid inviolate,
Today and evermore
Sin-soiled and weary children wait
On thee, their hope, O sacred gate, O ever open door!

The poet of a pure obedience is occasionally present in *Spiritual Poems* (1896) but these are mostly translations from a curious range of authors, Catholics and Protestant, from Prudentius to Verlaine, including obscure emblem poets such as Alonso de Ledesma; liturgical poets like Notker Balbulus (did Gray meet Notker through Rémy de Gourmont's *Latin Mystique*?). This anthology forms a devotional 'imaginary museum' and reflects the self-conscious relativism and eclecticism of the 1890s with its memory of Pater's 'all periods, types, schools of taste, are in themselves equal'. Designed by Charles Ricketts and published by his Vale Press, *Spiritual Poems* is a fine example of 'total art', its paper and typography reflecting the eclecticism and scholarly caprice of content. To do justice to *Spiritual Poems* one can appeal only to the variety of tone and metre; the fidelity to the spirit of the originals. Two stanzas from the version of Jacopone da Todi's *L'Amor mi mise* may be quoted:

Love setteth me a-burning,
When my new spouse had won me;
My piteous state discerning,
Had set his ring upon me, ...
All my heart broke with yearning.
Love setteth me a-burning.

My heart was broke asunder:
Earthward my body sprawling,
The arrow of Love's wonder
From out the crossbow falling,
Like to a shaft of thunder
Made war of peace, enthralling
My life for passion's plunder.
Love setteth me a-burning.[25]

As with his secular translations from the French, Gray often softens the jaggedness or astringency of his originals, blurring with a Pre-Raphaelite softness the disturbing elements. Some of the *Spiritual Poems* were written as early as 1891–92 and are contemporary with a number of the pieces in *Silverpoints*. A number of translations were rejected by Gray. Some, like a number of the published translations were virtually rendered at sight, resulting in a few errors and now and then a failure to catch a sharp antithesis.

One of Gray's legacies from French poetry is the continuous use of consonantal rhymes, half rhymes (and *rimes riches*), practised at that time by Gustave Kahn, the Irish poet William Larminie and several English poets of the period. In a translation from Madame Guyon (*Spiritual Poems*, p. cx) we find, for example, 'witheld' paired with 'melt' and in the *Blue Calendar* for 1896 (March), we find 'fair' and 'fare'. All this accents the provisional and experimental element in Gray's work. He seems to present himself, if we recall the rapid transpositions of *Spiritual Poems*, not merely as an acutely minority poet but also as an amateur. Only in his best work is the almost defensive note subdued.

Between 'The Phial', which appeared in *The Venture* of 1905, and *Vivis* (1920), a set of somewhat encrypted epigrams, Gray seems to have fallen silent. When his next secular volume *The Long Road* appeared in 1926 it was in an idiom quite distinct from the *poèmes noires* of *Silverpoints* and the baroque floriations of the religious verse of the later 1890s. The verses of his last phase prove that the poet in Gray was broadened by the strenuousness of the priest.

This new poetic identity emerges in a relaxed and subtly friendly but also sometimes caustic tone. 'The Long Road' itself is a symbol for human life, a very familiar *topos*. Writing to his sister, Gray observed:

> The Road symbolizes life, and its monotony is varied with excursions of the excursionist's own invention. The episode 'Along Wenlock Edge' is a march not in space but in time: from the 1st April to the 31st December. The poem contains familiar, strange reflections on the nature of a road, an artificial river flowing both ways at once.

The journey then is not a progressive single event; it is rather an accumulation of various tours, visits and incidents. Some of these tours are imaginary, most autobiographical. The poem moves towards death and its conquest, through joy in the natural scene and hope in an after-life. For the most part the style is 'prattling', an accomplished 'low' style that recalls William Empson's 'Autumn on Yan-Nueh'. The casual, intimate quality is reinforced by the metre, a five-line stanza with two short lines at the beginning and end, which can prolong itself naturally and unobtrusively into six or seven lines. With its muted assonances, the virtue of the style is that it preserves the diary-like sequence yet has sufficient flexibility to rise when required. The following passage may stand as an example both of mode and theme:

> The goose-gaggle's strength
> defined by cackling overhead
> of broods on Kebnekajse bred
> by one lithe bird a century led
> in great shimmering length.
>
> Or set out at noon;
> or take the road by rosy light;
> or woo the cool and velvet night
> to gather fodder for the sight;
> it all passes soon.

As cut off in time,
your history is soon compiled:
a flower observed; a playing child;
the hemispheric undefiled
where white cloudlets climb.

. . .

The known yet to know;
a river gliding from and hence
in utmost calm to thought and sense;
the effort and the recompense
at once ebb and flow.

The long-aged road
is tough, resilient and young;
becomingly abashed among
the singing streams of earth, so sung;
the scored, sacred road.

Its void's counterpart:
its breadth with huddling forms replete,
and ghosts of those these trudged to meet;
incessant thunder of their feet
and slow beating heart.[26]

In these later poems satire is frequent answering to a certain stylish acerbity in Gray's later self. The sanative disgust of 'Odiham' expressed in delicate but sharp shorthand humour is only one aspect of the later achievement:

Put his head
and anxious face
out of a car.
Seemed to have said:
Yell's the name
of this place;
seven, three, four.

Man addressed
tried to evince
interest,
as often before
and often since.
Said the name
of where they were
was Odiham.
Delighted, sir.

Fat, pale chap
seemed dissatisfied;
snatched a map
from those inside.

. . .

We know the way
to the south of France;
but Brodenham
is not in Hants.

. . .

He said: I said
Odiham.
Odium: hatred.
Odi: I hate.
ham: ham.
A ridiculous name
in that point of view.

He said: Are you
then a Jew?

He said: No.

He said: Oh;
I thought I'd like to know;
but I can't wait.[27]

Gray's patient love of the natural scene, and particularly of the spare, strong profiles of the Border hill country, provides him with accurate images. Here he describes the flesh of water in Ettrickdale, a 'winding dale' flourishing from primeval springs.

No lips of men have shaped the word
to name what all have often heard;
so willingly believe the noise
is like the uncreated voice.

The fiftieth time the lisping rush
has died upon a silver hush;
and faithful to the downward hue,
another element is blue.

White pathway in the darkening hills,
soft salve for nearly all your ills:
on bruise and scar a healing drip,
the wanderer's companionship.

A planet, rose on tender green,
tugs at its radius unseen,
and draws its complicated arc;
until it blaze against the dark.[28]

The 'Ode' which opens *Poems (1931)* follows with a curious, discriminating eye the delicate states of moving water:

where the toppling, the precipitous,
those of even pace,
the slow,
are for a long day pent.
Come to a metamorphic flow,
they wind, heavily changing place;
and in their winding smother
one another,
and know with other selves ubiquitous.

Grope upon the uneven prison floor;
deeper haunts and darker cells explore;
fill unechoing caves;
break, waves,
where banks are steep;
sob, sob along the tantalizing shore,
so low a sudden onrush were escape;
sink and almost sleep;
drown without place or shape.

Roam on the common face of the many waters' fate;
move at the will of the breeze;
rustle like the trees
in the liquid wind.
Float as a stony plate,
till the sun rescind
work in the stagnant air
of the jewel-making frost ...

. . .

Beyond the last town
shapeless dimensions all but lie;
weariness of mud brown
listlessly returns the colour of the sky.
Undaintily, long loaded jetties tread
its shallow filth, to find
the groping channel in its bed.
Its voice no more than a weak lap, an inarticulate moan;
films of ooze from fouler depths renewed,
a bobbing horror by squawking gulls pursued,
replenish its fetid breath;
in the watches of death
with riches piled and honour strown.

Dredgers grind.
Traders skulk
and await the signal to discharge
petrol or ores.

Pass it in the time in which a barge
fulfils its freight of stores
for a distant hulk.

While windmills still gesticulate,
dim, motionless, the river seems to wait
upon the first salt kisses of the ocean's lips;
where a white pharos heeds the ships.[29]

Such patience and quiet honesty before the average data of experience differentiates sharply this later poetry from the oblique strategies of *Silverpoints*. As 'On Aqueducts' shows, Gray can now control the 'subject' poem. And the religious lyric is now redeemed from the hymnodic trance that had vitiated the devotional collections of Gray's middle years. 'Speciosae et delicatae Assimilavi Filiam Sion' (reprinted in *Poems (1931)* from *Saint Peter's Hymns*) and 'Mane Nobiscum Domine' exemplify this advance:

Pledge of our hospitality, the bread
is broken by thy hands;
our quaking love, our most confiding dread
beholds and understands.

Food of our soul enlightens and updries
our darkness and our tears;
the breaker and the broken to our eyes
is all, and disappears.[30]

And in 'The Lord Looks at Peter' Gray achieves the ideal of the early *Blue Calendars*: a simplicity of assurance:

When not alone thine eyes, my God,
but all thy sacred body wept,
and every tear was ruby blood,
I shut my eyes and slept.

A night alarm; a weaponed crowd;
one blow, and with the rest I ran;
I warmed my hands, and said aloud:
I never knew the man.[31]

For his secular achievement, 'The Nurse Goes Her Night Rounds' may be cited as representative. Here, jagged enjambements mime very skilfully the momentary and blurred sense-impression of a patient in the dark and narrow world of his illness: an hallucination that blends into the healing figure, guardian and liberator, of the night nurse herself.

Droop under doves' wings silent, breathing shapes
white coverlids dissimulate; in hope
of opiate aid to round the ledge where gapes
the soot-black gulf in which obtuse minds grope

for very nothing, vast and undefined,
in starless depths no astrolabe can probe.
The moving form, as doomed to pass and wind,
unwind and pass anew, in sleep-dyed robe

of firmamental silence more than hue,
watches the doorway of the tired's escape
only. Fatigue gone on; I left behind

with moths' feet, wordless whispering; or find
reality, white coiffe and scarlet cape;
and dreams are what a dream should be, or true.[32]

By the late 1920s, Gray had become a formidable priest: the associate of Wilde, the ex metal-turner, was in 1930 to be installed as a canon of the Edinburgh diocese. His first cure had been in a dismal slum district of that city, and the conditions there had stung him into an interest in social reform. But in 1905 Andre Raffalovich moved to Edinburgh and built for Gray an elegant church in a respectable suburb. He died six months after Raffalovich in June 1934. For nearly thirty years between them they had maintained the style if not altogether the ethos of the 1890s in the dour northern capital.

Soon after this W. B. Yeats began assembling that eccentric canon founded on his own stagy ideology: *The Oxford Book of Modern Verse*. He had intended to include Gray and may well (and unenterprisingly) have confined his choice to the *poèmes noires*. At all events the executors, the Dominican Fathers refused their permission: from their own point of view publication would not at that time have been prescient and Gray himself had always refused to sanction any reprint of *Silverpoints*. The consequence, though, was that Gray survived only in the memory of his flock and his friends, and in the annals of the Order of Preachers and the Diocese of Edinburgh.

He had escaped the rage of Yeats's mythologizing in *Autobiographies*: he is barely mentioned, for unlike Yeats's old mentor, Arthur Symons, he had not died symbolically. Unlike

Symons, and like Yeats, he had subsisted through the dangerous middle years in a poet's development. And like Yeats's, his more slender gifts survived well into the twentieth century, survived and were largely fulfilled. He lived on to disprove the Yeatsian assertion that hearts filled with the dangerous wisdom of the poetic image could find no place for the Hound of Heaven. When his verse is collected, we shall see it coherently, see 'its somewhat beautiful oddity' as the oddity of a personal voice, a quietly compelling poetic identity.

Notes

1. Ts. Dominican Chaplaincy, Edinburgh.
2. In his as yet unpublished essay on *Silverpoints*.
3. *Silverpoints* (London, 1893), *v*.
4. *Ibid.*, *vi*.
5. *Ibid.*, *ix*.
6. Text from *The Sailor's Garland*, ed. John Masefield (London, 1904).
7. *Silverpoints*, *xii*.
8. *Ibid.*, *xiii–xiv*.
9. *Ibid.*, *vii*.
10. *Ibid.*, *xvi*.
11. *Ibid.*, *xxi*.
12. Ts. Princeton University.
13. *Silverpoints*.
14. *Sound*, ed. A.J.A. Symons (London, 1926), p.2.
15. I adopt the spelling in the ts. Dominican Chaplaincy, Edinburgh.
16. This and the ensuing unpublished poems are from ts. Dominican Chaplaincy, Edinburgh.
17. *The Long Road* (Oxford, 1926), pp.34–5.
18. *The Blue Calendar*, 1895, August. Unpaginated.
19. *Ibid.*, 1896, May. Unpaginated.
20. *Ibid.*, 1896, June. Unpaginated.
21. *Ibid.*, 1897, March. Unpaginated.
22. *Ibid.*, 1897, November. Unpaginated.
23. *Ibid.*, 1898, January. Unpaginated.
24. *Ibid.*, 1898, February. Unpaginated.
25. *Spiritual Poems* (London, 1896), p.106.
26. *The Long Road*, pp.24–5.
27. *Poems* (1931) (London, 1931), pp.30–1.
28. *Ibid.*, pp.22–3.
29. *Ibid.*, pp.4–5; 8–9.
30. *Ibid.*, p.38.
31. *Ibid.*, p.36.
32. *The Long Road*, p.45.

11

Lionel Johnson and 'The Dark Angel'

I

It may seem perverse to devote a whole essay to 'The Dark Angel'. Normally, the poem that receives this treatment such as say a Blake lyric, presents us with a deceptively simple surface. Alternatively, the texture may be snarled with allusions, like the 'Gerontion' of T. S. Eliot. 'The Dark Angel' falls between such extremes: without being charged, like Blake's lyrics, with a personal symbolic energy, it can be said to contain rich and even challenging allusions. But these allusions hardly play upon one another and reverberate like the muffled echoes and contrasts in a poem of Eliot. Still they subserve the two or three dominant themes; their role is not simply decorative.

Whatever power these allusions contain derives from a source beyond the poem. And, like the dominant themes I have mentioned, they are closely related to Johnson's history. Some knowledge of that history, and of the period through which it was lived, sharply increases our response to 'The Dark Angel'. This may well seem an invalid basis for admiration, or the bother of analysis. It remains a fact, though, that Johnson's was a *vie recluse*, a life strangely enclosed by literature. In a sense his life *was* a literary device. To this point I shall recur. And if not Johnson's finest, 'The Dark Angel' is certainly the central poem in his *oeuvre*.

The typical figures of the 1890s give us, as do the figures of few other periods, the sense of being 'a generation of Hamlets', sacrificed to their own values. Their lives may loom larger than their works, but the pattern of those lives invests the constricted range of their poetry with a further dimension. We are forced to make a constant reference backward and forward, from the text to the *milieu*, still with a sense that something eludes us. Loneliness, remorse, a gesture of illumination, a shadow of regret, the contrasts offer us little more. Their only other offer, indeed, is self-destruction. Baudelaire, submitting to degradation, can order it for the purposes of art; can use art as a means of exploring the spiritual world. But the nihilism of the *fin de siècle* poets seems unorganized: they were never to experience what Johnson called 'the slow approach of perfect death'. And, unlike Henry James, or George Moore even, they could not live uncompromisingly the life of art; they could not remain passionate observers. Their own art, then, finds itself in a series of precariously achieved moments. Unable to transform nihilism by decisive acts of faith, they explore the narrow poignant field.

Of such figures Johnson remains the archetype. Educated at Winchester and Oxford, of good family and sufficient means, he exhibits something almost of Rimbaud's ferocity of impulse in slowly murdering himself with alcohol, dying finally at thirty-five after a year's lonely illness. His life is one of morbid addiction to failure. He has homosexual impulses, but these must be stifled. Failing in personal relationships, he attaches himself to institutions, Winchester and Oxford, emblems of a happier past. But he values these institutions for qualities that are not quite real: qualities that his youthful self had projected into them. Even when he takes part in the life around him he does so in a manner that is curiously marginal. He supports lost causes, either ridiculous like the White Rose League, or unpopular as Irish Nationalism became after the Parnell *débâcle*. He turns away from contemporary literature, and from current thought, losing himself in theological minutiae, in archaic pedantries of punctuation and phrasing. True, he transforms the typical nineteenth-century appetite for certainty into what appears to be a decisive act of faith and joins the Latin Church. It is a purely intellectual conversion. His emotional responses remain fixed at an early stage. Unable to make abstract assents real, his mind hardens towards new experience. At an age when most men remain mentally adventurous, he can only fall back on the tired responses, the faded judgements, the by now phantasmal human relationships. For this slow unreality applies to the external world. His physical range narrows itself down to his rooms, a local public house, a few editorial offices: This solitude is self-created; it has the same hideous deliberation as the self-murder. Fear of homosexual passion; lonely drinking; siding with the failing minority, till it becomes a minority of one. But there is obviously part of Johnson's mind that passionately searches for some objective correspondence to a self-contained slowly receding system of ideas; there is part of his nature that passionately rebels against annihilation. This minority of one is delusive. The more he withdraws from the world, the more he senses the Dark Angel's shadow. Angel or beast? Last omen or the catastrophe of Grace?

On a poem that so neatly expresses the essence of its decade as 'The Dark Angel', we should be able to do more than pass a motion of indifference or, at the most, of contempt at the remaindered quality of some of its diction. For this is all that recent critics have managed to muster. F.W. Bateson compares Johnson's poem 'Oxford' with W.H. Auden's. One stanza of the Johnson poem is niggled with before the axe descends and Auden's poem is pronounced superior on all counts, but principally because it mentions undergraduates and has a crackling pun: 'Eros Paidagogos/Weeps on his virginal bed.' John Heath-Stubbs, like Prince Rupert at Naseby, despatches 'The Dark Angel' in one dashing onslaught that extends to the length of a sentence. One's audience is sure to be with one so why bother with the dull routine of substantiation. There is, finally, Graham Hough's analysis of Johnson's work as a whole: but even Hough hardly goes much beyond stressing the poem's psychological interest and paying tribute to Johnson's depressing command of the poetic *lingua franca* of the day.[1]

My own approach to the poem is, broadly speaking, in theological terms. Theology is an unfashionable mental discipline these days. Many of my readers, those who are atheists or agnostics, reverent agnostics or even reverent Anglican agnostics, may be inclined to retort that theology is unfashionable because we recognize either that it is a science without a subject (there is no God) or with a subject about which nothing can properly be said (the attitude of Wittgenstein). The answer to this is that, even if theology is based on an illusion or represents an attempt to make language assume a task for which it is unfitted, it has, and ought to have, as much meaning for the critic as myths, or metaphysics, or even poetry has, as an attempt to organize persistent and very important human interests and attitudes; and even for the atheist or the agnostic the correct, or at least the most fruitful, approach to theology is the phenomenological one—the attempt not to judge and dismiss a system of ideas from the outside but to feel through it, to experience it sympathetically, from within.

The critic brackets off ontological and even epistemological questions. He does not ask (there would be no point in his asking), 'Was Johnson right in believing in Christianity?' or even, 'What reasonable grounds had Johnson for his beliefs?' He asks, 'What would it have felt like to be Johnson having these beliefs, and how do they fit in with his general response to experience, and our critical judgement on that?'[2]

'The Dark Angel' is couched entirely in religious language: its subject is a metaphysical despair; its object, complete clarity about the self. Søren Kierkegaard's *Sickness unto Death* vividly depicts this type of religious neurosis and provides us with convenient working generalizations. The sickness is despair at being oneself, proceeding from immediacy to self-reflection and so to the more complex forms of the religious dialectic. In 'The Dark Angel' we can plot this development down to the *peripeteia* of 'Do what thou wilt ...', the acceptance of despair, the confronting of the Other, the fear of assimilation; when in Jungian terms assimilation would lead to wholeness. The contingent cause of the poem though lies in the weakness of the will when faced by certain temptations like drink and sex.

Lucifer may, like the Rebel Scot of John Cleveland's poem, possess the gift of ubiquity; but he is not continuously present to individual consciousness in the way the poem suggests. One must distinguish between the active tempting of the Evil One and the mere seduction of sin; between irresistible impulse deriving from the senses, and habit. What is most evident is the *pervasive* quality of the evil. The Devil of theology is finite in that he can affect us through the senses; can control the disposition of our bodies—can count on one's being weakened by illness (like Johnson), by melancholy or poverty; but he cannot touch the will directly, even though by nature the will is corrupt. Should we, so far as the conscious general symbolism is concerned, rule out dualistic pessimism (of a Manichaean order), it is clear that the Dark Angel must be a part of Johnson's psyche; not something which can in the last analysis be distinguished from it. This other part of the psyche, this other self, is the shadow without which the substance would no longer cohere. It is almost as if the theological Devil were being used as a stalking horse. Johnson wants apparently to unmask the Devil, but what if having done so he finds his own face behind the mask? Like Jonas Chuzzlewit, the murderer, he will become afraid not *for*, but *of* himself. And how will Johnson escape the other or lower self: by redemption or annihilation?

Here it may be objected that I am already putting the question in psychological terms. After all, our descriptions of the inner life are no more than convenient working generalizations. One can simply enough substitute the descriptive abstracts of psychology for the theological drama of the soul. But to do this would be to lose sight of the poem's moral structure. Moral theology, assuming a God who created us and on whom we are absolutely dependent, deals with absolute obligations; psychology, even though it is as fundamentally suasive as moral theology, is more flexible and modest. It seeks to make men accept themselves and fit in with society; it brackets off the question whether either selves or society are ever what they ideally ought to be. One set of concepts, then, tends towards transforming the individual, the other proceeds on a care and maintenance level. The poem, though, is clearly an objective form reflecting not only a theological but a psychological situation—an adjustment not only to God's demands of the late-nineteenth-century social order. With both of these the self is at variance. In its detail, the poem resembles, as already suggested in Jungian terms, an attempt at 'individuation'.[3]

According to the Jungian hypothesis, among the strange wraith-like contents of the unconscious are three fairly well-defined archetypes: Animus, Anima and Shadow, of which the last two concern us here. The Shadow, of course, represents the inferior and less commendable aspect of a person; his uncontrolled emotional manifestations. We have met this figure in literature; for instance, Faust and his shadow Mephistopheles. When a person is under the influence of emotional disturbances, when he is 'not himself', or 'beside himself', there is a distinct *strangeness* about him. When the storm passes this strange presence disappears, 'but it merely returns to the Unconscious where it awaits its opportunity. Its influence is still there, less obvious, yet more subtle and cunning'.[4] Individuation consists in transmuting the tension between unconscious and conscious into 'an unbreakable whole, the individual'. In order to arrive at individuation, one must confront and challenge the dark side of the self: 'the meeting with oneself is the meeting with one's own shadow', a point at which 'I experience the other person in myself, and the other, as myself, experiences me'. In sleep, among dreams, Shadow and Anima celebrate an unholy 'marriage'. When the presence of the shadow is accepted and understood, it can be viewed as belonging by necessity to the waking self, while the self-subsistent anima is freed to create and live here and now as it does beyond the borders of a single life.

In theological terms, this can be expressed as a relation between the components of the self. Kierkegaard defines man as spirit: 'but', he continues, 'what is spirit? Spirit is the self. But what is the self? The self is a relation which relates itself to its own self ... Man is a synthesis of the infinite and the finite, of the temporal and the eternal, of freedom and necessity. A synthesis is a relation between two factors. So regarded man is not yet a self'.[5] In Kierkegaardian terms, then, 'integration' (the harmonious relation of Ego, Anima and Shadow) is 'the positive third term and this is the self' (a self capable of assuming a position *vis-à-vis* God, and so capable of despair and salvation).

II

After this cursory introduction, we may look at the literary origins of 'The Dark Angel'. It derives from a latin poem Johnson wrote to Oscar Wilde on receiving a copy of *The Picture of Dorian Gray*—'In Honorem Doriani Creatorisque Eius'. The major theme of Wilde's novel owes its development more perhaps to Gothic sources, to Maturin's *Melmoth the Wanderer* and to Balzac's *Le Peau de chagrin*: in each case there is a study in metaphysical despair. According to Mario Praz's summary: 'Melmoth has made a bargain with Satan, by which, in exchange for his soul, his life is to be prolonged; but he can still escape damnation if he succeeds in finding someone to share his fate.'[6] Melmoth's pilgrimage is a variant on the Wandering Jew theme and the attempt to find the double as lover and redeemer. In *Le Peau de chagrin*, the hero is offered, again in a game of souls, the use of a strange piece of leather which shrinks with every wish. After a familiar (but tragically brief) Faustian pursuit of knowledge, sensuality and power, the talisman dissolves into nothing and the hero dies. In Balzac, as in Maturin, the hero is one-dimensional: Raphael and Melmoth are only a state removed from the lowest forms of despair: 'despair at not willing to be oneself; or, still lower, despair at not willing to be a self; or lowest of all, in despair at willing to be another than himself'.[7]

Melmoth and Raphael live on the plane of self-reflective immediacy. Despair in their case does not come about from tribulation, from something that breaks in from the outside, but by reflection from within oneself (suffering has passed from the passive to the active stage). In Maturin, as in Balzac, the element of predestination is apparent: each hero gives in rather easily. With *The Picture of Dorian Gray*, there is again the compact as, of course, in the *agape* of 'The Dark Angel':

> Apples of ashes, golden bright;
> Waters of bitterness, how sweet!

But, as allegory, the Portrait is morally more flexible than Balzac's piece of leather. It can suggest another self, and the *dénouement* is more personally horrifying than the end of Raphael in *Le Peau de chagrin*. Melmoth the vampire is looking for his waking-self; Dorian Gray looks for and finds his shadow.

Before considering the actual relation of Dorian Gray to 'The Dark Angel' let us briefly recapitulate the stages between. The parallels between Johnson's 'In Honorem Doriani Creatorisque Eius' and 'The Dark Angel' are fairly close:

> Amat avidus amores
> Miros, miros carpit flores
> Saevus pulchritudine:
> Quanto anima nigrescit,
> Quanto facies splendescit,
> Mendax sed quam splendide!
> Hic sunt poma Sodomorum;
> Hic sunt corda vitiorum ...
> Et peccata dulcia ...

The note is one of enthusiasm over Wilde's moral insight, though the 'mendax sed quam splendide' reminds one of the comment of the Fathers on Pagan virtues, that they were no more than splendid vices. In 1893, parts of 'In Honorem Doriani' were embodied in another Latin poem, 'Satanas'. This later poem is frankly theological; it covers the same ground as '*In Honorem*', but the history of the individual soul is now related to the moral conflict in the universe. Parts of its detail and actual phraseology carry us forward to 'The Dark Angel'. 'Satanas' ends on a note of genuine dramatic surprise:

Vae! non stabit in aeternum
Regnum, ait Rex, infernum:
Sed dum veniat Supernum,
    Dabo vobis victimas.

And this reminds us of the *peripeteia*:

Dark Angel, with thine aching lust!
Of two defeats, of two despairs:
Less dread, a change to drifting dust,
Than thine eternity of cares.

Here Johnson for a moment forgets himself and sympathizes almost with his tormentor. He is certainly, at that point, nearer to the formal and ritual objectivity of 'Satanas'. There the 'troop of passionate powers' rend the heart of the sinner: the passions themselves, furies, 'sorores avidas'. Johnson records the pains of Satan and the damned aloofly as though watching from another plane some interesting tragic spectacle. But if he can for the moment look upon the 'Rector Tenebrarum' as a tragic hero submitting to *force majeure*, this aesthetic trance is soon dissipated and we find ourselves uncomprisingly in the middle of our life's way with the towering threat:

    dum veniat Supernum
Dabo vobis victimas.

Up to a point, then, one may enjoy the drama of salvation and damnation *qua* drama, even perhaps with a sense of irony at one's own personal destiny being involved. When we move though from 'Satanas' to 'The Dark Angel' the sense of omen becomes plain. The centre has moved from angel to man. What was seen only as a warning in the poem to Wilde comes home now with horrid triumph. 'The Dark Angel' is at once a justification of failure, an attempt at reassurance, an exploration of lost territory.

In Johnson, as in Wilde, we find a curious ability for standing aside and watching the personal drama develop. 'To become', as Wilde puts it, 'the spectator of one's own life is to escape the suffering of life'. In Wilde's case the *débâcle* was sudden; in Johnson's protracted—but both of them accepted in an oddly detached way the consequences of their actions as though in some deeper sense they remain uninvolved. Wilde remains in England to suffer imprisonment; Johnson knows that he is killing himself with drink, but says 'I do not want to be cured', even looking forward in his mind to the time when, a shabby spectre on the model of Simeon Solomon, he will be cadging halfcrowns from his friends. One cannot claim, as one can with Baudelaire, that this detachment stems from a genuine objectification of the moral problem. It is rather a matter of escape from one level of the self to another (this is connected with the dialectic of resignation).

Johnson's poem is a late example of a text about the 'double' or second self in Romantic literature. E.T.A. Hoffman is cardinal for few of his writings escape from 'double projection', mostly associated with the demonic pact. Peter Schlemihl in Chamisso's story sells his shadow, which becomes highly successful in its autonomous career, resorting first to blackmailing and finally dominating its original owner. Hans Andersen in his tale 'The Shadow' rehearses the *topos*, focusing in particular on the role of the double in frustrating the original self in the love relationship.[8] All the psychological variants are embodied in the work of Jean Paul. What may be accented now is the option of depersonalization and that of multiplication of the personality (anticipating Wilde) and the sense that to destroy the shadow-oppressor would be to destroy the self.

Victorian poets were also acutely aware of the 'divided self', but to them it is often presented through a strategy of indirection as part of the audience requirement that the poet should renounce Romantic subjectivity. Johnson's poem is lyric autobiography and as such contrasts with the treatment of theme by his master Pater. In 'Denys L'Auxerre', for example, Pater presents Denys as an incarnation of Dionysus torn to pieces not by the equivalent of the Titans but by modern Bacchants, the God sacrificed to himself. Denys is a dopplegänger, no one can determine the relationship of the God and his surrogate. Denys exhibits a passive attitude to his own sufferings as does the prophet of Dionysus in Euripides' *Bacchae*, but the prophet or surrogate there disappears, mysteriously reassuming his Godhead. The 'Imaginary Portraits' of Pater correspond in their genre to the dramatic monologue: the author is not on oath, and fear of encountering the shadow is strongly distanced by historical setting and narrative form. Rossetti too was haunted by fascination and fear of the shadow. He touches the theme in the unfinished 'Saint Agnes of Intercession' while the drawing *How They Met Themselves* has been described as an 'interchanging, receding and recurrent movement of line and form, consciousness in identity and of otherness'.[9]

That classic of psychology, Otto Rank's *Der Doppelgänger* (1914) takes a Freudian line so that the mirror-water imagery in double literature is stressed as a sign of what the shadow represents: Narcissism. This readily applies to the *The Picture of Dorian Gray* or to *How They Met Themselves* but is not specially helpful in discussion of 'The Dark Angel'.[10]

What then is the relation of picture to man? Had Dorian been a self on the simplest level, without possibility or necessity, then no problem could have been posed. As soon as he wills to be himself, he calls 'the shadow' quite literally into the picture. Lord Henry Wotton's gloss stings Dorian into recognition of himself and to make the Faustian wish that he may stay youthful while the painting takes on the weight of his years (and his sins).

Those, however, who propose the picture as mirror rather than shadow may find confirmation in the notion that Dorian gives his 'self' away to the picture; by doing so far from acquiring freedom from moral constraints, and the capacity to fulfil the potentialities of the self, he has in fact no will and therefore no self and no dynamic relation to the picture. The relation of picture to man is certainly not that of conscience to sinner. Conscience, even when tricked or defied, gives to each separate act its moral significance—'the aboriginal Vicar of Christ' so Newman terms it. Conscience does not lessen the sense of self even though we become more scrupulous in committing the will to a train of thought or a series of actions; even though we limit the potentialities of the self. Or, to put it another way, 'a man who has no will is no self; the more will he has, the more consciousness of self he has also.'

Dorian views himself as an artist in life, shaping himself. Perhaps his error is to act rather than to contemplate. A little earlier, in the dialogue 'The Critic as Artist' Gilbert, who seems to represent Wilde's own point of view, applies some amoral lessons from Pater's *Renaissance*. Historical sympathy, impassionated contemplation, ensure that there is no 'dead mode of life that one cannot make alive'. And there follows the famous passage on Heredity:

> By revealing to us the absolute mechanism of all action, and so freeing us from the self-imposed and tramelling burden of moral responsibility, the scientific principle of Heredity has become for us, as it were, the warrant for the contemplative life, it has shown us that we are never less

> free than when we try to act. It has hemmed us round with the nets of the hunter ... We may not watch it, for it is within us. We may not see it save in a mirror that mirrors the soul. It is Nemesis without her mask. It is the last of the Fates, and the most terrible. It is the only one of the Gods whose real name we know.[11]

Wilde recalls the sense of liberation expressed in the 'Conclusion' to the *Renaissance*, and Pater's more evocative 'vibration of long past acts' working their way out in the present. We escape the self by becoming a hundred selves. Dorian, however, like his author (did not that 'voluminous tenderness' descend from Sir William, his father?) had inherited a stormy family past and could not abstain from action. Lord Henry Wotton plays the truly Wildean role of inaction but remains lonely and ageing at the end of the book. A triumph of misunderstood or parodic Paterism, he gets everything wrong. As for Dorian, he comes to realize that the boast that art, the art of life, has nothing to do with action can be proved, though disconcertingly. It is the picture which acts as much as reacts, circumscribing Dorian's attempts to repent, which are revealed, rightly or wrongly as Aesthetic religiosity, a higher form of hypocrisy. Acting may involve the transition from art (clarity and progression—the dead modes are numerous) to life (chaos and circularity), and once imprisoned within the mirror image one cannot act to save oneself. As criticism has indeed recognized,[12] the *Picture of Dorian Gray* amounts to a self-indicting text, one that undercuts the whole 'Aesthetic' proceedings of the 1890s. So far from the subject being unconditioned physically and morally, the picture's body, Platonically or vicariously, expresses the soul's corruption. The picture conditions Dorian, who has in a sense, lost his body. His attitude towards his image is one of loathing and delight. It is precisely this sequence that Johnson touches on in 'The Dark Angel'. He too had a dubious heredity (both of his brothers seem to have been unstable, one attempted suicide). But where Wilde has secularized the Aesthetic dilemma, Johnson touches on it in religious terms. That Johnson should have chosen as an alternative to the healing process (confronting the shadow) the composition of a lyric poem reminds us that the centre of his life was artistic aspiration, whether one views it as a broken aspiration, in that the life failed altogether in organizing itself for literature or broken in the realization that the quarrel of his sensibility with his religion could not be resolved in tragic terms. It is notable that what the Dark Angel poisons are not acts but contemplations, with the exception of the 'Banquet': the attempt to act leads to intensified despair. And if the mirror as emblem is eschewed, it is because from the time that 'The Dark Angel' was written, or earlier, Johnson had a hatred of his own image. He refused to have himself recorded in the photograph or the drawing. A late photograph, taken in circumstances perhaps that he could hardly refuse—a direct request perhaps from one of his surrogate mother figures, Alice Meynell or Katharine Tynan Hinkson, bears some of the marks of Dorian's portrait in its later stages: a haunted, seamed child's face, eyes trapped, the soul indeed imprisoned in the body.[13]

'The Dark Angel' is not Johnson's last word on the subject. In a series of painful poems no longer hiding in symbols he says:

> My hatred of myself is pain
> Beyond my tolerable share
> . . .
> Of myself to live ashamed
> Is ever present agony.

and asks that his desire shall either kill him at once or leave him the leisure to repent. His last word is to be found in 'To the Saints', written a year or so before his death. In these triplets, he is still able to evade the sin of despair, though he comes near to it in the stanzas on the Will:

> Freedom and weakness in my will I know:
> Ah, is it malice, conscious and aglow,
> That into paths of death persuades me so?
> . . .
> Said I, that I have knowledge of my will?
> False! False! Blind born, blind I continue still
> I do not know myself, only my ill.

III

> Dark Angel, with thine aching lust
> To rid the world of penitence:

The 'dark' of this vocative serves two purposes: dark as the darkened Seraph, but dark too in the sense of 'unknown'. To unmask Satan, according to Loyola, is to conquer him: the difficulty is to know what is happening on the other side of the hill. You tabulate the positions he has already invested: art, nature, personal relationships, as if that could help. Johnson's life, at this time, had begun to break up, and the poem sets out rather desperately in a search for answers. But 'dark' is also the signature of the shadow: here as elsewhere the two aspects of the danger interpenetrate: 'We are betrayed by what is false within.'

We know of two passions a fallen spiritual being can experience: pride and its derivative, envy. From the moment, or by the fact rather, of his Fall, the Angel experienced both these passions: pride in his separation from God and apparent autonomy; envy of what he had previously enjoyed, and of the hypostasization of Christ. This 'ache' of envy and pride indicates duration and intensity. Duration—Christ was sacrificed from the beginning of the world; there was a metaphysical Fall (of Satan) before the moral Fall (of man, or of this creation). Intensity, because 'the Devil's despair is the most intense despair; for the Devil is sheer spirit, and therefore absolute consciousness and transparency; in the Devil there is no obscurity which might serve as a mitigating excuse, his despair is therefore absolute defiance'.[14] In this sense the poem opens, as it finishes, on the eschatological plane. The reference to the Sacrament of Penance confronts us as a large general statement corresponding to the last two lines: 'Lonely to the lone I go:/Divine, to the Divinity.' If the world were rid of penitence, it would be formally rid of Grace: it would be given over entirely to despair, the second despair of the Tempter. But this vocative 'dark' represents a challenge. However much the Shadow battens on the substance, it can only reflect it: however wide the darkness spreads, it remains the absence of light: the notion of evil as the *privatio boni* (deprivation of the good) is to be found in the Fathers. Origen defines evil as 'The accidental lack of perfection': evil only exists because God's purpose for the creation was not fulfilled; it will disappear when the fulfilment occurs: it will 'perish of its own darkness'. However, the effect of the *privatio boni* may well be, as Jung suggests, the autonomy of evil as embodied in Anti-Christ, or Shadow. And if autonomous, the possibility of wholeness of the self through integration of the Shadow is lessened. Indeed, man himself can become a second creator: the creator of evil if he hypostasizes, and attempts to manipulate the Shadow. This is the extent of your ambition, is it the extent of your power?

Malicious Angel, who still dost
My soul such subtile violence!

The statement here is held in by the colon. As the poem begins and ends with a large working generalization of origin and destination, so, too, the argument proceeds in a fairly rigid dialectic. 'Who *still* dost', he knows the answers already, as if that were of any use. This oxymoron 'subtle violence' signifies intellectual no less than physical assault; but we might also derive from it the sense of sustained; the violence is continuous like that slow local pressure, after an atomic explosion, that pushes over a house.

Because of thee, no thought, no thing,
Abides for me undesecrate:

The onset of metaphysical despair will make us turn inward in the hope that we can find the smaller distortion, of ourselves, not the world. All my human activities are wrongly directed, and all things are indeed 'made double', but not in the harmoniously connected manner of the book of *Ecclesiasticus*.[15] That 'undesecrate' looks back to the Sacrament of Penance. Ideally speaking, the view of the world as naturally sacramental might be maintained: it is still God's creation however wounded, as Satan is still God's creature however darkened. No creature can lose its central goodness. If it did so it would no longer exist. This 'undesecrate' is typical of the negative diction, of the passive constructions, that haunt the poem. Thus we find 'unfair', 'untortured', 'uncomforted', 'impieties'. This is suggestive of the constrictions of the *vie recluse*; but it hints also at the *privatio boni* as defined in the Fathers and Aquinas—the absence of real good from a real subject. The characteristic of evil is that it cannot make, only mar what is already existent: it tends towards non-being, yet never attains it.

Dark Angel, ever on the wing,
Who never reachest me too late!

The Dark Angel is naturally depicted in his realm—Prince of the Air, the noon-day devil who flies by night. He appears here as a bird of prey moving, on the authority of Aquinas, with a velocity far in excess of light. Now for the corollary. We cannot *see* the evil, we can only translate from experience the terms used by the enemy. The paranomasia 'ever' and 'never' may seem to start a paradox. Clearly it refers to the double *role*, Angel and Shadow. The pattern of inner and outer has been established by 'thought': Father White cites blindness as an analogy. Blindness is real enough, but consists in the absence of sight from a real man; as darkness is real but consists in the absence of light. This, then, can imply: I am warned by temptation that you as Devil are on the wing; *but as shadow you are already there*. The stationary quality of the victim means both that additional grace never seems to be given me to avoid you, and the enclosed life I live gives me little opportunity of hiding from you in society or through diversion.

When music sounds, then changest thou
Its silvery to a sultry fire:
Nor will thine envious heart allow
Delight untortured by desire.

Why should we begin with music here? It seems something of a transition in the sense that it would be more natural to begin with poetry or, even more naturally, with social relationships. The construction is once again a passage from the particular to the general statement, though it could well be questioned whether the particular occasion is presented in adequately concrete terms. Music is the most accessible emotionally of all the arts; the art which has the most immediate effect on the senses, on the animal nature. It is also a catalyst—'all art aspires to the condition of music',—the credo of Pater and Verlaine, the condition to which the present poem aspires. Music represents cosmic harmony: the Greeks spoke of 'the harmony of Zeus'; the morning stars sang together; Lucifer fell, star of the morning. This hope that music will lead to purgation is an oblique means of mentioning the Aesthetic heresy. It represents the first of the distractions from despair, proposed in order to avoid recognizing despair and confronting the Shadow. Many trances, including mystical states, are self-induced with the assistance of music, and this might seem an opportunity of arriving at individual harmony without including the lower self. Music suspends the real chaos and permits us to dwell in ambivalence without synthesis. The 'silvery' leaves a sense of cool pure order: the moon against the sun of 'sultry', with its overtones of disturbance and desire. The immediate associations of silvery are not only chastity and repose—the Anima, but also pale, spectral, disembodied fantasy; in short, the life of the imagination. If one of the factors in recognizing the Shadow is despair over one's self, then imagination, 'the possibility of all reflection' is a first, but finally illusory means of escape for it is often the grammar of the Shadow.

This contrast of coolness and rest with warmth and movement persists through the poem. But not only lust and chastity are opposed for 'The ardour of red flame is thine,/And thine the steely soul of ice.' This coolness reflects a passionless withdrawal from human values into the *vie recluse*. For this reason we begin not with the natural world but with human skills. The domain of art represents, for Johnson, a moral problem that is less acute in the domain of social relations.

The 'envious heart' gives us the second spiritual vice. We can shift the primary meaning along these lines: the devil himself is envious of the beauty of art, since it is a mode of apprehending God. The poet himself is perhaps envious of an art form in which he cannot create, over which he has no control, but which can control him by its sensuous power. The aesthete in him would like to create an autonomous world, according to whim: 'Thou poisonest the fair design/Of nature with unfair device.' Like Satan, he cannot emulate the natural order by creation; or, if he does, through the 'gracious muses' of the following stanzas, it remains *mimesis* only; a shadow creation; the fruit of the closed world of the imagination. 'My aim is to write great poetry: but to do so I require liberty of subject-matter and liberty of sensation.' The 'untortured' here looks back to the original Latin sense of 'tortured'; that is, twisted or distorted.

Through thee, the gracious Muses turn
To Furies, O mine Enemy!
And all the things of beauty burn
With flames of evil ecstasy.

These 'gracious Muses', then, are not merely courtly and enriching, they are full of Graces in the theological sense: they can sing in Hebrew as well as in Greek. As a terminus of its own, poetry can represent another form of abstraction, so that they become Furies, the female attendants of Proserpina. In 'Satanas', these goddesses are equated with the passions that have rent the soul during its probation here:

Gaudet Rector tenebrarum
Immolare cor amarum
Satiare furiarum
  Rex sorores avidas.

The Furies in the ancient world were certainly seen as agents of damnation and despair, not agents of retribution and restoration in the Aeschylean sense—in the *Oresteia*, the Furies are tamed by Athene and become the guardians of the City, of the *mores* of the Athenians. Instead of purgation, poetry induces forbidden passions. In Dante the Furies become images of the fruitless remorse which does not lead to penitence (*Inferno*, 9.49.)—'one vehemence of useless tears'. The second pair of lines in this stanza seems very much of a ninetyish cliché. The general statement 'all the things of beauty burn, etc.' might follow as justly from the previous stanza, or from the stanza which describes the rhythms of the natural world. Still, it does show us delight in the actual process of being tortured by desire that constantly feeds itself through its own substance, that can never be quenched and suggests, too, something of a Dionysiac frenzy, pointing us forward to the burning waters of the *agape*.

> Because of thee, the land of dreams
> Becomes a gathering place of fears:
> Until tormented slumber seems
> One vehemence of useless tears.

These lines as a whole have a stronger movement, probably by contrast with the rather frail preceding rhymes: 'enemy' and 'ecstasy'. Could there be a more positive statement of the intended healing process? No doubt it would be satisfyingly logical to establish the world of the unconscious at the beginning of the poem, or somewhere nearer the 'hinting tones' and 'haunting laughs' of a later stanza. Still, Johnson lived in the partly pre-lapsarian world, before Freud; and a respectable causal chain extends from music and poetry to the dream. The military metaphor of 'a gathering place' is well caught up by the 'troop' of 'beleaguring' powers in the verse that follows. He is harping again on the world of fantasy, or the closed world of nonsense: might it not seem a way of escaping from the harsh logic of belief? There will be the times, say the manuals of the Latin Church, when you will wish that none of this were true. Not even the world of the creative imagination can change it; nor can the healing trance of sleep. It is from the unconscious, from the chthonic world, the Shadow rises. He is passing from one nightmare to another: the passage from waking and sleeping carries him through hinting tones and haunting laughs to the shapeless cries, the gaping mouths, the undecipherable gestures of sleep, more horrifying because of the absence of direct moral content. A pitch may be reached where reality is only known by the pressure of evil, evil that transcends itself. I may sleep, but the Shadow is unsleeping.

The last two lines have a certain concision. This 'vehemence' is a synecdoche by transposition, and the prose meaning is a shedding of tears that leads not to resolution but to exhaustion. It is in these lines, I think, that the painful moral insight is for the first time reinforced by a distinctly personal tone. We have had the general statement that the Angel never reaches him too late: but somehow the sharp syntax and the tensely particular meaning here have a more genuine pathos.

When sunlight glows upon the flowers,
Or ripples down the dancing sea:
Thou, with thy troop of passionate powers,
Beleagurest, bewilderest, me.

For Romantic philosophers the unconscious and nature are closely connected. C.G. Carus, uses, for example, specimens of intelligence and purposive action in unconscious manifestations of life, human, animal and plant, as proof of an unconscious (unconscious to us) mind. For Schelling, nature is an unconscious thinking. We can pass then from the world below sleep to the natural world with the hope that there the Demonic power will at least be mitigated. Nature can be seen as 'a partial revelation, a participation in, the divine Mind'. I use this elaborate analogy because there is obviously more to the stanza than a mere contrast between the peace of the outer world (away from the Rhymers' Club, Irish Nationalist Committees and the Fleet Street bars) and the turbulence of the interior life.

This sunlight glowing and rippling suggests Nature herself to be unimpassioned, apparently unfeeling, but perfectly at peace, because without consciousness as we know it. The ordered movement of dancing contrasts with the rapid vicious movements of the passions and the bewildered movements of their victim. 'Passionate' here is, thus, less of a ninetyish cliché than 'flames of evil ecstasy'. Rather, it is the precise word for these *sorores avidas* kept on the move by the energy, the sting of their damnation. Nothing can be further from the instinctive, happy movements of natural order. But this instinctive blindly happy quality of natural objects can be sinister: it may be a silent hint of withdrawn purpose. There is a tacit analogy between it and the person who is not aware of himself as spirit, not reflective; incapable of the metaphysical despair which begins the process of healing. The landscape suggests high summer, but the counterpart follows: corruption after innocence; the profile of despair; the darkened archetype of the *Paradisum Voluptatis*: A.W. Patrick comments: 'L'intention manifeste est d'éxciter la répétition des consonnes "gl", une alliteration peu heureuse et d'enricher la pensée par la substitution d'un decrivant non la lumière déjà suffisamment indiquée, mais le mouvement.'[16]

Within the breath of autumn woods,
Within the winter silences:
Thy venomous spirit stirs and broods,
O Master of impieties!

The spirit stirs in the breath; broods in the silences; haunts waking and sleeping, society and solitude; the dying life here, the living death of 'an eternity of cares.' The reference to decay and immortality is clear. 'The woods decay, the woods decay and fall', and the ruin of vegetation is clearly analogous to the ruin the Dark Angel effects in the human soul. The word 'venomous' suggests the Serpent lying in winter sleep, but stirring at a footfall. And the last line seems to play an unwilling tribute.

The ardour of red flame is thine,
And thine the steely soul of ice:
Thou poisonest the fair design
Of nature, with unfair device.

Lust and pride reappear in this flame and ice; but there is a glance too at the two Hells of the Schoolmen: the wilderness of perpetual flame; the icy torment. This notion of variation in the eternal punishment of the damned was based on Job 5:19, 'They shall go from excessive heat to the waters of the snows.' (See St Thomas Aquinas, *Summa Theologia*, lq. CIX.3). The damned pass from one extreme to the other (as quickly as one passes from a state of Grace to mortal sin, as quickly as the Dark Angel himself); they pass from giving themselves in lust to withdrawing themselves in pride. One thinks here of Dante's notion that there is nobility in sinning greatly: 'sin greatly or not at all.'[17]

Questo misero modo
tengon l'anime triste di coloro,
che visser senza infamia e senza lodo.
(*Inferno* 3.34)

The red flame connects with the autumn woods, the steely ice with the winter silences. These silences refer back to the 'silvery' of an earlier stanza, suggesting chastity because of a virtual withdrawal from life, the *vie recluse*. It is how such a withdrawal is used, purposively or not, that matters. The 'fair design' of nature violently counterpoints the 'unfair device' of the Dark Angel. Design here is teleological in the highest sense. Nature is invested with order, purpose, rhythm and beauty. 'Device' hints at stratagem: something of a heraldic flourish or challenge superimposed on a durable ground; 'design', corresponding to Hopkins's inscape and 'device' to the limp shapes of a demon-haunted nature. But it is 'unfair': it cannot cohere even. The Evil One can only disorder, render aimless, cheapen, distort what is shapely with a lying mirror. The 'poisonest' recalls the 'venomous' of the previous verse; the serpent brooding under the fall of leaves; Eden desolate; the rhythms of the seasons broken.

Apples of ashes, golden bright;
Waters of bitterness, how sweet!
O banquet of a foul delight,
Prepared by thee, dark Paraclete!

Music, poetry, communion with the natural world, these are all attempts at diversion from despair. We shall now encounter something more dynamic. For this invitation to an *agape*, a love feast, is more than a distant mockery of the Sacrament of Communion. Let us look at it, though, in this sense. Throughout the poem things are 'made double'. On this outer level of interpretation, then, the *agape* signifies that particular metaphysical horror: of eating and drinking the sacred elements to one's own damnation. Both elements are taken—what presents itself as the terrible marriage of Shadow and Ego is about to be consummated; priest, victim, and real presence in one. In a sense it amounts to an ascent from nature to nature's god; a last attempt to discharge the burden of his love before it becomes poisoned. If he cannot communicate with the unreflecting lives round him; if he cannot escape, that is, from consciousness of himself in despair, despair at being himself, can he rely on the offer of Grace? Is resignation, the awareness that eternity is the other part of the dialectic, to be the only refuge? He cannot be present and lose himself at the point where God meets Man most surely, most graciously, most in Person. The offer is made; but in place of the very body and the very blood what is offered is the apple of damnation, and wine that does not quench, but stimulates thirst.

Christian sacrament and infernal banquet are juxtaposed. The lines, though, involve a further *topos*: the banquet of sense, or of the senses, rather, hierarchically ranged from higher to lower; from those that operate distantly, sight and hearing, down to smell, taste and touch, those that are more or altogether immediate. The banquet of sense has its own contrary: the Platonic celestial banquet as glossed in the fifteenth century by Marsilio Ficino; the senses are tempted upward, where in the sensual banquet they are tempted downward. Both the celestial and its parodic sensual banquet would be known to Johnson, a close-reading man: Chapman's *Ovid's Banquet of Sense*, for example, or *Timon of Athens*, where the banquet having satisfied all the other senses, a masque is brought on by Cupid to enchant the sight (I, ii, lines 129 ff.). There is an obscure example in *The Tempest* where Ariel figures as harpy, and one may connect the harpy figure with the 'foul delight' of the banquet stanza in 'The Dark Angel'. Milton rejuxtaposes pagan and Christian banquets in *Comus* and most elaborately in *Paradise Regained*. This banquet of sense is also troubled by harpies and contrasts with the angelic banquet of which Jesus partakes as reward for 'standing', at the close of the poem. In spite of Satan's expressed views on how Jesus should be tempted, the actual process is not precisely manly, though this may be because the arch fiend is putting down the 'dissolutest' Belial who tempts himself while plotting a scenario for tempting Christ with women. Satan transforms the desert into the background of a Renaissance painting; the offscape is flushed by the Botticellian beauties tapering away into the distance. The temptation is aesthetic—these are not Belial's sort of girl; but the point for 'The Dark Angel' is that the Messiah is tempted also by a suite of delicious boys (temptation has to be total, for Adam fell totally):

> Tall stripling youths rich-clad, of fairer hue
> Then *Ganymede* or *Hylas*
>
> (*Paradise Regained*, II, 352–3)

Ganymede means 'pathic' as we know from an *ébauche* that Milton sketched out for a play on the subject of the destruction of Sodom: 'the course of the city each evening, every one with mistresse, or Ganymede gitterning along the streets or solacing on the banks of Jordan.'[18] The apple is a primary sexual symbol. In the poetry of antiquity it refers to the brimming shape of a woman's breasts; it is the fruit not merely of intellectual but of carnal knowledge, and its appearance recalls lost Eden as well as the lower senses. These apples are 'golden bright'; they have a Hesperidean tinge suggesting effort and danger (the kind of effort involved is condemned by society). This epithet 'bright' seems vapid, perhaps, but suggests phospherence, rottenness. For these apples have been culled from the orchards of Josephus. 'The shadows of the five cities are still to be seen as well as the ashes growing in their fruits, which fruits have a colour as if they were fit to be eaten, but if you pluck them with your hands, they dissolve into smoke and ashes.' (*Wars of the Jews*, IV, 8, 4, and Deuteronomy 32:32)

Hic sunt poma Sodomorum;
Et sunt corda vitiorum;
Et peccata dulcia.
('In Honorem')

Rex veneficus amorum
Vilum et mortiferorum.
. . .
Cor corrumpens suaviter
. . .
Fructus profert; inest cinis:
Profert flores plenos spinis
. . .
('Satanas')

Like the offer to Faust, the offer to Raphael in Balzac's *Peau de chagrin*, like Dorian Gray's wish that the portrait may age while he remains perpetually youthful, this banquet is a meeting with the adversary; a mutual recognition; the decisive moment in a lifetime. Art and nature have been diminished as distractions; this offer refers to social relationships. He is a little coy about what kind of relationships; but the 'unfair' of the previous stanza; the 'cheap and death-bearing loves' of 'Satanas' clarify matters. The real apple is full of juice, of sap, the movement of life. These dead sea fruits are infertile like love between man and man.

It is barely surprising that homosexuality should join intemperance at this board. Like the Renaissance, the later nineteenth century was a great period of Greek studies—Johnson himself as an accomplished classic, and these studies gained particular impetus from the preoccupations of poets peculiarly sensitive to the *mal du siècle*. J.A. Symonds' studies of inversion in the ancient world, and his devotion to 'blue breeched gondoliers', Swinburne's fascination with the androgyne, Roden Noel's luscious poem on Ganymede are merely three among many examples. One must clearly distinguish the cult of male beauty from the cult of romantic friendship, the sentiment, let us say, behind 'In Memoriam'. But in Johnson's case the two are confused. His responses hardened early. At Winchester he is said to have been one of the leaders of a homosexual circle (though evidence comes from Lord Alfred Douglas.) Yet the Lamia's banquet is not for a moment believed in. Not merely is the offer a substitute for the communion with that greater society that transcends the societies of earth, the economy of Christ's mystical Body; the loneliness from which it promises relief is not the cause of metaphysical despair. The question of art or contemplation (of the human scene or natural beauty), or even personal relationships, is not the cause of despair, is quite irrelevant to despair. Despair comes directly from the self.

This recognition is part of the healing process: it means an addition to despair, because consciousness of self is increased. So we come to the role of 'the dark Paraclete'. This word *Parakletos* means not only comforter, but theologically 'He whereby the Begotten is loved by the One begetting and loves His Begetter', as Augustine puts it. He dwells in man to co-operate with Grace. Here the Paraclete is the dialectically opposed indweller, who accompanies each decision with his own response. Yet he does not open out towards Grace but towards the terrifying depth of the ego.

> Thou art the whisper in the gloom,
> The hinting tone, the haunting laugh:
> Thou art the adorner of my tome,
> The minstrel of mine epitaph.

Superficially this refers to scruples, to hypocrisy, to imaginary and relished fears. 'Satanas' gives us:

> Venit autem vitiosa
> Species infamia:

Veniunt crudeles visus,
Voces simulati risus

The real note, though, comes over as pathetic irony, and on this ground one might defend the second pair of lines from any charge of being rhetorically false.[19] They catch the earlier reference to music and poetry in the mocking way of dreams, but the deeper meaning seems to be: what the world will see is an outward pattern of failure which corresponds hardly at all to the condition of the inner life. They don't, for example, understand the significance of the sacramental offer: through the forbidden experience I might express my feelings towards my kind (though it would be an effort to pick people up in bars or be picked up; through the trance of alcohol I can come to terms with objective reality, forget I am undersized and an old Wykehamist.) My resignation is based on a fierce metaphysical contest. But there is something here of the actor's pleasure in deception. The adorner adds something to what is known already: my hidden life has itself something of the depth and mystery of a work of art. There is something also of the perverse pleasure in self-corruption we discover in Dorian Gray, and the shadow retorts, when one attempts amendment: you are luxuriating in a new emotion; you are hypocrite, using your personal religious feelings as the raw material of art. *Voces simulati risus:* In 'Satanas' the howl of the damned sounds like painful hysterical laughter: how seriously we took this science of debauchery! There must, too, be a vivid reference to the voluptuousness of hiding a secret that threatens to escape one's silence, whose existence one hardly admits to oneself. These voices are the noises in the ear of the dispsomaniac, chiming with the typical feeling of pursuit and persecution. And, if any comfort lay in the reflection: 'I can destroy the shadow by destroying myself', like a transformation in a nightmare the thought might come: I am deceived. Sully Prudhomme has some strange lines:

Like his own shadow man down here,
A little living darkness, a frail shred
Of form, sees, speaks, but with no clear knowledge;
Saying ... 'By you my feet are led.'
Man shadows but another angel who,
Fallen from high is but a shadow too.
So, he himself an image is of God,
And, maybe, in some place by us untrod,

Near deepest depths of nothingness or ill
Some wraith of human wraiths grows darker still.[20]

Who is the shadow? am I? is it? For all I know the world may be the sport of an evil demiurge, and if virtue is, in the classic definition, 'the love of universal being' then this might dispose of the argument that an evil demiurge could never make me with such a conscience. Everything is made double: the still small voice has its brutal relatives. And these sneering laughs in darkness, these smothered echoes suggested by the paronomasia 'hinting' and 'haunting', lead up to the flat statement of despair:

I fight thee, in the Holy Name!
Yet, what thou dost is what God saith:[21]

the comma before the Holy Name makes it come out with a desolating weight. This is absolute zero: I was tricked. But might one not be consoled, thinking of the Adversary's role in Job: God uses evil for his own ends: evil fulfils the purpose of good? This 'saith' can mean either 'as God tells us' (i.e. through the Old Testament) or 'as God ordains it', though by foreseeing evil, as Samuel Clarke tells us, He does not command it to occur: an act is not retrospectively true, it only becomes true when it happens. (Clarke puts in philosophic form what Milton and others painfully taught themselves to accept.) These lines, then, in plain prose, are despairingly paradoxical: I fight you in God's name, yet you are doing what God tells you to. But have we not been already warned of the Dark Angel's masks? 'The Devil is but God's master-fencer, to teach us to handle our weapons.'

Tempter! should I escape thy flame,
Thou wilt have helped my soul from Death.

Temptation is constructive: it can advance our hope of Heaven; it can elicit Grace. From this point he certainly 'accepts the universe' in some broader sense as moral. So on to the eschatological plane:

The second Death, that never dies,
That cannot die, when time is dead:
Live Death, wherein the lost soul cries,
Eternally uncomforted.[22]

He is nerving himself. This is the medieval notion of Hell, *Revelations*. Chapter 20, verse 14, gives us 'And death and hell were cast into the lake of fire. This is the second death.' And Augustine has several allusions to the 'second death' in *De Civitate Dei*, xx, vi. and in xxi, iii:

> For the death then shall be eternal, and the soul that suffers it shall neither be able to live, having lost her God her only life, nor yet to avoid torment, having lost all means of death. The first death forces her from the body against her will and the second holds her in the body against her will …
>
> They that are not of this society are destined to eternal misery, called the second death; because there even the soul, being deprived of God seems not to live, much less the body, being bound to everlasting torments. And therefore this second death shall be so much more cruel, in that, it shall never have end.

This is reflected in Donne when he describes it in his fifteenth Sermon as a state of 'Eternal dying, and not dead'. In that eternal instant of horror, the soul imprisons all the content of its past action. (The 'uncomforted' recalls the Paraclete, the veiled sharer of the love feast.) This 'live death' resembles his present condition. Again, the thought might come that he could do without the rewards if he might only feel himself freed from the penalties. To distract, almost, from this thought:

> Dark Angel, with thine aching lust!
> Of two defeats, of two despairs:
> Less dread, a change of drifting dust,
> Than thine eternity of cares.

This 'aching lust' of the first stanza we can read directly with 'thine eternity of cares.' 'Satanas' gives us:

> Vitae eius mors est finis:
> Crux est eius requies.
> Qualis illic apparebit
> Cruciatus, et manebit!
> Quantas ista quot habebit
> Mors amaritudines!

'Death is the purpose of his life.' But before non-being can be arrived at, the ground of being must be shattered: the aim of the shadow is night: the end of Lucifer is deicide, death of God (though in the process he kills himself). What are these two defeats and consequent despairs? With 'Satanas' in mind, it seems certain that the defeats are the metaphysical Fall and the Cross, while the despairs, as we have seen, are deprivation of God and deprivation of death. Lucifer fell by pride and would rise by the same passion. (Suarez in his *De Angelis*[23] suggests that Satan desired a hypostatic union with God, in the manner of Christ's hypostasis.) Aquinas, anticipating this speculation, objects that, for Satan, this would be tantamount to wishing to cease to be, and no one can purpose that in a metaphysical sense. This hypostasis is the counterpart of the dialectical relation between Shadow and waking self, the urge of the unconscious to assimilate the conscious. Compare, too, Jung's notion of a divine quaternity, with its fourth and evil hypostasis.[24] In such a context Johnson's reference to 'drifting dust' becomes considerably pointed. What the Shadow represents in mystical or, indeed, in average Christian experience, Walter Hilton tells us, is the human burden: Grace does not rid us of the burden, but helps us to bear it: 'the soul is not borne *in* the shadow, though he feel it; but *he* beareth *it*.' Incapable, unlike Baudelaire, of the strength to suffer and be spiritually lucid about his suffering, Johnson does not revolt against it, but becomes resigned. He does not accept his suffering, as a final condition of the whole man; as a *terminus ab quo*, for the artist. The despairing self, at this point, is self-convinced that the 'thorn-in-the flesh' gnaws so profoundly that it cannot be abstracted, no matter whether this is actually so, or whether his passion makes it true for him:

> The dialectic of resignation is commonly this: in order to will to be one's eternal self, and then with respect to something positive wherein the self suffers and it is this self that man despairingly wills to be, detaching himself from every relation to the power which posited it ... *Not to will to be oneself, contenting oneself with the thought that after all this will disappear in eternity, thinking oneself therefore justified in not accepting it in time*, so that although suffering under it, the self will not make to it the concession that it properly belongs to the self.[25]

This 'drifting dust' by no means represents the orthodox sentiment, *cupio dissolvi et esse cum Christo*. Rather, it is a reduction to the atomic universe of Democritus one associates with it. At this point, the argument would seem to be posed between Lucretius and Augustine, both persons in Johnson's interior dialogues, a world of flux, without moral absolutes, so that the poem is resolved by being undercut.

Less dread, a change to drifting dust,
Than thine eternity of cares.

We have forgotten the teleological harmonies of 'the fair design'. And Johnson's own deliberate exercise in self-murder becomes in this light logical. It may be as well to paraphrase these lines: Of two defeats, of two despairs, a change to drifting dust is less dreadful than *thine* eternity of cares. The emphasis on *thine* suggests that the 'change to drifting dust' is, in some sense, *our* loss as against *thine* (the Dark Angel's) eternity of cares. It happens to bodies, not to spirits. Dust to dust, ashes to ashes ... In other words the Old Testament is echoing at the back of the poet's mind no less than Epicurean or modern materialism. But then *thine* eternity of cares may be also the eternity of the cares experienced by the damned which Satan, himself as the greatest sufferer among them, presides over.

By the general logic of the poem, though, the first defeat becomes the human defeat by death (the dissolution of the body), and the first despair is perhaps merely despair of the soul's survival; Death may be the end. The second defeat, which more properly belongs to pure spirit, is the defeat of the wish to die and the second despair is the despair of redemption. 'Materialism may be true after all, and that is consoling, for to people of my temperament the central thing in the Christian religion becomes Hell.' There can be no direct affiliation of ideas, but Victorian Broad Church Christians were forever worrying about eternal torment, which, they thought, made Christianity immoral. One thinks of the anecdote about Dean Farrar. 'Drinks on the house, o' man! Old Farrar says there ain't no Hell.' And more cautiously another Dean, Plumptre, puzzles over the same problem in his *Spirits in Prison*. He went and preached unto the spirits in prison (I Peter 3:19).

More broadly the dualism here between body (drifting dust) and spirit (eternity of cares) will help us to the Plotinian eschatology of the last stanza. The drifting dust, as it were, falls away to nothing in the poet's imagination, to moral unreality, and *when* it has done so there is nothing left in his imagination to individuate spirits. What is purely spiritual as such must be good and must of its own nature go back to God. The effect is a psychological one of relaxing, letting go—letting the dust fall far away, letting fall the cares, since they are no longer to be the poet's concern. This, then, is the general logic of the stanza: (a) either materialism is true, in which case I have been worrying myself sick about an illusion—this whole poem has been about nothing, or (b) even if it is not true, it is still true that our human bodies are destroyed and what remains is pure spirit, and (c) I have been imagining pure spirit eternally tormenting itself and seeking to destroy other spirits, but (d) what is really pure in my spirit must be taken up to the source of all purity, and it is right that what is impure should fall away from me and be destroyed:

Lone unto the Lone I go;
Divine, to the Divinity.

More profoundly, the immanence of a kind of evil spiritual power in physical existence is the dominant theme of the poem up to the last two stanzas: the notion of the destruction of physical existence, or its transformation to 'drifting dust', brings in, as something of a release, the notion of transcendence. Because the poet can see the situation of damnation, therefore also he is *beyond* it. The pathos here stems partly from the release being somehow mechanical—the Lone to the Lone, the Divine to the Divinity, like iron filings to a magnet, with no more need for worry, effort and self-torment on Johnson's part. The metaphor of gravity, of physical attraction, or of things mechanically arranging themselves into their separate species, underlies both the drifting-dust image and the divine-to-the-Divinity image. It may be that only the Dark Angel himself, with his 'eternity of cares', is left separate, responsible, individuated. From a Freudian point of view, it could be said that this is a pure death-wish statement: the confidence in this kind of unindividuated immortality is the death wish in a very transparent disguise. The answer to the constant nagging of temptation and remorse, to the inescapable anxiety of being alive, is the certainty that there will come a time when this nagging is no longer relevant, this anxiety no longer necessary.

The first line of the stanza is an epistrophe of the first line of the poem. A radical shift of attitude has taken place, amounting almost to a reversal of fortune. Earlier, the Dark Angel is depicted in majesty, shedding its baleful radiance over the soul. Now Johnson so far forgets himself as to feel pity. This is an analogue of the victim's pity for the tormentor; a pity that was known in German concentration camps. The Angel's suffering is far greater than mine; it is only his own torment which makes him torment me.

But even with our reading of the penultimate stanza the poem is not resolved; or resolved in an odd enough way.

> Do what thou wilt, thou shalt not so
> Dark Angel, triumph over me:
> *Lone, unto the Lone I go*
> *Divine, to the Divinity.*

'If we ask', Santayana remarks, 'what the alternative to these despairs may be, and what will issue from the triumphs he still hopes for, we find nothing positive, nothing specific, but only transcendental spirit, still open to every thought and to every torment, [the] words are the words of Plotinus and the Christian mystics but here we do not feel them backed by either the Platonic or the Christian scheme of the universe; they are floating words.'[26] Still, Johnson might plead the wording of Psalm 82, vv6–7: 'I have said, ye are Gods'—words used by Christ (John 10:34), which Coleridge thought referred to the first apostasy, the Fall of the Angels.

The actual quotation from Plotinus appears at the end of the *Enneads*:

> That which is Soul can never reach an absolute Unreal. Moving downwards she will come to Evil, and so to an Unreal, but not to Unreality-absolute. And if she hasten upon the contrary road she will come not to another but herself. But to exist in herself alone and not in the Universe of Being, is to exist in God. He that sees himself made one with that supreme Self, possesses in himself the counterpart of the Supreme; can he but pass over from himself to God, the Image to the Original, he has reached his journey's end. He will lapse again from the vision: but let him again waken the virtue which is within him, again know himself made perfect in splendour; and he shall again be lightened of his burden, ascending through virtue to the Intelligence and thence through wisdom to the Supreme. This is the life of Gods and of the godlike and happy among men; a quittance from things alien and earthly, a life beyond earthly pleasure, a flight of the alone to the Alone.[27]

Here, then, is the counterpart in personal terms of 'dum veniat Supernum', of the drama of individuation. If we recur to the 'drifting dust', though, it still seems that Johnson attempts to resolve matters by accepting either materialism, or an ideal pantheism, to which any idea of personal salvation remains irrelevant. The soul is itself part of the mental history of God recollected at death. This doctrine of the One makes little of the principle of individuation, a principle underlying 'The Dark Angel', without which the poem would be void of significance. Moreover, we cannot defend it on the ground that this confusion is overtly expressed; the poem purports to be an argument directed towards and arriving at an expected conclusion. We are responsible for our actions; we become what our actions make us. Where otherwise would be the point of the Offer? Yet one can still read the poem entirely in the light of the Plotinian *regressus*. The blight on art, on natural beauty, on human relationships, what more need that signify than the soul's inmost wish to abstract herself from illusion, to 'stand out' of the world of objects; so that rightly using that part in him which is divine, he may bring it back and lose it in the One. He will escape his lower self by being a self no longer. He is not, then, perfecting the self, he is transcending it; he is not overcoming his weakness, but avoiding, by rising above, the conflict. The public symbolism seems altogether at variance with the poem's inward situation.

IV

So far I have been concerned with isolating the special set of experiences, to which Johnson is responding. I have, I hope, shown that this response is deeper than a cursory reading of the poem perhaps might indicate. The action of the poem is made more easily accessible to us by its speaking of the Devil of theology. But this brings its own dangers. Johnson's problem is to find public symbols for a private drama, and to present those symbols in action with sufficient vigour, so establishing them as general truths of the life of the spirit. Whatever symbol is used it must give the impression of containing more than overt value. But by equating the Shadow so firmly with the Devil of theology he not only risks the rigours of the stock response, but involves the poem in a set of undesired associations. At the time the poem was written, the ordered progress of the nineteenth century, its complacency and materialism, had made it rather awkward to take the Devil seriously as a universal immoral agent. The only place he inhabited familiarly was the interior life of those for whom the social order had no place; not the populace, but the practitioners of minority art. And if one did encounter him in literature he came all too frequently encased in aesthetic frivolity, wearing the patched mask of Catholic Diabolism—a convenient literary fiction for *fin de siècle* neurosis. Johnson would have remained more faithful to his intuition had he described 'Him' in vaguer terms; for the angel was doubly 'Dark',

dark with evil and dark because unknown: the Shadow is at once so personal, so foreign to the self. Perhaps his haunting anxieties and painful insights are better expressed in 'The Precept of Silence':

> I know you: solitary griefs,
> Desolate passions, aching hours!
> I know you: tremulous beliefs,
> Agonized hopes, and ashen flowers!

But Johnson did, in the last analysis, see the problem in a less limiting manner as an attempt at psychological healing; as an attempt to reconcile the contradiction between private sensibility and institutional religion; between the truths of the visible Church and the truths of the heart. The promise is cleanly enough defined, but the wrong conclusions follow: after contemplating the Angel with horrified intentness, Johnson escapes through the eschatological trap-door. When the last vibrations of that great promise of a self-sufficient divinity have died away—'Ridiculous the waste sad time/Stretching before and after.'

'The Dark Angel', then, records confused feelings and their illogical, though not necessarily dishonest resolution. Yet, there is little corresponding tension and confusion in its language, or in its argument. The argument ascends like a series of syllogisms. Whenever a general situation is invoked it is presented in abstract terms, and the general clarity and dignity of the design is betrayed everywhere by timidity of diction and rhythmical prettiness. The secondary nature of the imagery, the negative diction, the fondness for passives, all contribute. The relation between experience and expression is more than logical. But, joining the contemporary pursuit of the disembodied lyrical sigh, as did Verlaine or Dowson, Johnson fails; he captures no more than a mood, a perilously balanced moment of insight. When we encounter the hesitant, searching rhythms, the often ugly constructions of Hardy, we hear a man's voice stumbling in perplexity, anger or resignation. He talks to us directly, without any self-pleasing ordinance of language, and we feel at that moment, however local the occasion or individual the sentiment, that he is also speaking *for* us. The more individual his rhythms and diction, the more they appear to approximate to the common voice. But Johnson's sensibility and diction, like those of other nineties figures, seems deliberately peripheral.

And as Johnson disguises resignation as affirmation, so he blurs, wherever possible, all distinctions, 'The Dark Angel' has no polysyllabic rhymes, and this certainly aids the transitions from line to line; enables the argument to move rapidly. Yet consider these pairs: 'enemy', 'ecstasy'; 'silence', 'impieties'; 'me', 'divinity'. 'Penitence' and 'violence' are again typical of these feminine endings, suitable perhaps for suggesting the languid apartments of *The House of Life*, but less unsuited perhaps to the Angel,[28] though more appropriate to the victim.

This to say that the poem's style corresponds to the life it is recording. It is finicky: it is the product of the unstable invalid Johnson was. Its very purged and closed-in effect reflects faithfully the suffocated qualities of the *vie recluse*, a clouded life, shut in deliberately, lived behind closed doors and heavy curtains. A life where nothing is resolved; where the frontiers between fantasy and reality are dangerously frail. And this finds its reflection in the frailty of the rhymes, the poem's neatly propositional form and suavity of texture. To his friends, his acquaintances even, Johnson was something of a self-contrived 'character': his life seemed almost a literary fiction in itself. Yeats (a dubious authority to be sure) tells us of those elaborate imaginary conversations recounted by Johnson so often, but never varying in detail and with the hesitations and rapidity of spontaneous utterance. Gladstone or Newman or Jowett would deliver themselves of utterances characteristically sententious, epigrammatic, of a noble unction. Johnson's life was not so much lived through literature. In a certain sense it *was* literature: the only discipline to which he responded, by which his life was transformed. Still, the poem is not about the *longueurs* of an enclosed life; it concerns an experience of metaphysical horror which should change the nature of subsequent experience; which should encounter the problem of aestheticism; the problem of knowing one's own damnation before death; the problem of dipsomania and Grace. Contrast with these vague and abstract descriptions of the seasons, the ruined garden and the memorial love-feast become a theatre for harpies with something of a similar order from a metaphysical poet writing in a language more ready with abstract general statements. Maurice Scève, the sixteenth century French poet, is depicting union here (the actual connotation of rivers and seas) and in God, what Plotinus describes in his last *Ennead* and what Johnson hints at in 'The Dark Angel' (for the flight from generation to essence is a flight from the imperfect love of objects to the perfect love of God). Scève is insisting, though, on bodily union of lovers in Heaven as promised to us by the resurrection of the flesh, and this pre-baroque solidity is helpful to the metaphor.

A si hault bien de tant saincte amytie
Facilement te debvriot inciter,
Sinon debvoir, ou honneste pitie,
A tout le moins mon loyal persister,
Pour unyment, et ensemble assister
Lassus en paix en nostre eternel throsne,
    N'apperçoy tu de l'Occident le Rhosne
Se destourner et vers Midy courir,
Pour seulement se conjoindre a sa Saone
Jusqu'a leur Mer, ou tous deux vont mourir?

Albert Beguin[29] calls attention to the admirable image of the River Rhone leaving its apparent source to rejoin *its* Saone to follow a single path to *their* sea where *both* die. How much this inner geography of souls is reinforced by the familiar geography of Scève's own countryside! Furthermore, this beautiful extended image does not depend on cramped language and complex statement. It leaves an impression of *density*, without sacrifice of music.

Johnson's closed life of fantasy and invalidism is the natural breeding ground of Angels. In silence and darkness these serene terrible creatures from another world of being may be tempted into visitation. The great poets of angelology, Hölderlin, Baudelaire, Rilke, are also poets of loneliness. Though Baudelaire had a wide circle of acquaintances, he possessed scarcely a single friend. Hölderlin lived his life in the isolation of madness, and Rilke buried himself in a tower to write his greatest poetry. The use of Christian symbolism charges Johnson with great responsibility. 'The Dark Angel' challenges masters. In the great Christian poets, spiritual experience is mysteriously and finally embodied in the symbol, 'the shining mystery of the Cross', so that from being a descriptive abstract of a personal state, the symbols themselves acquire a vitality of their own. Baudelaire, believing in Hell, dubious of Heaven, records his vision with an acute truth and power: *Debris d'humanité pour l'eternité murs.* Johnson tries to circumscribe the abyss by his neo-scholasticism, his cultural reference (we may take the references tacit and explicit to Dante, Plotinus, Crashaw, Augustine and Lucretius, as part of the Alexandrian quality of the later nineteenth century). Like Baudelaire, Johnson cannot reconcile what is positive in the secular world, material progress, the triumph of reason, optimism, with the realities of the spiritual world—suffering and evil.

But as Patric Dickinson finely observes of 'The Dark Angel', it 'is not great speech' in Baudelairian mode, 'but a terrible soliloquy spoken in the long small hours of his room in Fitzroy Street.' It is also, as we have seen, a rehearsal of *topoi*, of the *doppelgänger*, of the contrast of heavenly and sensual banquets while the last and most impressive part of the poem conducts an argument between Augustine and Johnson's favourite poet, the materialist atheist Lucretius. George Santayana observed that Johnson never really felt that though the divine world may surround us, still 'there is sin and damnation within us'; rather, at the deepest level, he felt the precise opposite; though the poem is ostensibly about Augustinianism and its horror: double predestination and the second death, Johnson transforms himself into a Valentinian or Basilidean Gnostic, bearing the suffering, but still Docetic Jesus within him, and circumscribed by an unredeemable physical world of which neither oneness with nature, nor the distractions of art, nor the sacraments, nor even physical death itself, will ever furnish an adequate evasion.

Notes

1. F.W. Bateson, *English Poetry* (London, 1950). J. Heath-Stubbs, *The Darkling Plain* (London, 1950). G. Hough, *The Last Romantics* (London, 1949). Professor Hough's general comments on Johnson are, as we might expect, most perceptive. There is a good though brief discussion in G.S. Fraser, *The Modern Writer and His World* (London, 1953). A full bibliography of criticism is given in *The Collected Poems of Lionel Johnson*, 2nd ed (New York, 1982).
2. Sir William Empson, without doubt the finest British critic of this century, was hard on an earlier version of this piece. He was at that time wrestling like Milton himself with Milton's God and my deadpan account of eternal suffering displeased one in the flush of his indignation at the neo-Christians. Without proper commitment, they had revived the sentiment: 'This last pain for the damned the Fathers found/They knew the bliss with which they were not crowned.' Johnson, however, according to Yeats, was on the other side, though only in a specialized sense could he be called a neo-Christian. Those who denied the eternity of punishment after death were too far gone to recognize their own absolute vulgarity. To Johnson, Empson's wish to transform the Christian tragi-comedy into comedy would have

possessed some dim analogue with Nahum Tate's *rifacimento* of *Lear* where Cordelia is saved and marries Edgar. The point goes with the pain.

Empson also observes that the more I attacked 'The Dark Angel' the better the poem seemed. Precisely the effect I had intended. I had only attacked the poem, or rather grumbled about it a bit, on instructions from the editor of the volume in which this piece appeared. Explication without judgement, I was sternly told, was a nullity: take Dr Johnson as your model. I am happy to revise or cut what was purely a shadow aggression, for I have no real objection to the poem whatever, and as I have Walter Pater for master I make no pretence of grading poems in relation to poems by other poets. And if I happen not to like something, I don't write about it.

3. C. Jung, *The Integration of the Personality* (London, 1940), pp. 20–21, 27, 70 *et passim*.
4. The common ground between Psychology and Christianity is illuminatingly discussed in Fr V. White, *God and the Unconscious* (London, 1952), though John Sanford in a recent study insists on distinctions. See, *Evil: The Shadow side of Reality* (New York, 1981).
5. S. Kierkegaard, *Fear and Trembling and the Sickness unto Death*, trans. Walter Lowrie (Oxford, 1941), p. 146.
6. *The Romantic Agony*, trans. A. Davidson, 2nd edn (Oxford, 1951), esp. pp. 116–20.
7. Kierkegaard, p. 86.
8. German prose writes such as Arnim, Tieck, Brentano and Heine, and German poets such as Lenau, Morike and Dehmel touch the theme, while it also makes its appearance in De Musset's 'Nuits' and in Maupassant's 'L'Horla'. Poe is a virtuoso of the double story, and Dostoevski employs it pungently in *The Double* and *The Brothers Karamazov*. In the Scots traditions there is the splendid *Confessions of a Justified Sinner*, while Stevenson in several stories touches on the double in various roles: enemy, redeemer, lover. Among the English, we may mention Kipling's short story 'At the End of the Passage'.
9. Nicolette Gray, *How They Met Themselves* (London, 1947), p. 25.
10. Other secondary literature includes the Introduction to Albert J. Guerard, *Stories of the Double* (New York, 1967), which contains Claire Rosenfeld's study 'The Shadow Within: The Conscious and Unconscious Use of the Double', and C. F. Keppler, *The Literature of the Second Self* (Tucson, 1972) which appears to be reconstructed Jungian in approach and which usefully distinguishes the roles and çategories of the figure. See also H. Tucker, Jr, 'The Importance of Otto Rank's Theory of the Double', *Journal of the Otto Bank Association* (Winter 1977–8), pp. 59–65, which compares Rank's hypotheses with those of Keppler and the rather literalist Robert Rogers' *A Psychoanalytic Study of the Double in Literature* (Detroit, 1970). H. Tucker has translated Rank's work as *The Double: A Psychoanalytic Study* (Chapel Hill, 1971).
11. *The Artist as Critic: Critical Writings of Oscar Wilde*, ed. R. Ellmann (New York, 1969), pp. 322–3.

12. See, for example, Donald R. Dickson, '"In a Mirror that mirrors the soul": Masks and Mirrors in *Dorian Gray*', English Literature in Transition 26, 1 (1983), pp. 5–15.
13. In her copy of *Poems* (London, 1895), though, Katharine Tynan Hinkson had a photograph of Johnson which she describes as the only photograph taken in his adult years. The date is 1891. Louise Imogen Guiney is another person who might have requested the later image.
14. Kierkegaard, p. 115.
15. *Ecclesiasties* 42: 22–5. 'All things are double one against another ... One thing establishes the good things of another.'
16. A.W. Patrick, *Lionel Johnson, poète et critique* (Paris, 1939), p. 221.
17. And, to come nearer home, of Browning's *The Statue and the Bust* and T.S. Eliot's Introduction to Baudelaire's *Journaux Intimes*, or Luther's *Pecca fortiter*.
18. *The Works of John Milton*, ed. J.O. Mabbott and J. Milton French, (New York, 1938), xviii, p. 234.
19. In his essay on James Clarence Mangan, Johnson comes near to analysis of his own case: 'The miseries ... were primarily of his own creation, realities of his own imagination, and therefore the more terrible; they were the agonies of a child in the dark, quivering for fear of that nothing which is to him so infinitely real and dread ... "a something enchained", as Saint Augustine has it, *sua ferrea voluntate*, by the iron chain of his unwilling will.' This essay appeared first in *The Academy* for February 1898 and was reprinted in *The Prose Writings of James Clarence Mangan*, ed. D. J. O'Donoghue and M. B. Gill (Dublin, 1904), pp. xi–xii. Sanford, p. 62, observes that 'The Shadow expresses itself in all kinds of fantasies. These, particularly if sexual, produce guilt which in turn brings one horror and fear'.
20. I am giving a faintly altered version of Arthur O'Shaugnessy's translation, *Songs of a Worker* (London, 1881), pp. 196–7.
21. A.W. Patrick, p. 221, prints an earlier version of this stanza from manuscript:

    I fight thee, in the Holy Name!
    And yet I know thou dost God's will:
    Tempter! Should I escape thy flame,
    Thou wilt have saved my soul from ill.

    The critic comments: 'Par la suppression du "I", le second vers devient plus énergique; par la personnification, le dernier prend un ton plus dramatique. Le substitution de "helped" pour "saved" évite une expression et un alliteration malhabité. Le mot "Death" fait une terminaison plus forte que le faible son "will"'.
22. In an earlier version of the poem published in *The Second Book of the Rhymers' Club* (London, 1894) Johnson has: 'wherefrom the lost soul cries', which is perhaps more poignant but suggests Hell as a place rather than a state.
23. *De Angelis*, Lib. 8. Cap. 18, quoted in *Satan: Etudes Carmelitaines* (Paris, 1948).

24. See C.G. Jung, *Mysterium Coniunctionis* (New York, 1966), 2, p.112, *segq.*, and *Collected Works* VIII pp.136 *seq.* and 160–62 (New York, 1962): The attributes of this feminine principle are darkness and sometimes evil. The absence of the feminine in the Christian pantheon has been inadequately compensated for by the exaltation of the Virgin Mary. There is a long way to go, though the Jesuit work on Mary as co-redemptrix is a promising start. The 'Wisdom' of the Jews could have been promoted, though Milton identifies it with the Sacred Muse, the female Urania. There are also the Sibyls. The Saint Simonians recognized the need for a second, female Messiah, but the lady, due to epiphanize at Constantinople, that Byzantium which mediates between East and West, failed to appear.
25. Kierkegaard, p.204.
26. G. Santayana, *The Middle Span* (London, 1947), pp.67 *seq.*
27. I quote from the translation by E.R. Dodds in his *Selections from the Neoplatonists* (London, 1923), p.124.
28. It was natural for Rossetti, as it was unnatural for his imitators, to write English as if it were a romance language. He was brought up in a household where Italian was spoken daily.
29. A. Beguin, 'Sur la "Mystique" de Maurice Scève', *Fontaine*, Tome VII, 36 (1944), pp.74–97. *Dèile*, Dizain 346. The shift to personal pronouns in the last two lines is masterful. Perhaps this quotation from William Pitt the Elder may further clarify the metaphor by showing its use for satiric purposes. He is comparing the coalition of Fox and Newcastle and the junction of the Rhône and the Saône: 'At Lyons I was taken to see the place where the two rivers meet; the one gentle, feeble, languid, though languid, yet of no depth; the other a boisterous and tempestuous torrent. But, different as they are, they meet at last.'

Index